T0354867

WHO AM I?
WHERE AM I?
WHAT AM I DOING HERE?

A TEXTBOOK FOR LIFE, LIVING, AND REALITY

A. F. KENTON

authorHOUSE®

AuthorHouse™
1663 Liberty Drive
Bloomington, IN 47403
www.authorhouse.com
Phone: 1 (800) 839-8640

Published by AuthorHouse 12/10/2019

ISBN: 978-1-7283-3711-1 (sc)
ISBN: 978-1-7283-3714-2 (e)

Print information available on the last page.

This book is printed on acid-free paper.

CONTENTS

DEDICATION

This book is dedicated to Seth, Jane Roberts and Robert Butts. It is through their co-ordinate efforts that they have provided me with the key that I have been looking for all of my life. I have used their material throughout my book without special notations, because I feel that they are so a part of me and my thoughts. I'd like to thank them for being themselves and for what they have given to me in doing so.

I also want to thank two other people James E. DeBiasio and Marilyn Bryant who were instrumental in my research and to St. Germain for spiritual guidance. I'd also like to thank Susan Steel, Bill Wunder and anyone else who I unintentionally forgot. Additional special thanks to my wife Karene for her support and our children; Wayne, Kim, and Wendy, who shared their reality with me.

FOREWORD

When I graduated from high school, a long, long, time ago, I remember signing a yearbook for a special friend of mine with a message something like this, "I am a victim of my time and environment". I remember that I did feel that way and believed that back then, but now I can't believe I could have been so wrong. Then again, it was correct at the time. I attribute a lot of that thinking to the average public educational system that seems to foster such ideas.

Neither our society or the public educational system seems to offer any alternative philosophies other than the here and now. It does little to promote positive mental growth and indirectly does, through demonstration of the educational systems procedures, encourages submissive behavior. This system in turn offers one very little hope but to view one's self as a victim of circumstances beyond one's control. I don't believe private or religious institutions offer any better educational alternatives that I would consider free thinking processes. This doesn't necessarily mean any of these systems are bad, but they sure don't encourage individualism to its maximum.

College education and even philosophy courses do little to encourage one's self esteem and growth either. All these institutes do is to basically teach greater tolerance for different beliefs, but then again, you get what you put into anything (I'll explain that statement later in the book).

It wasn't until the late 1970's, early '80's did anyone offer me an alternative answer to the "victim syndrome", and this came about in a strange way. In short, I came across a book in a book swap store. Its title was "Seth Speaks". It is a book by Jane Roberts. Actually, it is a book written by Robert Butts, Jane's husband, who transcribed information from an entity called Seth who was speaking through Jane, who was in a trance, now referred to as channeling.

This book contained some interesting information, but what struck me most was a phrase which was repeated a number of times in a number of ways. Seth kept saying, "You make your own reality". It is a hard phrase to understand as a victim; yet, it is even harder to dismiss. To really understand this statement requires the reading of the rest of this book.

"You make your own reality". A stupid simple statement. How can it possibly mean anything significant? Well, let me say this, it is the major thought form that can change one's beliefs from that of victim to one of total responsibility for one's self.

Seth, Jane, or Robert never did explain this statement to my satisfaction and with Jane's death there was no more information. So, it was up to me to make my own reality. By the way, one does not create a new reality over night. It takes time, insight, and the desire for truth. That is, it requires an intensive study from outside sources, from which come inner responses.

I personally had no intention of writing a book on belief systems or explaining how one makes their own reality, but I felt the need to do so or justify my own thoughts. Once I started, the book wrote itself. But the major event that triggered the actual writing was the tragic mass suicide at Jonestown, Guyana in South America. There, approximately 288 people blindly followed Reverend Jim Jones, to their death. They so believed in his religious cult teachings that they all became victims of his beliefs.

My book was completed shortly after that event, but I did not have the courage to have it published. It is somewhat ironical that my decision to proceed with its publication falls on another similar tragic event in Waco, Texas. Here we have another victim syndrome belief system of David Koresh and his religious following in another type of mass suicide.

So, there you have it and there you don't. This book was written because of events and/or thoughts of others. In a sense, the book too is a victim because it was the result of other causes. But a book is not a person. Also, I take full responsibility for its existence. Lastly, the book is specifically written to destroy the victim syndrome. It is somewhat easy to live one's life as a victim, it is quite another thing to take full responsibility for one's life and thoughts.

This book is unusual in a number of ways. It is supposedly a text book, but it will probably never be used as one in any major educational school system. The book was also intended as a guide for determining one's reality, which effects moral behavior. Yet, no hard and fast rules are ever mentioned but one. What this book does do is to question everything that we accept in this physical reality as tangible and says that it is first intangible. Can the average person accept that responsibility?

Because this is supposedly a text book, it is quite technical and may be boring with a lot of the definitions of common words in the earlier chapters. But, it is designed to educate! At the same time, you will find many areas of humor and references to popular songs and/or pop culture. There is also some original poetry throughout this book that is both serious and light in nature, but all of it has hidden meaning.

In determining one's reality, one must talk about the tangible and intangible or physical matter and spirit. To do this requires great care and balancing of theology and the occult or new age thinking. To take a black or white approach to these subjects would affect the credibility of both the book and myself; therefore, I have avoided what I call pattern recognition or areas of popular thought in order to discourage one from using emotions rather than rational thought processes.

This book will tell you everything you need to know about life, living, and reality. The answers are also known within you, because you make your own reality. However, our reality is also a joint venture or journey. There are a lot of forces out there that affect us and unless we are conscious of them, we can all become victims of these beliefs. The choice is up to you.

Happiness is not something in and by itself. It is the understanding and recognition of recognizing one's self and one's knowledge of this conscious recognition is the key to taking control of your life and the making your reality. If nothing else, you must understand this. How you use this information is up to you.

I would like to end this dedication on a positive note; however, I feel I would also be doing you an injustice if I did not tell you the consequences of doing nothing or not changing. To do this, I also have to make reference to the prophecies found in the bible and occult literature. Examples of these prophecies can be found in the Book of Revelations or the writings of Nostradamus. Basically these sources and others condemn us to a fate of massive destruction and earth changes. These events need not happen if enough people learn how they make their own reality and do something in a positive creative manner through loving, caring, and sharing. You make your own reality, but in doing so, you also affect mine. Let's try to work together, because the results are bigger than all of us.

INTRODUCTION

I would like to begin this book on an equal plane of understanding; therefore, I will try to make the language of this text as simple and plain as possible. My hopes are that in keeping it simple, I can communicate with as many different people as possible and at all levels of life and or social standing.

Communications is probably the most important thing one will learn in his or her life time, and it doesn't stop there. Most forms of communication are so obvious and so common place, that this interaction is taken for granted and really never considered to be that important by most people. Communication takes on so many different forms that these patterns are overlooked. It is not just a matter of verbal and written speech that one forms a common union of thought, an agreement, or an exchange of ideas. Communication is the action or reaction of the spoken or written word expressed in attitudes and/or emotions, either negative, positive, indifferent or uncommitted. Therefore, it is important that you and I communicate to form a common union of thought and a communion of mind and spirit; to progress and grow in a positive, creative, and loving manner. These same thoughts will again be expressed at some length in the latter part of this book for it is an important ingredient in the well being of all concerned.

At this point, I feel that I must express some of my own personal feelings, or those ideas about which I feel strongly. I would like to consider myself an optimist and a realist; however, I am sure that there are many persons who may consider my thoughts extremely unrealistic and somewhat pessimistic. The latter will not be covered in the normal or conventionally accepted form of communication, but it will be covered. As to the matter of reality, or what is realistic, I will try to address myself to these questions in properly definable terms.

Unlike fact or truth, there is the area of emotions. I believe each and every person likes to be noticed and praised by his peers for actions which contribute to the well being of mankind, either mentally or physically. This book was positively motivated to do good or to make a contribution to mankind; however, I also know that it was negative thought or fear of failure, that delayed the actual writing of this book and its publication. It is these emotions that drive us and I am no exception. The elements of time, emotions, and consciousness make a difference in our beliefs and/or the controlling factors that affects so many of us.

I feel I have so much to say and have so little time left to express everything. Then again, perhaps my biggest fear remaining is that what I have to say will be misunderstood because I will not be properly able to communicate those positive creative thoughts to others in the same way that I personally feel or believe them to be. These beliefs or this book, can make a difference in changing one's life and it will create greater happiness.

This book is something on the order of a "do-it-yourself" type text book. That is, the material contained here is designed and organized to present you with a plan, thought, or ideas, which you can implement to bring about the emotional changes necessary to bring you greater happiness. It may be the driving force that can change you to undertake a new positive and creative direction in your life. The thoughts presented in this book do not in themselves guarantee you more positive mental growth. You must do do it yourself and in so doing you will improve the well being of all concerned. Reality is a matter of belief, and belief is another form of matter controlled by the unknowing mind.

Most of the material which is presented in this book, is not really new; rather, it is a collection of ideas taken from the past and from within. The contents have been organized to provide guidelines which relate to everyday life situations. It is hoped that his material is presented in such ordinary and practical terms that the complexities of life appear simple and beautiful. With this new knowledge and a few simple truths, it is expected that you will gain a new awareness and a happier, fuller life through the use of increased higher consciousness.

To improve or change anything, requires concentration and or work.

Consequently, those things which are desired and valued above all else, are those things which require the most concentrated efforts. Material things of great worth are valued for short periods of time, but these things cannot or may not stand the test of time to give them great value. Immaterial or intangible things, are more difficult to value because they usually cost you nothing to begin with and they usually can not be used frequently; therefore, the knowledge and or use of the latter is difficult to evaluate. The knowledge or information imparted in this book, is of the intangible variety; however, it is also a type of commodity that can be used daily but won't wear out. Hopefully, this common usage factor can and will impart great value to both the user and the receiver, thereby giving this knowledge a type of tangible quality or sustenance, which will actually grow in value with time.

It is common knowledge that people can relate better to other people, than they can to ideas and concepts; therefore, I would like to just say a few words about the problems I had in putting this book together. Also, I do want to emphasize that this book is about reality and therefore does discuss morality. Perhaps, I am subconsciously repressing the use of the word morality because most people have some strong feelings concerning other people telling them what they should or should not do with their life in relationship to others.

It is my belief, that many people are like me in their relationship with others. That is, they prefer to associate in small groups with people of like interest, but like the access to larger and bigger organizations and or more influencial people. They like their privacy, but they also want to be one of the gang. The problem arises when one of the group or organizational goals, conflicts with one's own personal goals or desires. How one resolves this type of problem is a question of morality or what is right or wrong? Can one choose a solution which does not offend someone or deter a relationship with another? Hopefully, this book will answer that question in a positive and very firm, **"YES!"**

Most of the contents and ideas for this book were thought about, back in the early 1960's. However, it wasn't until some 20 years later, did I get up enough courage to write this book. The reason for these lost years, was due to my fears and the very powerful unseen force of our society, the establishment, or whatever you want to call it. The unforeseen pressure or fear of being different and fear of isolation caused by non-conformity is very strong in all of us. The desire to please one's peers and/or society as a whole, dominates and controls most people's behavior and causes, and I am no different.

Those friends and/or associates, with whom I did speak to in confidence about my ideas concerning positive creativity regarding our reality were somewhat in agreement about my concern for acceptance of this subject matter. They too, felt that the subject matter must be cleverly done or hidden to conceal the true nature of the book. That is, they suggested that I should write a fictional book that had a message or moral to the story. Something like an Aesop Fable. Other suggestions offered in order to get wide coverage or exposure to these ideas was to incorporate this knowledge or information into the popular themes of sex, violence, or an expose' of some kind.

In my opinion, most people read books for light entertainment or escapism. No one wants to read a book that is going to be a mind bender. Especially, one that requires strange new beautiful and simplistic thoughts that are intended to expand or exercise the mind. Even though a lot of people are caught up in this physical fitness craze, the mind doesn't seem to be fair game or fall under that category of exercise.

Everybody knows that books written or directed toward attitudes or behavior are usually put out by some weirdo. That's why most major publishers don't get involved in such books. Only private individuals, institutions, and cults or religious groups publish such material that pertains to certain limited ideas, which small minorities can relate to and feel some form of gratification or reinforcement from such strange isolated ideas. Such books are designed to persuade people to convert, repent, and or to join a supposedly worthy or worthwhile cause. Unfortunately, this book does none of the above. You make the decision! You make it happen! And you create your own personal reality!

In school, you were taught to question, what are the author's credentials for writing such a book? Only people with advanced educational degrees of study, are authorized to write such serious type books. The only exception to this unspoken rule, is if you have devoted your entire life or career to this field of endeavor, or someone has had some miraculous revelation or experience bestowed on him. I personally do not qualify for any of the above; however, I have been looking for something all of my life, and I think that I have found it.

Considering the subject matter in regards to morality, you might come to some kind of conclusion, that a person has to have lived a saintly life to write such a serious book. Also, such a person would automatically be setting himself apart from the day-to-day conflicts, confrontations, and changing environment and necessities of life, to be able to properly relate or adapt his thoughts, into practical everyday knowledge. Surely, anyone living such an isolated, boring or inactive life, would be dull and not worth reading. Well, I don't fall into that category and I don't intend to tell you my life history either. In any case, I will tell you that I am an engineer and manufacturing consultant by trade and am artistically inclined. I have not had a dull and boring life. Being passive in my work environment, has never been one of my attributes. Maybe such a life would have been preferable; however, it didn't work out that way.

As to the accusation of being a religious fanatic, I don't think I qualify for that either. I don't ask you to follow me, for I am not the way or anything like that. I seek nothing from you, nor do I ask you to join me or support me in anyway. I do not have wealth or a position of great importance or influence, that you can gain from being associated with me in any way. All I have, is a beautiful idea, that can work wonders but requires some effort that is greatly rewarded and returned from whence it came. This book per se, is not religious nor anti-religious. The concepts contained in this material may have religious connotations; however, the ideas presented here are probably more universally acceptable thoughts about life and reality than, maybe, theology. The fanatic part is up to you. If you consider an individual with no outstanding credentials, who writes about morality to be a nut, weirdo, or whatever, then, maybe I fit into that fanatic category. You will have to make that decision.

To help you arrive at that decision, I will give you a little extra help by telling you what I think you may gain from reading this book. The answer can only be speculative at this point; however, it is hoped that the "I," the individual or reader, will learn more about himself, his being, his origin, his internal makeup, his purpose, and why he behaves the way he does. Hopefully, he will also learn where he is, so that he can put this information to better use in practical everyday terms. By learning more about himself and his world or reality, man will remember what he is doing here.

I don't see any reason to believe that you, as a reader, can not arrive at anything but happiness from reading this book. That is, I expect this result to happen if you allow yourself some time to think about the substance or sustenance contained on these pages. Give it a chance. Do not do anything that does not make sense or that is not fun. Be yourself if you can, or if you dare.

I will conclude this introduction with an original poetic prose that I put together some years ago, on or about the time I read my first book by Jane Roberts, Seth, and Robert Butts. I find it appropriate to place this and some other original works throughout the book. Poetry is usually quite personal in nature, because it indicates a pattern that may not be entirely recognizable to its reader; however, this little mental exercise is sometimes very rewarding the truth is understood. It is not always obvious or apparent from the words or outside appearances, but it is its internal form that makes poetry so appealing to some. I hope you share my thoughts.

THE FLOW OF LIFE

Life is not unlike a drop of water.
Born of physical matter,
Created by chance or design by forces
known and forgotten by man.
From an astral heaven,
rained down to an earthly apparition.

Like a drop of rain, I grow in substance and am exposed
to an environment which conditions my direction both
consciously and unconsciously. My being is in a state of
confusion, driven, guided, directed, and pushed like in
a stream of water.

At times, I am in the main stream of swift currents and
great awareness, only to be caught up in obstacles which
slow my progress and submerge my abilities and qualities.

My course is mostly uncertain and full of twisting, turning,
swerving, and changes which I do not do if left to
my own volition. Do I in fact have consciousness? Do I
actually have knowledge, wisdom, or freedom of choice?
I think not!

Although I harbor the hopes, desires, and dreams of myself, my creators,
my friends, my enemies, and my acquaintances, I am a reflection or
image of something greater and beyond all comprehension. I am swept
along a never ending current to an unknown ORIGIN. Do I in fact
exist? Am I a means to some other end? I think so! But the time is not
yet his plan.

SECTION I

WHO AM I?

Physical Reality

CHAPTER 1

In Search of A Start

What is a beginning? It is a point of reference or focal point that sets a limit. It is a designated position in time and space in the reality of physical matter, as we know it that can include intangible thought. It is a concept beyond which nothing like it, ever existed. A particular and discrete unit or entity independent and not directly relative to other things. A starting point, if you will.

To be realistic however, what is to say that this point, this position, this idea or concept can not be found to exist in part or parts of other already existing forms of physical matter or thought. When talking about non-physical, intangible thoughts and ideas, there may be no way to identify a beginning, or starting point. But surely, when talking about physical reality and life forms, there are limitations of a beginning and ending.

Even if there is more to life, as we know it, or as we are capable of understanding it, we are still limited to a beginning and an ending. Supposedly, there is no identifiable substance to life, either before or after those limitations; therefore, it is not practicable to consider life beyond those points. We are primarily concerned with the conscious being in this physical reality and those things, which directly relate to or affect that being. Therefore, something which doesn't exist in our reality can't affect our reality....Or can it?

It is with that crystal clear understanding and/or confusion that we begin to explore the purpose of this book and that area of thought, that has been on everyone's black list, unspeakable list, or taboo list of unpleasant subjects which everyone tries to ignore, hide, or just plain refuses to recognize as an existing problem. I am referring to the subject of reality and morality. This book is intended as a guide in the formulation of one's reality and its relationship to behavior. It is with this intent in mind, that we begin this book, and what a better way to begin a book, than to ask another question.

Why would anyone in their right mind and living in such a permissive society and age, want to write a book on life and/or behavior? Especially, a book intended as a guide for formulating and practicing acceptable moral conduct for young adults.

It is obvious, that such a book is destined for trouble or the trash heap, or both. The subject matter is not necessarily a best seller, even though there is a lot of individual thought on or about morality. It is because there is so much thought on the subject, that so many people stay away from discussing the matter intelligently. It is a vast wasteland. There are so many different thoughts concerning the subject of morality that few can agree on any specific rules of conduct; therefore, most individuals are basically left up to their own devices and/or conscience, to decide moral issues, and perhaps, that isn't altogether, a bad idea.

Moral behavior is a difficult subject to talk about rationally. It has succumbed to peer pressure and/or the environment to regulate or enforce certain unwritten rules and regulations. However, such a system of moral discipline is not always effective and often has conflicting thoughts or ideas, depending upon one's interests, social status, wealth or benefits to others.

How this type of system or pressure works is something similar to the following: Two or more people get together over a few drinks and engage in conversation which generally leads into discussions about other people and their relationship to others. This is usually one of those casual, loose, strike-up-a-short-friendship type conversation and usually involves talking about a person or relationship of common interest. It is seldom a very deep, serious conversation with few constructive ideas or suggestions for corrective action of a long run nature. Rather, the answers, if any, are emotional and usually amount to such stereo type answers as: A) He ought to be shot! B) Break his arm or leg! C) Punch him in the nose! D) Hang him up by the .....! E) All of the above. This is a kind of "an eye for an eye", "tooth for a tooth" type of approach to the invisible and/or the unwritten quasi-legal laws of the land. These half hearted meetings normally result in impracticable solutions that deal outwardly with inner conflict. Even though results are somewhat questionable, the verbal outlet does seem to produce some type of positive re-inforcement to the participants.

It is because of conflicting interests and other motivating personal goals, that most people are turned off or are indifferent to the subject of morality. It seems to be that the golden rule has changed to: "Do unto others before they do unto you!" Morality is fine so long as it benefits me but when it requires something from me to give to someone else, forget it, Mac! I'm not giving up anything.

Hopefully, this example is over-exaggeration, although, it is a conscious or subconscious fact that must be considered. More likely, the negative attitude stems from utter despair, frustration, and the futility one feels in confronting a moral issue. Unless a person has certain powers to reward or punish, as in "Child/Parent" relationship, or an "Employee/Employer" relationship, there is little chance that a moral issue can be enforced or sustained. Even in this relationship, one may be able to control an immediate local situation for a short period of time, but overall, a long lasting effect is nil unless other people, or that person affected supports that behavior pattern and/or enforcement of same.

This attitude problem is also the direct result of the inequality or justice under the current rules, regulations, and laws of this country and all nations. This problem is also the result of the internal conflict within one's self. It is the same or similar situation one encounters when one deliberately makes a false statement, otherwise known as a lie. One knows that it is wrong or untrue, but one avoids the conflict or prefers the results offered by the false statement.

There are many forms of communication where words and actions cnflict. Because of the ambiguities of the written and verbal language, one can even influence the language sufficiently to change the meaning or intent of any law. Accordingly, if one argues long enough and has sufficient resources, one can change the law or laws to suit the needs of those involved.

Today, our social-economic culture is confronted with so called liberal and permissive attitudes, based on, or fostered by past indifference. The children of the affluent 50's rebelled into the 60's and wreaked havoc with

3

the social norms in the 70's. Now, the children of these children, are adrift in the 80's and the 90's, because the moral structure that once was, is no more. The rebellion from inequality and the concept of "we", is now the indifference or acceptance of "Do your own thing", and the concentration on the person known as "I".

There is little concern today, for the well being of the other guy. The philosophy of "Being thy brother's keeper", just isn't considered to any great extent in the western society any more. This attitude change reflects the growing acceptance and permissiveness of the individual to seek out his own course of action or destiny, but, this also means, "Whatever ye sow, so shall ye reap." Man is more on his own now to do as he pleases, but he must also suffer the consequences of his actions. Like "hey man...far out!" Whatever he wants to do, is cool. "Dig it?" "Let him do his own thing!" If he wants to burn himself out or waste himself, let him go.

When viewing this new type of attitude on a one-to-one basis, most people will accept this philosophy. Nevertheless, we still are predominately a collective society, sharing many of the same ideals and common ancestry, consequently, many of the older populace views these changing attitude tendencies of the younger generation as divisive and destructive. There are many more who predict doom and gloom and possibly a collapse of the Western way of life. A "Fall of the Roman Empire," if you will.

This new anti-culture, is believed or viewed as a threat to the cohesive force of society. I believe that this new attitude problem is not actively seeking to destroy anything, however, it is thought by many that it is creating apathy or a void in unity or a dropout culture. Consequently, this collective attitude noticeably changes and breeds more and more extremist groups, whose intent is to re-establish morality under their own creed, rules and/or interests. This is like "Jumping out of the frying pan, into the fire." People are conforming to non-conformity!

Knowing all of this, why then, would anyone with the knowledge of these conflicts of interest, indifference, ambiguities and sheer apathy want to write a book about life, reality, and morality? In fact, how could anyone write a constructive, intelligent, rational and comprehensive book on the subject? It is obvious that the odds are against the success of even a sincere effort to write such a book. But maybe, that void in society is real. Maybe the new interest groups or subcultures are a far greater danger to the cohesive force of our society, than the apathy. Maybe, just maybe, someone can offer a new thought or idea that can serve as a unifying element, or at least, the basis for some type of unity in a positive, constructive way.

How does one begin to write such an ideological book? Well, I suppose the classic answer would be, "very carefully" or "don't even try." However, I have expressed a need or concern regarding the subject matter. I have my own doubts about such a venture, but I also think it is a necessary endeavor. I don't believe the knowledge of moral behavior has ever been put into the proper prospective or digested sufficiently for proper consumption in relationship to the meaning of life. So here it goes!

I agree that the subject of morality is difficult to approach in a rational way because it deals primarily with the emotions. Current trends in morality toward more freedom of expression do not normally reverse themselves, and few people are willing to submit to strict rules or pattern themselves to conform to rigid inflexible laws for the greater good of all. These thoughts and ideas have been tried and are still being tried out primarily under the name of communism[1]. Don't get me wrong, this is not the only "ism" or ideology; however, it is in theory, one of the better systems. Too bad it doesn't and can't work in reality.

Getting back to the subject at hand, few people are about to make concessions that would affect their so called freedoms or liberties to do as they please, and how they please. Even if such a rigid system was to be adopted, it would be almost impossible to enforce. In short, I agree that to impose strict rules or even guidelines for social and moral behavior are not practical nor healthy in the normal sense of the word.

Attempts have been made in history to change behavior patterns. The most overt of these actions are the so called wars of national liberation, which most of the western society refers to as terrorism. Other attempts or justification for the voluntary or formal acts of adoption by existing governments for drastic behavior changes, fall under a category we refer to in this country as a state of emergency. This latter situation is usually or supposed to be used when there is some severe problem affecting the lives of a great number of people. The enactment of such a law is supposed to be temporary until the threat has passed or the situation returns to a near

---

[1] Note: This book was written before the break up of the Soviet Union, but communism still in part exists.

normal condition. What normal means is anybody's guess however, I think it means, that which maintains the status quo.

In any and all situations, any means to impose external controls or controls contrary to one's existing beliefs and/or behavior, is almost impossible to enforce. Any permanent change or mass compliance to such a request, must come from within those individuals involved; This is an interesting statement, so keep that latter factor or statement in mind. The state of emergency, enforced by supposedly legal means, is a very powerful means to affect changes and consequently, will receive the greatest support of those involved. Given the proper circumstances and conditions, for a long enough period of time, overall morality can change drastically. However, such a change requires the proper circumstances or a convincing emotional appeal for unity of action for a common good.

Considering that I am not advocating any forced compliance, either overtly or covertly, I think I am safe to say that I am not expecting any revolutionary change based upon the contents of this book; however, it would be nice to get a few people to try to apply some of the thoughts advocated here. Most major changes usually originate in small groups and get tried out and/or modified before they get incorporated into the mainstream of life and this is how it probably should be. Any real worthwhile changes in life are born of time, space, and patience. Meaningful changes must withstand the test of time and space. This is the meaning or media of patience.

Perhaps, the greatest difficulty in dealing with the subject of moral behavior, is the problem of emotions. This is probably the main reason why it is so difficult to get everyone involved to think and/or agree to the same or similar form of action. The problem also involves a question of one's closeness or relationship to everything and everyone involved. Rational logic gives way to the emotional fear of losing something or being restricted in some way; consequently, one reacts out of a need or attachment than he does so much from real physiological needs to sustain him. That is, the person or persons involved respond to an outside stimulus that causes him pleasure or pain. This is nothing more than a reaction to the laws of cause and effect. Without the element of conscious rational thought, there can be no agreement. Few people are willing to give up something they find pleasing or satisfying in some way, shape or form.

In reality, an emotion is a function of the mind and can be controlled rationally, however, this requires an area of understanding of one's self. The mind works on many levels. This is evident alone by the words: Thought, Idea, and Belief. Supposedly, the words all refer intangible functions of the brain. Why then, are there so many different words to describe the same thing or process? Without going into real in depth explaination at this time, these different terms would seem to verify this multi-level functioning of the mind. Later on in this book, I will devote a great deal of time to this aspect.

Perhaps the word, emotion, does not describe a function of the brain so much as it does a level of consciousness. Emotions are more an awareness of one's thought processes manifested upon the physical senses, in relation to one's involvement or mental positioning. Emotions are the intensity of one's beliefs manifested upon the world about one's self, resulting in either action or reaction. You might say that emotions act similar to the gas pedal on a car, whereas, the function of the mind or thoughts are more like the road or destination one is headed for, be it known or unknown. How conscious you are of all this determines which roads you select and how well you steer the car. Your physical body is like a vehicle that must be attended and properly monitored in order to get you where you want to go and hopefully safe and well. You shouldn't go stepping on the gas pedal without knowing the condition and performance of the vehicle in a relationship to the road ahead.

The functioning of the mind is also complicated by the function and forms of communication. The difficulty of language meaning makes it imperative that we go into specific detail on the words being used in this book. One can use and say the same words in the same way and mean different things. It is important that we all agree on definitions and relationships, or we will lose the continuity or oneness of thought. Verbal speech is a difficult thing to understand, and if you include slang, forget it. You have heard of the generation gap and there has been some acknowledgement of what is being called a creditability gap; therefore, I caution you to make an attempt to agree to those or this form of written communication in order to form a common union of thought. Hopefully, through a careful building process based on written communications, we will build a bridge or structure upon which we can all stand and proceed to some agreed upon destination.

Getting back to the mind, I have purposely stressed the meaning of thoughts and emotions and how they work or function within the individual; however, the control over these functions is something else and I believe that the control over emotions is the primary motivating factor for all behavior. I believe that definite tangible results and over all objectives can be achieved by a re-education of this so called response center or function of the conscious mind.

The example of the car and destination helped to illustrate the function of the mind. Now, instead of trying to improve or modify the vehicle, we are going to try to improve the driver. The idea of this book is to make the individual more aware of the destination and keep his eye on the road, so as to avoid unnecessary and unexpected hazards and accidents along the way. Hopefully, once the destination is known, one can regulate, control the speed or gas pedal, and to be aware of and to recognize problems or situations which delay or hinder the journey of the vehicle and individual. Once this awareness is accomplished or under control, then we can even possibly improve the road or take short-cuts, or even to change the road and destination without getting out of the car.

You see, reality and morality are serious subjects. They are much more important than casual bar room conversations, or fashionable at family and social gatherings. Behavior requires much more thought and time than can be given at these type of gatherings. The exchange of experiences and/or life situation type stories is interesting, but it can also be confusing and misleading to impressionable people. Talking about experiences is a kind of subversive or indirect teaching form or method, either intended or not. The typical opening line of such a teacher begins something like this: "If I were you...." or, "When I was a kid...". Such conversations merely relate one's personal experience to another situation which may be entirely different or relate to an entirely different time basis and/or morality. What this conversation does do is to tell you more about the person doing the talking than about the proper direction or course that should be taken; however, if the person speaking is a so called person of rank in the social-economic community, he may influence a number of people to follow his example or way of thinking. Such influences are neither good or bad, but one should still consider the consequences of his own actions. In other words, "Think twice before acting!" in questionable or similar situations.

Let me clarify the latter thought. I am cautioning you not to accept blind actions or stereotype responses to certain situations. Man learns by experiencing and to some extent by witnessing and example. One can be warned of the danger of fire, but unless one directly experiences its negative harmful effects, one can not really understand or appreciate that danger. I am not saying you must experience everything yourself to fully understand and comprehend. What I am saying is that each and every person is a unique, one of a kind type of individual and that no two people act or react in the same way given the same situation.

The reason for this difference in thought and action is quite complicated, but I will only say at this point, that no two people see things in exactly the same way. That is, the actual situation really takes on the characteristics of those involved. It is a reflection of themselves that they are looking at. If for example, one is looking at a half color, say fifty percent of red and fifty percent of orange, one person may say that it is orange and another may say that it is red. They are both right as long as they can relate to the same color, even though they may see it slightly different. Whether, they actually see something physically different is of no importance. The important thing is that they both agree that they are talking about a color or visual perception and not two different physical senses.

The issue of morality is not like dealing with the tangible physical properties of say fire or color. Rather, one is trying to relate to something you cannot see; consequently, the effect on the individual can be drastically different from one person to another. Something like using two different senses to experience the same thing.

Up to now, we have been concerned with the individual and how he relates to morality. We have also talked about the need for perhaps more uniformity of thought, or at least the control over this form of thought by the individual in a society or social order. You would think that as long as everyone minds their own business, there shouldn't be any problems or reason to concern ourselves with the issue of morality. "Right on!"... you say; "Wrong!"... I say.

"No man is an island unto himself...", and it is just that simple. Nearly all of our actions somehow affect or involve the lives of other people or things, and these actions directly or indirectly affect morality. All of this inter-relationship is a form of communication that affects our fellow man, as well as ourselves. The results of these inter-actions are either pleasant or unpleasant to varying degrees of intensity. However, most people don't even think about any form of communication as being anything but a natural part of life. Consequently, there really isn't any effort or thought put into such encounters or conversations. Such forms of communication are usually designated as idle chat or casual talk aimed at nothing in particular. Such conversations are more an act of acknowledgement of a status relationship than they are of meaningful dialogue. This is a form of recognition that requires little or no effort on the parties involved. In fact, this is an acceptable form or pattern that you might call mental conditioning for it sets a precedence or attitude or a form of behavior that is expected. It is an acceptable custom or tradition set by the society or culture, and it is probably universal in nature.

When dealing with morality, one must also talk about society's customs or social norms. Everyday life here, is not the same as everyday life elsewhere. What is acceptable as natural here, others may think unnatural elsewhere. Most people are unaware of these differences until they are in another country or culture. It is only then, that they notice the differences. That's because, in their own country, they accept these customs and traditions as natural because they see and use them every day of their lives. Such behavior may be considered mental conditioning or brain washing. This is not something that should be considered good or bad, it is just a way of life, or pattern that has become acceptable in that particular society.

When that same person is taken out of his immediate environment, he may find himself confronted with new and strange differences. Therefore, in order to survive, he either learns to accept these new patterns of life style as his own, modifies them, or he can go back from where he came. He can also try to fight the system with some success; however, that will usually end up with that person experiencing a great deal of isolation, loneliness and perhaps, physical harm. Vis-a-vis, racial and religious confrontations. In any case, the individual will undergo a type of growth process or change which will, in some way, affect his behavior. That also means that the environment, which is shaped or affected by its residence, will greatly determine the law of the land or customs.

What I'm getting at, is that what is considered natural or unnatural, depends more on where you are or who you are talking about. This relationship is called conformity. If you accept those dominant patterns of the land, you are considered one or part of the establishment or land, because indirectly or directly, you support those patterns which are common or dominant. If you do not accept those patterns, but you do not interfere with anyone else, you are tolerated as someone existing in that society. If you fight the patterns, you are often considered a fugitive or criminal. Patterns of behavior that are contradictory to customs are considered unnatural. Natural is the law of the land. But, if you believe that everything is learned, that also means that nothing is natural.

What is normal or natural, is all relative to the immediate environment. That is, people learn how to act, or get along with their fellow man, for the benefit of themselves and/or mutual benefit. Even within that same environment, circumstances or people can change, which can result in an entirely different behavior. This learning of how to adjust or change is not so much a forced change, but more of a voluntary action on the part of all individuals involved. This adaptation is done in order to keep life experiences pleasant and to avoid the consequences of conflict.

This desire to get along and avoid unpleasantness, is a form of mental conditioning. It is in this way, that mass attitudes or social norms develop. Large groups of people get together with alike ideas and thoughts for a common interest or benefit and because of the number of people involved, these ideas become beliefs or social norms. These attitudes can develop along geographical, racial, religious, business, trade, or other lines, or divisions, of unity where large groups of people share the same interests. Now, this mass or group belief doesn't necessarily make the thought or resulting action either right or wrong, but it is acceptable, which may be confused as meaning right or wrong. Another way of looking at this process, is that people are taught and they learn to react, rather than to think and act along creative lines.

As one can see, to attack or criticize existing morality or behavior patterns, is very difficult to do creatively and/or constructively. Such an endeavor is very risky and therefore, requires great care to avoid unpleasantness to all involved. Morality has both positive and negative effects on thoughts, ideas, and beliefs; therefore, one must not destroy a belief without offering an alternative, and hopefully, a better idea. It is not practical or beneficial to tear down without thoughts to build and replace. What needs to be done, is to see where we are before we can decide where we are going. What we need to do, is to see what can be used to build upon, to establish a broader, more firm base of communication so that everyone can relate to fires and colors in the same way, without having to suffer the consequences.

Therefore, this book is not intended to directly attack any existing morality or behavior patterns. There will be no attempt to evaluate existing acceptable standards of conduct or moral issues, rather, this book is written with the intent in mind to explain just what one can really believe in, or really exists in the realm of truth as we know it and can be proven beyond a doubt. Hopefully, once everyone can agree on the same point of reference, we can build on that point, everything imaginable and then some. With this truth and knowledge, one can achieve personal gain, satisfaction, achievements, growth and creativity in life's journey back to his origin.

This book is intended to explore the so called rational physical world of matter. It explores the limitations of the physical being and the "I" concept. This section of the book will cover the subject, "Who am I?", in the conventional sense of the world we know. Section II will explore and answer the question, "Where am I?", and deal with a new expanded concept or the "I" concept. Section III will conclude the book and deal with the question, "What am I doing here?", or explain how this new "I" concept can be used or put into practical everyday use.

Now, you might ask another question, after having a brief idea of the contents of this book, and that question might be, "What does that have to do with morality?" The answer to that question will not be obvious to the reader until the last section of the book. Not until the three questions of the amnesia patient are answered, can he begin to start anew. A new beginning. A new start, with new and expanded limitations of the "I" concept and life. Not until he has found himself, can he properly relate to other forms of life and matter. A new morality! A new beginning!

So where do I start this book? To put the reader in the proper frame of mind, to be convincing, to be as objective and unbiased as much as possible, I must take you away from your present society and environment and cultural behavior patterns. I must try to isolate you, to dispel all preconceived ideas and notions that our current society, our way of life is the only way of life or the best way. Nearly all cultures in history have believed that their way of life is or was the best way, but, as stated before, the idea of something better is relative to all people and it is just that which they are seeking as their fulfillment in life.

A constructive step in understanding morality is to understand ourselves, and what better way to understand ourselves than to study the use of languages and observe the cultural behavior patterns of another society. Perhaps, then we may see ourselves better. So, this is where we begin, or is it? Let me say, that this one beginning. This is a beginning for a search for truth in the physical world of matter. In section II, you will experience a second new beginning. A beginning unlike most people have ever experienced. A beginning involving unknown knowledge of an intangible quality to this physical world of matter. Last, in Section III, it is possible to start on yet another new beginning; however, this beginning depends upon you!

To help you on your way, the following proem may provide you with a clue to what life is all about. But this is also a puzzle within a puzzle that requires more than meets the eye.

THE QUESTION AND ANSWER

To all who exist in this Piscean world, there is question
and doubt, as to what life is all about.
Life is a puzzle, a riddle, of which we know little.
A journey of time, a nursery rhyme.

The answer to life is given, but it is also hidden.
Seek and ye shall find is only a state of mind.
The Purpose of life is known, and is tied to that
from which we have grown.

The answer lies separate and apart
and is in another form of thought.
There is one, separated in two, composed of seven, expressed in nine,
conceived in many, in search for and equaling the sum of one.

We are all born of the same age and reflection,
but have chosen and frozen different moments
of our own selection.
Our life, our reality, comes from our personality,
which exists and resists, like a sea of mist.

The Concept forms the foundation and relation
of life's participation.
The Name is our present point of focus that is our path or wrath.
The Part expands and experiences our being and seeing
into this world and touches the next.

To those who see the Aquarius dawn, be patient!
There will be comfort and direction in knowing the connection.
The answer to life is not in question or doubt,
but in the seeking and application of our final route.

CHAPTER 2

Reality or Morality

So, we have now determined our reality. Where do we go from here? Before we proceed with the individual, or "Who Am I", we must explain a little more about how our reality works. To do that, we need to know and understand who or what is the element of control that affects our behavior as an individual and as a society. We are all individuals and therefore the element of control rest within each one of us. Meaning nothing can affect us unless we allow it by giving our power away. We decide or have decided how we and/or our society will function or not function. We have made selections that determine the limits of our own power that those powers of control we have given to those that we decided will govern us.

The element of control is therefore shared responsibility and how we choose to recognize the tangible and intangible energy forces determines our physical life or our reality. Man interprets or sees things as black and white, good and bad, yes and no. That means that man lives in a dual reality, or the tangible and intangible world of opposites and possessions. There would be little interest in relationships that do not add or subtract value to elements that control matter or possessions, because man would neither gain nor lose anything from such a relationship. The intensity of the need or value determines the behavior of the individual to that relationship that is in question.

Relationships are based upon wants, a needs, or preferences in relationship to the individual or who we are or want to become either knowingly or unknowingly. Therefore, the way we behave or relate to everything is determined by each individual. To show you how that reality works, let's take a looks at another earlier statement. We said that man controls himself and his behavior by imposing intangible rules and laws upon himself in order to sustain physical life in a familiar or friendly environment. This environment is a collective mind of the dominate species of man or what we call society. As we said earlier, these rules or laws are supposedly designed to restrict or prevent certain unacceptable behavior and bring stability to relationships between man and nature.

While much group behavior is consider good and desirable, it also limits or restricts thinking to some extent and creates mass patterns of acceptable thought or beliefs known as conformity. By the way, the word conformity has no value until the individual places value on it. That is, it means neither something good or bad by itself.

Left to his own consciousness by himself, man has no problem with rules or laws. Basically, he is in a world of his own even while he is amongst a lot of people. It is only when he has to interact or relate to his fellow man that he may encounter problems. If there is a difference of opinion or thought regarding a matter that affects two or more people, then that difference of thought must be corrected to a ruling of unity, or what will be recognized as real. The legal court ruling on the matter may decide the issue in favor of one person or thought; however, the enforcement of the matter is yet another issue that may have to be resolved. Fortunately or unfortunately, these rules and laws are subject to interpretation and enforcement. Also, being intangible, they can be controlled or manipulated to some extent. How much these rules and laws can be controlled depends on a number of factors, but let's just say that there is no black and white, only shades of gray.

Again, rules and laws were initiated for the greater good of all man kind. A bad relationship or conflict usually ends up before a ruling authority for determining who is right, or whose value judgment or intensity is greater. People usually seek to gain or fear losing something from a ruling in their favor. An oath or the appeal to spiritual authority or higher consciousness does not always insure that man will always use his goodness to the benefit of all involved. Personal gain or greed is a motivating factor that causes a lot of bad behavior. This in turn causes people to make false statements, otherwise known as a lie to manipulate the truth which may affect the ruling of the authority. Supposedly, one knows that it is wrong to lie, but tries to avoid a conflict or prefers the results offered by the false statement and/or consequences of the same. Whatever the final decision or ruling that is rendered by the authority, becomes law. Indirectly, this decision is suppose to unify thought and reality, but it also sets a precedence for future similar cases; therefore, there is more at stake than the immediate ruling.

The question of a false statement or lie brings up an interesting thought. Is there such a thing as a false reality? The answer to this question is no, there is no such thing as a false reality. However, at the same time, you have learned a little about man and his duality in this reality. That means that each individual controls his or her intangible reality, but also shares a common physical reality. To the individual, any and all realities are real. However, within a predominately collective society that shares many of the same ideas and common ancestry, this reality maybe considered false, because it may not be a shared reality. Unless another person or group can accept that which is in question, it does not exist in their terms; therefore, even in mass consciousness there can be minorities that consider or recognize conflicting or dominate thoughts as a false reality. Who or which statement is correct is determined by your definition of your reality or what you want to experience.

Now, that last sentence brings up other interesting thoughts that must be pursued further. Above all, there is the statement that thought can be manipulated; therefore, carefully attention must be given to words and definitions when communicating with one's fellow man. Even when there is agreement on definitions, words have multiple meanings and there is still the prospective of the individual involved. In other words, the individual may know what you are trying to say, but his use of words or connotations effect his interpretation and that may really change the meaning or response to such a clarified communication.

Because thought is intangible, it is subject to interpretation. That thought basically comes down to the question; does everyone hear and see the same things? Again, like above, the answer is yes; however, do we all interpret or recognize what we hear and see the same? The recognition factor is the key to that answer and therefore, that means that thought can be manipulated and controlled as well by society's rules and laws. These statements about thought are designed to bring you aware that everything is not what it seems to be or can be. That is why you will find a lot of definitions and explanations in this book of relatively simple words with complex meanings or interpretations.

Let's get back to our last definition of reality, which we said is a combination of universal and society laws. We were talking about control and conformity and/or mass beliefs for the greater good of all. How does our behavior effect our reality or does reality affect our behavior or are both statements correct? As stated before, the question contains the answer. Both or all statements are correct. However, the correct answer depends upon the relationship of the individual to his own consciousness. On top of that, to answer that statement in accordance to our physical reality, we need to know what that individual is seeking in his relationship to the world around him.

A good lawyer knows how to manipulate intangible thought to explain anything he wants it to be, but he still has to work at it. Man, on the other hand is somewhat like a free lance artist creating his own reality as he goes without a lot of preparation or thought. That is, he is aware of others and their relationship to himself to a greater degree than even his conscious mind is aware of, but he chooses those things with which he is familiar or within a certain comfort zone of acceptability. Therefore, he conforms to certain patterns which he and society recognize as good or favorable.

That last statement means that behavior is a learned activity or a controlled response pattern of conformity to the society in which that person resides. An individual's actions or response can take the form of a physical activity or an intangible communication response, but it must also acknowledge the boundaries of that society. That is, one is taught to recognize and behave in predetermined or controlled pattern in certain conditions or situations and how this is done is just as important as if it is done. Why? Because these recognition actions and responses are patterns of acceptance or acknowledged control that are learned behavior taught to the individual at a very early age. Such pattern behavior has a certain amount of free choice; however, as stated before, most people respond in a predetermined or predictable manner based upon their knowledge of acceptability.

The conformity thought process has inadvertently brought us to another interesting starting point. Supposedly, children have no preconceived idea of what life is all about and how to survive in this physical world we call realty. Childhood, or the beginning of learning what you, the individual and physical life is all about is completely based or dependent on a parent and other older human beings teaching their knowledge of this reality. This is true for a rather lengthy time period in the life of the individual and it is questionable if this process really ever stops. Therefore, associations and dependency are very powerful factors in one's life.

To live one's life is to demonstrate or show what one has been taught and accepts as their reality. Amazing! What if we have all been taught a lie? Then again, maybe everything is just as it is suppose to be and we know what we are doing and what reality is all about. If we are not right about that last statement, we are sure of at least one thing, we are what our parents want us to be or to the best of their ability to convey their understanding of our reality.

The lack of true knowledge, dependency, and fear are powerful tools for human development and behavior conditioning. These forces are basically forms called negative reinforcement. One quickly trades, knowingly or unknowingly, independence for safety and not wanting, within certain limits, for acceptance into this group behavior or society. On the opposite side of negativity is positive reinforcement. This is learned behavior based upon rewards. The latter is usually a little harder to administer and is somewhat selective in its application. That is, it requires a relationship with people and opportunities which are not as common or as easy as punishment. Through pattern repetition of what to do, how to do it, when and where to do it, one eventually succumbs to a reactive learned response and way of life that is acceptable to the society in which the person lives.

In our world or within our society there are many different groups or sub-societies; therefore, it is difficult to get mass thought to agree on a local, much less a world wide basis. It is no wonder that there are many different opinions about behavior and why the subject is so difficult to talk about. Also, the subject does not necessarily lend itself to pure logic and the greater good of all man kind. That is, man is motivated by material interests or the control of wealth which in turn affects the control of people and social standing or power within a community. Competition for these resources or positions of power leads to conflicts of interests and that can lead to unpleasant experiences which may result from both positive and negative forces to control or modify behavior to conform to the will of those who have greater wealth and control. The equality of man is talked about a lot, but is not commonly practiced. Self interests usually always are the normal dominating factors affecting one's behavior and/or ones reality.

Now, how behavior and man's rules and regulations are imposed upon society is another interesting story by itself. Normal behavior is learned from childhood and is subject to repetitive conditioning or learned behavior based upon rewards and punishments. This is actually an ongoing process throughout society up until death. That is, reward and punishment is a way of life that may not be overtly practiced as it once was, but just the same it is there and it is practiced because it works. Meaning, the desire to be part of society leads to uniformity and that leads to conformity, which is more easily controlled and that is the whole idea behind the unwritten laws of morality. But remember, behavior is a relationship. That is, it requires the individual to acknowledge the element of control and once the relationship is terminated however briefly, so too does the control factor revert back to the individual.

Because laws and rules are written by one ruling group of people for intended good of all involved, they are also interpreted by another group of people charged with carrying out the law by punishment or negative reinforcement. Laws are made as guidelines for self disciple. That is, they are supposedly written to explain correct behavior and declared the law of the land for all to obey and follow.

Unfortunately, a lot of people only become aware of what is or is not the law is by doing something which conflicts with someone else who deems this persons actions illegal or against the law. As mentioned, this happens only when man enters into a relationship that is not on a mutually beneficial basis. There can be no conflict when all are in agreement. We also know that words can be manipulated for ones purpose and/or meaning. Because of the ambiguities of the written and verbal language, one can literally change the meaning or intent of the law. If one has sufficient resources and argues long enough, one can change the law or laws to suit the needs of those involve.

Even if the laws were interpreted the same way, they may still be implemented or enforced differently, because the element of control changes constantly. What one person does one time may not be acceptable at another time. What has changed is time, space, and the relationship of the individual to the element of control. Individuals in mass do make a difference. Given the same action maybe only one person may be deemed wrong and punished for his behavior. Why? Because control resides within the individual until he relinquishes that element to someone else. Knowingly or unknowingly, the individual chooses that which he wants to experience. The tangible application of power or the control of intangible thought forms results in unconscious patterns of recognition, which may threaten society or affect the need to enforcement of laws of conformity.

Society or mass thought is a collective thing; therefore, if enough people observe false or inappropriate application of laws, then there is and must be a change in the law or the enforcement authority. Actions or reactions of enough people can create mass thought that can direct intangible forces to change or correct a condition as a result of the knowledge of the inequality of justice under law. Naturally some people may view the lack of uniform discipline or implementation of such actions or non-actions as discriminatory or repressive.

Inconsistent applications of the law can result in bitterness and disrespect toward authority and/or the law in general. If one law or rule is misused or the authority is misused, then a house built of cards may soon crumble. There is a relationship. Now this may sound like a liberal idealistic way of thinking; however, if this pattern is how reality really works, then we are in big trouble. Why? Because laws can and are used to control both the negative and positive actions of people and mass thought can be manipulated for both good and bad. To get around the legal issues of good and bad, morality is more commonly used to manipulate behavior. The subject of morality is difficult to approach in a rational way because it deals primarily with the emotions.

Still, with all of our differences we are predominately a collective society, sharing many of the same ideals and common ancestry, consequently, there is surprisingly great cohesion and conformity that holds our society together. A lot of this cohesion is due in part to religion. Historically the great majority of our population shares what is call western European culture. Attempts have been made in history to change behavior patterns or to eliminate the people, sects, or organizations that do not share the same beliefs. Recently, most of these actions are the so called wars of national liberation, which most of the western society refers to as terrorism.

Other attempts to control or justification for drastic behavior changes, fall under a category we refer to as a state of emergency. This latter situation is usually or supposed to be only used when there is some severe problem affecting the lives of a great number of people. The enactment of such a law is supposed to be temporary until the threat has passed or the situation returns to a near normal condition. What normal means is anybody's guess however, I think it means, that which maintains the status quo.

In any and all situations, any means to impose external controls or controls contrary to one's existing beliefs and/or behavior, is almost impossible to enforce. Any permanent change or mass compliance to such a request must come from within those individuals involved; This is an interesting statement, so keep that latter factor or statement in mind. The state of emergency, enforced by supposedly legal means, is a very powerful means to affect changes and consequently, will receive the greatest support of those involved. Given the proper circumstances and conditions, for a long enough period of time, overall reality and morality can change drastically. However, such a change requires the proper circumstances or a convincing emotional appeal for unity of action for a common good.

Most major changes usually originate in small groups and get tried out and/or modified before they get incorporated into the mainstream of life and this is how it probably should be. Any real worthwhile changes in life are born of time, space, and patience. Meaningful changes must withstand the test of time and space. This is the meaning or media of patience.

Perhaps, the greatest difficulty in dealing with the subject of moral behavior is the problem of emotions. This is probably the main reason why it is so difficult to get everyone involved to think and/or agree to the same or similar form of action. The problem also involves a question of one's closeness or relationship to everything and everyone involved. Rational logic gives way to the emotional fear of losing something or being restricted in some way; consequently, one reacts out of a need or attachment than he does so much from real physiological needs to sustain him. That is, the person or persons involved respond to an outside stimulus that causes him pleasure or pain. This is nothing more than a reaction to the laws of cause and effect. Without the element of conscious rational thought, there can be no agreement.

Few people are willing to give up something they find pleasing or satisfying in some way, shape or form.

In reality, an emotion is a function of the mind and can be controlled rationally; however, this requires an area of understanding of one's self. The mind works on many levels. This is evident alone by the words: Thought, Idea, and Belief. Supposedly, the words all refer intangible functions of the brain. Why then, are there so many different words to describe the same thing or process? Without going into real in depth explanation at this time, these different terms would seem to verify this multi-level functioning of the mind.

Perhaps the word, emotion, does not describe a function of the brain so much as it does a level of consciousness. Emotions are more an awareness of one's thought processes manifested upon the physical senses, in relation to one's involvement or mental positioning. Emotions are the intensity of one's beliefs manifested upon the world about one's self, resulting in either action or reaction. You might say that emotions act similar to the gas pedal on a car, whereas, the function of the mind or thoughts are more like the road or destination one is headed for, be it known or unknown. How conscious you are of all this determines which roads you select and how well you steer the car. Your physical body is like a vehicle that must be attended and properly monitored in order to get you where you want to go and hopefully safe and well. You shouldn't go stepping on the gas pedal without knowing the condition and performance of the vehicle in a relationship to the road ahead.

The functioning of the mind is also complicated by the function and forms of communication. The difficulty of language meaning makes it imperative that we go into specific detail on the words being used in this book. One can use and say the same words in the same way and mean different things. It is important that we all agree on definitions and relationships, or we will lose the continuity or oneness of thought. Verbal speech is a difficult thing to understand, and if you include slang, forget it. You have heard of the generation gap and there has been some acknowledgement of what is being called a creditability gap; therefore, I caution you to make an attempt to agree to those or this form of written communication in order to form a common union of thought. Hopefully, through a careful building process based on written communications, we will build a bridge or structure upon which we can all stand and proceed to some agreed upon destination.

Getting back to the mind, I have purposely stressed the meaning of thoughts and emotions and how they work or function within the individual; however, the control over these functions is something else and I believe that the control over emotions is the primary motivating factor for all behavior. I believe that definite tangible results and over all objectives can be achieved by a re-education of this so called response center or function of the conscious mind.

The example of the car and destination helped to illustrate the function of the mind. Now, instead of trying to improve or modify the vehicle, we are going to try to improve the driver. The idea of this book is to make the individual more aware of the destination and keep his eye on the road, so as to avoid unnecessary and unexpected hazards and accidents along the way. Hopefully, once the destination is known, one can regulate, control the speed or gas pedal, and to be aware of and to recognize problems or situations which delay or hinder the journey of the vehicle and individual. Once this awareness is accomplished or under control, then we can even possibly improve the road or take short-cuts, or even to change the road and destination without getting out of the car.

You see, reality and morality are serious subjects. The exchange of experiences and/or life situation type stories is interesting, but it can also be confusing and misleading to impressionable people as a means to influence behavior. Talking about life experiences is a kind of subversive or indirect teaching form or method, either intended or not. Conversations merely relate one's personal experience to situations which may be entirely different or relate to an entirely different time basis and/or morality. What conversations do is to tell you more about the person doing the talking than about the proper direction or course that should be taken; however, if the person speaking is a so called person of rank in the social-economic community, he may influence a number of people to follow his example or way of thinking. Such influences are neither good nor bad, but one should still consider the consequences of his own actions. In other words, "Think twice before acting!" in questionable or similar situations.

Let me clarify the latter thought. I am cautioning you not to accept blind actions or stereotype responses to certain situations. Man learns by experiencing and to some extent by witnessing and example. One can be warned of the danger of fire, but unless one directly experiences its negative harmful effects, one can not really understand or appreciate that danger. I am not saying you must experience everything yourself to fully understand and comprehend. What I am saying is that each and every person is a unique, one of a kind type of individual and that no two people act or react in the same way given the same situation.

The reason for this difference in thought and action is quite complicated, but I will only say at this point, that no two people see things in exactly the same way. That is, the actual situation really takes on the characteristics of those involved. It is a reflection of themselves that they are looking at. If for example, one is looking at a half color, say fifty percent of red and fifty percent of orange, one person may say that it is orange and another may say that it is red. They are both right as long as they can relate to the same color, even though they may see it slightly different. Whether, they actually see something physically different is of no importance. The important thing is that they both agree that they are talking about a color or visual perception.

The issue of morality is not like dealing with the tangible physical properties of say fire or color. Rather, one is trying to relate to something intangible and cannot see; consequently, the effect on the individual can be drastically different from one person to another. We have been concerned with the individual and how he relates to morality. We have also talked about the need for perhaps more uniformity of thought, or at least the control over this form of thought by the individual in a society or social order. You would think that as long as everyone minds their own business, there shouldn't be any problems or reason to concern ourselves with the issue of morality.

"No man is an island unto himself..." and it is just that simple. Nearly all of our actions somehow affect or involve the lives of other people or things, and these actions directly or indirectly affect morality. All of this inter-relationship is a form of communication that affects our fellow man, as well as ourselves. The results of these inter-actions are either pleasant or unpleasant to varying degrees of intensity. However, most people don't even think about any form of communication as being anything but a natural part of life. Consequently, there really isn't any effort or thought put into such encounters or conversations. Most conversations are more an act of acknowledgement of a status relationship than they are of meaningful dialogue. This is a form of recognition that requires little or no effort on the parties involved. In fact, this is an acceptable form or pattern that you might call mental conditioning for it sets precedence or attitude or a form of behavior that is expected. It is an acceptable custom or tradition set by the society or culture, and it is probably universal in nature.

When dealing with morality, one must also talk about society's customs or social norms. Everyday life here is not the same as everyday life elsewhere. What is acceptable as natural here, others may think unnatural elsewhere. Most people are unaware of these differences until they are in another country or culture. It is only then, that they notice the differences. That's because, in their own country, they accept these customs and traditions as natural because they see and use them every day of their lives. Such behavior may be considered mental conditioning or brain washing. This is not something that should be considered good or bad, it is just a way of life, or pattern that has become acceptable in that particular society.

When that same person is taken out of his immediate environment, he may find himself confronted with new and strange differences. Therefore, in order to survive, he either learns to accept these new patterns of life style as his own modifies them, or he can go back from where he came. He can also try to fight the system with some success; however, that will usually end up with that person experiencing a great deal of isolation, loneliness and perhaps, physical harm. In any case, the individual will undergo a type of growth process or change which will, in some way, affect his behavior. That also means that the environment, which is shaped or affected by its residence, will greatly determine the law of the land or customs.

What I'm getting at is that what is considered natural or unnatural depends more on where you are or what you are talking about. This relationship is called conformity. If you accept those dominant patterns of the land, you are considered one or part of the establishment or land, because indirectly or directly, you support those patterns which are common or dominant. If you do not accept those patterns, but you do not interfere with anyone else, you are tolerated as someone existing in that society. If you fight the patterns, you are often considered a fugitive or criminal. Patterns of behavior that are contradictory to customs are considered unnatural. Natural is the law of the land. But, if you believe that everything is learned, that also means that nothing is natural.

What is normal or natural, is all relative to the immediate environment. That is, people learn how to act, or get along with their fellow man, for the benefit of themselves and/or mutual benefit. Even within that same environment, circumstances or people can change, which can result in an entirely different behavior. This learning of how to adjust or change is not so much a forced change, but more of a voluntary action on the part of all individuals involved. This adaptation is done in order to keep life experiences pleasant and to avoid the consequences of conflict.

This desire to get along and avoid unpleasantness is a form of mental conditioning. It is in this way that mass attitudes or social norms develop. Large groups of people get together with similar ideas and thoughts for a common interest or benefit and because of the number of people involved, these ideas become beliefs or social norms. These attitudes can develop along geographical, racial, religious, business, trade, or other lines, or divisions, of unity where large groups of people share the same interests. Now, this mass or group belief doesn't necessarily make the thought or resulting action either right or wrong, but it is acceptable, which may be confused as meaning right or wrong. Another way of looking at this process is that people are taught and they learn to react, rather than to think and act along creative lines.

As one can see, to attack or criticize existing morality or behavior patterns, is very difficult to do creatively and/or constructively. Such an endeavor is very risky and therefore, requires great care to avoid unpleasantness to all involved. Morality has both positive and negative effects on thoughts, ideas, and beliefs; therefore, one must not destroy a belief without offering an alternative, and hopefully, a better idea. It is not practical or beneficial to tear down without thoughts to build and replace. What needs to be done is to see where we are before we can decide where we are going. What we need to do, is to see what can be used to build upon, to establish a broader, more firm base of communication so that everyone can relate to fires and colors in the same way, without having to suffer the consequences.

Therefore, this book is written with the intent in mind to explain just what one can really believe in, or really exists in the realm of truth as we know it and can be proven beyond a doubt. Hopefully, once everyone can agree on the same point of reference, we can build on that point, everything imaginable and then some. With this truth and knowledge, one can achieve personal gain, satisfaction, achievements, growth and creativity in life's journey back to his origin.

This book is intended to explore the so called rational physical world of matter. It explores the limitations of the physical being and the "I" concept. This section of the book will cover the subject, "Who am I?" in the conventional sense of the world we know. Section II will explore and answer the question, "Where am I?", and deal with a new expanded concept or the "I" concept. Section III will conclude the book and deal with the question, "What am I doing here?", or explain how this new "I" concept can be used or put into practical everyday use.

Now, you might ask another question, after having a brief idea of the contents of this book, and that question might be, "What does that have to do with morality?" The answer to that question will not be obvious to the reader until the last section of the book. Not until the three questions of the amnesia patient are answered, can he begin to start anew. A new beginning. A new start, with new and expanded limitations of the "I" concept and life. Not until he has found himself, can he properly relate to other forms of life and matter. A new morality! Another new beginning!

To properly understand how the mind works and to be objective and unbiased as much as possible, I must take you away from your present society and environment and cultural behavior patterns. I must try to isolate you, to dispel all preconceived ideas and notions that our current society, our way of life is the only way of life or the best way. Nearly all cultures in history have believed that their way of life is or was the best way, but, as stated before, the idea of something better is relative to all people and it is just that which they are seeking as their fulfillment in life.

A constructive step in understanding morality is to understand ourselves, and what better way to understand ourselves than to study the use of languages and observe the cultural behavior patterns of another society. Perhaps, then we may see ourselves better. So, this is where we begin, or is it? Let me say, that this one beginning. This is a beginning for a search for truth in the physical world of matter. In section II, you will experience another new beginning. A beginning unlike most people have ever experienced involving unknown knowledge of an intangible quality to this physical world of matter. Last, in Section III, it is possible to start on yet another new beginning; however, this beginning depends upon you!

To help you on your way, the following proem may provide you with a clue to what life is all about. But this is also a puzzle within a puzzle that requires more than meets the eye.

CHAPTER 3

Journey to Understanding

In trying to write a plain and easily understandable book, one runs into all kinds of problems with the words and the language. Rather than to bore you with the problems of grammar and semantics in a technical manner, I would like to present you with what seems to be a perfectly simple, clear cut question that I want you to answer to the best of your ability.

Question: Let's say that we are going on a trip. We are going from Princeton, New Jersey to Mt. Shasta, California. Now I want you to consider all the problems and obstacles and decide the best way to get from one point to the other.

Simple.... right?

Wrong!

What appears to be a simple problem concerning a journey can become quite an education. The question, as it was worded, only gave you two locations. The rest of the problem was really up to you. Therefore, each person who is trying to answer the question is going to come up with a different answer. Why you ask? Because each person will draw upon his own personal experiences and knowledge. That is, a person usually understands a problem in direct relationship to that which he has experienced. Such experience is usually referred to as empirical knowledge or first hand experience. Something like our statement about learning about fire, but it can also refer to a process of thinking.

So where is the problem? You might ask.

The answer is actually contained in the problem. Everyone who considers the situation, draws on experiences and an environment which is slightly different from everyone else. Because each and every person is different to some degree, each person considers the obstacles and/or difficulties of making such a journey differently. There are no limitations placed on this trip; therefore, each and everyone was permitted to make this trip in the best way in relationship to who is involved.

The word "BEST", is the key word or limiting factor in this problem. "Best" really has no value until one assigns it a meaning. The word "best", only takes on meaning in relationship to the object or objective in this case. One must set limitations in order to arrive at an answer for the word "best". To arrive at "best", we must know: Who is involved? What is involved? When? (in relationship to time). We know where (two assigned points), and why it is necessary to make the trip is not relevant at this time. It is only when these factors or limits are known, that we can get many more people to agree on what is "best".

Even with limitations now placed on this journey, you are still dealing with a theoretical situation in that you are left to your own knowledge of resources available to you. That means to bring this best answer or solution to reality, you must take into consideration the most practical, workable solution that you can afford and/or is convenient to you. In other words, you must bring theory into physical reality. This is still a personal relationship to the word, best, even with a new set of limitations.

The choosing, or selection of the best way or solution to the question takes on a cause and effect type of relationship. It sets up a limitation that affects other limiting factors. Something like a chain reaction. That is, for every action (cause) or selection taken to accomplish a certain task, the end result is brought about in relationship to that action (effect). Each selection is a limiting factor which in turn limits the effect until the task is complete. The journey is over! This is the same process that a computer utilizes to arrive at an answer, but because a computer cannot think, it must be given all of the limiting factors and options. Unless the information has been programmed, there is no way an answer can show up that was not already there or known.

Let's look at some of our options. I believe most people automatically think in terms of one's self, or a single person going on a trip. I think everyone also thought that the fastest way to get anywhere these days, is to get there by air. If money was an issue, or time was not important, this option was probably turned down by a lot of people. Besides, these two points are not very convenient to major commercial transportation facilities. To travel by car requires much more time and effort in both physical and mental sense. The cheapest way to get anywhere would be to walk, if you had the time and/or desire. If I were to have asked you this same question some fifty years ago, your answer would have probably been to travel by train. Prior to trains, you might have said horse and/or wagon. If I changed the time frame even more, who knows what your answer might have been. After air transportation, what comes next?... "Beam me aboard Scotty or Mr. Spock?" If we increased the number of people involved, then your answer may have also changed. If you loved water, you may have considered sailing. The answers are as endless as there are people. Perhaps the mode or style could be more important to you than the means.

If you considered driving by car, it might have to be a luxury car, or a sports model. Maybe the car didn't matter as much as the power plant or means of propulsion, say a solar powered or all electric vehicle. In any case, a means of conveyance must be selected to which you feel most comfortable. Best is a relationship of all options available to you versus your means to pay, render services, or compensate others. That which you select must also be equal to that which you have or are willing to give in the form of various energies. This last sentence or two may sound a little confusing; however, I would rather not go into a long explanation at this time. It will come up again.

After the means of conveyance has been selected, then we must consider the route to be travelled. We may select easy or difficult routes, and these in turn, may be direct or round about. We may be more selective of the road or ground surfaces such as: smooth concrete highways, gravel back roads, or we may blaze a new path cross country. We may select roads taken by friends or others known or unknown to us, or roads hardly travelled at all by anyone. We may get help before our trip, or along the way. We may even get no help or help which actually delays or hinders our trip. We may ask for help or it may be given to us voluntarily. We may also have to pay for the help along the way in the form of time, money, or some other form of compensation. We may choose a scenic route, a very rugged route, a nature type trail, a very dry desert route, a snow blown route, a route through very wealthy neighborhoods, the poor slums of populated cities, or the farms of the rural countryside. This best analogy could go on and on; however, I believe that I have made my point. We have again made a selection of a direction or road to follow which will directly relate in some way to that which we want to experience or must experience in order to get to where we want to be.

So you see, the best way may not be the fastest, nor the easiest. In addition to the fastest and easiest comes cost, speed, convenience, style and a host of other limiting factors which predetermine your selection or defines or places a value on the word, best. To re-emphasize, "Best really has no value until one assigns it a meaning." Again, this value is in direct relationship to that which you have or want to experience.

Now, before we move on to sociology and observing the cultural behavior patterns of others, I want you to think about all of the trips and journeys you have made that went exactly as planned within the limitations that you had set. I bet you are having trouble lifting one finger, or perhaps you were smart enough to remove the restrictions or limitations on such trips so that you could just experience or adjust to the unexpected which you undoubtedly made provisions for. Perhaps the pop poster phrase pertaining to Murphy's Law, "If anything possible can go wrong, it will!" comes to mind.

In this latter paragraph, what I am saying is that the human who is supposed to be solving this problem of "A best way," is incapable of consciously foreseeing all of the difficulties and obstacles that can or will interfere or affect such a trip. Therefore, the word best again is relative to that which one experiences or has knowledge of. If one has never experienced such a trip, how is one supposed to plan or prepare for such a journey? Best is an accumulation of fact or factors that relate to both known and unknown causes and effects within a known environment. Even though factors are both known and unknown to the individual, they may not take place in an environment which is known. Or is it? This question too, will be addressed later.

This book is an exercise or journey between two worlds; therefore, the problem and/or destination may appear very unclear and uncertain. This book, this journey, is the story of being or life. Without explaining the destination, I will try to provide you with the answers to the obstacles preventing you from the positive, creative life and greater happiness. I will not explain your journey for you; however, I will provide you with the knowledge of knowing the right way. The selection is still up to you. Only you can select happiness! And only you, will know that your selection will lead to happiness, for it is only relative to you. This knowledge is not a private thing. Others will know that you have found happiness; however, for themselves, they will not be as certain and it will take them a little longer to know.

This journey that I am about to take you on is so unusual that it is difficult to imagine. Therefore, it is important that the wording be carefully selected so we can avoid as much confusion as possible. Just like our example of the word, best, other words are relative to the individual even though they are common usage type words. Environmental usage and conditioning has changed the value to a lot of the written and verbal vocabulary and language.

As I mentioned earlier in this book, "Communication is probably the most important thing one will learn in his or her lifetime...." Therefore, it is important that we convey the proper meanings; however, words in themselves do not assure us of proper meanings. What is required is a commitment imparted by both the sender and receiver. This is the common union that I referred to. This union is a joining or bonding type process known as communion, or the becoming of one mind or thought. It is not absolutely necessary that we achieve this communion level; but this level would assure us of the exact or true meaning of the written word. It is so easy to misinterpret others because of the failure to even achieve a common union.

Most communications fail because one or more person does not make a commitment to recognize, or become conscious. They are not interested in forming a common bond. They only hear or read what they want, so the information or communication only benefits or reinforces themselves and their beliefs. Communication takes work, creative work. One who is inherently selfish or self centered cannot communicate anything unless it directly relates to his own being. He cannot communicate any greater thoughts because he is unwilling to work at it and make a commitment and recognize the importance of everything, there is.

It was not my intent to get off on the subject of communication again so early, but it is a very important part of life and it is little understood and yet used excessively and often wrongly for the wrong reasons. I have known people to talk incessantly and have found it very difficult to determine just exactly what they were saying or wanted to say. In this latter case, the communicating party fails to listen to what he wanted to say. That is, he is more interested in being noticed than he is in forming a bond to positive creativity. Communication is a form of power. It requires attention and concentration. It is work! It requires an active and passive, or sender and receiver type relationship. To hold one's attention or point of focus is a sense of power over the recipient. It commands one's time and attention.

It is my desire that we communicate in at least a common union to begin this journey together. It is hoped that we will arrive at the same destination together; however, it is not that important that we go in the same direction or go there in the same way. It is only important that we begin and that we seek a positive, creative approach in seeking greater happiness. The results will, hopefully, be the same, but it is not necessary that we can attain the same values in getting there.

In this journey that we are going to take, you as an individual, will hopefully learn that the trip can be somewhat more interesting than the purpose or end result. You may also discover that anything of great value usually involves more difficulties or effort than those things which come easy. Something which cost a great deal does not exactly constitute great value. Those things which are available and/or known to you, but denied to you, usually have greater importance or value than material possessions. Then again, this is a relative thing. Example: Remember when you were a teenager and you were not of age to engage in the social custom or establishments serving alcoholic beverages? Also, do you remember your same feelings toward drinking once you reached that mystical legal age?

The idea of putting worth or value onto an object is an interesting subject in itself and not one which I am about to explain in any great depth in this chapter. Usually, tangible physical objects can be assigned a fixed or monetary cost or worth; however, intangible items such as thoughts, ideas, or beliefs do not or cannot be affixed such cost but they have value. There have been some attempts to place fixed costs to the intangible and it is a growing concern. Basically, this is the system utilized in the business world to affix salaries and consulting fees to individuals or groups or for specific functions resulting in an end result known as a service. Again, this is a relative thing, in that it is directly related to whomever is in control of that immediate end result or service. It is an integral overall cost that must be assigned and relates to the well being of all concerned in the unit or organization that seeks these services and/or end result.

One must adjust or conform to these limitations or values either self-imposed, imposed by others, or both. The acceptance of a position in the business community or services type industry, constitutes worth or value within certain determined limits of that community or industry. Somewhere along the line, someone or group decided that certain, specific skills and/or services were worth or valued over others. More than likely, this assignment had to do with what was called, the free market, which is based on a supply and demand exchange of money for services. This is our cause and effect relationship at its grandest. Supposedly, easier skills were more abundant and therefore cost less than skills which were not in as great a supply, but needed. This situation would account for some of the discrepancies and inequalities for services rendered today, but not all.

Even in the world of tangible goods, there is inequality of worth or value and monetary compensation because of this supply and demand type market system. This exchange system is somewhat like our word, "best", in that "best" is relative to each individual. That is, the demand for certain commodities or goods and services, is directly related to that which one has or wants to experience. What I am saying, is the same thing that I have said earlier. You can't have "best", until you set up limitations on that which you want to achieve, or the end result. In our market or society, a lot of like goods and services are exchanged without too much difficulty; therefore, that would tend to indicate that there is a lot of uniformity of like opinion and people. However, the only thing this uniformity really indicates is that there is a lot of acceptance of this system, not that there are equal values.

In our society, the free market system tries to compensate a little for the intangible qualities or value of the individual. That is, some people are more capable of producing the needed results or better results than others. These results, in turn, are related to time and the overall concern for this quality we call "best". The individual who adjusts or conforms to or within the limitations set by those in control, normally tries to compensate such individuals because they have greater value to the overall concern and/or end result. In other words, a tangible end result is, or can be, improved upon by an intangible quality and in turn, those responsible are rewarded for their efforts above those who do not work within those limitations.

In the latter situation, the word "best" does not relate to the individual so much as it does to the overall well being of that unit, group, company or society. Perhaps, the word "best" can be defined as that which benefits and/or perpetrates the overall organized unit. The term benefit, is another one of those limiting or relative term words which again is directly related to the majority or whoever is in control of the immediate end result. In this case, even though we are talking about a larger unit than the individual, the limitation(s) must be set by an individual acting in behalf of the larger unit. The final structure must allow for a group or organized participation; however, the limit is still set by one, with the approval of others. "Best", therefore becomes a majority or consensus of opinion in relation to the group and end result. It is not a question of morality as it is, a desire to experience a specific environment related to a journey or act of movement in a specific direction.

Earlier, I said, "Those things which are available and/or known to you but denied to you, usually have greater importance or value than material possessions". But, what about those things which are not known to you? What about the value of something which is unknown to you? Obviously, since it is unknown, it can't be relative. It can't have value. Or can it? The value of gold has been known almost since the beginning of time. But minerals, such as uranium, platinum, etc., were of no ones concern or interest back then. Why? Because there was no relationship to the form of matter or mineral, to anything useful to man until fairly recent times.

Now, that's interesting!

Why? You ask!

Because, that means that values and/or relationships change. That means that everything has value; however, its value or importance is dependent upon its immediate relative nature or usefulness to man in a certain time frame. This is a form or movement in a linear direction that can also be considered a form of growth. To put it in a more simple way, the individual or person(s) uses or does something to accomplish something else. By repetitive actions and slight variations, this something gradually changes into something else that accomplishes the task or end result faster and/or better than the original something. That means that there is a form of growth or change that can also be likened to a journey; whereby, you continually meet new encounters and/or experiences.

Hopefully, this book is a journey to make the unknown, known and relative to each individual who reads it. This book is a book of knowledge which relates to both the known and unknown worlds of the multi-dimensional self. It is a practical guide for dealing with the world around us. It is a journey to rediscover our own understanding. This is a book that will show you the relationship of values upon the individual and how that affects and controls who you are, where you are and what you are doing here.

Man is at a crossroads in his life right now, and the direction that he takes, will affect himself and this reality we call earth. The direction he chooses or selects, is very important to his own well being and the greater well being of all living things. Whether he chooses a new road or continues on the road he is on now, is up to him and no one else. Reviewing past experiences, it is reasonably certain that man will continue on the path that he is on now. That doesn't necessarily mean that is good or bad, it just is. However, it is also reasonably certain that that experience will also be filled with some happiness, with pain and suffering being dominant. If that is good, then there is some question as to what this reality is all about and hopefully, this will be addressed within the contents of this book as well as the question of morality.

Man is a collection of habits, customs, traditions and patterns that make up his behavior. Therefore, his journey and the road that he takes, is likely to be one with which he is familiar. Not necessarily because he likes it, but because he knows what to expect. One can seem to tolerate or adjust to good and bad, so long as it is confined to or held within certain limitations of acceptability. What that means is just about anyone's guess. I guess a good answer is for you to just look around you and see what acceptability is. I suppose you could say that acceptability is that which is manifested into physical reality. Whatever man has created, is therefore acceptable. That again doesn't mean that it is good or bad, it is just acceptable.

Now, that last statement covers a lot of ground. That covers all those things tangible and intangible that are considered good as well as those things that are considered bad. That means that good is the freedom to do what you want when you want, but also means that you can be poor, starving and/or destitute. On the other hand, bad can be considered a violent criminal act that takes from those who have for those people or persons who do not have. This may be for the purpose of one's own survival or one's own gain or wealth. So what is right and what is wrong? Hopefully, this question will be answered.

Our trip or journey from Princeton, New Jersey, to Mount Shasta, California is more significant than might meet the normal eye. Not only is it a trip that involves the traversing of a great distance, it is also a symbolic journey that involves other dimensions. That is, Princeton is supposedly a well-known learning center in this country and society. It is also, or was, the last home of the late Albert Einstein, one of the major movers and thinkers in this latter day world. The other location, Mount Shasta is supposedly shrouded in mystery, folk lore and is supposed to have powers that are mystical in nature. These two locations, these two points or positions are somewhat in two different worlds, even though they share the same geographical reality. That is, one represents one of the best things that our culture or our man made society has to offer, and the other extreme or position is something that cannot satisfy that same culture or society as something that is relevant and worthy of any significance or attention. One is known as something beneficial and the other is known for nothing or shall we say, frivolous in nature or man.

This book is a journey from the known to the unknown. It is a trip worth taking. One's reality is not as simple as most people seem to think. Then again, it is and it isn't. That is, we all relate to the outside physical world through our physical senses. What about that which is intangible? Does that have a reality of its own? If it doesn't, why doesn't it? What makes one's reality real and the other, not? What about dreams, how does that fit into the rest of this questionable nonsense? Does our world end where our physical senses won't go any further? Why can't we perceive beyond our physical senses, or can we? Questions, questions, questions! Are there any answers? YES ... There are!

Our chapter began with the questioning of the word - "best", but now, it even goes beyond that. The word - "best", can only relate to this physical reality...or can it? Here we go again! The problem of communication is that it usually involves a one-on-one basis. That is, it requires a sender and a receiver and it must relate to everything in a linear sequence that has a starting point and an ending of some kind. To convey information or descriptive data in any other way, would not constitute communication of an understandable nature. Information must be displayed or organized in certain patterns that in themselves, have smaller or shorter beginnings and endings. They must be organized patterns that form a structure of thought. Any other patterns are not recognizable and are therefore, ignored or discarded as irrelevant and that is the problem(s) that we face in this physical reality.

Other worlds may exist, however, because we cannot relate to them, we ignore them and become unconscious to these other patterns. That doesn't mean that they don't exist. It just means that we fail to recognize or utilize such patterns. You might say that there are many or more roads or paths to travel than meets the eye; however, it also means that only one road will be chosen. Maybe it is possible to come to crossroads, look down and beyond the corner without even moving and seeing what is in store or what life has to offer in the way of challenges and growth for each individual, and then decide which way you want to proceed. Maybe you can't see everything, but you like the relationships or new challenges that lay before you. But it is more often than not, that which is familiar to you that makes you decide to proceed in the current direction and relationships with which you are accustomed, be it good, bad or indifferent.

This book is a journey to understanding that which is and is not. It involves a process of growth, expansion, or movement in a new direction. Man grows in many ways, but unless his growth can be related to value, there is no need or purpose to life, as we know it. Just ask anyone down and out in any major inner city. It is important that each individual recognize and understand values so that he can relate to his environment. He must learn to grow, expand and change, or his value to himself and others, ceases. The end result is achieved. So you see, beginnings and endings are important, but only in the way they relate to other things. A journey is a form of growth, in that it involves more than just the self. It is relative to other things. It involves expansion of the tangible and the intangible and it is relative to each individual.

The word - "best" is a relative term that only relates to that particular individual. What is best can be better answered by asking the question; "What do you want to experience?" A trip or journey is a growth process that enlarges one's area of knowledge. That is the purpose of this book. It is relative to each individual. Each person will receive, expand, or relate to that which he can recognize and wants to experience. There is more here than meets the eye. You must need to know where and how to look for it. Hopefully, this book has all the answers, or at least it tells you where to find the proper answers. We are at the crossroads. Where do we go from here depends upon you. Let us begin our journey, but let us begin with a little mystery. The following is a little piece of prose that may get your interest to continue your journey.

In an abstract way, "It's Almost Tomorrow", reflects the current thoughts of frustration that constantly surfaces through one's lifetime; however, it also ends in a prophecy or possible probability based upon understanding or the lack of it. This is a relationship of beginnings and endings that relate to growth or a journey into consciousness.

IT'S ALMOST TOMORROW

It's almost tomorrow, and I have yet to change.
The stars in the universe illuminate the darkness, interrupted
momentarily by soft billows of moonlight mist, which move
slowly on, deliberate, but unsure of their journeys end.
There is a somber sound of silence, the essence of which
conveys a joyful fear.

The moment appears suspended, as if a segment of life were
slowly evolving and becoming a physical reality.
Consciousness seems absent, but a sense of wanting, wishing,
holding and hoping for a new and better day is present.
Man and nature are temporarily at rest.
The world sleeps with anxious thoughts and illusions of peace.

Flickering starlit shadows reflect the fading images of
progress and knowledge.
That which is, is not what it appears to be.
Visions of truth are like lifeless forms of the night,
without shape, substance or meaning.
THE BRILLIANCE OF WISDOM IS IN DARKNESS!
The night is almost over and the dawning is to begin.

The brilliance that once was, will again return.
But, not until the true ancient past is re-discovered,
the plague of the three sunless days of Egypt returns, and
a new Stonehenge is built for a revised 17 year calendar.
Until then, I cannot change, for it's almost tomorrow.

CHAPTER 4

The Sociological Identification

Now, let's see....where do we begin?

I guess we'll begin just where we left off.

Our new beginning and our new journey begins with the word - "growth". As you have learned, growth is a relative word that involves the number two or more. By proper definition, growth pertains to an increase or progression of sorts, but it is also a word that sets limits. That means that two or more objects, items, or points, are involved. Actually, it is a series of short beginnings and endings.

To grow indicates movement or change of some kind. Growth involves time and space of anything that can be identified in a linear direction. That means that this identifiable object had a starting point or beginning and that its present situation in time and space is related to its start or its end result. Perhaps you may remember a basic concept of science that says, "all matter is in constant motion". That means that there is change taking place, but you may not be able to observe it. It also means that the object is no longer in its exact same condition or position to its original beginning. To make it simpler yet, it means that if we draw a straight line, we have a beginning and an end. Growth means that we are at some point along that line of progression.

Why all this concern for the word - "growth?"

It is because, growth is what life is all about!

Man is said to grow in four ways. These are: mentally, physically, spiritually and socially. Of these four, spiritually is probably the least understood form of growth and socially, is probably the least thought about form of growth. There is little that has to be said about mental and physical growth. Most people have a very good idea of what is meant by growth in these two areas because they can definitely relate to them and they are noticeable. This is somewhat like our science concept that puts all matter into motion. I guess people can see the motion of this matter or growth much easier than growth of the spirit and that of sociology.

In dealing with the subject of growth and man, it is necessary to get into some rather technical areas of study. This is something, I would like to avoid; however, I see no way to get around it. This is a polite way of saying that we are going to be discussing some rather boring information that a lot of scholars think is important and make a big deal over.

The subject concerning the growth of man falls under many classifications; however, the two areas that we are most interested in, are those of Anthropology and Sociology. These two classifications or limited areas of study, concern man's physical growth in relation to his fellow man.

Anthropology is primarily concerned with the study of the physical and mental characteristics of the various racial groups of people. It is a systematic study and classification of people by a variety of criteria, all of which is artificial or intangible. That is, man or scholars have set limitations that supposedly identifies people into groupings based on; biology, religion, politics, ideology, occupation or any other division that may involve or affect or influence other people. Whereas, Sociology deals with all of the above, but primarily it has more to do with its organizations, institutions, and society. In short, it deals with human values.

Like any other supposedly intelligent, clear cut and dry subject worthy of study, you get what you are looking for. Depending upon which source or authority you read or study, you will find that man is classified into either one, three or five major racial or physically structured beings or species. For simplicity sake, let's go with the idea that all the races are a variety of a single species and then go with the anthropologists who claim that the environment affects physical or biological changes. That is, man over a period of time, has evolved physically due to adaption to climate, food supply and even culture or self imposed practices. Other divisions or limitations which may be noticeable are the learned habits imposed by technology, economics, religion, language, social organizations, and culture.

Now, here you have some of the identifiable limitations affecting the growth of man. But, it should be understood that man is not committed by his physical or learned habits to any particular variety of behavior. Culture is not biologically transmitted. Culture only transmits tradition. It is culture, with its ideas and concepts of good, bad, right and wrong that bind men together. It is these intangible ideas and standards that form or bond people together for a common purpose and growth within certain defined limitations. This union, in return, gives each individual a sense of not merely who or what they are, but of what they are likely to become. It is shared experience which relates to the individual and the larger group. This is our sociological identification. This is our accepted self imposed rules of behavior known as morality.

This acceptance or identification process is, a supposedly strange involuntary act committed on our part at birth. We identify and assume responsibility from day one, whether we like it or not. By the age of three, our identification is almost complete and irreversible. Our identification process is both an active and passive relationship. These early years are formidable years of acceptance and passive learning habits. It is in the later years that the active response and teaching habits are most noticeable; however, this reinforcement of values is a constant progressive process involving great responsibility.

This identification process is a conditioning program based on a stimulus and response type relationship which is extremely strong in molding the individual. The end result of this process is a conditioned individual that acts or responds rather than thinks in most cases. There is a certain amount of tolerated thinking; however, it is also somewhat limited or directed in certain areas which do not affect basic beliefs. This conditioning program can be thought of more like action-reaction situation or our analogy of beginnings and endings, otherwise known as limitations. Things are not thought of as either right or wrong, they just are. These unquestioned responses can therefore be classified as beliefs. Such responses or beliefs are the bases of civilizations and cultures. These intangible actions or responses of a mental or physical nature form relationships that have tangible qualities or values that hold people together. Again, this is our sociological identification.

At this point, you should be aware that both you and I are part of a larger group. Therefore, it is totally impossible that either of us can be totally unbiased in our mental processes and attitudes concerning other cultures and groups. We are conditioned to respond with likes and dislikes rather than to think intelligently and logically. However, we are given free will to make such important decisions in regards to other relationships. We can make logical decisions against our conditioned likes or responses, but the odds and chance for doing so are against us. We are products of our environment! Not victims!

This larger group that I belong to, and probably yourself, is known as the western civilization or culture. This sociological group has spread itself more widely than any other group of people that has so far been known. The size of this group and its technological achievements dominate all the peoples of the world. The main characteristic traits of this group are its predominately European historical past and its Christian society or form of ethics. There are exceptions to this criteria and in fact there are numerous varieties or subcultures within this grouping, as there are in all cultures.

These subcultures lead us into a kind of gray area that should be talked about briefly. Just like our problem of determining the number of physical races, the number of subcultures is compounded. It becomes very difficult, if not impossible to classify all of these subcultures and it also depends on who is doing the classifying. Again, this is a relative situation which varies with the results that one wants to be achieved. For sake of argument, we will say that these larger groupings of people can be broken into smaller groups according to their special interests. That is, these new smaller groups exhibit strong characteristics that are noticeable and therefore can be separated or classified as a group that represent special interests or limitations.

The only trouble in recognizing these subcultures is that you have so many special interests that people can belong to a great many different special interest groups. Therefore, you can be counting or classifying the same individual to one or a dozen special groups. In effect, you will be counting the same person more than once. It is therefore also possible that the same person can be in effect for or against himself in some specific issue or action. Example: You can have a lawyer who is a member of a gun club organization, and then you can have a group of lawyers introducing legislation to eliminate guns. Therefore, the question of classification loses some of its importance when you delineate the lines of limitations.

Some of these groupings are very important, such as the grouping of people by occupation and/or purpose in life; whereas, the classification of say religion, which primarily denote the style of worship, is of a lesser importance. Then again, this classification is only relevant in a peacetime situation. If you had a condition of say, a religious war over idealogy, then it would be very important to know this classification. It is again important to note the end result or purpose of these limitations and how they relate to a specific situation.

One last note about subcultures. These cultures within a culture, or smaller groupings known as organizations, families, tribes, classes, cliques, etc., can also be known as a minority. Now, a minority means to be part of the total, but belonging to that part which is not in control or to be fewer in numbers than the larger distinguishing limitations. One must be careful when designating a minority as to not confuse apples and oranges. That is, one must be careful not to count one person into more than one minority grouping. To do so would change the issue or problem and not the quantity for or against something. Remember even though one belongs to a minority, that does not necessarily mean that, that person supports that minority and/or their beliefs.

The implied meaning of a minority connotes inferiority, because one or that particular group is fewer than the overall total; therefore, they are supposed to be subject to the will of the majority. In actuality, there is no clear cut majority or consensus of thought; rather, there is this overlapping of minorities that make up the whole. We are a society or culture of individuals. Control, is the self imposed limitations or value responses of the individual to the greater overall total or end result to society. You notice, we have come back to the number one or total again.

So you see, the important thing to remember then, is not so much the division or classification of the minority or subculture, as it is the overall unit, governing body, or control factor. It is the relationship of the individual to the end result that is the controlling factor. Unless the individual supports the control unit, that body cannot function. How the individual functions in this relationship is difficult to determine. Basically, this is our cause and effect relationship or action/reaction behavior which is reinforced, intensified or given importance or value by a stimulus response type behavior pattern, all rolled up into one. In effect, you have an action (special interest) that has certain tangible qualities of force, even though it consists of intangibles, that is intensified or given existence relative to the stimulus response type reaction.

I'll bet that last statement was clear as mud. To try to simplify that point, I'll try to give you an example. Suppose we say we have a square block that some group thinks is important. This block gets tossed into a bunch of other blocks of supposedly equal importance, size, shape, etc., how does one notice this block. This is our cause and effect relationship. The only way for this block to be noticed is for some action to occur by some form of stimulus, and the intensity of the stimulus depends on the intensity of the response desired. That's like saying the height to which I raise that block, affects or directly relates to the impact or impression that block makes upon the total relationship of all the other blocks. The amount of exposure or attention affects the response, but it is the qualities or weight of the block that is significant and that is something extremely difficult to pin down. That's the unknown quality that cultures play on behavior patterns.

Cultures determine modes of behavior in action, thought, and intensity. Cultures impart intangible building forces of self imposed limitations that control. It appears that the relationship is held together by a constant variable that has its own set of rules. That is, in the act of growth, we increase and progress in a certain linear direction on an almost pre-ordained manner based on evolving limitations or at least a line of probable actions. By making selections, one sets into motion certain counter responses or actions that in turn continuously sets in motion a process of growth or change in a specific linear direction. This is really a series of short beginnings and endings.

This is a process of growth or a type of conditioning program that we alluded to earlier in our childhood, except, now the situation is so common place that we no longer can consciously relate to the process. In effect, this indicates or concludes that behavior patterns are predictable, as well as that of cultures. This is also our computer type example that concludes that unless specific information is put in (enacted or programmed), there is no way an answer can show up that is not already known, because input limits output to a specific known answer. There is no thinking necessary or involved in this process. It is a progressive path of short beginnings and endings.

Let me elaborate a little more on this patterning process. We acquire our knowledge and behavior by experiencing and observing the interactions of the world around us. These experiences are reinforced by drawing on past history and/or memory of similar situations. In a sense, we are conditioned somewhat like laboratory animals; except, we are given a greater latitude and freedom of movement than our caged friends. Just the same, we reinforce our beliefs by the system of stimulus and response type patterning. That is, we are rewarded for proper behavior and punished or not acknowledged for improper behavior. This is a form or process of limitations. Through repetitive situations, a specific response is generated which becomes automatic and can therefore be called, a belief. Because our laboratory or our environment seems almost limitless and non-confining, we are unaware of our own conditioning. Cultures are in a sense, nothing more than groups that conform to a specific patterning behavior.

Now, to conform means to adapt and adapt means to change. This kind of indicates that everything grows and changes. Like our scientific example of all matter is in motion, these changes may be so slow as to be imperceptible. Therefore, although most things appear to be the same, they are in fact, different. Even in the most controlled environment designed to prevent change or to hold standards, there is in fact, change taking place. How can that be? You ask. Well, these changes again are so slow as to be unnoticeable or insignificant, but it again points out the fact that the item relates to something or some person and therefore, is identifiable. To specify one quick and easy example, I just want to say that all items in this physical reality relate to time and space. That's like saying that if I move an item physically, I have in some way affected a change to space. Even if I don't move the item, it will change in relation to time itself and possibly by some form of expansion (growth) or contraction (resistance).

In any case, it is a common everyday process of growth to adapt to one's environment. Each and everyday, there are a series of changes taking place that need special or slightly different actions to accomplish the same or equal desired end results. Most people can adjust to these changes with little difficulty. However, to adapt to another culture is something which is quite difficult and cannot be done effectively. One can tolerate and adjust to differences and changes to a certain extent or within limitations; however, one cannot normally act contrary to basic beliefs no matter how hard they try. That's like the old saying - "You can take the city boy out of the city to the country, but you cannot take the city boy out of the boy".

Sure, it is possible to live within other cultural environments, but one would never become part of these new environments mentally. It is in effect, quite another world or reality, and one cannot relate to something that was never there to begin with. One can go through the physical motions of conforming, but one can never achieve mental compatibility, because the early learning habits that teach beginnings and endings, was not there to begin with.

The willingness of individuals to impose self limitations or to conform to specific behavior patterns, seems strange. The idea of mental compatibility has evolved over a long period of time, just as the physical characteristics of the various races has evolved. Man has discovered through the years that there are great advantages enjoyed by living together in a common relationship. Left on his own, man had to be concerned about his food, shelter, and security. His daily tasks were totally directed toward providing for himself and family. In small groups, he could share or specialize in various skills which could provide to the greater well being of the group concerned, thereby, giving him more time to enjoy some of the rewards and pleasures that life had to offer, as well as some of prestige, pride, wealth, position or control that this new organizational structure gave him.

Supposedly, man has progressed to a point where he no longer must perform daily activities or functions which are solely aimed at his well being and that of his family. Now, man has grown into a interdependent gregarious individual who seeks certain specialized functions in support of this greater organized unit called civilization and cultures. This evolution is deemed to be greatly beneficial to all of society because it has allowed individuals more time and freedom to seek and develop more creative endeavors and more beneficial achievements to help strengthen his particular culture. Therefore, the adaption of man into organized units was done voluntarily in an effort to improve his own lot from the necessities, wants and the boredom of repetitive routines, which consumed his entire life.

Modern man, in the western civilization, no longer thinks in terms of interdependency; however, it is still there, it still works, and it still is the underlying strength that makes this culture what it is today. It is this organizational structure that has allowed us to progress in the more technical areas of creativity and to enrich the lives of all mankind. Today, we have reached a point where, "Man is learning more and more about less and less." That is, man is specializing in such limited areas of study, that the knowledge he derives from such specialization is no longer information that aids in the general well being of all, but rather, it only contributes to other individuals of specialized studies. This information or specialization is supposed to trickle down to benefit all; however, this route or time span becomes longer and longer as specialization increases.

The dependency and specialization of people, has continued to grow and intensify over the years, but man has gotten so accustomed to this relationship that he no longer thinks in terms of dependency and shared responsibilities. In fact, because of his increased specialization, some of these people can no longer relate in a constructive manner to living off the land and providing for their own survival. One does not normally think about dependency when there are so many sources of supply and alternatives which one can utilize to fulfill his wants and needs. This is something like the adage, "Out of sight, out of mind." It is a relationship that is now considered uncommon and therefore, not even thought about. This lack of thought or forgetfulness is reinforced by all the overlapping and backup systems of the supply and demand type marketing structure that civilization has constructed, but just the same, there are limitations. In such an environment, even the word survival, no longer has the significance it once had.

In a land of plenty, one thinks more about his wants and himself than in shared responsibilities and the greater good. The reason for this change in attitude is simply because the values of such ideas cannot be properly related too. In an affluent society, wants, seem to create more wants and the value of such wants, diminish as they are possessed. "The more you get, the more you want." The importance or value, is lost. That's because value is not necessarily in the object or possession, but is the means or way of accomplishing the end result. As a modern travel agency slogan once read, "Half the fun is just getting there." In such an environment, happiness or satisfaction cannot be properly achieved, because value is an intangible quality that relates not only to the possession, but to the individual as well. The filling of wants does not constitute great happiness per se, as the relationship involved in accomplishing the end result or possession, which is indirectly, a form of self enforced responsibility.

In a realistic relationship, we indicated that a selection and in this case, a possession must be equal to that which you have or are willing to give, in the form of various energies. That's something like saying that one deserves or has earned the right or privilege to the end result through personal efforts or actions. This possession then is directly related to a cause and effect relationship, but the amount of efforts or actions needed to accomplish this task relate more to a stimulus-response type assessment to the word, value, in that it establishes its degree of importance to that individual. Therefore, since the effort or value is a personal assessment, the relationship of the possession to the individual may not be the same to each individual who experiences this same possession. Given the same end result, the value may be different to each individual who experiences it.

The idea of dependency and responsibility does not relate to modern western man's environment, as it may in other cultural environments. In our culture, the value of these intangible qualities is not known or possessed, nor are they sought; therefore, they have no major tangible values or importance at this time in relationship to this culture. But even though this culture may not value these qualities, there is still a relationship. This is a cultural relationship which you unknowingly agreed to by engaging in or partaking in the physical life experience. You may or may not agree to the worth or value of an object or possession, but because you are part of a greater organized unit, you may unknowingly agreed to fulfill your obligations of and to that greater unit. You may try to resist this integration or interaction, but just the same, it is there and it is the dominate force that prevails in determining your behavior.

So this is what social identification is all about. It is about the growth and journey of a larger organized unit that is bound together by dependency and responsibility to the overall well being of the individual and the organized unit known as culture. This grouping is a tight knit structure that is specified and functions as a single unit, but it is only as strong as its weakest link and this link is called value. It is a difficult intangible link or relationship that does exist and does work; however, in the western culture, this force lacks value or the limitations of other societies.

In our civilization, the idea of dependency and responsibility is openly denied, because the relationship is difficult to determine and confusing to the average individual. Just the same, it is there, and the importance of this relationship can only become quite noticeable during a time of crisis or in the event some major disaster known as a state of emergency, that might affect our marketing system of the distribution of goods and/or services. It is this identification of intangible qualities that have a tangible binding force and growth in a linear direction of probability.

I will close this chapter with a poem that has mixed thoughts. There is a connection or link that binds man to one another and I think you can see that in this piece.

THE CONCEPT

In the beginning, God created the heaven and earth
and filled it with consciousness.
That conscious entity manifested itself into the physical
being known as man.
From infinite energy, without form, came a world of images
and limitations.
And one image, MAN, was given dominion over this world.

Mutual deliberation became the basis of this reality and
civilization of probability that we know.
This progression of thought, this world, and this moment
is now our home.
This is the present environment we have chosen to expand
our experiences of becoming.
However, we have forgotten our true origin and inner awareness
in our spacious present.

We are from one, we are of one, we receive from one, and we
give to one, in a multidimensional manner.
Yet, we are more than the sum of one's parts.
We are past, present and the future.
We are, we were, we will be.
The selection and choice is of our own and his guidance.

The element of time is a concept of mind and our projected world.
At this level, we are subject to deception and trials of
our own volition.
At the next level, we will remember the concept of good,
better and best.
Before then, we must approach another step in the evolution
of our becoming.
We will once again, and soon, recognize and remember
all that we have forgotten.

Until that moment, inequity will prosper and multiply and
wreak havoc with the quality of life that could have been.
This trauma will cease when the entities of one will be
the enemies of none.
Man, with a renewed understanding from within, shall again
join God and his creation on a new venture in this world.
There will then become a true heaven on earth and peace among men.

CHAPTER 5

The Learning Process

What better way to start a new chapter than to start with another definition. This time, however, this word was used quite frequently in the last chapter without any special attention to its meaning and/or limitations. This word that I am referring to is that of possession(s). I used this word interchangeably in reference to objects or tangible things, as well as intangible thoughts and ideas. Some people might perfer the use of the word property, instead of possessions. However, property carries too many other conotations. Even this word possessions, and its usage needs a little explanation as to its meaning and its relationship to the individual.

The word possession, refers to either an intangible quality or tangible item which belongs to, or is part of something or someone. It belongs to that thing or person because of some form or bond that holds or connects these items and/or person(s) together. This bond is called a relationship; however, it can also be identified by other limiting descriptive words. This bond or relationship is something which is shared by two or more items and/or persons, but it does not necessarily change or affect those things involved. In fact, these items and/or people involved, gain from such a relationship and in a sense, they become one in character, or can be identified as being part of one thing or person because they form or have a beginning and ending.

I think an example may be appropriate here. Let's say that we have a wooden chair. This chair is put together with parts (small beginnings and endings), which are in turn bound together by glue and nails and the efforts of an individual(s). The materials used in the construction of this chair are all tangible items which can be seen. In this case, the glue and the nails are the tangible binding substance and the limiting words that describe their qualities. In addition to these tangible substances, the chair is also a result of work and effort of the individual(s), which is of an intangible nature which cannot readily be seen, except for the quality and/or time and materials used in the appearance and end result.

Now, the bonding forces do not stop with the end of the construction of the chair but it is another small beginning and ending. Because the chair was made by someone, it belongs to that person, unless that person is employed by someone else for the purpose of making such things as chairs. In the latter case, the chair belongs to whoever controls that company who employs the worker. But in the latter situation, the chair only temporarily belongs to the company. The chair serves as a means to another end for that company and/or persons involved in the building of chairs. The chair will be sold to yet another person(s) for the monetary sum in exchange for the chair.

So you see, there is a bond which identifies the chair to the individual, as there is a bond between the parts to the overall end item. Each has a number of beginnings and endings. The overall efforts of the individual resulted in either the construction or procurement of the chair. The efforts of an individual result in an end item and in that item becoming a possession of someone or individual. The bond that holds the chair together is tangible and can be easily identified as a specific ingredient or substance of matter which has a function or purpose. Whereas, a chair left unattended or unguarded in a no man's land, has no visible, observable relationship to an individual. It is abandoned and therefore worthless. It has lost its value to man but has begun a new relationship with the elements of nature for its return to its origin.

In the latter situation, unless someone can recognize or identify the owner or maker of the chair, there is no relationship and therefore this would not be considered a possession. The chair belongs to no one, but just the same, these bonds of ownership are there in time and space to some extent and therefore represents a possession. It is only the individual who is not connected to the chair by visible means that is missing. Even if the chair could be identified as a possession of someone, because of its unnatural setting or position in time and space, its relationship is questionable. That is, the chair is beyond the limitations of a possession, even though it was a possession at a time and can still be again, it is now only an unnatural object subject to natural laws and/or destined to be reclaimed as a possession of our physical world of matter.

In the last chapter, we identified the word possession as meaning, that which is sought to fulfill wants and desires for the purpose of happiness or the greater well being of all. Then we said that in the western civilization, the possession itself has become the most important form identifiable with the happiness of the individual, but it is also a form which has considerable or variable qualities and depends on the individuals involved. In short, the western culture equates happiness to tangible material possessions, or thinks of wealth and/or possessions as happiness. This latter interpretation is slightly different from our earlier variety of the word, possession.

Just to remind you, we said that a possession is something which has a kind of form, either physical or non-physical, and is part of, or belongs to something else, even though it is something in and by itself. A possession is related to an individual in a position of unity because that person has expended some effort or energies in a cause and effect relationship to acquire that something. That is, a possession is the result of an individual's wants or desires after he has identified that which he is seeking as either happiness or his well being and his willingness to part with certain energies and/or tangible efforts. Tangible efforts here, relates to monetary compensation derived from physical or mental energy. Monetary compensation is the most common denominator of tangible efforts.

In short, a possession is an end result or entity in itself. This end result, in turn, has a being all its own, but one which the individual exerts a form of control or ownership over for his own use, needs, wants or whatever purpose he desires. A possession belongs to someone or something; therefore, it is related or relative to that person or thing by a bonding element, connection or force, just as an individual relates to a culture. Therefore, possessions relate and are acquired for the greater well being of that particular individual. Possessions add to or enhance the individual in some way, shape or form first mentally and then physically.

Perhaps, one of the most interesting things about possessions is that they relate to the individual in such a way that they function as the basis of certainty about which the individual patterns his life around. That is, the individual accumulates possessions for the purpose of trust, comfort, familiarity, and/or assurance from objects and things in a world of constant change and motion. Therefore, even though a possession is an end result or entity in itself, the end result of a possession by an individual is relative to his stability, comfort and peace of mind. In effect, the individual creates his own personal reality from the world about him, through a process of selection and efforts designed to benefit his well being through the accumulation of possessions either tangible or intangible.

These possessions then, serve as a form of patterning or recognition of a designed nature in an otherwise and supposedly hostile environment, for the purpose of the end user or individual so that he can function in the world about him. In a sense, the purpose or intent of these possessions is to share a broad common base of familiar objects with and from which to communicate that individual's being to those of others. The broader the base or possessions, the broader the individual can relate to others. One can use or convey his thoughts and feelings through possessions, for possessions are a form of communication, which helps to serve as a communications bridge or common basis for the understanding the world and this relates to the greater well being of the individual and that of his culture.

Now, all of the preceding was a rather lengthy definition and explanation of a simple word called, possession. In fact, I may have overdone it a bit. But, I think this explanation was a necessary evil, because I would like to explain another interesting word that is very similar to possession but has a meaning all its own even though it is related to possession. The word that I am talking about is that of knowledge, or to know. This word also gets a little complicated; however, this word relates to the individual in a slightly different manner. Unlike the word possession, which controls, or limits, or unites someone or something to that of another, knowledge can be used to define or separate the limitations of the physical world in its relationship to the individual. However, both words are meaningless until they are related to someone or something. That is, you cannot have a possession or knowledge without the individual being involved.

Knowledge is a form of possession. To know is to possess. It belongs to, and is controlled by the individual in a specific relationship. Unlike the word possession, knowledge cannot be identified by another singular limiting descriptive word or proper noun. Therefore, to know is to possess, but to possess does not necessarily mean to know totally. That's because knowledge has a quality or form of certainty which cannot be broken down or divided further but where that limit is, is endless. That is, it is the smallest unit that can be identified with a specific beginning and ending. It has certain specific qualities that make it different from all other identifiable things of mind and matter. It is the real nature or quality of a thing and is not dependent on external circumstances or other conditions which create a final result but it does require a form of recognition which is relative to the individual. One does not have to know everything about a possession for it to belong to him, but he does need to know its relationship to himself if nothing more than to acquire items for their worth and/or value sake. That is not necessarily true of knowledge.

Knowledge cannot be bought or achieved as an end result in an indirect relationship as can a possession. Knowledge can only be acquired through the concerted efforts of the individual involved in a direct relationship. That is, the want or desire to know, must come before the end result or possession of knowledge. To acquire knowledge, one must make a determined commitment to comprehend, recognize, and identify its relationship to himself and then work toward that end result. One can be given knowledge, but unless that person is receptive to its relationship or importance to him, he will not retain or possess that knowledge. Knowledge does not belong to an individual because of money or any other common denominator except direct involvement. One must purposely seek knowledge to acquire it, because it requires special attention to detail and/or relationships which only an individual can control through possessions.

Knowledge requires the individual to use analytical thought processes to separate and isolate that which one is seeking. It requires the individual to identify that particular unit (beginning and ending), and then see what this unit is and how it is connected to or relates to the overall problem. Knowledge then, is the accumulation of certain identifiable units into their smallest parts and the understanding of how these parts are different, but in turn, relate or connect to one another. It is the knowing of these units and their differences that constitutes knowledge. Knowledge is the recognition of separation or the identification of small beginnings and endings, recognizable by a common union that is related to the individual.

When possessions are the manifestation of matter into useful physical objects of man to use as he pleases, knowledge is the equivalent in the mental state of being. Knowledge is that intangible quality that relates to the real physical world, but cannot be seen. That is, thoughts about the world are first perceived by the mind and are then manifested into physical reality through the application of energy to create new forms of matter that can be controlled. Man takes his knowledge of nature and natural laws to design or re-arrange matter into specific creations for a specific result or possession.

The intangible quality of knowledge makes it much harder to come by or acquire than do physical possessions. That's because the physical senses are so much more dominate than are one's conscious mental abilities. The power of the mind is strong, but the physical senses detect specific physical limitations that affect our reality. Mental images and thoughts can easily be changed or altered and may not affect our physical reality. The seeking of knowledge requires greater wants and the ability to comprehend specific relationships in regard to absolute certainty. The same intangible qualities that make knowledge so finite or absolute, also make it so infinite or limitless. One can never know all there is to know, because one can never relate to or be conscious of all there is.

For a moment, let's go back to our example of a chair and the binding force or relationship of its parts. In this example, it was said that the end result of physical efforts was the construction of a chair, and this end result constituted a possession. Now, how knowledge differs from that of a possession is in the fact that the individual(s) must know ahead of construction, what the materials will be and how they will be put together. One has to know how these parts go together and how to hold them together in a permanent or fixed position for the end result and/or the efficient benefit of the work effort. Unless one knows the end result, the work effort does not or should not start.

In a competitive situation, where you have other people making chairs, it is important to know or ensure that the construction or end results are restricted to certain prescribed limitations. That is, one does not normally want his work efforts to exceed the value or cost of the end result. Therefore, one must know in advance what the necessary limitations are in the fabrication of the chair in relationship to his ability to maintain his competitiveness and/or his stability or well being. In this case, the knowledge or knowing of the characteristics of wood, and the shape of the parts, and the finish, automatically limits the individual to certain specific methods of construction and the existing equipment available. The media, tools and the individual involved are all limiting factors in the construction of the end result.

So here you have a chair, a final result or possession. However, this unit was first conceived by the mind to serve a useful purpose. Then that idea was analyzed and broken down from its idealized concept and function to its overall construction, next its parts, then the binding elements, the fabrication methods, the work effort and the cost of these efforts in relationship to the final cost. All of these factors were conceived in the mind of the individual before actual construction even started. Knowledge preceded the end result or possession. Without the accumulation or possession of knowledge, construction could not begin. Again we are confronted by small beginnings and endings that forms an interconnecting union.

All of these explanations were necessary to lead you up to a point in the understanding of relationships. Possessions and knowledge form a relationship, and the relationship of these items to the individual, form in effect, a triangle. These three elements make up what I call, the learning process. These three elements make up a complete subconscious pattern or structural unit; however, to bring this structure out into physical reality, two more elements must be considered and they are time and space. So our triangle now becomes a pyramid that has depth or dimension to it. These five elements form the basis of our physical reality and are needed to manifest the world about us. These elements make up our environment and learning process that relates to all.

Now, even though the learning process has been identified, there is still one major element missing. What is missing, is the binding force that holds these five elements together. It is the interior content or space between these elements or corners that is still unknown. But this is simple enough. What else can have form and cannot be identified itself? The answer is understanding. Understanding is that inner content, it is the force that allows man to function in the physical world. It is the unmanifested force that holds and separates everything and relates everything to everything else. It is the understanding of the five elements and their relationship that creates the world about us and allows us to operate and function for that purpose.

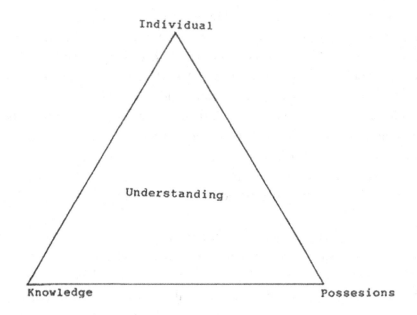

Illustration #1

The Learning Triangle

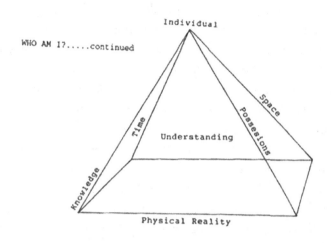

Illustration #2

The Learning Pyramid

Without understanding, the five elements mean nothing by themselves. It is one thing to know something and another to possess something, but these things alone will not help or add to the well being of the individual. One must understand how knowledge and possessions relate to the physical world before they can belong to or benefit mankind. This is a world of physical matter, and one cannot properly relate to something which cannot be manifested into matter for the use of the individual. It is the triangle that symbolizes the mental learning process and the pyramid that makes this learning process relate to the physical world about us, and it is understanding that holds everything together. These structures represent a relationship of understanding. They are building processes or systems which must be used by the individual to fulfill wants and desires. These elements and their relationship then constitute the learning process.

Because man is so accustomed to operating in the physical world about him, he seldom questions or understands this learning process. However, it is there and it does work on a constant ongoing basis. But, it may be extremely difficult for the individual to see this relationship of the elements in the learning process; therefore, I will try to give you a quick example of what is involved. But, before I give you this example, I want you to imagine an unrealistic situation. What I want you to do is to put yourself in an isolated environment. This is difficult to do, because you really have never experienced anything even close to this situation. But let's try.

First, let's start out with something simple. Let's say that you are the only person left on this earth. Now for some reason, you are killed or eliminated. Your demise or removal from the learning process would leave a gap or space which understanding could not fill. Therefore, there would be no need for knowledge or possessions, because they would not really add to or benefit you in physical reality. So, the elimination of the individual from this physical reality and the learning process would virtually eliminate the need or purpose of the process.

Next, let's say that you, the individual, had no possessions. You would find yourself in a world of physical plants and animals, but you would not be able to exercise any control over these objects. You would be without clothes and you would have no food or shelter, because you could not control any part of your environment; therefore, there would be no learning process. Even if you had the knowledge of everything about you, you still could not use these things to sustain yourself. Without possessions, you would find yourself in a relatively hostile environment. Man, or the individual, must have the ability to use energy or nature for his own benefit. This is the purpose of physical existence, or the individual will soon perish and again there will be no learning process.

To know requires the ability to separate or distinguish the world about you into distinct identifiable items or units. Unlike possessions, which binds everything together to the individual, knowledge separates everything. Without knowing differences, one could not distinguish things from one another and would not be able to function. Possessions would not be any good without the knowledge of how to use them in relationship to the well being of the individual. Therefore, one would have to know or have the knowledge of objects in order to use them for his survival and benefit. Without knowledge, again, the individual would soon perish and again there would be no learning process.

Without understanding, these elements and how they relate to one another in space and time, man cannot exist. Without the learning process, life as we know it would not exist. Without one, there would be no need, no purpose and no meaning to life. But, it is the inner content above all that determines or limits our outer world of physical reality. It is the understanding and/or access to alternate unmanifested non-linear realities above all else, that brings meaning to the world about us. It is understanding that shapes our world and gives it some semblance of order and form of a tangible nature.

It is interesting to note that the word understanding and the word meaning are almost the same or synonymous to one another. The word understanding refers to standing among, or to know the meaning or implication; whereas, the word meaning, refers to a degree of importance, or halfway, or to have in the conscious mind. Both of these words basically denote a position or relationship which would put them in between two extremes or center position. This is just where we placed the word understanding in our triangle and pyramid. This implication is important. Like our culture that binds people together in a mutually beneficial relationship, understanding binds people and the physical world together in a greater relationship.

Beside understanding being the binding force in our learning process, it also serves as a value quality. As stated before, the acquiring of knowledge or possessions does not or cannot stand alone, because there is no relationship. As the consciously understanding increases, so do the relationships increase, and that expands the knowledge of things, and that in turn, increases the possessions or abundance of things in the material world. Therefore, the real value of knowledge and possessions comes from understanding and the giving away of this understanding in the form of knowledge or possessions. The quality or value of knowledge and possessions comes with use and understanding. The more something is used, the more skilled or adept one becomes in the understanding of that knowledge or possession. Therefore, value normally increases as understanding increases or one gets close or more accustomed to the patterns. This is true up to a certain point, and then this understanding normally grows or changes into something else in a progressive manner into something of more value, but related to the original. Again, we are confronted with beginnings and endings.

It was mentioned several times before, that value comes from effort. In the preceding explanation, we said that value comes from use. I don't think that there is any contradiction here, because use requires efforts of some kind. But, through understanding, the effort can become less and less as the understanding increases. That is, the more one knows about something, the easier and faster it is for him to achieve the proper end result. Therefore, understanding can vary the effect of knowledge and possessions, but understanding requires great efforts and energies and patience which few individuals seem willing or able to expend. That is, understanding seems to take a lot more energy than most people are willing to spend, are unable to spend, or for some unknown reason, don't want to spend. The problem with understanding seems to be that it takes much too much time, a concerted effort, an attention to detail and/or relationships, the ability to recognize and above all, patience.

Because the human body is composed of physical matter, he can best relate to things which are also of physical matter. His senses are equipped to identify and feel the physical forces of matter around him. Therefore, he can respond much quicker and easier to things of a tangible nature. Therefore, his efforts and energies are directed to things of this nature which have limitations or beginnings and endings. Knowledge and things of an intangible nature such as alternate unmanifested non-linear realities are relatively unimportant or secondary to that of physical matter, because matter can directly affect the body and/or physical senses. That is, one can see what one is up against with physical matter and can choose to join or avoid that which is confronting him in his immediate environment.

Another possible reason or problem concerning understanding and knowledge is that efforts in this direction, usually do not necessarily have an immediate end result or benefit to the individual. People are normally reluctant to do things without something in return. That is, people want to see some sort of response or return for their energies and efforts. Apparently, the element of time is very important to the individual and effects a lot of his judgements and decisions to select one thing or another. Changing life styles and attitudes have an effect on the time element. Most people no longer want to wait or lay careful long range plans, they want to experience things right here and now. Therefore, the physical senses are satisfied immediately.

The same problem that affects knowledge and understanding, is the same problem that limits the individual. That is, it is the self imposed limitations of conscious understanding and knowledge that constitutes the world of the individual in relationship to his environment. His physical reality is only as big as his triangle of conscious understanding, or his learning process. Man restricts himself. He will learn only as much as he wants to learn. He can do and function only as much or as far as he wants to learn. He can do and function only as much or as far as he is willing to expend his conscious energies. The alternative or consequences of his actions, is to live within his triangle or existing framework of his self imposed limitations and to be comfortable or know how to accept that which he indirectly expects and/or is willing to tolerate.

As mentioned earlier, understanding occupies the center position of our learning process. But, this does not necessarily mean that the individual will always chooses this position, nor does it assure him of proper learning or growth. Man limits or restricts himself; therefore, he can also position himself anywhere within the triangle or learning process. The ideal location would naturally be in the center where he could share an equal balance of understanding knowledge, self and possessions in time and space. But the individual exercises judgement and free will. That is, he evaluates that which he wants to experience, either consciously or unconsciously. Therefore, he can select or choose those things which he considers important, useful or beneficial to himself. It is his selection, based upon his value judgement, of what he consciously or unconsciously wants or desires, that determines his position within the learning process.

Let me repeat that again for my own sake. The individual first has wants and desires, which were basically a result of previous selections. Please remember that, it's important. Then, he selects certain absolute knowledge which relates or leads to a position in relationship to a specific end or desired result. Through his conscious knowledge and understanding of relationships, which is in effect the connecting of short beginnings and endings, or groupings of similarities, the individual sets out to change, alter, or influence things in a cause and effect manner. That is, he selects the proper relationship or position that again connects or leads to his hoped for or expected end by using energy and effort to create a predictable (within limits) desired result. This selection process is primarily a system of elimination which narrows or limits the mental and physical actions of the individual and/or material manifestation.

That means, that man uses energy to create mental thoughts and images of his desire first. Then he consciously goes about bringing these intangible qualities into physical tangible reality. Subconsciously, man has the ability to access all probabilites in unmanifested non-linear realities. However, man chooses patterns based upon physical reality and understands certain positions of relationships that he somehow connects to and identifies with and exhibits certain variable qualities. Therefore, man developes unconscious controls and/or possess these thought patterns or mental routines which becomes part of our behavior, and all of that constitutes the learning process. It is a process of expansion and growth of recognition.

CHAPTER 6

Self Control

In learning about "Who Am I?", we are learning about life, and life is basically nothing more than a learning process. You may wish to add to this explanation; however, you will not delete learning as life's main function. In the last chapter, we actually learned about the learning process itself. That is, we identified the elements of the learning process, what they are, how they function, how they relate to one another and how understanding holds everything together. What I did not explain is how one sets this learning process into motion. What really starts it?

It was also stated in the last chapter, that knowledge and possession control the individual in a specific relationship. Our chair example and subsequent explanation of this learning process indicates that this specific relationship is primarily a process of selection or self control based upon understanding. That means that the individual must first be exposed, drawn and/or take an interest in something, then he must focus in on that thing by a selection or value process which narrows one's reality and limits actions that are initiated to reach or accomplish the hoped for end results. Sometimes, these limitations are already set by that of another individual, or previous selection, or the consciously known information available to us. In any case, the selection process is a system designed to accumulate knowledge and posses more understanding, so that the individual can, in a sense, enlarge his triangle, or to grow.

The actual selection process is a mental conscious process of knowing and understanding relationships. However, in order for this mental process to be effective, one must be able to visually see the results of these mental processes take form in physical matter. This manifestation of thoughts into matter gives the mental energies or efforts respectability or a certain form of predictability and reliability. In short, it makes everything worthwhile or believable. One has extreme difficulty operating or functioning when there are so many options or alternate means available to achieve the same desired results. Therefore, the manifestation of thoughts into matter limits the options and narrows the choices so that the individual can more clearly see that reality which he is seeking.

The conscious key or motivating force behind the individual and the learning process then is selection. To make a selection, means that there are several or more ways of achieving the same hoped for or desired end result. Therefore, to make a selection requires knowledge and understanding of certain relationships based in a linear time sequence. Knowledge becomes the source of the choices or options available to the individual; however, man has limited himself in knowledge, so he has also limited his conscious selections. That is, knowledge is somewhat fixed to some degree, therefore, his responses are predictable to some extent. But, just by knowing and understanding relationships, his choices or options become much greater than his limited knowledge and/or is non-linear in origin. Then again, conscious understanding is still limited by the individual's efforts and energies to see and identify similarities and differences.

One might ask at this point, if there are so many ways of achieving the same desired end result, then why is there all this concern about the learning process, selections and limitations anyway? The reason for this concern has to do with position and side effects. That is, most people primarily think of themselves first in relationship to others; therefore, their efforts usually create side effects, reactions and counter responses to actions one sets into motion in order to accomplish his end result. The desired end result of an individual who is out of step with his fellow man or is just self centered, is rarely accomplished without affecting the environment which is shared by all others.

Each individual, in his journey through life, leaves a trail or path behind him somewhat like a motorboat through water. That is, the results of his actions spread out and continue to do so long after that individual has passed that same point in time and space. The individual who is basically self centered or oriented in this position, is usually unaware of the effects that his decisions or selections have on the world about him. This is true, so long as he continues along in a straight line and never looks back. Should the individual turn around or reverse his course, the wake or waves are quite noticeable and have enough energy to affect even the swiftest boat. Therefore, care should be exercised in making selections, because they affect more than just self, they affect everyone.

It is the conscious linear time selection process that gives direction to one's life. It is by this means that man progresses and grows in this physical reality. It is his choice to select knowledge or possessions when and where he chooses. His selection determines his growth and understanding or lack of it. Selection is the force that makes the learning process work and allows one to grow and expand his awareness of all there is. There is nothing wrong with creating waves and/or rocking the boat so to speak, so long as you are willing and able to help those who are affected or floundering because of these waves. Don't forget a very important rule of science which states, "For every action, there is an equal and opposite reaction". Again, care should be taken when and where possible to make the most practical selection.

Perhaps I should define the word, "practical" stated above; however, I think that this is another one of those words where value is in the mind of the beholder. That is, it is like the word, "best" that we used as our first example to explain relationships. In that example, we said that it is a word that is related to the individual's experiences, efforts and consequently, his idea of values. It is his experiences in the visible physical world that he draws on to make his next selection. It is a process of elimination whereby the individual purposely takes specific actions designed to lead to or achieve a specific end result or understanding of new relationships and purposely avoids other non-linear alternatives. You might better call this selection, strictly a process of elimination; however, it is both a positive and a negative process.

The actual selection process requires a value judgement. This judgement is the conscious or unconscious act of selecting, determining or forming of an opinion about something based upon known facts available to the individual concerning that person, place or thing. Supposedly, this judging requires the individual to think things through as far as he can or wants too, in order to decide on a specific course of action designed to achieve a benefit to that individual and possibly all concerned or affected. Unfortunately, the individual exercising free will, will often forget to include the part about "all concerned". That's because his value of others, all concerned, is not the same as that which the individual places upon himself.

If you are able to pay attention, you may have noticed that I have just used the word value in slightly different context than that which I have used twice before. So far, I have used the word, value, to denote efforts and energies used and given to achieve some end result; however, in the previous paragraph, I have used value as that meaning importance. Therefore, let's take another look at this word. The official definition of the word value means, the quality of a thing in relationship to importance. Very interesting! Isn't it? Again, I am dealing with a word that denotes a position. Just like our words, "understanding" and "meaning". However, unlike these words of position, this word denotes extremes or a variable location. The individual is still within the learning process triangle; however, his selection will fix his location somewhere closer to one of our five learning elements. Somewhere off center.

This selection process, or judging of values then is actually a positioning process. That is, the individual mentally reviews in his mind the positive and negative known relationships and understanding of both linear and non-linear actions that can or will affect certain wanted or desired results, and then selects from non-linear reality that which he thinks is the best possible way to accomplish this want or desire. His selection then, moves him off center and leads or directs him to where he wants to be consciously within the learning process.

The selection process and/or value judgements take place on the subconscious level in unmanifested non-linear reality. These alternate realities bring up the question as to whether or not all of these selections are based upon a conscious evaluation or value judgement basis, but based on emotion or emotional ties to the subconscious level(s) of unmanifested reality. However, although subconscious emotions play a part in making selections, it is the individual who made the previous conscious decisions and selections that put him into a strong emotional relationship or position to begin with; therefore, the individual believes he makes the selection based upon reasonable conscious known data or his knowledge of relationships based upon physical reality. Whatever the end result or action is it is the individual who makes his own reality! He is in control of this positioning process both consciously and unconsciously. IT IS NOT A CAUSE AND EFFECT SITUATION OF RANDOM COINCIDENCES OR IRRATIONAL THOUGHT.

In making selections, man makes a commitment and embarks upon a type of imaginary subconscious journey, if you will. But, before this, you might say that man is basically at rest, until some stimulus arouses something within the individual sufficiently to create wants and desires, somewhere within our learning triangle. Then, the individual somehow (I will explain that latter.) activates the use of energies to overcome the inertia or the natural force of gravity to center one's self around a nucleus or home position, in order to reach the outer edges, or that which one is seeking. This outward movement or journey is a process of growth that allows the individual to enlarge his learning triangle. However, once the individual achieves the end result or gives up the quest or desire, he then returns to his point of origin or center point or home position from which he started. That's because man likes to surround himself with that which is familiar to him. There is a great deal of comfort and assurance in familiarity or certainty, and man always seeks to return to the security and safety of this home position.

It may be difficult for some to imagine, but each selection is a process of growth that allows the individual an opportunity to reach out mentally. That is, the making of a selection is like the exercising of the physical body. However, instead of toning up muscle, one is toning up the mind. To exist, in this physical world of matter, one must constantly use that which is given or available to him to build or create, so that he does not degenerate and/or is overcome by the natural forces of resistance or gravity. That which is inactive tends to be dense, heavy and slow; whereas, that which is active tends to be light, airy and fast. THEREFORE, THE PURPOSE OR FUNCTION OF MAN IN THE PHYSICAL WORLD OF MATTER IS TO LEARN THE USE AND CONTROL OF ENERGY. This will be explained in depth latter in this book.

The last statement about purpose and function does not necessarily contradict my opening comment in this chapter that says, "....life is basically nothing more than a learning process". In fact, this latter statement tends

to explain the learning process and clarifies the true purpose of life and/
or learning and growth. It seems rather inappropriate that such important
matters of life can be explained in so simple and few words. This brevity, in
fact, tends to make such simple statements inappropriate and unbelievable.
Life seems so much more complicated that it almost seems to need a lengthy
complicated explanation similar in fact to the trials and tribulations that
one encounters daily. I'm sorry if I disappoint you; however, it just isn't
so. But perhaps my explanation later on may help to relieve some of your
doubts and anxieties as well as to put you back on the path to your being
or becoming.

Getting back to our subject of energy, it is energy that provides the
stimulus or motivating power to seek or reach out and grow in the learning
process. Through the application of energy, one overcomes the natural
forces of gravity and resistance of matter to seek its nucleus or center.
One rarely thinks of energy as a means to bring about change, or for that
matter, an entity in itself which has a being or existence in mind and
matter that can affect reality. Energy is that one common unit found in all
things. It has the latent powers to affect unbelievable drastic changes or so
subtle changes as to be imperceptible. The understanding of relationships
is the understanding of energy, and this knowledge provides the tool to
alter, change or influence all things in ways different from their original
qualities.

My explanation about life and its stimulus, energy, may be difficult
for many people to accept. There isn't much written about this matter,
nor is it thought of or spoken of often. Given years and years of parental
guidance and conditioning and maybe religious matters, and experiencing
for one's self the knowledge of physical and biological sciences, one seldom
encounters any correlation to energy as the most important aspect of one's
physical life. This is probably due to the inability of anyone is properly
define, separate or isolate that which is called energy. Everyone knows how
it works, but no one really knows what it is in and by itself. Therefore, why
would anyone try to explain something they don't understand?

Energy can rarely be related to just one type or form; however, today
we are probably more familiar with electrical energy than any other form
of energy, except maybe atomic energy. Man no longer relies primarily on
animal or water power to ease his physical energy labor burden. His use

of mental energies has relieved him of many of the time consuming chores based on old means of energy conversions. Man has come a long way and has discovered that energy has the ability to change things or get things done, but he still cannot isolate it sufficiently to define it better than to say that: it is a force or power capable of vigorous action for doing work and overcoming resistance. Maybe now you can appreciate this general lack of concern or interest in explaining energy.

I think a better explanation of energy might be; it is the ability to change, expand and/or transfer in a sequential manner, the expansion and contraction of atoms through a similar cohesive bonding force. The regulation of such an energy force would be controlled by a point or position in proportion to that which one is trying to energize. That is, if you wish to accomplish something, you must use energy. To do this, you must transmit a force to that which you wish to accomplish either mentally or physically in order to overcome its position, or non-position. The speed with which this task is accomplished, depends on the force or position from which one is transmitting this energy. This new definition still does not isolate the substance known as energy; however, I believe, it may better explain how it works.

On second thought, I would like to take this explanation one step further. The ability of energy to expand and contract, also has the ability to draw or move more dense matter out of its center or in any direction so desired. You might compare this motion to that of an oscillating cycle or an ocean wave that moves or is activated by environmental conditions. The motion depends upon the area that is activated or the point or position of the force. This force is then transmitted through a media or special conversion units to affect certain specific results. These results will differ depending upon where the energy is applied. You might better be able to observe the results of this center point by watching a piece of equipment designed with an eccentric shaft to produce vibrations in a limited area. Such a machine will produce different patterns, routes, or directional flow depending upon how and where the eccentrics are placed, because this in effect, actually changes the center point of the energy flow outward into physical reality.

Perhaps another item that should be clarified, is the use of the word, "energy" in relationship to the individual and this thing I call a center point or position. It may be better that I discontinue the purely scientific analytical language to that of a more compatible common street type language that may relate to more people, if I haven't lost most of you already. Because of word associations and a certain prejudice that is conveyed in such language, this explanation will be brief and I will again revert back to the language of the text.

In speaking about this thing called energy and the center point, I am talking primarily of that which is known as one's will. So that we are all in agreement, the word will, is defined as: the power of self direction or self control in the direction of deliberate action or attitude toward others. Will is the ability to mentally and physically control energy. Will, is the movement of this center point and the application of energy from this point to any direction so desired. Nothing is impossible! It is only the ability of the individual to properly orientate his being or center point to achieve the desired results. The problem is not in the application of energy so much as it is the ability of the individual to focus in on the location of this center point and this ability is related to one's understanding of relationships and value on both a conscious and subconscious level. The factor of time and space in the growth process also tends to make it more difficult and confusing for one to properly orientate himself and locate this center point.

In referring to the center point or position with our learning triangle, the individual rarely seeks nor does he ever achieve returning to the exact center of this process. That's because, in reaching out, the individual learns about himself and the world about him and temporarily alters the shape and size of the learning process and its limitations. But, within the existing framework of this process, he develops certain tendencies or likes which he finds useful and beneficial to his being and uses these more often than other alternatives. These likes and dislikes might be referred to as characteristics, because the individual favors these patterns and is somewhat predictable in his actions and/or behavior. That is, the individual attains or lacks special skills or knowledge of patterns which are or are not valued over and above that of other people. All of this is nothing more than the understanding of the relationship(s) of beginnings and endings. This is known as behavior.

Behavior then is the favoring of certain paths or patterns. In actuality, these patterns tend to serve as familiar landmarks or markers along a path that one can trust in his coming and going in the growth process. One's favoring or likes and dislikes would then be considered a biased point of view or position which the individual has taken in regards to his new center of focus or point within the learning process. These patterns are what make each individual different from one another. It is this point of view or collective views that in turn tends to stimulate this reaching out and growth process in all. Therefore, you might want to compare this center point to that of trying to find the North Pole. In order to locate that point, you have to decide which pole you are seeking. There are in fact, the magnetic north pole and the geographical north pole and/or true north. Each serves a purpose and function.

In determining this center point, we are also talking about two opposing forces. One is that of resistance and the other is that of motion or energy. Both forces are necessary for stability. Together, they act or perform a positioning process similar to that of the "X" and "Y" axis found in geometry and is the basis of computer technology applications and/or Computerized Numerical Control operated equipment. In relationship to the individual, each force has advantages and disadvantages which are dependent upon that person's wants and desires. Neither force is all good or all bad.

The value of the forces is determined by the individual and is equal to his efforts, which are activated by willpower, and results in the selection of a position. The amount of efforts or energies used are in proportion to the position or degree of importance one places upon the end result. That is, the value of anything is dependent upon the positioning which controls the efforts of the individual and vice versa. Self control is then the key to life and growth, and few people realize this fact or power of the self in making or determining one's own reality.

The exercising of self control is not properly understood by most people and therefore life, as we know it, may appear meaningless to those many people. The reason for this confusion is this thing called free will. That is, the individual has virtually total control of his being, except for self imposed limitations or those powers which he has given to others. However, this total freedom also creates the illusion of total chaos or disunity. That's because all of these options or alternatives orignate in alternate levels of unmanifested non-linear reality. When one has access to an unlimited environment, self control appears not to have meaning and seems not to terminate with the desired end result. Therefore, many people may conclude the options of such efforts are futile and are consequently meaningless. Such a conclusion overlooks many facts which will be covered later; however, the important thing to remember is that there is an inner center point, and when and if that point is reached, one will have created or achieved absolute total unity and balance.

One of the problems encountered in discussing life and/or the virtues of life is that one normally thinks of one's self and the fulfillment of that entity. Therefore, most people are preoccupied or obsessed with the dominate characteristic of life which is the physical sensations of one's being. In talking about one's being, one may not in any way, shape or form, be able to relate one's self to any other aspect of his being. I have already indicated earlier, that most people tend to dwell on end results and possession as the most important thing to one's happiness or fulfillment. However, let me remind you again, that this is only one aspect of the learning process. There is a great deal more to life than the accumulation of objects and sensations.

The manifestation of life in this reality is expressed by the corners of our learning triangle or pyramid; therefore, most people tend to dwell on these outer edges or limitations, as I have indicated previously. Occasionally, the individual will seek some guidance from within, which is the bases of non-linear reality, but more often than not, he tends to look or seek his answers from the outside world. That which is composed of physical matter, seeks comfort in physical matter. But matter is a form of energy, and energy is the common unit found in all things of the physical outside world of matter and the inner world of spirit. Therefore, there is a bridge. It's just a problem of understanding relationships. In section II of this book, I hope to make this relationship become more clear.

So long as the individual chooses or selects an equal balance of motion/energy and resistance, outside and inside of himself, he will remain healthy and grow. However, if he should choose to position himself constantly on the outer edges or any extreme of our learning triangle, his growth will be poor and deformed. To the physically healthy, one must seek an equal balance of all there is and utilize those abilities which are given him.

However, the biggest problem involved here is that the individual is usually unaware that he is in fact caught up in a routine or pattern which does not permit real growth. You might say that before you can solve a problem, you must know that a problem exists. The answer to this situation is simple; however, I am sure it's so simple that most people will not agree with me that this is the proper answer. The answer is in seeking this thing called the inner content or understanding. Remember, that's what holds the learning elements together. If you possess many more negative thoughts about life and/or people in general, I am sure that you are out of balance, and I am sure that deep down you know this too. The human entity is a marvelous thing that projects interesting manifestations of health and general well being to one's physical self in an out of balance situation as another means of getting one's own attention. What is meant by that last statement is that intangible mental thought can create conditions of physical illness.

A very common mistake that most people make in this growth situation is this concentration on the corners of physical manifestation. To dwell on one of our learning elements is to put one's self at the extreme limitation of the learning process. This is O.K. so long as one does not constantly choose to stay at this position. Should one, in fact, select this point, one enters into a form of possession, and to possess totally is a form of greed. Greed is the accumulation of anything in excess of one's needs, or a form of positioning dealing with self imposed limitations. Greed is a negative form of creativity that impedes growth. Greed may achieve positive or monetary goods up to point, but it soon loses its value and requires more and more motivating powers to satisfy the individual. Consequently, the individual may gain from greed over a relatively short period of time; however, in the long run, such a position imposes more limitations than it actually achieves in relationship to the well being of the individual.

As you may be able to see by now, by making a selection(s), one takes a position and sets into motion certain actions which result in specific counter responses or actions that in turn continuously sets in motion a process of change or growth in a specific direction. You create your own reality! These selections then set limitations in a progressive linear direction, which may or may not be predictable, depending upon the position of the individual. The relationship(s) of the selection process to the individual is a matter of self control and results in a type of patterning system or responses. That is, the individual learns to associate a certain selection pattern, meaning a series of beginnings and endings to that which will usually produce a certain or predictable result; therefore, that person will more often than not select that pattern because he knows what to expect within certain acceptable limitations. These patterns or patterning then becomes, in a sense, part of ourselves or characteristic of that individual. This is just like our cultural identification analogy. The individual accepts limitations for his greater well being and seeks comfort and assurance in a stimulus-response type selection process or behavior pattern.

I would venture to say that not one of us, as an individual, thinks about or considers ourselves to be pattern oriented or to be controlled by a predictable routine type behavior. However, I will also agree that all of us are, to a greater degree than we care to admit., very pattern oriented and predictable. More so than most of us consciously think. If you can be truly objective about this matter, and really take a look at your own life and analyze it, you will discover that you are in fact a bundle of patterns. So much so that one appears to be almost programmed to do and perform basic routines the greater part of one's conscious life. For a little variety, one seems to trade off certain frequent routines for ones that are less frequent, but just the same they are routines that vary in cycle and are only disguised by time and space.

I am sure you're going to want an explanation of this last statement, so here it goes. To begin with, let's take a look at some of the more simple identifiable routines that are performed daily. One begins the day with what we call the awakening of the conscious mind. Simple enough. Everyone does that. Next, nearly everyone tends to his own physical being. That means, he tends to all the bodily functions and makes sure everything is in working order to begin the day. Next, he concerns himself with his identity or personal grooming. He does certain things which he feels makes him look and feel like that which he wants to be. Next, he pursues those things which perpetuate his physical conscious being. That is, he partakes of physical nourishment, then pursues that which will provide for his security and/or shelter for himself and well being of those whom he is related to physically and mentally. At the end of the day, he retires to a state of rest or to identify with his spiritual unconscious self and grows.

With the exception of that last sentence, I am sure you will agree with everything I said about daily routines. However, you may still take offense to the idea of patterning, because you may think that patterning requires one to do something exactly as one did it before. This is not true. One does not mean duplication when confronting a pattern. All one requires is an outside framework or limitation to qualify as a routine. That is, there are certain things which are required in duplicating or an identical state; however, there are still options that can be exercised even within a routine. You may not wish to acknowledge these basic functions as routines, but just the same, they are.

Without sounding too fatalistic, you might say that man is destined to perform like robots. However, I think this too is carrying it a little too far. Remember, I have repeatedly said that you make your own selections and/ or routines. You have a choice! You make your own reality! Repetition is not altogether bad. Remember the saying that: "practice makes perfect". To become proficient at anything, one has to experience that thing many times before he masters that extension of himself. That is, through identifying with the mental and/or physical process(es) that one is learning, that individual in a sense becomes one with that tool or process and therefore, is able to accomplish tasks much faster by knowing and understanding that thing which then becomes a possession to some extent. But as I have cautioned before, even the simplest and the most complex routines can become detrimental after a long period of time. The key is the learning process. You will continue to grow so long as you are in control of this process and not become a slave to it.

To sit down and analyze every action to determine if it is a routine or not, is not that important. It is what you can learn from routines that might help you grow. That is, do not question if an action is a routine or not, ask why this action is necessary. Where is it leading me? Is there another way which has better benefits for all concerned? Etc., etc. If you undertake an action, make sure you are aware of its end result, and try to make that result happen in the most proficient and/or effective way possible. You can make a difference! Your actions influence others in some way, shape or form, just like our example of a motor boat passing through water. You do leave a lingering trail behind you.

It may seem to you that after a thorough analysis of yourself, that you are left with few major selections that are not routines. This statement is also not true. You might say that man is a very creative being that constantly builds structures in which he dwells. Man limits or controls himself! These limits are either mental or of physical substance that determine one's growth. How the individual fills these structures is comparable to his selection process or free will that he exercises outside these self imposed limitations or routine structures. You might also like to compare one's life to that of watching a black and white movie or TV picture. Free will lets you convert this picture into color as you think it should be.

Don't get me wrong about routines or patterning per se; except, remember my statement about absolutes. To remind you, I said that an excess or extremes of anything is a form of greed or negative growth. It leaves no room to expand or grow. One is locked into a confining location and surroundings of his own choosing. The limitations are absolute and totally confining. But there is also another side of growth that should also be explored. That is, the abandonment of total limitations is also detrimental.

One can embark on a journey outside the world of physical matter and mentally lose his way, because he has a tendency to lose his reference(s) or markers along the way. One is relatively secure within the learning triangle, or close by it. But if one should stray too far without proper cautions or references, one may soon perish or lose one's self and/or never again return mentally to that position known as our physical reality. In the latter case, there is a point of no return. Or is it... "no deposit, no return?"

So you see, everything that we have been talking about indicates that the ideal situation is a relative balance of motion outward and that of resistance in the outside and inside realm of the individual. Growth constitutes that area in which the individual can function effectively within specific limitations or a known environment of his own choosing. The world of physical matter gives him that opportunity to work out problems in a linear progressive manner without too much confusion of absolute freedom. Self control is the way and means by which one grows in this progressive manner. The speed of this growth is determined by one's ability to understand relationships and to use energy and free will to the benefit of all concerned.

We are not done with talking about the functioning of one's self and his being; however, we have explored and may have found out, or at least we have a little better understanding of, how the individual works or operates in this world of physical matter. We have not really discovered exactly, "Who I am", but we know how the "I" functions. It may be of interest, that the explanation of "Who I am" is a continuing ongoing process. In the meantime, before one can really explore one's own being, he must also know what belongs to him. That is, you have discovered that you are related in so many ways to so many things, that it is difficult to determine what it is that really makes up you and your environment or that of the society in which you live.

We have discussed limitations in regards to our own being; however, we have also talked about growth. You see, we seem to be always talking about balance. Again, life is a marvelous, fantastic thing that offers so much or so little. It depends on each individual. You make your own reality. Through self control, you determine your growth mentally, physically, spiritually and socially, or the lack of it. Your center point or position is the controlling factor, but how you position this point depends on will power, which seems to be greatly influenced by emotional relationships which cannot be easily identified. However, we will try to cover this subject a little better, later on.

You may have also noticed that all of the foregoing discussions refrained as much as possible away from words that indicate extreme conditions. I have purposely stayed away from all statements that say this is true in all cases, or that it is the best way, or that it is right or wrong. And yet, I indicated to you that this was a book about our reality and morality. Up to this point, little reference was made to this subject. However, we need to set some ground rules before we discuss this subject, and I will be talking about the establishing of morality and the concept of good, bad, right, and wrong after we agree upon a common foundation. It is hoped that such a long prelude might help you better understand the concepts that are involved in these determinations and the effects upon the individual. It is also hoped that you may better understand the limitations of these artificial borders and how to control them or live within these limits and still maintain your balance and grow.

CHAPTER 7

Behavior

Let's begin, or continue our journey of growth by looking at group patterning or social growth. We have, up to now, talked about the individual as a single entity and how he functions in relationship to the world around him. We have made references to other people in connection with the individual and we have also talked about sociological identification, but we did not elaborate on how the individual behaves as a group or a group behaves as an individual.

There is a definite message that this chapter has to convey in our progression to discover that known as the self or "Who am I?"; however, to write about it in a straight forward way will not convince you of its importance and/or the tremendous powers that control or influences the individual. Therefore, I feel that I must reinforce my argument by resorting to examples of knowledge which you can directly relate too. This is necessary to get you to look at and analyze that inborn and inbred mental patterning or conditioning that we all have to some extent. Until the individual or you, learns to understand the importance or significance of yourself or your part in this so called real world around you, you will be a victim, so to speak, of your environment. The idea of this chapter is to convince you of your own importance and power you have to affect your own reality. To do this, you should look at this information and all information with an inquisitive asking eye. You should analyze everything given to you in a way you have never done so before. You should not accept things as they appear to be, but again you must not isolate yourself, balance is the key.

What I am saying, is that I want you to look at perhaps familiar information in an unfamiliar way. I would like to convince you to abandon your routine behavior of patterned learning habits which consist of short beginnings and endings for a more objective way of interpreting and/or recognizing your reality. This is a difficult task, and it is made even worst by the fact that most information is somewhat pre-digested or biasedly reported and passed on to other people. However, I would like you to try and exclude likes and dislikes associated with words, actions, and/ or existing values. Let's try to understand behavior and values for what they are and are not. It is totally impossible to exclude all understanding and information not experienced directly; however, I would like you to question such information and perhaps use it only for comparing and not for making judgements and/or selections.

To explain behavior and values, we are going to rely on information that has been collected, and compiled by others for the purpose of understanding the inner workings of large groups of people. Now again, this information is not experienced; therefore, you should question its accuracy and/or conclusions and/or observed reporting of supposedly factual information. We will use this information for comparing, but we will not use it to control or direct our own selection processes at this time.

One of the best ways to understand and study values is to observe them in action. To cite examples or differences of values within our own society is asking for trouble. That is, there is no way the reader is going to sit back and take such information in an acceptable passive manner, when we are talking about something that might directly or indirectly affect him or the guy next door. Whatever logical reasoning power one possesses, would be overcome with emotional ties to basic beliefs, and that would destroy any attempt to lead us to a truly desired or intended unbiased understanding of ourselves. Therefore, to do this, we must rely on and study the behavior of other societies or groups of people.

To achieve this objective or new understanding, let's refer back to an area of study mentioned before. Let's talk about anthropology. To remind you, this subject matter, deals primarily with the study of physical man and his behavior, rather than man's organizations and institutions that is covered by sociology, which is also referred to earlier. There will still be crossovers in this explanation; however, here we are concerned with human behavior. Any explanation of man must also include that which he surrounds himself with, or that which is familiar to him; consequently, it is difficult to talk about physical man without talking about both areas of study.

The study of man, is the study of man's customs and traditions. These routines or practices probably constitute the major basis of man's conditioning or limiting of his behavior patterns. These patterns limit him and serve him by providing him with those so called landmarks that I referred to in the last chapter. That is, man uses customs and traditions to identify and reinforce his own being with that of a larger, greater force or being which has somewhat tangible qualities. Man looks to his immediate surroundings for comfort and security. He looks to his family, his society and his sub-cultures for acceptance and assurance that he is somehow important, and that he is in some way, shape, or form, contributing to that greater force or entity in either a positive or negative manner. You see, man must make his presence known, and to do this, he must enter into a give and take situation. Again, we run into balance. This relationship, or contribution, or involvement, enlarges the overall learning process of both the individual and that of his society, group, and/or environment.

In the last chapter, I indicated that routines may affect human behavior patterns more significantly than individual creative actions. However, I also indicated that the individual is rarely aware or conscious of such controlled or limited behavior patterns. That's because customs and traditions are patterns, values or guidelines impressed upon the individual from early childhood. They are actions and/or learned unquestioned responses to beliefs. Therefore, these customs and traditions are linked to both the logical rationing mind and the powerful emotional control center. Therefore, these routines not only affect the characteristics or relationship of an individual to certain tangible possessions, but they also affect the way people think and act.

It is interesting to note and reflect back to an earlier statement I said sometime ago, that man basically limits himself to a cause and effect type behavior pattern which is heightened or give more importance or value in a stimulus-response type relationship. Again, you have the mental logic system being given more energy or value by that of the emotional control center. I also said or compared the self imposed limiting behavior of the individual to that of how a computer works. Now I am prepared to go one step further and maybe out on the limb to say that customs and traditions are in a basic sense, the same as computer programs. That is, they are like routines rather than normal actions of logical thought. One learns or is conditioned to respond to specific stimuli, which conclude with known or predetermined results or actions within certain acceptable limits of probability. The end results are similar to a multiple choice test; however, the amount one experiences is heightened or diminished by the emotions.

The logic and emotional functions of the individual determines one's behavior. The above paragraph tends to indicate that the emotions rule or control the individual; however, let me remind you, the individual actually makes those decisions and selections which brings that person into that particular situation where the emotions take over and/or control the individual's actions. You might want to compare this thought process to that of a railroad track, because one mentally throws the switches (makes selections) of the logic system which starts one off in a direction to get to somewhere or something for a specific reason. However, the length of time one stays on that track and/or the experiences that are encountered is determined by the emotional center. Because of the power of the emotional center, one sometimes forgets the reason for taking that track or the end results one was seeking.

This again is a case of balance, where one compliments the other, and you make your own reality and select those things which you want to experience. The way one experiences reality is determined by the relationship of the conscious self or being on an emotional level with that of one's physical senses and not the mental logic reasoning powers of the conscious self. I will refine this statement later on, but briefly, one uses the physical senses for nearly all conscious input to the learning triangle or in his growth process. Therefore, emotions tend to dominate the individual, because the emotional center is tied to and/or responds to the physical stimuli; whereas, the logic system has no such connection.

It looks like here, we have landed on a very important statement that has tremendous implications. However, I do not wish to elaborate on this subject at this point. The main thing to remember is that the physical world and/or self must relate or relates best to that which is similar to its self. That means that man is composed of physical matter and is equipped to detect physical stimuli and responds to the same physical matter or the human body mechanisms. That is the reason for the emotions to rule or control one's behavior more so than the logic reasoning system of the mind. It is difficult, if not impossible to detach one's self from the physical world in which he dwells, nor should he, but he should also be consciously aware of the unmanifested spiritual world in which he also resides. Again, we are talking about balance.

Getting back to the subject at hand, we were talking about customs and traditions, before we got sidetracked onto emotions. Speaking about tracks, each culture, society, nation, group, etc., has its own set of tracks, guidelines and/or limitations on nearly every conceivable word, thought or actions, past, present and future. The way people act or behave is to a large degree, in a direct relationship to the customs and traditions of that group in which the person dwells. As indicated by the chapter on social identification, it is difficult to really isolate and identify a specific group as that which sets all these legal rules and regulations as well as the informal customs and traditions which people observe. However, there is such an entity or force, be it singular or multiple, is not important. What is important, is that these words, thoughts and actions have to some extent or another, preconceived values attached to them to make them either good, bad, right or wrong to some degree. These predetermined values are in turn, directly related to the overall control of the individual and consequently, the group.

A rough guideline to discover these intangible values, is to observe trends (short beginnings and endings). That is, one can and should observe obvious behavior patterns in everything and everybody from a very simple act to those which are complex, and from literally, soup to nuts. Certain things are favored, liked or preferred above other things to a greater or lesser extent. This is like one's personal taste or diet, but it doesn't have to be food that is the nourishment. Then again, when it comes down to mental thought processes or patterning, another old saying might be appropriate here. And that is, "When in Rome, do as the Romans do". Here, I am referring to one's basic sense or ability to perceive differences and/or to adapt to a new environment that has different prefered patterns with specific beginnings and endings.

To emphasize that last statement, I think a little explanation is in order.

The context of this old saying is basically some good advice for individuals to use in order to get along with people in an unfamiliar environment. It is saying that one should try to blend into that new environment in order to accomplish in the best way possible, that reason or result that brings one to that environment. This is accomplished by trying to dress, groom, speak, eat, act and to conform to those customs and traditions of the land. Doing and performing all of these acts does not make you one or part of that new society or group; however, it does minimize your own differences which can hinder your task(s), or bring unwanted attention and possibly even scorn by others in that particular group. One normally performs or acts effectively in an environment of ease and relaxation with the trust and confidence of those around him, and to accomplish this, one must be capable of generating or responding to those around him on an equal basis. This means to stress the similarities or positive virtues in everyone and thing and not to emphasize the negative differences. This is accomplished by observing and following the patterns of that society or environment.

So, you see, this innocent little old saying has some interesting ramifications. It is saying the same thing that I have been telling you all along, that duplication and conformity is encouraged and reinforced as something that is good and right. To do as the Romans do, is behavior patterning in its most obvious condition. However, most of the patterning which I alluded to earlier, takes place within our own society or group(s) and is more of a subconscious level of thought than is indicated by this old saying. In this lengthy explanation, I am in a sense, comparing customs and traditions to that of a group, rather than that of an individual. But in this case, the group behaves as an individual. That is, the group finds it beneficial to be as close or similar to one another as possible in order to appreciate and/or respect one another's individual behavior. The idea is, if everyone shares the same things, they must also appreciate and respect the same values; hence, the consequences are self imposed limitations, otherwise known as conformity. This is nothing more than the performing of actions and/or the sharing of patterns that have short beginnings and endings.

We still have a little problem here that needs to be straightened out. In our explanation of customs and traditions, we basically said that these values are characteristic of a particular group, or are relative to that group.

Earlier, we said that the word, best, and subsequently, values too, were relative to the individual. How can both statements be true and not conflict with one another? The key to this problem is this thing called, self imposed limitations. The individual is part of a larger group and he imposes limitations which fit himself and that of a particular group. One does not need to comply or limit one's self totally to that group, because that group as stated before, can not be totally isolated and/or identified itself. Even if that group could be totally identified, it is still a collection of minorities or sub-groups organized to control or accomplish a specific task or certain favored interests. It is in itself, not a total inflexible absolute that controls absolutely, nor should it be. It is a framework or structure in which the individual can help fill or to add a little color.

Because of these self imposed limitations, it is difficult to determine who limits whom. Does the individual limit the group or does the group limit the individual? I believe, you will find your answer to this question in our discussion on balance. You have a lot more influence than you really think you have. You make your own reality and if you think you have something good, you will find that you have a following or group, with or without your conscious knowledge or approval. The only element that is missing from this group is that of control. Who controls such a group? The answer is simple! Anyone who wants it or believes in it most and is willing to initiate some action that will bring about a more wide spread knowledge of this good thing. Hence, we have a new control group within that group, that you started, whether you know it or not.

This group, like you, has an interest or cause that affects its immediate surroundings or environment. The effect(s) or action(s) of this group, on behalf of you and/or your ideas, has the ability to change existing relationships. That is, patterns or routines that had been set prior to your idea, will affect or change the status quo and in effect, sets up new relationships. The resulting changes, or lack of changes, depends upon stimulus, values or position of you and/or the interest group. The amount of energy that is generated or stimulated, affects, advances or enlarges the involvement or growth of this particular interest and/or interest group. The response, in turn, affects time, space and physical matter, or to put it in more simple terms, one's environment, just like our motor boat syndrome example.

This exaggerated situation is a classic example of our learning process, triangle or pyramid in action. In this example, an individual is somehow affected by someone or something in his environment. The way that person reacts to this cause, stimulates him to affect a response of some kind. The way this individual reacts to a situation or problem, is characteristic of that individual and is somewhat predictable. This patterned response is known and classified as behavior; but in effect, it is actually that individual's learning process routine. That is, one selects a series of specific patterns to arrive at an understanding of relationships. This process consists of switches (selections) of a yes-no, or go-no go computer like routines. In this manner, one is able to direct energy and relate knowledge of experiences which he knows will affect certain specific results in the way of physical changes to bring about possessions or a desired result. Voila!....and there you have it. The learning process is complete, or rather, it is an on-going and continuous overlapping process until its energy is overcome by a greater resistance.

In my attempt to clarify the problem of values between the group and the individual, I actually explained behavior and the learning process again. But, throughout these explanations, I have also and again referred to limitations. Therefore, the point to remember in all our explanations, is that man limits himself. The purpose of these limits is a matter of control and stability. To radically abandon limits and controls, one runs the risk of losing the learning process, or more specific, the understanding of relationships. In a sense, without these controls or limits, individuals have little common ground on which to agree and/or relate to. In a more humorous contemporary way of putting it, I recently saw a picture of an ape with the following caption that read: "Just when I learn all the answers, they go ahead and change the questions on me". You cannot have proper growth without responsible limitations.

Perhaps, I should now elaborate on the words, responsible limitations. But to do this, let's go back to my earlier statement I made that said, that all words, thoughts and actions have to some extent or another, preconceived values attached to them. Also, I think it might not be a bad idea to clarify the actions of groups at the same time. What I am going to try and do here, is to kill three birds with one stone, so to speak.

I believe that perhaps everyone, including myself, might have generalized that all words and actions taken in behalf of, or to benefit specific interest groups is considered good and right. But, if I were to say that, we run into problems. First, the word benefit would have to be defined and limits set on the desired end results expected, before we can have or be able to place a value on that or those actions of that particular interest group in question. This is difficult, if not impossible to do, and yet, this is absolutely necessary unless we want to run the risk of saying those actions taken by that interest and/or control group of say, the German people in the second world war. In this case, this interest or control group set about the deliberate act of human destruction for a supposedly good and right reasons which was the supposed purification of the German race. This type of same logic or situation exists in nearly all conditions of war or violence, where all people involved are supposedly acting in behalf of good and right reasons for a proper end result. It's also interesting to note that after that physical conflict of interests, only one interest group is right and that group is that one which controls the final outcome.

In all these situations, a particular action was right and/or good so long as that group remained in control. In these cases, and perhaps most cases of conflict, the old adage; "Might makes right!"... is correct. However, such logic is illogical. Therefore, we find ourselves moving from a position of belief and support of interest and control groups to that of suspicion and caution, and/or non-involvement in any organization. Now doesn't that sound a little close to home? In any case, the quality or value of action resides in the control group which supposedly is acting in behalf of a majority of people and therefore, or, because of this relationship, their actions are assumed good and right. The actions of this or any control group do, or may have preconceived agenda(s) that are supposed to be responsible to all interests. But are they?

In our chapter on sociological identification, we said that people organized themselves, limited themselves and become specialized in order to derive greater benefits and to decrease the burdens that a totally self sufficient individual would have to face if he were all alone in the physical world. Well, in undertaking this relationship, man has reaped great benefits and tragedies as well. When man entered into this relationship, he assumed certain responsibilities to his fellow man to aid him by providing greater benefits than that individual could provide by himself. This relationship worked fine up to a point; however, once man was relieved of a greater part of his problems, he sought more than his share of the wealth than the land could provide. In a sense, he became greedy and possessions still weren't enough for him, but with possessions, he found he could exercise great power over his fellow man. Wealth gave him prestige, pride and control because of his position within the group and his immediate environment. With this control, man continued to seek enlargement of his environment and consequently, he conflicted with others nearby. Times have changed, but this quest for power and position has not.

Today, those people elected or brought into power, or for that matter, put in any position of authority or control, are given responsibilities to fulfill certain legal or mutually agreed upon rules of conduct. However, more often than not, these same people confuse their responsibilities with that of temporary absolute power. That is, they confuse the guidelines of their responsible behavior with that of the endowed power or right of and by their position. Rather than to manage the affairs of many to help and aid them, they tend to control or manipulate their brethren. This may or may not be done on a conscious level. However, it appears as if there may be an indirect desire or wish to control people for supposedly good intentions, help or even humanitarian reasons, but just the same, the reason is often overcome by the power or position of the authority and not the other way around.

The reason for this use of power may be founded in a simple explanation. It may be a lot easier for people in authority to issue orders or direction, rather than to manage the affairs of their fellow men. It requires a great deal of effort to mange properly, and by just issuing directions, these people do not have to worry about a proper balance or quality to life and living conditions of the many instead of the select few. It is simpler to just suspend the mutually agreed upon rules for those rules of their own liking and/or interests. Therefore, that is one of the reasons why it is said; "Might makes right", or why good and/or right exists only with that group or interest that is in control. That's because people or persons in control tend to interpret existing rules and laws to their own beliefs and/or their special interests take precedence over those of the majority or will of the people and remember, a majority is nothing more than a collection of minorities that is constantly changing. Effective power must be concentrated or directed in order to overcome resistance.

Perhaps, these last few statements are a little harsh, or they may at least come off that way; however, it may also explain away a lot of problems people have in dealing with people in authority. There does seem to be a definite lack of ability or insensitivity on behalf of authoritative figures to try to properly balance different thoughts and beliefs on the way things can be. Then again, this problem that individuals have with authority may also stem from the inability of authority to control or enforce such power to correct or influence change adequately or fairly. Again, authority gets its power to control from the same people who seek this same power in return. If the people refuse to cooperate with authority, then authority has no power to control. The whole purpose and intent of this latter explanation was to try and indicate and identify perhaps some of the inconsistencies or discrepancies in the rules and regulations which are designed to limit behavior. However, what we got, was what we want. You make your own reality.

The concept of our legal judicial system is somewhat offset or balanced by customs and traditions. The only difference between the two concepts is that the point of control or position of the limits. That is, our legal system and customs and traditions, vary only in the fact that one system has an identifiable single source of control; whereas, the latter has no known source. Consequently, customs and traditions are a way to get around formal laws, rules, and regulations from sources of authority. They are, in effect, an informal way of limiting and controlling without a direct power source. However, just the same, customs and traditions are a force of direct authority which is vested in each and everyone. Therefore, it does have the power or threat of physical punishment or negative reinforcement per se to make it just as strong as our formal legal system. Together, these two systems or forces, balance each other out. And again, we return to our concept of balance and/or position.

Directly and indirectly the legal and the informal systems are designed to limit or control one's behavior. The important feature of control rests with people designated or responsible for the administering or controlling of these limitations; however, the actual control rests with the individual himself. All the systems and all the powers on earth cannot and will not limit or control an individual, if that individual does not wish to limit himself to the guideline so identified or indicated to him. The alternative to variance is physical punishment, isolation or death. However, we said a long time ago, that there are usually more benefits gained by a group sharing responsibilities than there is if one where self sufficient. Therefore, more often than not, the individual will choose to comply or limit one's behavior.

It might be interesting to mention here, that civilization used to administer to or tried to invoke its will of control upon the greater populace by legal means of enforcement or authority mentioned previously; however, today's societies tend to stress the more positive side of limiting behavior or by appealing to or working with the emotional center of the mind, rather than the logic center. That is, in times past, one witnessed and felt the power of physical punishment and logically concluded that it would be more beneficial to comply or limit one's behavior to that of the interest or control group in power, or at least, that was the thinking of the people in authority back then. A review of past history indicates that these efforts were not very successful.

Today, man has to some extent, learned that physical punishment or the threat of such punishments doesn't really work. Rather, it may achieve temporary limits or goals; however, it really only delays the problem or source of conflict, it doesn't solve or resolve the problem. Therefore, man has tried to use psychology to positively reinforce the need or benefits of such self imposed limitations. That is, man is now attempting to persuade the mind and appeal to the emotional center of the mind to make such changes. As I mentioned before, the emotional center deals with the physical senses and therefore tends to have greater control over the individual than the logical mind. Also, by working with the mental capacities, less physical efforts and energies may be expended to obtain the desired end results and they may be obtained faster. Therefore, all indications are that limitations are still being forcefully used, but in different ways, and probably, with greater results. So, individual behavior is still a personal matter; however, the matter is becoming more difficult to identify.

Now, there are still a few things that this chapter is lacking in respect to explaining behavior; however, I think you may have a little better idea of how it works. I never did get into the examples of societies and behavior patterns in action. This is still a very important part of this book. To discuss a subject in an indirect way is one thing, to experience a whole way of life is another thing. So let's talk about people. People just love to talk about other people. It's a favorite past time of people to analyze other people's good and bad points, especially the bad points. Whole industries and tabloids are built around this area. It seems so strange to me that there are supposedly so many rotten and bad people around, that you begin to wonder if any decent people exist. At least it sounds that way if you believe everything you read or hear. But of course, you know all of this already. You know, because talking about people is a favorite American or national past time. In the next chapter, you might get an idea of what behavior really is all about and this might change your idea of people as well.

CHAPTER 8

Patterning

Lights!
Camera!
Action!

As you can tell, this chapter was written and somewhat inspired by the recently televised Motion Pictures Academy Awards, which are given out annually to members of their profession. The trophy, or Oscar, as it is referred to in that profession, is given out to a number of different categories involved in the making of films as well as several special areas of acting and film classifications. Again, limited patterns of recognition for behavior in action. The categories getting the most attention are those pertaining to best actor and actress and best film of the year. These are the glamour categories or popularity contests that are supposedly the top position anyone can hope to attain - or obtain, like a possession.

You would think that we are finally away from that dull, boring, technical information that I have been feeding you for sometime now, but let me show you something interesting. Above, we are talking about self imposed limitations or classifications imposed by a special interest group in order to provide a lead or direction to their profession. By honoring or rewarding and/or awarding trophies to these various sub-groups, this profession or a main group is attempting to influence the direction of growth, as well as the center position or point of reference for others to follow. Interesting, isn't it? You just can't get away from it! Reinforcement and limitations are all around us, and yet we never really see them. A lot of that problem has to do with consciousness. We'll get into that later.

Anyway, the reason I chose to start this chapter out this way is because I see an interesting analogy between the acting profession and our own lives in general. I also thought it was a clever way of getting your attention after some rather slow thought provoking ideas that really require some mental efforts. Lastly, people generally pay more attention to things that they can personally relate to and/or have had a day to day diet or exposure to high media coverage items. Now I wonder where I heard that before? In any case, I see in a slightly distorted way, that we are all actors playing in a long running series or full length feature entitled, "Life". Exciting, isn't it? I wonder how much it will gross? Better yet, I wonder if there will be a sequel?

Enough of this questionable humor. Let's get serious. That would make an interesting song title! Anyway, the point I'd like to make, is, that acting is an interesting profession. It is supposedly a vocation that is nothing more than an individual expressing physical and emotional actions of another supposed individual or fictitious character in a short dramatized study or story. The real skill involved on behalf of the individual is that he must be convincing and as close to real life situations as possible and still maintain his own identity as well as that of the person and/or part that actor is trying to portray. This is difficult to do, because if you never have experienced a true life experience, it is difficult to act in a convincing fashion. The ability of an actor to make this transition and convey the proper emotion, pretty much determines how well the motion picture is received and patronized. Naturally, the story also plays some part in it; however, it is the acting that really makes or breaks the film.

You might say that how well one plays or acts his part in real life, determines how well he or she is also received. There maybe no awards given in this performance; however, the amount of popularity or patronizing one experiences, is perhaps, sufficient reward for a good performance in life. The only major difference in one's performance in life and that of an actor, is that the individual does not have to memorize words or learn a script. Otherwise, there is little difference. Both situations primarily use the physical senses to understand and express one's self in this physical reality, and both accentuate certain actions by using emotions to dramatize those experiences which are really important to that individual or actor.

This emphasis on the physical senses and emotions is because it is in this same manner by which we communicate or outwardly transmit understanding. That is, and you have heard it before, that which is of substance must reciprocate in a like manner in order to be properly understood. Like poles attract, opposites repel. This idea of communication is a complicated thing, and not to be treated lightly. An actor actively seeks and trains to master certain fundamentals of the physical anatomy in order to control certain muscles which are utilized to portray states of emotional excitement and/or compassion. These same muscles are often used to also control the tone or inflection of the voice and/or speech. In any case, the art of acting involves a great deal of effort and energy directed at working with the muscles and physical senses.

The ability of an actor or individual to express and communicate his thoughts, feelings, and emotions to others, is also a form of control. In the act of communicating, one is trying to transmit his thoughts and beliefs about the real physical world about him and its relationship to himself to those about him. That is, he tries to persuade and convince others to enter his world of reality, so to speak, in order to gain control over the situation which confronts that individual at that moment. There is strength in numbers. If that individual can successfully convey his thoughts, feelings and emotions to those about him, then in all due respect, he ought to be able to control the situation to his liking or desired end results. In effect, he possesses a form of power and energy that can change physical reality, or at least, his immediate surroundings. Therefore, it is obvious that communications is a form of control and power.

The power of communications to control is also emphasized or demonstrated by the fact that all organized civilizations, societies, and cultures try to manipulate or control communications to some extent. In fact, in this country, the Constitution grants the freedom of speech, press, assembly, and worship, as its first amendment. Perhaps now, you may be able to understand a little better the reason why communications is so important. It is because communications has the power to control, the power to affect changes, the power to affect reality. It is also this same power to control, that limits the boundaries of nations and people. That is, the ability to communicate effectively determines the amount of physical resources or power one can control to supposedly share the wealth or benefits of the land and people to all that can be organized to communicate in a mutually beneficial relationship.

In any case, we were talking about acting before I went off on a tangent. What I wanted to say is that acting is very similar to true life. We are all acting in this full length feature called, "The Game of Life". We are all acting or playing our part in a growth process that involves experiencing the use of energy in some form or another. It really doesn't matter so much if we win or lose, but how we play the game....or is it? "Everybody loves a winner!" It seems that everybody has to be a winner at the game of life, or so our current philosophy or trends in society, so indicates. This is an interesting concept. I'd just like to know what they mean when they say, "Winner".

To understand this game, let's take a look at some of the games that have been played, that are slightly different from the one which we are now playing. To do this, I will, for the first time, deal with major data composed and compiled by others. There are a few good case studies or research works that stand out as being exceptionally well documented. However, let me remind you again, you get what you are looking for. At the time of this writing, there was an accusation concerning perhaps the most influential anthropologist of modern time. I am referring here to that of Margaret Mead and her book on the Samoan culture, entitled, "Coming of Age in Samoa". *

Although the point I wish to make concerns differences in behavior patterns, which are the contents or findings of Margaret Mead's research study, I also want to caution you in your own growth and development in your own learning process. That is, I would like you to review this information for examples of contrasts, and yet, I want you to remember that differences are only in the mind of the beholder. Differences only exist, if you want them to exist. You make your own reality. You set your own limitations. To emphasize my latter concern for your well being, let's review the controversy that appeared in publications before we get into the research work on cultures.

In short, the article indicates that another anthropologist, named Derek Freeman disputes Ms. Mead's results as being incorrect. The main thesis of Mead's work was

* TIME Magazine, February 14, 1983. Article under "behavior" written by John Leo. Reported by Joelle Attiner/Boston and John Dunn/ Melbourne.

supposedly a study that was basically an attack on conventional mores of the time, around the 1920's and 30's. In her book, she contended that sexual promiscuity of the Samoan culture encouraged a happier, freer lifestyle. Freeman suggests that Ms. Mead's study was an act of self-delusion; whereby, she isolated herself from the major segment of the Samoan society and relied solely on informants who told her what she wanted to hear. That is, her questions were arranged or patterned to reach a certain pre-destined conclusion. Supposedly, Ms. Mead chose not to work with a cross section of the populace and never consulted the male dominated culture or so says Mr. Freeman. Consequently, Ms. Mead portrayed a romantic vision or version about the south sea island culture.

To understand this biased problem a little better, you also have to or should have some knowledge of Ms. Mead and/or the times in which she lived. There is great probability that Ms. Mead accomplished or fulfilled the end results of her own self imposed limitations to which she herself, was subjected to during her own educational learning or patterning process. You see, in addition to knowledge, one is subject to and is taught certain learning patterns in higher educational institutes. In any case, Ms. Mead was subject to the teachings, of yet, another anthropologist, named Boas. This fellow was in turn, committed to the belief that humans are born as blank slates and shaped by their cultures. Also, at the same time, there were a number of other people who subscribed to the idea that heredity, molded behavior. Among the most noted supporters of this latter cause, was Nazi Germany, which actually tried to alter human behavior by controlling and directing bloodline genetics.

As you can see and tell, this study had both political and ideology overtones, as well as scientific value. Boas' teachings were theory. He needed certain findings to substantiate this into reality. Enter Margaret Mead. Boas' idea was to find a culture relatively free of adolescent stress in order to come up with the blank slate type behavior and/or culture. Surprise! Ms. Mead found such a culture on her very first attempt to make a scientific study on the subject. This same situation occurred to yet another student of Boas and that was Ruth Benedict, who wrote "Patterns of Culture". This latter book is used a lot in the following pages.

As you can see, it is believed that Boas told his students what to look for, and they found it. Again, we are confronted with short beginnings and endings that leads or creates a pattern of growth. Apparently, this also leads one to question all such reports or studies, but strangely enough, it really doesn't. Man basically accepts reports or findings of people with credentials of supposed knowledge and higher learning. Ms. Mead and Ms. Benedict found what they were looking for and it served their desired end result. They neatly catalogued their studies and identified the differences as they were taught to do. Naturally, they had to end up with the results they did because of their own patterning behavior.

Patterns are like my earlier statement on sub-cultures. That is, they are very difficult to distinguish and consequently, you get overlapping areas. In such cases, the color that one is seeking is in reality a shade or hue of the original. However, because of this confusion and/or chaos, it is also easy to fit or impose limitations at the same time. This situation or lack of continuity and the need for such limitations or logical patterns simply results in someone arbitrarily assigning an identity or value to such a pattern. You will find that very few people will argue with such findings, unless they have something to gain in identifying with a specific study. The reason for this is clear and simple. Our physical reality demands that we separate and identify information into patterns for easy assimilation in our learning process. Unless we are directly affected, we will normally let other people make these determinations for us. This is one of the benefits of living in such a society or culture.

In effect, Ms. Mead's book was not so much a scientific study of foreign culture as it was a critique of Western civilization. Supposedly, she indicates that Western civilization encourages fidelity, competition, overheated sexual arrangements, a tight nuclear family, guilt, stress and adolescent turmoil; while the supposed primitive Samoans live in an environment of cooperation, adolescent bliss, casual family ties and easy sex, all without any signs of guilt or neurosis. The success of this study and/or book propelled Ms. Mead to the forefront of the liberals and their causes. Her works were frequently quoted to stress and promote new ideas and hopefully, new learning patterns. Ms. Mead became the focal point and in fact, took part in shaping and influencing public opinion. If her research work should be discredited in any way, she will always be known for her success in swaying the minds of liberal educators and psychologists in a way not intended but very effective anyway.

To emphasize my point about controversy and that you make your own reality, I'd like to quote a few more conflicting studies about others and their research. The article that I am using for reference here, indicates the following: "Robert Redfield's 1930 study of Tepoztlan, Mexico", found warm, laid back peasants. Oscar Lewis studied the same people in 1951, finding a culture in which murder, gossip and cheating were rampant. Early reports on African bushmen labeled them the "harmless people", later research revealed a distinct aggressiveness. Bronislaw Malinowski, in a famous 1923 study of the Trobriand Islanders, found that the area's young boys grew up without the Oedipus complex, a refutation of one of Freud's presumed universals. But last year, Anthropologist Melford Spiro, using Malinowski's own data, said, "Malinowski's conclusions were unwarranted". Well, I hope you get the idea. Be careful what you are looking for, because you will find it!

In my attempt at credibility, I seek comfort in someone else's work to prove my point. I am taking the easy way out, as do a lot of other people in our society. Perhaps this is a protective safety valve type approach to living. That is, in the supposedly moderate approach to life, people are afraid to offend and risk controversy or takes sides on an issue. They try to take a flexible approach to matters; however, they sometimes mistake this balanced type of living for something else. They sometimes take this approach only until an issue or element of control is perfectly clear, then they usually take sides. Remember, everybody loves a winner, or wants to be on the winning side.

Another reason for reliance on predigested or compiled information, is for personal gain or favor. That is, if one is good or skilled in the art of human engineering, one can rest relatively secure in a position of authority or siding with those in control. By a means of manipulation, one can use this interdependence in our society to escape responsibility or use it as a way to blame or transfer wrong to someone else. You know the type of people I am talking about. They are the ones that take the credit when everything goes right, but never accept blame if things go wrong. It's always someone else's fault. That's because these people were either supplied with wrong information or the information came from other sources or people with supposedly academic credentials; therefore, the information and/or decisions must be right and good, or else it is the fault of that academic institution for not teaching these support people properly. Do you believe that?

The last reason for relying on such compiled information, is for a matter of expediency. I have to plead the latter case. I have already qualified the inherent problems associated with such studies; therefore, I have little to personally gain from the use of such information except, time and possibly, some relationship of association on your part with the examples cited. It is also interesting reading. As mentioned before, the following examples come from Ruth Benedict's "Patterns of Culture". She found and neatly categorized three cultures; One supposedly designated as Dionysian, the Dobu Indians of New Guinea, another is classified as Apollian, the Zuni Indians of Southwestern United States and a third group, is somewhere in between the other two, the Kwakiutl Indians of Northwestern United States and Canada. Now, we are still talking about patterning, so I will continue this chapter; however, there is a slight change to this patterning, therefore, for the rest of this chapter, I will classify these sub-cultures with sub-title headings.

GROUND RULES OF PLAY

If we are finally going to talk about anthropology, we have to set some limitations or ground rules by which we are going to play the game. That is, anthropologists classify people or cultures into two main groups. They are either Dionysian or Apollian. They came up with these names because the study of people began to flourish around the time of the Greek Empire.

Dionysian refers to people who pursue arriving at a value of existence through "the annihilation of the ordinary bounds and limits of existence". He seeks to attain his most valued moments by escaping from the boundaries imposed upon him by his five senses, to break through to another order of experience. His desire is to press through toward a certain psychological state to achieve success. Some analogy in modern times can be stated in terms of drunkenness, and/or the use of drugs as a means to justify an end goal. That which exceeds normal physical boundaries or creates states of non-ordinary reality, is a goal and is wisdom sought and valued, by the Dionysian. I have recently heard a lot of reference to our younger generation of non-conformist children, as our drug culture. You may draw your own conclusions or change their name.

The Apollian culture refers to those who seek states of being outside normal reality and the boundaries of the physical being but without outside aids. Such people have little or no idea of nature or the means used by the Dionysian. In fact, the Apollian finds such means to outlaw such practices and/or pursuits from conscious life. He simply lives on a day-to-day basis and experiences that which is within the realm of his perception and/or inner senses, a middle of the road type approach at that, with no extremes. His altered states are achieved by meditation and/or diet control or fasting. Sounds something like the question of balance in the learning process, I told you about before.

THE DOBU INDIANS

The Dobu Indians are a group of people that exhibits Dionysian or great excitement and extreme behavior patterns. Their culture lives or lived in the Southwestern Pacific off New Guinea, on a smaller island appropriately named, Dobu. The island lies just south of New Guinea and near a group of fertile islands, called the Trobriand. The latter group of islands, are relatively low and quite beautiful; however, Dobu is a rocky volcanic island, that is poor in just about everything. In fact, the island is so poor, most neighboring people have left the Dobu alone and this relative isolation makes them prime candidates for a research study.

The primitive natives are primarily fishermen; however, even the waters around this island, are not very bountiful. Therefore and consequently, these people are relatively fierce and at one time, were considered barbaric and cannibalistic. In any case, they don't have a very good reputation as being friendly. Because of the scarcity of everything, the lifestyle of these people were considered hard and their hostile environment is a main contributing factor to their social behavior, or lack of it. You might say that these people pattern their life style on a kind of negative approach to social customs as we know them, because survival is the dominant thought among these people.

In looking at this culture, it is difficult to see any form of organization. In fact, this is characteristic of their society. There are no forms of organized institutions, and leadership is fragmented. Most of these people are in a continuous state of war with one another and any outsider or nearby neighbor. Lawlessness and treachery are a major trait of these people. The dominant theme seems to be, cheat as much as you can, and that personal gain or achievement is derived at another person's expense. Hostility is a way of life and culturally accepted within each village, with slight differences. Hatred, suspicion and distrust, are common thoughts harbored by these people. Man is considered bad and friendship is regarded with terror and not at all practiced. Yet, a bad man in their society, is considered poor in material goods. This negative attitude even goes beyond living. That is, these people believe in magic and the supernatural. There is nothing natural in life, and that all things are caused by, or are a direct result of man. Even natural death is still considered to be murder by human hands, but no one knows by whom.

As you can see, these ideas are radically different from those of you and I. Before the white man controlled this area, no outsider would venture into this area except to kill or raid, with but a few exceptions. One of these exceptions, was a rare and unusual form of trade or commerce they refer to as Wabu-Wabu. Perhaps our equivalent of a sham. This is a practice or style of trade whereby the Dobu would promise you anything in order to get the goods and run, without in fact, delivering anything in return. The Dobu did not abide by fair trade rules at all. This is a kind of something for nothing approach to life, or just another form of stealing.

Another example of their unusual behavior, can be seen in their marriage customs. Marriage must take place with a spouse from another tribe. There are no marriages of people within the same tribe. It must be an outsider, or it is not a marriage. How this occurs, is interesting to say the least! When a boy grows old enough, he is encouraged to seek a mate among the neighboring tribes. He is permitted to sleep around, if you will. That is, he is encouraged to sleep with as many neighboring females as he wants and if she in turn, is willing. He may have sexual relationships with as many as he desires; however, this still does not constitute a marriage. Marriage must begin with a hostile act of the mother-in-law. That is, if the young man sleeps with a woman all night or stays beyond sunrise of the following morning, he is likely to see the mother-in-law blocking the doorway of the house. The young man is then considered trapped. Supposedly, this usually happens when the man gets tired of roaming. In any case, the friends and neighbors in the village see the event and hear the bellowing and join the impromptu ceremony, which consists of the couple coming out of the house and sit outside, surrounded by all those who wish to take part. The couple is officially married after a period of silence and staring which lasts about a half an hour. The young man then becomes a member of his wife's village. Then, the mother-in-law puts the young man to work doing chores around the house or working the garden. This is still part of the ceremony. Also, or during this work period, the village crowd is encouraged to abuse and ridicule the new husband.

Now, there are still other obligations in this marriage that include the young man's relatives and family. Although the rules of marriage are informal, they are very strict and demanding. This union also becomes a strong bond which carries obligations for families to have sexual relations among each other's mates. Adultery is common and accepted. To complicate matters even more, the new couple live under the rule of each parent's village or alternate living in each other's village. Other obligations are the sharing of garden fruits and vegetables, with one exception. To these people, the jam is a cherished food item and is treated almost as an entity itself with certain or specific blood lines. He maintains his jams and she maintains her jams. If the marriage is dissolved or the man dies, then all his shared food is tabu to his children and they become members of the mother's village. But for a period of one year after the death of the husband, there is a period of mourning and great demands on the part of the man's village. After that time, the wife and the children may not enter the husband's village again.

There are some other strange or foreign beliefs pertaining to magic and supernatural powers that greatly affect these people's daily lives. Among these, is the belief that nothing is possible without magic. A good crop is a confession of theft and magic, but a harvest is always kept secret for fear of theft. Suspicion of magical spells which are infested in disease charms is always feared to paranoid lengths. This can result in starvation if the food is thought to be contaminated and can only be cured with another counter spell. Spells are placed on trees and/or persons and are supposed to cause misfortune, but is good for the individual casting the spell. Therefore, materialism is not sought in this culture because of the fear of these evil spells or curses by others. As mentioned, death is caused by magic and sometimes a little help from poison. A death in retaliation for another threat is known and called, Budo. Apparently, this is a common practice, or else it wouldn't have a special name.

Although this is a relatively negative type society, they do have conflicting customs or beliefs on bad or wrong behavior. Among these, is the idea that any meeting between opposite sexes not married, is regarded as illicit if she does not flee. That is if she is seen by a villager. This taboo therefore, requires the husband to guard his wife while she is gardening. Also, she is not supposed to talk to anyone outside of her immediate family and never to outsiders. Another strange custom that is thought to be bad or evil, is, that no one must uncover themselves in public even when they are all alone with their own sex. If the men are out fishing and must relieve themselves, they must get into the water so they do not show themselves. They are not suppose to speak of sex either, but as you can see by their pre-marriage custom, sex is on their minds often and favored by all.

The Dobu are prudish and passionate people, consumed with jealousy, suspicion and resentment. A good man is one who has many conflicts to his credit and has moderate prosperity. Everyone believes he is successful due to his thievery, killing by sorcery and cheating. As mentioned, theft and adultery are valued as well as superstitious charms. Magic and witchcraft are also favored. A bad man has been injured by misfortune or by conflict, in which he lost out to the better man. A cripple or deformed man is always bad. He doesn't even have to do anything. Anything you can get away with, is respected. There is no legal system and there is no such thing as mercy or kindness, nor do they get involved in challenges or insult. Resentment, is their motivation which will bring anything to pass in spite of others. To kill another man, one seeks out his company and spends several days in a close relationship. And so it is!

THE ZUNI INDIANS

The Zuni are an indian tribe culture located in Southwestern United States, living along and between the Colorado and Rio Grande Rivers. This tribe is supposedly the descendants of the great ancient cliff dwellers which are located in the arid plateau valley of the San Juan River in Colorado and the bordering areas of Arizona and New Mexico. Although these people also live in a relatively harsh environment, they typify the Apollian quietness or non-aggressive attitude. Their outlook or lifestyle is completely different from the Dobu Indians off New Guinea. But like the Dobu, the land is again thought to play a significant part in the behavior patterns of this group.

This indian culture is based upon the belief in moderation, or a middle of the road type approach to life, staying within the known realm of their physical limitations or reality. They do not meddle with disruptive psychological states to break into another order of experience induced by frenzy or outside stimulants. The Zuni are an unusually peaceful group of people who were surrounded by many known hostile warlike tribes until recent times. Their once flourishing civilization diminished greatly over the years, but not as a result of wars or direct conflict. The reason for this decline, is wrapped in as much mystery as the reason for the supposed abandonment of the now famous cave dwellings of their ancient ancestors. These are very secretive people as are most of their ceremonial practices.

These people believe that one should not indulge in any form of conduct, too much or too little. This attitude seems to foster a somewhat passive society with very little fighting, arguments or even, punishment. There is no sense of good and bad and therefore, there is no form of guilt or sin within their society. They, as a people, seem not disciplined and there is no motivation to seek a position of authority. Even the sacred ritual of marriage, is held with little fervor. Death too, is considered a minor event, followed by a relatively brief mourning period. What little authority they have, is shared in a decentralized way with no main source of command or rule. Therefore, these people practice a type of permissive society, but one with strict guidelines where aggressiveness is discouraged and quietness and moderation, are encouraged and the norm. Survival and their group way of life, seems to be their main desire or goal.

The Zuni seek comfort and experience life in a passive way without external stimulus and they desire not to improve upon what already exists. This leads to a feeling of oneness, where man has a direct relationship to nature, in the same way that animals run free in nature without interference. In such a situation, change would then occur only if the natural balance of things was upset. In this environment, a kind of inter-relationship exists where each individual is independent of one another and yet, dependent on the land and its people to work together to conserve and treat their surroundings in such a way as to allow nature to support all things. This is a kind of self imposed limitation or responsibility of conservation which may be a direct cause for the tribal social behavior of moderation for these people.

As mentioned, the Zuni are very ceremonious people. Their daily life is centered around religious practices which are believed to be supernaturally powerful. Great emphasis is placed on rituals and exact details, especially the ceremonial dances for rain or fertility. Their culture is basically a theocracy with six secret societies of priests. No other aspect of their existence seriously competes with the dances and religious observances. Marriages and divorces, are casual and individually arranged, because individual matters are not considered that important. Rather, the Zuni search for supernatural powers and seek membership in one of their religious societies. Their culture only requires the individual to learn by intense and extensive ritual methods in the proper order of things. They are also taught not to indulge in the search for membership exclusively, or in excess, or as part of their religious rites. They do not use drugs or mind inducing vegetation, nor pain or pleasure to achieve an enlightened state of being.

In the pursuit of religious power, the Zuni tend to pattern their culture into a single principle or belief. However, this type of approach or pursuit of values, tends to also lead some groups within this culture to actually reject the principles or unity of mind. At the same time, this rejection also serves as a unifying force. Their ideas of individualism, are naturally disruptive in nature, at the same time, it is the single most important or dominant drive that is evident in their behavior pattern and consumes their whole cultural pattern. This is quite unusual, because most cultures are multi-theme oriented.

Our explanation of this group of people would not be complete without explaining some of their customs in detail. Therefore, we will begin with their marriage custom, just remember, individual matters are not considered important. In this society, there is no courtship in marriage. There is very little prior encounter between the sexes before marriage. When a boy decides to get married, he goes to the girl's house to taste her food. The father then asks the boy if he has come for his daughter. If his reply is yes, the father says he cannot have her. However, if she is willing, the mother makes their bed and they retire together. After a period of four days, she then dresses in her best and presents gifts of corn flour to the boy's mother. There are no other formalities and little social interest. There are no property rights or economic exchanges.

The rules of conduct and divorce are just as simple. To get a divorce, the woman merely packs up all of the man's belongings in a neat bundle and sets them outside. He has no recourse. He simply returns home, finds his belongings outside, picks them up and returns to his former family. There may be some weeping on his part and his family; however, the rules do not provide for violent emotions. In spite of this simple procedure, most marriages endure. Bickering is not liked, and most marriages are peaceful. But, no matter what happens to a marriage, the woman of the household remains with the house for life.

Wealth in this society exists to some varying degree; however, it is not as important as one's ceremonial role. Membership in one of the religious societies outweighs wealth. Personal gain is incidental, but can be accomplished modestly. However, the Zuni distrust individualism. An individual who excels at a competitive game is often barred from future events. The idea is that people should be interested in the game and equal chances and not the individual who plays the game. Moderation is key. This is again, something like our earlier concept of balance in the learning process; however, you might also consider this to be in an extreme condition in regards to the time element. That is, this moderation or balancing is done on a daily basis, rather than over the lifetime of the individual.

Although individual efforts are encouraged, authority exists to a limited degree; however, it is not sought. Selected men of council are chosen against their wishes. No one seeks such a position, but when elected to it by others, they are bound to serve. This attitude toward power involves leadership and consequently, no one in this position wishes to excel; therefore, the leader(s) seek to distribute their power or share responsibility with their people. Such an attitude toward power encourages independence and cooperation on an equal basis of moderation.

THE KWAKIUTL INDIANS

The last group of people that Ruth Benedict wrote about, ceased to be a viable culture or society in the late 1800's. Much of the information was handed down in writings by others and the remaining descendants have been integrated into the western culture. The Kwakiutl used to exist as a culture along the Northwestern coast of the United States and Canada, from Alaska to the Puget Sound region of the State of Washington. Perhaps, the best known feature or artistic trait for which they are known, are their sculptures known as Totem Poles.

Unlike the previous indian cultures studied, the Kwakiutl lived in a land of plenty. The land was good to them, but they were not farmers. Most of their wealth came from the sea, hunting, fishing, and wood working which were their major occupations. In fact, their people were extremely gifted in wood working, producing boxes, planks for houses that were uniform, furniture, utensils, boats and very lavishly decorated items, not to mention joints and the joining of wood in such a way as to be difficult to detect, and this was all done without the use of metal tools.

On a whole, this culture had great materialism as primitives go, and an almost inexhaustible supply of goods without an excessive expenditure of labor. They were a vigorous, often overbearing people with no common order and a zest unequalled by neighboring tribes. Its values were not those commonly recognized by other cultures, but again the affluent wealth of the land is believed to be a major reason for this type of behavior, Perhaps the major difficulty that this culture had was the problem of language. The culture was really composed of several tribes, each speaking a different language, but also sharing the same customs.

The culture was rich in material wealth and wealth was highly sought. Because of this situation, their culture developed around a system known as Potlach. This is a kind of way to conduct economic warfare. This was a means to show wealth and strength, with an unusual custom whereby each party involved in such a conflict, was actually a loser. Physical wealth was complex. The natives used Dentalia sea shells as money, but real wealth was determined by the amount of moneys owed to them in interest which was extremely high. Native copper was also exchanged, but its value would constantly change and depend upon the latest transaction.

Marriage was also tied to wealth. One could get ahead and improve upon social standing by marriage and the bestowing of wealth associated with this institution. Marriage was treated as a business transaction with property rights and possessions. At the time of marriage, the daughter would receive wealth from the father and the new husband would control it.

Children born of marriage were given only the name of the village until it was time for them to have a name. A name was arrived at in this system of Potlach, That is, the children would be given blankets to distribute to their relatives; thereupon, the children would be repaid with a name and interest. Territorial ownership and commodities, as well as non-material things such as names, myths, songs, and privileges, were all signs of wealth and controlled by a family. The use of the family name was the right of the oldest born. In this manner, name and rank were given. Each time something was given, known as Potlach, a new name was bestowed upon that person.

Tribes were organized in lineages and societies with supernatural powers. Their calendar year was divided into two summers and two winters. In the summer, the lineage society was dominant, in the winter, the supernatural society dominated and used secular names and common names were taboo. Although wealth was the dominant trait of these people, religious rank and privileges also played some part in their behavior. One peculiar sect of ceremonial dancers were known as the cannibal dancers. This was the highest ranked society. These dancers strove for ecstacy and consequently, would lose control of themselves. Attendants would actually have to tie them with ropes to restrain them. During their dance, these people would actually take bites out of the arms and legs of spectators, and could eat from a slave specially killed for the ceremony. These dancers usually did not really eat or swallow their morsels of human flesh, but just the same, they were savage and barbaric and yet treated special. Supposedly, because of their altered state of being, it took four months of retraining to be able to bring these individuals back to re-enter society and another four years before he would again act normal.

The greatest act of nobility and/or rank, was the use of Potlach. Wealth was used to shame rivals. Everyone tried to distribute their own wealth more than others. These other people could not refuse accepting such wealth without admitting defeat. That is, unless that person could bestow a gift of equal or greater value, it was a sign of defeat. This bestowing of wealth was a way to gain in social position. Rarely, did they fight one another with weapons, but with property. However, murder was also a way to gain in this society and the man who killed another would take the name of the man he murdered, his dances, crests, supernatural powers and anything else that may have belonged to the other person.

The obsession for wealth was the object of the Potlach system. Wealth was so great in this culture that much of it was put away and never used, except for exchange and/or waste. The object of Potlach, was to show one's self superior to one's rival by possessing or destroying wealth. To out-Potlach a rival, was to succeed to heap scorn and ridicule upon one's opponent or guest. However, there were some rules placed on a chief in such Potlach ceremonies in that, he could not destroy property that would impoverish his people. In other words, there were certain understood taboos on Potlach. But to lose, was a complete disgrace and often resulted in suicide.

Now, this society, the Kwakiutl was determined to be a mixed or middle of the road type culture; however, according to the ground rules, it definitely has a tendency or leaning toward the Dionysian, rather than Apollian cultural pattern. The system of Potlach was a kind of relationship based upon the values of material goods and spiritual intangible items. How Ms. Benedict concluded this position is not explained very thoroughly nor can the records be verified any easier. However, it is an interesting group of people and it does relate to both material goods and spiritual matters in a somewhat moderate degree.

OTHER VARIATIONS

There are a lot more variations of human behavior than is represented here in these studies, and some of their characteristics are equally unusual and interesting. However, the purpose of this book is not to write about anthropology, but it is about the individual and that of morality. The latter issue, we haven't really pursued in depth. But before we leave this subject of cultural behavior, I thought that I would just mention a few more examples of different behavior in other parts of the world.

Among one of the more interesting variations, is found in Australia. The primitive aborigines use to practice a segregated society where the men and women would have completely different and separate social lives. In fact, this was an exclusive male cult whose fundamental trait is the exclusion of women. In fact, they would punish any woman who happened to intrude upon a man's secret ceremonies. A woman was put to death if they even knew or heard anything about the adult male rites or ceremonies.

On the other side of the world in Africa, there is another culture that is exclusively female dominated. In this society, beauty is identified with obesity. At puberty, girls are segregated, sometimes for years and fed sweet and fatty foods. They are also not permitted to exercise and they are attended to by others to groom and care for them. After this period of time is over, she is paraded through the village and ends up with her getting married.

In other parts of the world, there are situations where tribes living relatively close to one another have completely different life styles. In British Columbia, Canada, there used to be one tribe of indians that included both boys and girls on the same terms, or equality, in puberty rights. While very close to them, the Carrier Indians used to ban or isolate their children for years as part of their puberty rites.

Lastly, the Eskimo has or had a custom that permitted the killing of another without any retribution for no reason whatsoever. This was not a frequent act, however, it was similar in fact to animal behavior, or the survival of the fittest type approach to life.

ILLUSION OR DELUSION

Now, what I have tried to do in the foregoing, is to educate you or increase your learning triangle by trying to create a relationship of what was, to, what is. I have also tried to lay the groundwork or guidelines by which we can talk about morality intelligently. By using these examples, I have tried to expand your learning process or change your center point by demonstrating the knowledge of limitations and its relationship to patterning and the individual to a specific society.

The detailed examples from Ruth Benedict's "Patterns of Culture", is somewhat of an illusion, in that, the behavior of the people depicted, may or may not be what it really was in reality. Based upon our system of creditability or academic credentials, you will have to agree with the findings or results. The only thing that I can be sure of, is that it was an accurate account of what she thought she saw or heard. You must be the judge of these studies, because you make your own reality. You must make a selection to decide what you want to believe, for reality is a matter of belief and belief is another form of matter. When you make your decision, you create, change, or you retain your learning patterning. You have the option or ability to make it fact or a delusion. Is it an illusion or delusion? Maybe, Ms. Benedict was a bit overacting or performing a dramatization of a real life situation. Maybe, the lines of control are not clear enough for you to take sides, Maybe, there isn't a side or winner.

Most people are self programmed or patterned to think that they only have two choices or selections. You do have a third choice which I advised you of before we started this chapter, and again reminded you in the last paragraph. The earlier suggestion was to merely observe the examples for contrast and differences. However, these examples were also inserted to show you different forms of patterning and the dominance or dominant role that customs and traditions play in determining moral behavior. These subtle patterns are fixed in all of us at a very early age and are reinforced by social experiences or empirical knowledge. These patterns then become forms of limitation that may finally develop into that known, as a belief. This is the ultimate. You can't go any further. The end result is an unconscious response to an outside stimulus.

These studies or examples of behavior patterns were also a good study of relationships of how and why societies function and think along specific patterns. The behavior of these people is colored, edited, or arranged by the limiting factors of customs, traditions, and institutions which are set up by these groups of people to control participation in their societies. Environment and heredity play some part in determining behavior; however, the dominant limiting factor is the actual human institutions set up to control or organize the society into a singular homogeneous mass that is able to communicate in more than words and actions. It is a form of shared responsibility to one another working toward certain tangible goals or desired end results.

I would also like to bring out another observation from these studies, and that is, that a society is of relatively minor importance. That is, a society can be regulative in nature and law but not necessarily equivalent to social order. Habit or customs may supersede formal legal authority. Even in our civilization, the law is a crude implement of society. Above all, a society is not separate from the individuals who compose it. No civilization has an element that is not contributed by an individual. You do make a difference!

Anthropology is the study of human beings as creatures of society. Human behavior is the manner in which customs function in the lives of the individuals who compose these societies. Custom is behavior at its most common place. Custom is the predominant role that plays in experience, institutions, and in patterns of thinking. Even philosophy cannot go beyond or behind these imaginary walls or limitations, self imposed. Good, bad, right, wrong, true or false, still require or need to reference a particular tradition, culture or some form of precedence, in order to affect behavior. The life history of an individual is first and foremost, an accommodation or accumulation of patterns and standards of tradition handed down in a particular society or culture or cultures.

From the moment of birth, the environment into which one is born, shapes his experiences and patterns his behavior. This starts at such an early age that it is difficult to discern if one is actually born as a blank slate or is a product of heredity. By the time a person is able to talk, he is already a creature of his culture; therefore, it is almost impossible to determine which force is more dominant in patterning. However, custom patterns seems to be the controlling factor in all cultures. Because of the subtlety of this force, its laws, and its variety, and repeatability, it remains the most complicated factor in human life and therefore, it must be the most difficult force to understand in its relationship to patterning.

Patterning takes many forms on both a conscious and unconscious level. If you are keenly observant or conscious, you may have noticed that this chapter was put together a little different from all the preceding ones. It was organized in a different way to make its point more credible. All of these changes still support one central theme that contributes to the overall well being of a desired end result or book. While being different from other chapters, it is but another form of patterning. This chapter happens to require more detail and support than a lot of others, because it covers more ground or requires more communication to make it more understandable; consequently, there are more variations that are needed to support its one single concept. It is a book within a book. A pattern within a pattern.

In a sense, this chapter is similar to and supports the idea of pattern variations or cultures. The complicated nature of this subject matter somewhat determined its own pattern, because it needed a different type of mental relationship or environment to make it more acceptable or believable. Again, we are reaching out beyond our existing learning triangle and therefore, we need some support or landmarks by which we can find our way. The point I want to make from all of this confusion is that patterns exist in all areas of life and can change from environment to environment and that depends <u>SOLELY</u> upon the individual. You make your own reality! It's just a matter of conscious identification and belief that results from an understanding of relationships. You respond to a situation based primarily on patterning which is the controlling factor; consequently, you normally become a product of your environment, be it victim or not.

What better way to end a confusing chapter than to end with a confusing riddle of a poetic nature. There is an external pattern, but what about an internal pattern?

THOUGHTS BY THE SEA

Misty morning by a misty sea,
Misty memories by a misty me.

Thoughts of loneliness, thoughts of despair,
Thoughts of confusion hang in the air.

A touch of blue, a touch of green,
A touch of sadness settles serene.

The mood is mellow, the mood is mine,
The mood of the moment is the mood of my mind.

Colorless water and colorless light,
Colorless appearing, but just out of sight.

An emotion of mind, an emotion of feeling,
An emotion that's colorless is not too appealing.

Endless motion and endless thought,
Endless changes, endlessly sought.

Illusions are plenty, illusions abound,
Illusions misleading are all around.

There's clarity in water, there's clarity in light,
There's clarity in living that's beautiful and bright.

Constant motion, constantly misleading,
Constant clarity that's often revealing.

To look is to expect, to look is to see,
To look is a vision that looks from me.

Images of time are images of place,
Images of mind are images of space.

Truth of this world comes from truth from within,
Truth from my mind comes from truth from him.

The mystery to see is the mystery of reflection,
The mystery of truth is the mystery of selection.

CHAPTER 9

Good, Bad, Right, Wrong

A rather interesting, catchy title for a new chapter, wouldn't you say? I could have added to this; yes, no, true, and false, to this title; however, I think that would be overdoing it a bit and I also think that would be over dramatizing it too. Besides, these words are used more frequently in dealing and talking about morals than are the latter four.

Normally, I start out a chapter explaining a definition of some word; however, what can be so difficult here? Everybody knows, understands and recognizes all of these limiting words. Right? Guess what?...you're wrong! Not only is that startling, the sentence itself is contradictory. If I am making the statement that says, "you're wrong", then that assumes that everybody knows the meaning of the word, wrong. Right? Perhaps, we better start out with an explanation and start all over again.

Suppose I were to say that these words are not understood properly. Impossible you say? You're crazy!...you say? Maybe you're right. Here we go again. This time, we're not going to start over. This time, we are going to take a closer look at these words to see what all is involved here. Obviously, it's not a simple question or statement that can be passed off as insignificant, if it has caused this much confusion in a new chapter. Like the word, best, that began this book and started us off on our journey, these limiting words are much more difficult to understand than most of us think.

To begin this investigation, I will help you out by telling you that we are not dealing with a question of semantics or the meaning of words. The problem lies much deeper than most of you think. That is the reason why it has taken us so long to get here from there. Basically, this book deals with our reality and indirectly how it effects morality, and yet, little has even been said about the subject except for a few hints or and/or references. This beginning was planned and necessary to build a good foundation and understanding of just what we are talking about

We are building a bridge to understanding and it must be properly erected in order to support everyone who wishes to cross. There are a lot of people out there on their journey through life; however, some people go around in circles, others stray off the main roads or get sidetracked, and others never know where they are going. Our bridge is a short cut. But it is strange how few people can find or see the bridge and fewer yet, how many will actually cross the bridge once they find it. And all of this has to do with the learning process and patterning. One cannot properly talk about the subject of morality unless he understands the language of communication. This chapter is an attempt to try to help those who wish to cross this bridge and to find a better way to get them closer to where they are going. I could say something here about the word, better, but I won't. I'll just leave you guessing for a while.

To accomplish this task of understanding, let's start out by reaching an area of common ground upon which everyone can agree. I believe it is not improper for me to say that everybody born under the sun, and then some, knows the basic concept or meaning of the words; good, bad, right, wrong, yes, no, true and false. That is, they can at least associate these words with or to actions and objects. I mentioned the key to this understanding in the last chapter, but I will again repeat it, because it deserves repeating. "Good, Bad, Right, and Wrong, still require or need to reference a particular tradition, culture, or some form of precedence in order to affect behavior". Now, this sentence just explained the reason for all of the confusion in the beginning of this chapter. It just told you that you know the use of these limiting words, but only insofar, as they relate to your own particular environment. They cannot stand alone or have meaning outside your personal learning triangle. They simply do not exist. Or do they? Oh-oh! here we go again.

As I indicated in an earlier chapter, one can move his point of focus to a location outside the triangle; however, he still must be able to find his way back. Therefore, whenever he ventures out beyond his limitations, he carries certain references with him. A lot of time these references are associated with these limiting words, but more than likely, they are much more related to the words; true and false, than our other limiting words. That's because these words refer to inner qualities as well as outer qualities. Spiritual and physical, if you will. In any case, one must be able to relate to matters of mind and matter to understand and function. Therefore, limits apparently exist to some degree, and that amount is what we hope to discover.

In a more realistic way of looking at this same problem, let's look at it from another standpoint, or the world of physical reality. Let's again look at the process by which your knowledge is acquired. As I mentioned earlier, from day one and on, your parents began a subtle conditioning program both intentionally and unintentionally. That is, as you grew, you began to be consciously aware of your parent's actions, reactions and a form of non-recognition to you and your actions. Through a process of inter-reaction with your parents and your environment, you began your process of learning either your limitations or a process by which you limit yourself.

The normal belief or understanding is, that you learn your own limitations. This is a process or conditioning program that begins with learning how to get attention or be recognized. You might say that this too, is a form of acting or over dramatization. That is, one discovers in this society that one gets attention by actions that stimulate or affect one's environment. The bigger the action, the more one gets recognized; consequently, one often over dramatizes his being in order to be noticed. By means of reactions and responses, one supposedly learns the limits of one's being in relationship to others and his environment.

To put it yet another way, the learning process or conditioning program primarily takes the form of over reactions on the part of the parents, to actions and/or behavior by the child. Through a process of repetitive actions and verbal commands to words or sound, the child begins to recognize and associates certain patterns and responds to this relationship of sounds and actions. That is, the individual begins to understand that certain patterns are associated with certain actions and/or sounds or combination of both. This knowledge comes from the child, the parents, and any other human contact with which the child can interact. The key to this knowledge system is recognition! One learns the limitations of this physical reality through a process of interaction and a stimulus-response type mimicking or behavior patterns with intended beginnings and endings that lead in a sequential manner to a growth type pattern.

As the child grows and progresses, he begins to understand the system of rewards and punishment which is associated with recognition and non-recognition. He, in effect, learns how to really turn on his parents or knows how to get their attention. All of these forms of recognition and attention are also forms of control that relate to the individual in a form of power which is relative to one's environmental conditioning and vice-versa. To put it more simply, the individual learns to control his own behavior to comply with the wishes of his parents and to conform with that of his society, or his parent's culture. However, in making these changes or creating a self imposed pattern of behavior, he is really not consciously aware that he is doing so. To him, he is merely adapting to his environment in order to participate, communicate and to perpetuate his being.

This logical conclusion that we have just drawn about self imposed limitations or patterns, brings us back to an earlier statement which we discarded. Earlier, we said that one learns, "...either your limitations or a process by which you limit yourself". Now, we indicated that most people believe that you learn your own limitations; however, in trying to prove this statement, we just proved that one learns to limit one's self. Therefore, this brings up more interesting questions concerning all our physical and mental limitations. However, we will not pursue those questions at this time. Rather, we really want to find out more about this question of behavior in regards to our own being.

Probably, the first words a child learns after certain nouns for recognition of, mommy and daddy, are the words, yes and no. In fact, it is usually the negative words that are learned first. In this case, we are talking about the word, no. No, refers to a restriction or a complete or extreme limitation. However, it often carries the meaning or connotation of bad, and bad usually carries the idea of wrong in most situations. The words, yes and no, are supposedly opposites of each other, for they identify the two limiting extremes of the same act or condition. You might say that they identify contrast like the shades of black and white; however, they convey an understanding more like that of a common traffic signal, that uses the colors; red, green and amber. In this case, no would be red, non-recognition is amber, and green would be yes. This analogy is far from being accurate, but it does represent most people's beliefs.

Getting back to our negative words, you have no doubt heard the word, no, used a lot as a child. Or the expression, that's a no, no. In the latter case, the word is used twice as a double positive negative for emphasis, even though its grammar usage itself, is wrong. But, somehow, the child understands and either corrects his behavior pattern or gets negatively re-enforced to remind him to correct his behavior. This word no, is recognized and associated by the child as a limit. That is, he understands that if his behavior does not stop or change from its current directed actions and probable or eventual end result upon the hearing of these words or command, then that act or behavior is regarded as bad or wrong and is subject to punishment or a reinforcement of a negative nature to drive home the point through an unpleasant or painful stimulus. Sometimes, the word, bad, is used in place of no. But, in any case, the verbal command is still reinforced with a negative force, if the warning is not heeded.

The next group of words that are normally learned by a child are those of, good and bad. Again, the word, bad, is learned and used primarily in the early years of the child, along with the word, no. Good and bad vary from - yes and no, in that they usually refer to a quality of an object, or something has in relationships to its physical properties, or the effect something has in regards to one's being. Yes and no refer more to the actions of that being. Even though the words, good and bad, do not directly control one's behavioral actions, they do in fact, affect behavior patterns. This is perhaps why these words are used so interchangeably with yes and no, and are often used wrongly.

The normal definition of good involves something that is beneficial, adds something, or is a positive form of recognition. Whereas, bad denotes something detrimental, lacking in quality, or subtracts from something. Again, these words are opposites of one another. But unlike yes and no, these words are relative to the object and the individual; therefore, they admit to slight variations because people and objects are involved, or an element greater than one. Yes and no control the actions of one element, the individual. Consequently, you might say good and bad, represent slight tints of black and white, but not quite gray. Another way to remember the difference might be to compare yes and no, to action and reaction, and the words, good and bad, to stimulus and response. The first set of words control the use of energy and intangibles and the second, determine the amount of energy or resistance of tangible matter.

As I said before, the problem with good and bad, is that it is relative to the individual. This is something like our word, best. What is best (good) for you, may not be best (good) for me. That is, a person may be given a positive yes to perform an action of say, stealing; however, the act itself or effect would definitely be considered bad in most situations, because it takes away or subtracts from someone else without proper compensation. Therefore, good and bad, do not control the individual's actions per se but appeals to his sense of values which are relative to his needs and/or desires, which in turn, may or may not affect one's behavior.

Now, to make matters worse, the words good and bad are usually associated with the meanings of the words right and wrong. However, the words good and bad refer to tangible objects or relatively easy identifiable qualities and values; whereas, right and wrong, refer to qualities which are not so obvious and cannot be seen as easily by those involved. In this situation, you might say that the words good and bad have a very physical relationship or meaning; whereas, right and wrong, have a more emotional type basis or psychological or mental relationship.

The words right and wrong usually convey severe contrasts of thought and are not generally used to denote contrasts of black and white, but large areas or shades of gray. These are transitional words that attach a quality or value to an environment or situation. These are complex words that involve great understanding or relationships. It is, therefore, noteworthy that these words are the basis of all legal judicial systems which are set up to try to determine the degree of an act in relationship to responsibility and/or conduct in a specific situation. To be specific, the word right, pertains to a form of fairness, truth, justice or a correct responsive action; whereas, wrong denotes false or erroneous acts that inhibit, oppress and suppress, or distort one's behavior from its pattern of acceptable conduct.

The word wrong, is probably the last common negative word one learns to associate with as a child. Unlike the word no, which is clear cut and dry, and tolerates no exceptions, and the word bad, which admits to a slight varying degree or quality of the object or actions of the individual, the word wrong is subject to interpretation to specific circumstances, situations, and relationships dealing with human organizations. That is, the word is associated with moral conduct and responsibility in a group environment, rather than individual limitations; therefore, one is dealing with elements greater than one and elements of an intangible nature. Consequently, this is a selection or determination of an action, based upon a multi-leveled structural organization dealing with conflicting or overlapping rules and/or regulations.

The words right and wrong then, are words that set limitations on responsibility in relationship to one's specific environment and/or culture. It is an artificial set of guidelines that controls or directs one's behavior in a group environment. Therefore, these words do not necessarily carry with them or involve rewards or punishment directly inflicted upon one's physical person in the form of pain or pleasure, as with good and bad, but rather these words form a system of communicating recognition, non-recognition, alienation and isolation, all rolled up into one. These words define limits of growth within an organized environment and also denotes a relationship to responsibility and conduct that appeals to one's inner sense of the greater well being of all and the supposedly correct acceptable behavior patterns one learns as a participant in a group environment.

Because right and wrong are subject to the understanding of relationships, they are the most difficult to learn and use properly. One learns or begins to associate these words when one enters into communication with other children, adults, schools, institutions and other various groups, that express subtle differences in relationship to both words and actions. Acceptance into these groups depends upon one's ability to understand and adjust to slight changes on a continuous basis. One learns to adapt to one's environment for the purpose of survival and acceptance; therefore, one must know and understand these limiting words and other forms of communication designed to control behavior if one wishes to function freely in that society or properly participate and share in the benefits that group has to offer or reward for such participation. In any case, the individual learns that the words right and wrong vary to some degree from group to group, and depends upon that group's particular interests or desired end result more so than his original concept of right and wrong.

This problem of identification, which is knowledge, or the learning of right and wrong is basically the same problem we identified in describing,

"The Sociological Identification", and the problem of classification. You eventually end up with overlapping and conflicting interest groups and you get what you are looking for. That is, one can be both for something and against that same something, depending upon which group he is participating in at the time. But unlike the sociologist, the individual can and does control himself and can therefore adapt to this conflict of interest relatively easily. He controls his behavior in order to receive some form of benefits, recognition or to just grow socially. Man is a rather gregarious being that must associate with others of his own kind to grow in a positive creative manner, which in effect, is another form of responsibility to the greater well being of the individual and the group.

I have made several references about the use of negative words and commands in one's early childhood. Now, I want to take a little special effort to explain the positive form of these words, before we go on to the last set of limiting words. It is interesting to note that the positive forms of these words are used and heard less frequently by the child in his early years. The reason for this is not very well understood and may tend to lead one to believe that we are primarily a negatively dominated and motivated society. However, if one were to consider non-recognition as a form of positive permissive approval, then one would get an entirely different picture of how this society operates. Non-recognition does not stop or inhibit in a negative manner one's actions; therefore, it must be considered a positive form of behavior, just as freedom is thought to be one of the most sought after quality in one's life. So, even though the negative words are heard more often, the positive words and the neutral forms of non-recognition combine to balance out the negative influences in one's behavior. At least, they tend to channel or direct one's patterning in a specific direction so that there appears to be an equal balance of standard acceptable behavior within a particular culture.

Because of that last sentence, I want to remind you that we are talking about limiting words and how they relate to our society and culture. If I were from another sociological group, such as the Dobu, these negative and positive traits or values that limit or restrict their society would be nearly opposite those of our own beliefs. That is, yes or non-recognition would be that acceptable norm or behavior regarding stealing and revenge; whereas, no, would be the command or form of communication for kindness and the aiding of a fellow neighbor or stranger. Therefore, this question of balance is an interesting thing involving the understanding of relationships within one's immediate environment and/or reality.

I believe, it is still somewhat understandable in any society, why one encounters less positive statements or commands than the negative. I think it is also understandable why non-recognition is a form of positive permissive approval. It is simply because the individual is in a process of growth and he will select, choose and develop patterning in those specific directions which offer the least amount of resistance. The individual will grow and base his selections in those directions in which he can most easily control his own being and that of his immediate environment. However, without the proper balance and/or guidance, one tends to lose his proper perspective of life and he becomes self centered and seeks self interests above those of others. Naturally, this situation normally results in greed and detrimental behavior in relationship to others of his group and environment.

It is difficult if not impossible to imagine a completely unrestricted, unlimited person who has never been preconditioned to some set of rules, standards or customs. However, I would suspect that our own experience might identify such people as criminals or possible leeches to society. The reasoning for this is because neither group is suppose to be able to contribute to or support the greater well being of a particular group. It is therefore believed, that negative restrictions must be placed or imposed upon everyone in order to assure a cooperative working relationship. For without the threat of negative punishment, or without opposition from a strong negative force, one will <u>always</u> take and abuse the rights of others. I believe that this is perhaps the logic that is commonly accepted by most people, and it might be entirely correct; however, I also think that there has been no well documented study that would indicate that this is in fact correct. However, remember, you will get what you are looking for; therefore, it is more important to know what it is we want to find. There is a need for balance and there seems to be a need for both positive and negative stimulus. However, this may be a biased attitude on my part, because of my own preconditioned mental patterns. Again, one cannot get away from patterning and conditioning.

In opening up this segment on negatives, I described the word no as usually being associated with the word bad, and bad as being associated with the word wrong. However, on a closer examination of these words, this relationship did not necessarily hold true. But, this revelation does not mean that the majority of people will understand the significant difference in these words nor will they use them correctly. It is difficult to change existing patterns and even more difficult to get everyone to agree to certain changes in verbal communication, especially since the trend is away from true or exact meanings of words in favor of slang and jargon of sub divisional groups. The latter manner of speaking again is a means of communication, identification, and separation within the larger culture. Consequently, it is becoming more difficult to understand verbal communication even though it is probably more important now than ever before. This thought leads us to our last set of words which have a potential and possible tendency to bridge the gap.

I classify the last set of words as limiting; however, there is some question in mind if they really are. The way these words are used in our culture is of a limiting and controlling nature; therefore, that is why I have included them in this chapter. The words I am referring to are those of true and false. I just used one of these words in the last paragraph to describe a condition of word usage and it was intentional. You see, these words describe an exact or accurate condition. These words, are like our words good and bad in that they pertain to objects or conditions rather than actions. But unlike the former words, true and false pertains to that which is. It is a quality that exists in spite of all else. It is neither good nor bad, it just is.

True and false also have an interesting relationship to yes and no. As you can see, these words also admit to no exceptions. They just are. But, while these words are exact, their average usage is not. That is, people use these words true and false incorrectly. When these words are used, one can only interpret them as either having a positive or negative meaning to whatever was just said. I am particularly upset that one of the major offenders of these words are a lot of school teachers who are suppose to be responsible for their proper usage. I am mainly referring to tests given in school, known as true and false question tests.

No doubt, you yourself have taken one or many of these type tests. I am not so interested in the questions themselves, but the usage of the words true and false in this situation. Normally, or in most situations, these questions refer to events or conditions and statements based upon human interpretations which are relative to an observer. Therefore, these questions are not so much a statement regarding an exact condition of what is or was, but an interpretation of what is thought to have happened. It is a relationship of the observer and the event only and not the exact nature of a thing. Consequently, such test questions really never tell you anything about the true nature of that event, but only an interpretation of actions, which are really considered right and wrong because they are based upon artificial standards of human origin. Even though a specific end result is or was achieved by a certain person or by a physical condition, it is still a human recorded event, if you will, and subject to an element of more than one or matters that involve specific circumstances, situations, and relationships, dealing with human organizations. In short, these are really questions involving right and wrong based upon the element of someone's interpretation, the subject of control of whoever dominated that recorded event, not true and false.

I will admit that perhaps my own understanding of these words is a little bit different from that of others and/or even the dictionary; however, I believe my point is correct and important. I am not arguing so much the definition of these words as I am the source from which one derives true and false, but definition is also affected because of this source or point of source. What I am saying is that these words, true and false, are not subject to interpretation; rather, their meaning comes from within an individual or the source object itself. It cannot be gotten from a secondary source. This is a special kind of communication which I will discuss in depth later, but for now, let's stay with current beliefs.

The dictionary defines true as: accurate, exact, certain, without varying, constant, reliable and trust. However, it also defines or uses these words to describe true: right, correct, real, in accordance to fact, agreement to reality, conforming to an original pattern, rule or standard. The latter definition is slightly different from the former in the fact that they require an interpretation or relationship involving a pre-existing pattern based upon human participation and/or conditioning. Another way to look at this difference is that the first definition uses words that are unlimited or virtually unrestricted; whereas, the latter definition usage is limited by human beliefs and patterning.

I am not about to argue with scholars, educators and the majority of people who have come to use this set of words to add emphasis to their particular communication they wish to convey. However, I do want them to be aware of the fact that there is a significant difference, and that difference cannot be communicated as truth to anyone else, because that information would then be coming from a secondary source and not its true origin. I don't believe many people will understand this point nor will they alter the way in which they use these words. Again, a rather firm pattern or routine has been established and it will not be changed or be altered radically unless there is a definite need and/or benefit to do so. There is no major benefit or incentive to make this change. A new pattern is not warranted just yet.

In describing the words good, bad, right, wrong, yes, no, true and false, you may have noticed and I have mentioned several times, that these words are grouped in pairs. I hope you will think it is an interesting observation as much as I think it is, because this carries with it even more interesting connotations.

All of these words are supposedly opposites of one another because they indicate two extremes of the same situation or condition. These words are used like black and white to indicate contrast and content; however, gray is also involved. I would like to think of these opposites in relationship to my explanation of growth. To refresh your memory, I said that growth can be compared to that of a line that has a beginning and an end. Again, you might remember our opening chapter that concludes that endings are really the same things as beginnings. Both are artificial limits that are set up to indicate extreme conditions or milestones one must reach before he progresses to the next level of experiences. Before one can begin this other level of activity, he must complete or finish a specific desired end result, which also serves as the basis for a new beginning. This is similar to grade levels in our educational system.

In describing opposites, we are talking about limitations of a singular subject. Therefore, in talking about contrasts of black and white, maybe we are really talking about gray and the absence or addition of black or white. The latter explanation would then fit our line of growth model. That is, growth consists of a process of learning or expanding in a particular time frame, which is also linear, within this environment known as physical matter or reality, which is also known as a plane of existence. The latter limiting element can also be considered linear, because it is singular in nature, or must be encountered or experienced in a progressive, chronological or sequential pattern to be properly understood, assimilated and possessed to be of any value to the physical being. This is nothing more than a series of short beginnings and endings. In any case, we are dealing with singular elements of a line nature, or elements possessing extremes and/or an average, normal, physical, condition, whether or not it appears that way.

Speaking about lines, it is also interesting to note that in geometry, a line is explained as a segment which if transverse to infinity, will eventually return to its point of origin, opposite from which it went. Again, we are dealing with an interesting concept. Such an explanation would then indicate that we are really not dealing with a line, but with a huge circle. The reason for this is because the only geometric shape that can be made with one line is a circle. The significance of this observation means that words which limit extremes of the same concept might or must involve things of a circular form or pattern. This circular shape may or may not be important to you right now; however, you might appreciate and understand this importance in its relationship to our explanation of self control and the positioning process of focusing one's self within the learning triangle or pyramid.

Just to remind you, we said in that chapter, that the positioning process was a selection process that one could control by the understanding of the relationship between one's self, knowledge, and possessions. We also indicated that the learning process involved the force of energy and the resistance of matter. That is, one can only change one's position by overcoming force with resistance or resistance could be overcome with sufficient force and this use of energy was limited by the individual to obtain a desired end result. Therefore, movement in a particular direction within the learning triangle was controlled by the amount of energy one had or has to use, in order to overcome resistance.

Now, with our knowledge of opposites and their probable form or pattern, we may be better able to identify our ability to control our position in relationship to our self imposed limitations. That is, our beliefs in right-wrong, good-bad, and to a lesser degree, yes-no and true-false (as it is customarily used - not the meaning that I have attached to it), may be the forms or patterns of resistance which I referred to earlier. The limits of our learning triangle and/or the positioning process may be influenced or affected by these lines, circles or orbits of limitation imposed by these words and/or our understanding of these opposites and/or extremes. Just like a baseball or golf ball, these words act like restrictive bindings that affect the overall performance and/or behavior of that item or individual. However, because words are of an intangible nature, they are probably less restrictive in controlling one's ability to adjust to different environments.

Perhaps the best way to observe this comparison is to look at our own reality for a guide or model that we can relate to. Surprise! We have two examples that make it doubly interesting. Strangely, or not so strangely enough, these two examples also represent extremes. In this case, these examples are related to each other through the dimension of size. These examples compare inner and the opposite, outer space. I am referring here to our model as that of a solar system with planets and a sun, or that of an atom with electrons circling about. Interesting, isn't it, that our model should also take on characteristics of extremes? Or is it? Another question that has significance, but one which we will not pursue at this time.

The point which I wish to make here, is that as one positions oneself within the learning triangle, one is also surrounded by intangible lines of forces that from now on, I will call inbalances*. These inbalances, in turn, affect or control one's behavior and one's perspective of one's own limitations. As the individual uses energy for the purpose of changing his focus point or position, he also affects the orbits of his limitations and vice-versa. That is, the orbits have an energy force of their own and tend to relate to the individual, therefore, these so called orbits of limitation tend to stabilize one's position, or make it difficult for one to change unless there is sufficient desire or need to make this change. Otherwise, the individual will remain complacent and as predictable as a computer program. But, should a change occur in position, so must a change in orbits occur. The effect of these changes may be temporary or permanent, depending on the

* INBALANCE - Author's coined word for an unbalanced but stable condition in a state or position of separation (see next chapter)

individual's needs, wants and desires of a positive or negative nature.

I feel an urge and need to clarify myself again. In the process of growth, one is constantly running into this positioning process and balancing of extremes and/or opposites of the same thing. One's selection creates forces, like waves which in turn affect others or other things in one's environment. These changes affect and relate in many ways to the individual depending upon the position he takes in regards to known limitations in his environment. The results of his actions reflect his new position. That is, his change from his original actions reflect his new position. This change from his original position may cause him to counter balance the effect of certain limitations and this might result in patterns or limitations that have very elliptical orbits causing certain extremes to dominate one's actions and the opposite extreme to have little or no affect on his behavior pattern depending upon where the force or energy was applied.

A change in position may also cause a sudden shift of another orbit to become closer to him, warming up the issues so to speak, and shedding more light on that particular set of extremes. This change may also put an issue in a more temperate zone with limitations much more hospitable and favorable to growth. In any case, this idea of uniformity and shape to intangible thoughts and/or concepts of opposite is known, but it is interesting to note this connection or concept of orbits, circles, and lines in relation to patterning. It appears that the similarities are there and the effects one can observe in one area of knowledge, may be the same for other items of an intangible nature. One's perspective of reality definitely affects the quality of one's life and the values one believes in and vice-versa. The position one takes in regards to the orbital planes, determines how one views these limiting extremes of a verbal nature. Consequently, the action or item really doesn't determine a matter to be good, bad, right, wrong, yes, no, true, false but it is a definite quality in respect to one's position that is the dominant factor that controls one's behavior.

What I have tried to show you up to this point is that there is a lot of confusion over some relatively simple everyday words that control our lives and/or limitations. Hence, this rather lengthy explanation and the reason for my intentionally confusing beginning to this chapter. To explain these simple limiting words is nearly impossible, but at the same time it is also necessary that they be defined. It is a must! We could not function as a society or group of people if we didn't understand these words. But to properly understand them, one must or should know how these words are used. Knowing words only defines, identifies, and separates them. To understand them, one must know how they relate to the individual and his form or pattern of communication. Therefore, my opening statement that good, bad, right, wrong, yes, no, and true, false, are not properly understood is correct.

For those of you who were disappointed in my lack of explaining or taking a specific position in regards to morality, have heart. There is more to come later. Even though we talked about words that affect morality, I did not fulfill my promise to really get into an in-depth discussion on this specific matter. However, before we can do this, we still must identify who we are, or more proper, "Who am I". Not until we have cleared up this matter, can we properly discuss other human relationships.

In this chapter, we have laid the ground work for how one operates or affects his own behavior by his own understanding of words and the position he takes in controlling and limiting their useage and vice-versa. We have also learned something about opposites and their possible relationship to unity and balance or forces I call inbalances, but this is about as far as I can go in describing "Who am I", without straying from conventional thought processes. Therefore, this will conclude the first part of this book, because this is all we can discover about the individual within the limitations of physical reality.

Even though the next section II of this book deals with the subject of "Physical Reality", it is really a series of transitional chapters dealing with a subject that everybody knows about and can relate to, called "Spiritual Reality". As mentioned, the next chapter is really a continuation on the same theme of opposites, which together form unites or unity. Now you know that is a ridiculous theory and can't have any justification for anybody in their right mind. Or is it left mind? What better way to finish a chapter than the way we began than in utter confusion and chaos. But doesn't that also mean a new pattern that man cannot yet identify?

SECTION II

WHERE AM I?

Spiritual Reality

CHAPTER 10

Physical Reality

I am sure that there are still a lot of people out there who may still have a few questions regarding my planes of unity theory and its effect on the element of control. However interesting my analogy of opposites to orbits is, I am also sure that no one, or few, will really ever give this concept any serious thought. You see, theory is one thing, practical reality is another. Besides, how can intangible concepts be proven, and better yet, how can one use this knowledge to any benefit? About the only thing that makes any sense in the last chapter is the thought or idea that there is no such thing as right and wrong, good and bad, etc., and everybody knows that situation isn't so or possible. Interesting...yes! Practical...no!

So what have we gotten out of this book so far? Maybe at this point, we better take a look and see just how far we have come on our journey to understanding just who we are? To be honest with you, it has taken me a little longer than I thought, to get from here to there. Or is it there to here? Or does it really make any difference? Again, we are involved in a controversy of opposites. Hopefully, we will eventually solve this problem once and for all, but not now.

Most of this book has been spent explaining how poorly we, as individuals, interact, and communicate with ourselves and others. We have also learned that man limits himself mentally and possibly, physically. We have also learned that man is not so much a free thinker as most of us have come to believe, but we are rather a collection of patterns and routines which controls behavior both on a conscious and subconscious level and in unmanifested non-linear reality. The result of these limitations has a tendency to restrict or channel man's behavior by imposing preset standards of acceptable conduct known as customs and traditions which is nothing more than a collection of short patterns with beginnings and endings that lead to growth in a linear sequential manner.

Now, one's conscious thought process and the unconscious desire for conformity leads one to think in terms of pre-destination or the idea that history repeats itself. If this is the case, then there may be some bad times ahead as most philosophers of doom and gloom seem to believe. However, the purpose of this book is to actually give you the answer to predestination and answer any other question you might have regarding life. It will also give you the way in which you can affect your own reality and possibly that of history itself.

On another more positive note, we have gotten to read and review the dictionary and we may have also learned or discovered something new about how certain words relate in a more technical way to the world of science and mathematics. That is, we have learned how the actual learning process has form and shape, and that the elements that compose this shape relate to one another through an inner content. We have also found out that we can control this relationship by understanding and positioning ourselves within this inner content and by the use of energy and resistance. The key to this control factor is the knowledge of positioning and the ability of the self to make one's own selections that make one's own reality. It is the conscious knowledge of one's self in relationship to understanding one's environment that determines the quality of one's life even though it originates on a subconscious level in non-linear reality.

Again, all of this information may be interesting, but it still doesn't tell us who we really are. It only explains in a new way, how we function in a group environment and behave the way we do. It really doesn't do a good job at that explanation either, because it doesn't tell us why we do, what we do, and for what reasons. In the last chapter, I explained what it is that maintains our positioning and controls our limitations. This explanation of extremes and opposites, gave way to circles of unity or oneness. More than likely, and hopefully, this explanation of balance has given you a little better understanding of why we do what we do, but again, it does not explain the question "Who am I". Perhaps, who we are, is really not that important as is how and why we behave the way we do. But, if we do not learn who we are, there may still be the possibility that we are missing something important in determining our behavior and in properly relating to a group environment, society, or culture. Maybe we are locked into a life of predestination of our own choosing through the learning process and patterning itself.

For all intent and purposes, our explanation of behavior does explain all conditions of both a tangible and intangible nature; however, it is also so abstract and that is difficult for the average person to relate too. Therefore, I will again try to explain this problem of behavior in a different way and in perhaps more easily recognized terms and conditions. The selection or positioning process explains our relationship to customs and traditions, but it doesn't explain why we prefer certain limitations over those of another and/or for what reason. Well, that's not exactly true. It does and it doesn't. I think the best way to explain this situation is through the use of an example.

Basically, we have talked about mental processes and the choosing or selecting of a position within a specific plane of unity; thereby, setting up a specific relationship which one has chosen to experience consciously. That is, one decides prior to an event of a tangible nature, where he wants to view or experience this exercise of energy. This is a cold or sterile way of saying that you make your own reality. An example of this might be a selection, on your part, to participate in a sporting event. This is a group activity that is not unlike one's involvement in a culture or society. The way in which you are going to experience this event depends upon your prior selections. That is, you may have selected to experience this event as a participating player, in which case your prior selections had to do with physical aptitude or skill. Or, perhaps you are a manager or instructor to the participants, in which case you are probably older than the players and you yourself have played the game with some success. Or you may be a financial backer or a paid employee of the stadium, in which case you have selected, or are skilled in providing specialized talents in money management and/or in providing services to the crowd in a way of security, food, drink, health services, or maintenance needs. All of these examples usually require selections of some advanced nature in the way of a conscious commitment to a specific pattern or routine that supports one's lifestyle or supports one through his life experience(s). In a sense, it is a positioning process or life responsibility one has chosen to experience.

On the other hand, one may choose not to make a commitment of such an advanced nature, in which case, one is more likely to be only a spectator. In this latter case, the individual chooses to use his time and money to relax from direct involvement in the sporting event and the use of his energies to that of mental conscious support for an exhibition of talent which is of interest. One's involvement as a spectator may also take one of several forms of support. This can take the use of energy and direct involvement or participation in an indirect way, or it may be that of a passive nature. The latter situation can also take several forms, the most noticeable being his position or seating within the stadium. This shows to some extent, his interest in the event. Another selection might be to listen to the event on radio or to watch the event on TV. In this case, other priorities made direct participation of an indirect nature unfavorable and/ or secondary to other matters.

As you can see, selections and participation in an experience can take many forms and becomes quite complicated and involved in itself. These examples and explanations still don't even touch the whole of the problem of positioning; however, it does represent a concept of selection and position of a more conscious tangible nature. You are directly or indirectly involved and/or participating in that event by just being conscious of that happening. It is only a matter of position and selection that separates you from the degree of involvement or participation in the event. Put another way, one's selection limits one's position, which in turn, limits one's experience. Again, man limits himself rather than he is limited by his environment. Interesting....yes! Practical....maybe? You will have to wait a little longer to see.

The preceding chapters only explained in an intangible way, how man learns to limit himself. It also explains how society and sociological pressures of customs and traditions affect man's behavior and/or restricts him or limits his growth. Man's environment basically sets limitations of a regulatory nature by setting precedent behavior modes or patterns that act as guidelines as to what is tolerated and accepted in a group environment. This might sound as if we are now saying that an environment is just as important as the mental positioning process. This may be true in the way most people view and experience the environmental conditioning processes; however, this need not be so. All mental activities precede physical action;

therefore, if one can learn to understand and be consciously aware of the positioning process, then one can control his own destiny and fate. You make your own reality! You need not be subject to limitations and/or the pressures of certain pattern relationships which you have selected, unless you wish to be a victim or experience an environment not of your own choosing.

Don't get me wrong, environmental conditioning is a strong and powerful force. However, one can change an environment easier than one can change a mental position. That's because the environment is a tangible form of physical matter that is easily identified to the physical senses and is therefore easy to relate to. One is consciously aware of a change in one's physical environment, but he is not necessarily aware of a change on a subconscious mental level. Once a person has consciously selected an environment, either to work, live, or play in, he has committed himself to an involvement and participation in the use of energy and the forces of that particular environment. He is directly involved in an event or situation of his own choosing. He has consciously chosen to participate in and shared some of himself, his being and energies, with that of a particular environment be it good, bad, or indifferent.

This involvement doesn't necessarily mean that this experience will be of a pleasant or beneficial nature; however, one's understanding of an environment and one's selecting and choosing of this particular time and place, usually assures one of some reasonable amount of control. Therefore, one's experience can usually be thought of as beneficial in a positive or negative manner. Even though the definition of benefit indicates or states: to do good to, or for, to receive advantages or profit, it also is anything of a contributing nature. Therefore, the individual can gain from an unpleasant as well as a pleasant experience even though it may be somewhat painful. This is a little contradictory to most people's way of thinking and the usual understanding of the word benefit; however, it fits into our concept or circles of unity. That is, there is nothing really good and bad in itself but is dependent upon a relationship of the individual to that environmental condition.

If we carry this thought a little further, the individual who is not consciously aware of his selections and his environment, then might be thought of as a victim of that environment; because the events and forces of that environment will have a tendency to condition and program him into relationships of compatible routines serving to perpetuate patterns of probabilities or predestination over which he has little control. This is a polite way of saying, if you don't know what you are doing, or why you are doing it, then you are not serving yourself or anyone else any good. To subject yourself to the will or forces of others for monetary compensation or some supposed beneficial gain without just or proper creative endeavors that contribute to the greater well being of all, is a very negative and detrimental to that greater well being of all as well as yourself.

Man has free will, but he is also a walking series of patterns; therefore, he is very easily influenced. The reason for his being gullible is because man is not conscious of his own powers and his abilities to determine his own future. He really doesn't understand the world of physical reality and his relationship to planes of unity. Man has the ability to fill in the open spaces and add color where needed; however, he must know what he is doing, and why he is doing it. If he is ever to gain control of his self, his position, his environment, or his point of focus in this physical reality. If you haven't noticed, we are again talking about a situation of balance.

The balance of one's mental selection activities within physical reality brings up the question of tangible and intangible forces of energy. One affects the other, and vice-versa. Selection provides the individual with an environment of his own choosing but that selection process does not necessarily add to or subtract from the individual. That is, there is nothing necessarily good or bad about a particular environment until one decides to interact with it. An environment just is, or exists. One's interaction in that particular environment makes one's experience either of a positive or negative nature, depending upon how one reacts to or with other forms of conscious energy forces within that environment and/or the prevailing acceptable standards of that particular dominant control group or society. Perhaps the only new element that we added in this long dissertation is that of one's level of consciousness.

By physical movement, one is able to position himself in a certain relationship to other forms and forces of conscious energy. Therefore, one affects his level of consciousness and/or involvement with movement or positioning of a tangible nature. This movement changes one's perspective of these energy forces and also serves as a stimulus to one's own powers and his use of energies in a responsive manner, if he so chooses. Because of the effects that positioning plays in affecting or determining one's behavior, one is often accused of, or thought to possess certain qualities of a particular environment. That is, if one should frequent or associate with an environment or certain people with known or predictable behavior patterns, one himself is often typed or classified by others as being like that environment or those people with whom that person associates.

The closer one gets to or associates himself to a particular known pattern, the more likely that person will be influenced by those dominate forces from that particular environment or people. In more simple terms, we are talking about the slang terminology, in a negative sense, known as, "guilt by association". In this latter situation, one does not even have to do anything, to be accused of wrong doing or to be implicated as possessing certain undesirable qualities, even though it may or may not be true. It is true, as far as others are concerned, because people see and are aware of behavior patterns and/or the effects of an environment.

Any form of action or behavior is neither good nor bad in itself in relationship to the individual unless other qualities or standards are imposed. This or these value systems are the indirect interactive relationship which make or determines the act or behavior as being either good or bad. Without these other artificial limits, the idea or concept of planes of unity would be quite clear and acceptable to everyone. This same idea also applies to all people or any environment. To the individual, there is no such thing as good or bad, until he imposes other artificial limitations, or someone else makes that determination for him. In the latter case, the individual has relinquished his rights of self determination to someone else and therefore becomes a victim of his environment. But again, the determination is a matter of position. That is, the individual becomes more concerned or aware of the group acceptance and/or environment than he is of his self or what he himself wants to experience. He tends to go with the flow and adapts to the acceptable patterns and predominate factors within his society or culture for speed, convenience, and other supposedly beneficial factors of group behavior.

So you see, reality or morality is not, or need not be, what it appears to be. These manifestations can and should be thought of as circles of unity or oneness that need only be identified. There is no such thing as the words good and bad indicate, until the action or behavior of the individual is compared to someone or something else which has the ability to enforce an artificial limiting standard of conduct. It is just like the word best; it cannot be identified until one first determines or selects a course of action or desired end result

One's reality is of one's own choosing. One selects that which he wants to experience; however, that selection and choosing is more often than not, of an unconscious or subconscious nature which contributes to one's learning process, and that in turn, sets up limitations and establishes patterns that control one's behavior. Therefore, one's state of being is primarily a result of patterning and the limitations that the individual has placed upon himself. Again, man limits himself, rather than he is limited.

Man has trained and has patterned himself to see and seek separations and divisions. His world consists of differences that appear because of one's position and the need of the individual to control his environment. That is, by separation, one is able to identify certain inbalances which man finds useful. On the surface, these inbalances may seem trivial and ridiculous to the casual observer. However, I think they deserve a lot greater attention if you are ever to understand the theory of unity. To do that, I think it is necessary that we go into a rather deep explanation of physical reality.

The word, physical reality pertains to a quality relating to the conscious senses. A proper definition describes it as that which is real, fact, actual, true, etc. However, it is also interesting that one definition describes it as the image made in relation to the meeting of light rays at a certain point or points. Now, as far as I am concerned, these definitions tell us very little about physical reality, but the latter definition does reference the words position (point) and the word "relation", both of which are very important. The dictionary relies on one's ability to recognize or interpret what one means by real, fact, actual or true. I myself like the reference to the senses, because it sets up a relationship of understanding of a multiple of things, but mostly it describes the individual (the recognizer) as having the ability to recognize and offer recognition to all there is or everything.

Man's world is composed of physical matter, which in itself, has separated itself, created or manifested itself from everything and nothing. That is, matter is a form of energy, composed of particles or atoms. To come from everything or nothing implies opposites or a positive and negative form and/or force. This means, that the positive form of matter must also imply a negative form of matter or anti-matter, however, we are dealing with the intangible again and therefore, it is difficult to relate to something that is not of like properties. Consequently, we cannot be assured of another form of energy, even though it is probable and relative. To make this point clear, I have to revert to that of another example to explain the words everything and nothing.

Let's say that the universe is comparable to a block of wood, stone, or metal. In a sense, this solid mass would or could contain every possible configuration of patterns and/or design, or it could contain nothing but the density of block itself. The shape of the final product really depends on the dominate force(s) that work or shape this block. Its final appearance might resemble something that we know to exist or something abstract. Its shape depends upon what is desired by the dominate person or people involved in its creation and/or their skill in working the materials and tools they have. The most important step to achieving the desired end result is the selection of what the end result should be; therefore, we are back to square one, or our block of unity which is everything and nothing.

The molding and shaping of the block of wood, stone or metal is easy for an individual to identify with; however, it is more important for him to know what it is that he wants to achieve. Once the individual begins to expend energies to achieve his desired result, he is pretty well locked into a course of action or predestination. It is extremely difficult to patch or correct a mistake once it is made, and it is almost impossible for it to look the same prior to a mistake, unless the whole thing is painted or covered over with something. It is difficult to correct an endless or limitless block of material even if one were to try to go back and make some type of correction.

It may seem and sound a little strange, but man really identifies better with the patterning and a form of organization than he does with the final end result. The reason for this is because he must then seek another new beginning and/or end result. Man is comfortable performing repetitive tasks. It gives him a sense of order or form that is fairly constant and self assuring to his own well being and value or worth of himself as a human being. He is contributing in a certain predictable manner and producing results with certain predictable qualities. What more can anyone ask for? Isn't this the ideal person?

Anyway, the point I wanted to make is that man sees and seeks separations in order to use inbalances to accomplish certain results. He cannot use this knowledge until he understands the relationship of one inbalance to those of others. Another quick example of this thought is the quality of wood to burn and its ability to be used in construction. In the first case, the wood is used in its original state without limitations. In certain other relations, this same wood can be used in some primitive or basic constructions such as our chair example earlier. It is not until wood is prepared or worked into certain sizes and shapes that it can be used most effectively. In a sense what man has done is to use his knowledge of inbalances to use a harder material such as iron or steel to cut the raw wood and/or to produce limitations on the wood. The end product is then used to erect a structural form that offers qualities of shelter and/or protection against the natural elements of the earth or physical reality to reclaim or change the energy and atoms into something else. As a shelter, the wood helps to retard or slow down the effect of the natural elements to break down everything which are subject to the forces of temperature expansion and contraction as well as the water moisture forces.

Once man has learned the basic knowledge of inbalances, he has the ability to control these certain forces for his benefit. This selection process, constitutes the learning triangle. That is, the knowledge of inbalances and the understanding of their relationship to other inbalances, results in the ability of man to control or possess. The aspect of control then becomes a possession as well as a material reality if he so desires to utilize his ability to manifest his energies for a material object or end result. The amount of knowledge one possesses is relatively useless until man understands the relationship of the inbalances and his ability to bring some form of order or patterning to the relationships. Again, possessions have no value until they can be used to change something or benefit someone. To possess totally is a form of greed and a selfish form of control that does not benefit anyone or anything.

In our description of everything and nothing, we talked about form or patterning as an end result; therefore, it should be noted here, if you haven't already understood it there, that patterning or form can support tremendous forces and energy. The key to controlling these forces is to identify these patterns and their relationship to physical matter. So as not to confuse you too much, let me remind you that the following description of patterning involves only physical matter or the theory of separation, which is also our term for everything.

Man takes for granted many, many, common inbalances as fact or that which is almost natural. Probably one of the most useful and common place inbalances is the ability of wood to burn and to be used as a heat source and catalyst in speeding up the action or reaction of other substances to change their form or pattern. Here, we are talking about areas of inbalances again. First, the natural condition or wood does not or cannot support a condition called burning, until an inbalance can be achieved whereby the molecular structure of the atoms in the wood are excited or energized enough to support a continuous and spontaneous chain reaction which results in a physical change of matter in the release of heat. The heat in turn is easily transferrable and can energize other substances and speed up molecular changes and/or motion to other substances to cause them to act or react in some new form or pattern.

Another common application of wood is in the construction of various structures. In this situation, wood which is precut or limited, is arranged in an unnatural way, in a form, shape, pattern, structure or whatever, to be utilized to produce results that are usually far beyond the natural abilities or characteristics of wood. Here, I am talking about the ability of wood used to make bridges, dams or barriers that can support or hold back forces much greater than unlimited or natural wood. I am also talking about the ability of wood to be arranged for the purpose of transmitting mechanical energy such as the early water wheel and other machinery found at the beginning of the industrial revolution. These are all conditions of inbalances, but how often does anyone really ever even think of these situations or conditions as such.

By using positive and negative forces, or inbalances, found in this physical reality, one is able to affect great changes in matter and/or one's environment. That's because physical matter varies in mass, density and other physical characteristics. Each element or substance has certain attributes, characteristics, behavior, or call it what you may, but by all accounts, call it patterning. Everything is composed of energy or atoms;

therefore, all matter possesses some form of unity or oneness to it. However, this idea of commonality or unity is really found in the theory of separation. That is, instead of a two part separation, such as good and bad or black and white, this situation involves multiple points or positions found more commonly on a sphere or similar in nature to a solar system, or the structural shape of an atom. Simply put, matter exhibits separate qualities, even though it is composed of a singular unifying element. It is only a condition or position of balance caused by patterning that creates this separation. It is the structure or pattern of the inbalances that exert forces that stabilize the inbalances. That means that the inbalance is stabilized internally and must require an outside stimulus to de-stabilize it.

Man identifies with separation, because man is limited, and that limiting quality implies patterns. These patterns, in turn, imply inbalances or a form of unity in an unbalanced, but stabilized, state or position. The problem of identifying this unity is due, in part, to the inability of man to see or understand its opposite, un-manifested state of being, which I prefer to use the word nothing in this context. Again, the reason for this problem lies in the fact that man identifies with matter or like things; therefore, man, who is unbalanced himself, cannot relate to unity the same way he can, separation. That's because everything which man knows and is familiar with, is in a state of separation and therefore unbalanced and limited. If everything were properly balanced, there would be absolutely no movement what-so-ever. To be balanced, in physical reality requires its opposite, which is nothing and unlimited. Naturally, this latter state of being is unnatural and therefore cannot be considered probable or relevant to man, even though it may exist. The problem of this logic cannot be found within the boundaries of limitations; therefore, the quest or question remains unanswered up to this point or position.

In our description of our universal block of wood, stone or metal, that had been shaped, or is an on-going process, the material removed was or is tangible. That means that because the matter removed was tangible, so must it be replaced with something tangible and that means it may be an air, a vacuum, or a liquid. That also means that the replacement substance must also occupy and be the complete reverse opposite of that which now exists or a lighter less dense form of tangible matter. From our point of focus or position, we can observe a singular pattern, even though and in fact, other patterns of separation exist in a balanced or limited position of an un-manifested state or position which is intangible. This describes our world of everything and nothing.

In an un-manifested state of being or nothing, the opposite of physical tangible matter is hard to describe. The main reason for this difficulty lies in the fact that this other world(s) or opposite(s) is unlimited and non-linear in origin; therefore, the patterns of tangible matter do not even have to be duplicated in its un-manifested self. That means that there does not have to be any restrictions as to size, shape, form, or time. That also means that positive and negative may not apply to the world of un-manifested matter. However, in comparing how the mind works in dealing with thoughts and ideas of an opposite nature, there is a good indication that there must be some reasonable likeness in their patterns and their relationship to identifiable objects, if only in the mind of the beholder, or man. Remember, the individual (the recognizer) has the ability to recognize and offer recognition to everything and probably nothing.

I hope you don't get too confused in my explanation of inbalances and opposites. The problem of this explanation lies in the fact that we are basically talking about two different sets of opposites that are still united. Those opposites that appear in physical reality are primarily of an intangible nature, but control one's behavior. Then there are opposites that exist in a state of separation and affect behavior on a subconscious level in unmanifested non-linear reality. The difference between these examples is in one's conscious position. One can accept the first example, because one knows the physical limitations or properties of matter or the block of wood and he himself is part of this reality and can sense its forms and patterns.

Physical reality is also contradictory to that of the world of un-manifested matter. That is, our reality tells us that two things cannot occupy the same space at the same time. It also tells us that, should positive and negative forces try to occupy the same space, there is often a violent reaction that results in the release of energy and/or destruction of some kind. On the other side, there is literally nothing. One cannot identify with something he cannot consciously sense. Therefore, man does not lend much credence or recognition to the theory of unity and an un-manifested state of being as much as he supports the theory of separation.

In describing the world of physical reality, I hope each individual can gain a little better understanding of the workings of how man relates to the world about him. The mental processes of choosing and the selection of a position has to do with inbalances and separation. Even though I am going to go into more detail on the patterning of the mental processes, this explanation should help you to understand my theory of unity better. It is my contention, that unity is very important in understanding life in this physical reality. Unless or until this concept is understood, people will continue to embark on a course of separation that will take them further and further away from a true reality of life and its purpose. Unity is the primary cohesive bond between man and "All There Is". Without this knowledge and understanding of this relationship, man, or many people, will never really know or understand life. Such people are captives of their own self imposed limitations. They are the dead, walking amongst the living. They are victims of their environment and subject to the fate of predestination.

To reflect on that last statement a little more, Alvin Toffler wrote two books, one called "Future Shock" and the other "The Third Wave", in which he describes this future of predestination of not less, but more separation. In fact, he has coined his own word to describe one of these new patterns. He calls it, "prosumer". This is a combination of the words, producer and consumer. In short, Mr Toffler believes that man is continuing on a course that will further divide and separate mankind from one another. He supports this statement very well by tracing the history of man back through time and then showing how there were three major changes that affected man's life and behavior.

These changes that Mr. Toffler talks about, primarily involve how man relates to one another. He describes how man was basically a nomad or wanderer, if you may, and survived off the foraging of the land or physical reality. He indicates that the first wave consisted of man becoming domesticated and uniting or becoming one with the land. That is, man learned how to support himself from learning how to grow and prosper off the land. This first wave was agriculture. The second wave consisted of the industrial revolution, which united and tied man closer together than ever before. Then man was subject to greater discipline and emphasis on time and schedules than ever before. Unlike the first wave that dealt in seasons and activities, the second required coordinated activities and standardization to produce mass goods of a similar nature. However, in becoming standardized, man also became separated and dependent upon those still involved with agriculture.

Mr. Toffler says that we are in the midst of the third wave right now. He indicates that the third wave will be the freeing and the separation of man away from the rigid schedules of that demanded by the industrial complex and more toward self determination, where man will or can produce that which he wants and needs and at the same time to sell his services to others who may find a use for his talents and skills. This is primarily the result of the computer age. This electronic marvel will allow man to do more things with far less energies than ever before. The consequences of computers is the lessening of dependence of other people for the purpose of supporting a unifying or collective society. Mr. Toffler does a great job of supporting his claims by citing many examples of diversification of interests and the difficulty of a lot of mass media type support organizations, such as newspapers and TV to retain their sales and/or their ability to influence people as they did once before.

Indirect and directly, Mr. Toffler is talking about separation and predestination. But he also stresses the continuation of existing necessary patterns of agriculture and industry to continue their functional support of man and his culture. The third wave indicates a greater amount of separation than ever before in man's relationship with his fellow man. Compared with a living plant that is supported by roots, leaves, and its main body, man is becoming more separated unto himself. The ruling of the majority is actually becoming a governing of the minorities. Whether or not this is good or bad is unknown at this time; however, without the buffering or conciliatory compromising of the larger majority, the extremes may tend to be a controlling situation. If man can maintain a proper prospective of the theory of unity and exercises his option of free will for the greater well being of man, then there is always optimism for a greater tomorrow. However, without the knowledge and understanding of relationships of unity, there is little patterning that can support this greater probability. You make your own reality!

One more thing, in regards to computers, although these systems are tremendous time savers and offer great savings of personal energies and time, they are in fact preprogrammed limiting systems. That is, you can only end up with a result with which that program was intended. This is a form of predestination. Computer programs are designed to produce a certain end result. If you are trying to end up with a mathematical calculation, such a pattern or program will produce that result. It doesn't matter if the numbers are different every time you enter a different problem. The problem is subject to predestination based on a set of limitations that do not change. Therefore, it may be significant to you to re-evaluate just exactly what patterning is, and how it can affect a certain limited result. Again, the answer from such a pattern is not necessarily good or bad in itself, it just is. It is more important what is done with the information than is the answer itself. It is a relationship that affects one's reality.

To clarify that point a little more, the computer is a mechanical tool which is designed to respond to certain input data, primarily in the form of numbers and symbols. This information is then processed by patterning. That is, the data is assigned a predestined organized system of computations (a fancy word for patterns) that require an answer or answers arranged in another form or pattern. In simple terms, given a problem that involves X, Y and Z, the answer has to be A. Because X, Y, and Z are subject to the laws or planes that must result in A. No other result is possible until or unless other new patterns are assigned tasks and/or values that override or are the controlling factors. These mechanical functions of the computer are called programs. They are, in fact, patterns. They cannot act, they can only react, based upon a stimulus or input that causes this information to be processed in a specific sequential manner that ends up with a result.

My reasoning for going into so much detail on computers is because of the possibility or probability of a constant add on of computer instructions that is taking the control or the result out of the hands of the individuals, who in turn believe that they are exercising their right of free will. That is, the computer is an excellent tool that aids man; however, it is only an aid. As man becomes more use to the beneficial effects of the computer, he will also become more dependent upon it as well. Again, this is neither good nor bad in itself. Should man decide to entrust all of his decision upon a mathematical formula or programmed patterns, it is his decision and selection. However, it should be brought to one's attention that all patterns have their strengths and weaknesses; therefore, care should be taken as to how much information one wants to control or how much information is going to control him. Again, you make your own reality!

ORIGIN

I think, therefore I am
is the recognition of what is man.
A venture outward from an inner source
and from which we use energy and force.

Spirit born unto matter
is the form to which we gather.
This is the environment in which we entered
and to which our energies are centered.

Selection is a matter of choice
that gives life meaning and its voice.
But attraction is the faction
that gives us satisfaction.

The universe in mental first
from which comes physical thirst.
Recognition is matter we perceive
or is it how we are deceived.

Real or imaginary,
we make our own reality.
What is and what is not
is in the mind and what is taught.

The original of ones being
is based upon our seeing.
Life is but a reflection
that escapes our detection.

Where we begin
is somewhere deep within.
Truth and love are there,
it's just a matter of care.

CHAPTER 11

The Structure of The Universe

In talking about patterns and physical reality, I keep coming back to the theory of unity and oneness. In the last chapter, I made reference to the fact that patterns (beginnings and endings) have strengths and weaknesses. All patterns and forms have inherent advantages and disadvantages which depends upon their use and/or application. An example of what I am saying lies in an old game that children would play called, "Scissors, Stone, and Paper". For those of you who may not have heard of or played the game, it is a game whereby one can guess and demonstrate with the proper hand symbol, which of the three objects dominate on a show of the hands. Should all three symbols appear, there will be no dominance or control, but should only two of the three objects appear, one will dominate. That is, scissors cut paper, stone breaks scissors, and paper wraps stone.

The reason why I keep coming back to the theory of unity is because it is the only structure that does not have a weakness and cannot be controlled as we know control. That is, it is the only unite that stands by itself. All other numbers are composed of the number one in multiples or fractions of the number one. Therefore, no number, no matter how large it is, is not or cannot be larger than the number one. In a sense a larger number acts much like a fractional or decimal number in relationship to the number one. You can have more than one object of something and accumulate more than one of something, but it is the same as the original or the first one that you started out with. Therefore, the number one is the dominating or controlling force of anything.

As long as I am still on the subject of opposites, I will also say that the smallest number that can be achieved is the number zero. Zero, is actually a void or nothing, and nothing is smaller than nothing in our physical reality. But since zero or nothing is actually something known, it does take on a neutral negative characteristic. Therefore, when nothing and everything or the number one are put together the number one dominates. This is expressed in a simple mathematical formula of $1 + 0 = 1$. That is because, in a physical reality, the positive form must dominate. This is also explained in my own coined word, "inbalance", which indicates that a physical object, form, or pattern, is really out of balance with unity, but that it is also relatively stable.

Before the universe was created out of everything and nothing, there was no such thing as time or space. That is a hard concept to swallow! The reason for this statement lies strangely in the theory of our learning triangle. That is, time and space do not and cannot exist, unless there is a relationship. That's almost like the definition used to identify sound. In that definition, to have sound, you must have a sender and a receiver. Therefore, if a tree falls in the forest, as the old saying goes, there cannot be any sound, because there is no one there to hear it. Man's physical limitations, will not allow the recognizer, to recognize that event with recognition. The individual must be present or in a position of consciousness, before a relationship of understanding can result.

I think that most people can and will accept the idea that time is a relative thing, because of Albert Einstein's theory of the speed of light and moving objects. However, the effects on aging and other biological processes are still a little difficult to comprehend. The problem in understanding this latter situation is because no one has ever experienced this concept in physical reality. It is a difficult theory to prove if not impossible until the physical living proof of two or more objects can be scientifically monitored as to their aging processes, in relationship to a set controlled amount of time and environment.

Just to jog your memory a little, you may recall that one of our definitions of physical reality had to do with, "the image made in relationship to the meeting of light rays at a certain point or points"; therefore, theoretically, time slows down the farther one gets away from the sun, or at least, it is not the same for a person who is at a position of rest and for another who is in motion. This is expressed in Einstein's Theory of Relativity and now famous formula $E = mc^2$ (energy is equal to the mass of an object, times the speed of light multiplied by itself - note the reference to the speed of light again in relationship to time.).

I had hoped to stay away from very technical matters, because of perhaps poor interpretations on my part to translate complicated matters into simple everyday terms. However, I do find it necessary to carry this conversation one step further. Before Mr. Einstein died, he published another important document, known as "The Unified Field Theory". Just the name of this theory alone, is interesting and relevant to my theory of unity that I have been suggesting; however, the Unified Field Theory, deals primarily with that of physical matter only. Therefore, any names and places or similarities to my own thoughts are, or may be purely coincidental, as they say about certain TV shows and motion pictures (even though it may not be.).

What Mr. Einstein tried to do in the Unified Field Theory is to try to tie together the mathematical formula that establishes this world of matter we call physical reality. His concept was based upon complex formulas involving ten sets of equations relating to gravity and six sets relating to electromagnetism. In short, he mathematically identified the patterns or forces that hold our universe together in a state (position) of inbalance, separation and stability. However, before this book was widely circulated, Mr. Einstein withdrew his original text or theory and claimed that it was incomplete and needed further refinements. After seeing what man did to his Theory of Relativity and using his formula of $E = mc^2$ for developing the atomic bomb, he may have avoided a full disclosure of this new theory for fear of misuse and destructive intents.

Mr. Einstein's "Unified Field Theory", is primarily based on the premise that matter is a product of energy, rather than the reverse, nor are they separate entities. They are one, or unified. This is exactly what I myself stated earlier in this book, but I really didn't explain it just that way but I used the words together to explain resistance and energy as the limiting factors involving self-control. I suppose then, we can also define physical reality a little different than what I chose in the last chapter as, "that which is relevant to the senses". Perhaps a better definition might be, the point or points at which energy enters into a state or position of inbalance, stability, and separation by creating a unified field of energy and resistance, resulting in a form or force which we call physical matter. This definition gets us away from the need of having a recipient as the determining factor, and/or the explanation of the tree that falls in the forest syndrome.

Strangely enough, Mr. Einstein himself did not believe that gravity was a force itself, but a product of the space-time continuum that relates to a field-energy concentration or pattern. He contended that gravity is directly related to other forms of energy and primarily electromagnetism. In simple terms, Mr. Einstein believed that gravity was the end result of a relationship that involved energy and resistance otherwise known as time and space. If this were so, then, time and space could be used and controlled by man, something like an electromagnet. Naturally, the consequence of learning to manipulate time and space could drastically upset this thing we call physical reality and which is the subject of a book called, "The Philadelphia Experiment" by Charles Berlitz.

Like our learning triangle, the unified field theory may be the basis for another self supporting triangle, called physical reality. Such a triangle would be composed of three elements known as: magnetism, gravity, and matter. The space in between these points would be reality, divided by space and time. For simplicity sake, we are only talking about what we call our manifested physical reality. The relationship or the controlling factor that would affect one's conscious desired end result would be based on knowing and possessing an understanding of the unified field theory or the relationship of energy. It is this theory that holds the structure of this manifested physical reality and/or universe together. This completes our second triangle. It is only a matter of consciously understanding the proper relationship of the energy elements and how they interact with one another that they can be controlled. It is only a matter of time that time can be controlled.

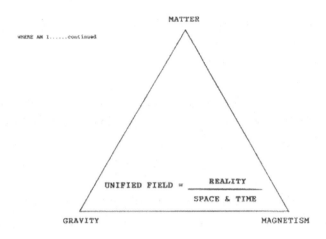

Illustration #3

And so it is. Physical reality is an entity unto itself. Self supporting and sustaining. Formed if you would out of a series of patterns or limitations that create forces of inbalance that allow for change, but are stable and separated out of a unified state or position. This position or state can also be explained in a way that adds credence to my theory of unity. Therefore, I would also like to go into an explanation of how this relationship called physical reality enters into being or existence in a unified field. To explain this, I must go into an explanation in an abstract manner, but also through the science of mathematics, which is very precise and absolute in itself.

Our physical reality can also be expressed in relatively simple terms. To explain gravity in more simple terms than that of Mr. Einstein, gravity is a product of separation. That is, it is caused by the forces that produce a state of separation or inbalance. In short, Mr. Einstein calls it a concentrated pattern of energy. I believe we are talking about the same thing. Opposing patterns or forces of energy are created that are striving for reunification; however, the forces of resistance are also at work and result in a slowing down, cooling, and hardening of energy. Without the resistance of matter, our physical reality would not be possible.[2] Creation begins only when one

---

[2] NOTE: A lot of the following information is based upon an unusual book by Elizabeth Haich called "Initiation". Another chapter to follow will again mention her and include her work.

force separates itself from unity and sets itself up opposite the creator as resistance. Therefore, gravity can also be thought of as those forces that are striving for reunification. Gravity is indeed the product of separation.

This product is manifested from the state of unity; therefore, it enters or departs from the sum total of everything which is expressed in the number one. This manifestation can also be depicted as a single dot or point which again is singular. All energy and forces of the universe are movements that emanate from one point, their own center, and radiate outward or away from their center point in circular waves or as spherical vibrations or oscillations. This example is demonstrated by the largest and smallest shapes or forms found in the universe, that being planets and suns on one hand, and atoms or molecules on the other hand. But probably the most interesting and most common form in nature is that of water. In its smallest form of a droplet, it is completely spherical in nature. On a global scale, it is also spherical. It is only on a limited basis, where water is confined to containers, such as a glass, does water exhibit the quality of being level or flat. Interesting, isn't it? It is also relative.

In any case, this point of departure represents the number one or unity. Upon entering a one dimensional world, if it could or does exist, this point would then become a line. That's because everything in a state of separation has a beginning and an end, or limiting extremes. But it is also interesting to note, that instead of progressing to the number two, we automatically achieve the number three. Even though we are talking about opposites or extremes, we are also talking about three factors. Anything that has a beginning and end must also involve a space in between, no matter how short that space may be. Therefore, the next logical number in a progressive reality is the number three.

Considering that we have started out in the most simplest manner possible and have only proceeded but to include two numbers, you may have noticed that there is no way to achieve the number two. Any movement of a point, must involve three factors. To achieve the number two, there must be some significant basis to establish the number two and its proper place in our numerical system. The only logical solution to this question must involve the splitting of unity and the establishment of opposites as two different realities. That means that the number two can only be achieved when those two opposites are set beside each other.

But, because unity cannot exist in a state of separation, it must project a reflection outside of itself. When such a division takes place, there is a sense of death to unity and the creation of limits that obscures the origin and concept of the number one. Supposedly, the word doubt, which represents a kind of separation within the mind, is closely related to the word double or the word which stands for the number two.

To make sure that we are correct in our establishing a basis for the number two, let's carry this logic a little further. In a two dimensional world as we understand it, we have length and width; therefore, our line would become a plane. Our line, which consists of a number of points or dots, would also mean that these points or dots would be projected perpendicular to the original line of force. Therefore, if the force or energy is equal, a flat square or plane that looks like a postage stamp will result having four sides and composing an area of limitation. These sides and the area in between would then be composed of five factors or the sum of the number five.

In our three dimensional world, we are concerned with length, width and depth; therefore, our line or plane would now become a cube. That's because, another force would have to generate a third projection relative to the first two forces. The only possible result of this force or pattern, originating from a singular point is that of a cube. This shape consists of six sides or planes and an area of limitation or inner content and would be representative of the number seven. Therefore, the number seven is the basis for all physical matter in the universe in its simplest form. Besides the biblical references, that is why our calendar is based upon a seven day week.

As you can see, there is no way to arrive at the number for two logically, other than the division or separation of the number one. That also means that the resulting manifestation, not the number two, is less than the number one that unity represents and that is because the other part is not manifested. But, in proving the existence of our world of physical matter and separation, we have just come up with another contradictory problem. The problem that I am referring to is the actual shape of the cube itself as the basis for physical matter. I have mentioned many times before, that energy and resistance are the two major forces that control our world. By explaining the shape of energy, I have just described a shape that seems relatively unstable or in a condition of stress. That's because, the points and/or corners of a cube are not equal distance from one another. Consequently, this variation in distance causes tension and unequal forces of stability.

So how is it, that the basic building block of the universe is unstable? Why, or how does physical matter maintain its relative stability or inbalance if it is in a constant state of stress? There must be something missing, wrong, or something we are overlooking, in the composition of matter. We cannot have a shape or pattern of force that is unstable, or else everything would return to a state of unity. Yet, the logic and outward appearance of the shape of the cube would seem to indicate that everything is correct. If it is an unstable shape, then why doesn't it break down and return to a state of unity? The only possible answer must lie or have something to do with the space in between, or its inner contents.

We have already discussed one shape that does show this kind of stability, and that was the shape of unity; otherwise distinguished as a circle or sphere. Now, obviously, this shape is the basic building block or unit that composes the more complex patterns and shapes found in a one, two, and three dimensional worlds. Just as the atom is the building block for molecules, this same thought form applies to all patterns or forces in a state of separation. Consequently, there must be a more complex pattern or structure that offers some form of stability. Since there is no two point geometric shape found in nature, we must go to a three point shape. Eureka! We found it! It is the shape of a triangle. Amazing! It is the only figure that can have each of its points equal distance from one another. You can check the rest of the numbers and shapes, but take my word for it, it is the only one that creates a pattern of stability. You may have also guessed this figure before, because of my references the to the learning triangle and the triangle that I called physical reality.

You may be asking yourself at this point, what does the triangle have to do with the shape of the cube as our basic building block for physical matter? The answer to that question is contained <u>within</u> the cube itself. I have explained how the three dimensions or planes provide the outer limits for our world; however, hidden within the shape of the cube, is yet another pattern based upon the triangle. To arrive at this inner shape, one must dissect the cube. To do this, start from one point or corner of the cube, say the bottom left, and intersect each of the three planes. This will bring you out to the two points or corners opposite and oblique to the original starting point. In effect, you are cutting off one corner of the cube, but if this were done four times, the resulting shapes would be quite different from that of a cube. It would result in a tetrahedron triangle, which is a four sided figure composed of four equilateral triangles.

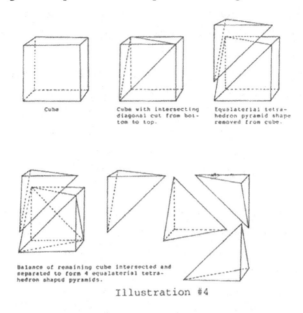

Cube

Cube with intersecting diagonal cut from bottom to top.

Equalaterial tetrahedron pyramid shape removed from cube.

Balance of remaining cube intersected and separated to form 4 equalaterial tetrahedron shaped pyramids.

Illustration #4

So there you have it, the cube is not a cube after all. It is really four tetrahedron triangles which are very stable, because each has points equal distance from one another. That means that there is no strain or tension and that makes the cube itself stable. That is, each of its corners rest on an inner equilateral triangle; thereby creating a condition of equilibrium and harmony in a relationship or state of rest. This harmony can also be demonstrated by flattening out each side of the tetrahedron into a flat single plane. The result of this flattening would be the creation of a single large equilateral triangle. Therefore, one should be careful of outward appearances. It is the inner content that is important. Matter cannot exist without it and that must also apply to man himself, because man is composed of matter. That means that man is composed of and controlled by the same laws as those that govern the universe and physical reality. Man too, has an outward and inner appearance and that is but half of his own unite or unity.

In describing our world of physical reality, I may have overdone it a bit with somewhat boring details; however, I also felt that this explanation was necessary to clear up the concept of unity and separation as a necessary and important factor in the creation of matter and man. If you have followed me up to this point. I am about to enter the most difficult or controversial part of my description of our own reality or realities. In talking about separation and the creation of matter, I have not said anything about that which is opposite matter in a state of separation. That which is opposite matter is the more controversial world of unmanifested reality and/or spirit.

In most cases, people tend to link the subject of spirit with that of theology and religion; however true to that reference, it also applies to a state or level of consciousness. That is, spirit is the opposite, un-manifested part of unity and therefore part of everything. If physical matter were to be compared with the number one, its spiritual opposite could be represented by a zero or nothing. Whereas, matter can be referred to as resistance, spirit can be compared to pure, unlimited energy. At this time, I would also like to link the usage of the word unity to that of God. This reference will not satisfy those who have a concept of God as a moral, all powerful being or entity that has absolute control and qualities similar to man himself; however, I believe it is the only undisputed, all encompassing explanation of God that is possible in a world based upon separations and limitations.

At this point, you may be asking, how is it that spirit can or is manifested in matter or man without destruction of both or the return to unity, if it is opposite to one another. Well, just as I explained earlier, there is a common relationship. That relationship is based upon a structural form or pattern found in both matter and spirit. For unity to manifest itself outside that state or position of being, it must take on or assume three factors, because any limited reality must involve a beginning, an ending and a space in between. These three factors can also be translated in terms relative to unity. That is, the beginning or one point of a triangle is the same as the recognizer, the ending or third point is the recognized, and the space in between or second point is the recognition. This is the resurrection. A state of perfect harmony and equilibrium. In a Divine state of unity this is a condition of complete consciousness, whereby the three are one and the same. Therefore, unity or God in a state of resting within himself is one in three or three in one. Put into a structural geometric pattern, this is the form of an equilateral triangle. This explanation is basically the same as the definition I used earlier to describe physical reality; however, the difference between the two is in the mental position or level of consciousness. This will become more significant as we progress.

Before I leave the subject of the triangle, I would like to make sure that you haven't forgotten that we were talking about one in three or three in one in a state of unity. When any force is manifested into physical reality, there is a separation and our one in three emerges and becomes one <u>and</u> three and that makes four. This relationship to physical reality is also demonstrated by the fact that hidden within the shape of an equilateral triangle is another triangle in reverse. This relationship makes our one triangle actually composed of four triangles of equal size. This brings us back to the shape of our cube and its inner content, the tetrahedron, which when flattened out forms one large equilateral triangle in the exact configuration as our triangle that represents unity. Voila, we are back to where we started, the shape of the inner structure or form of matter again. Amazing, isn't it!

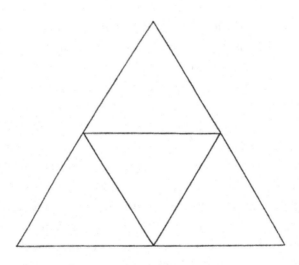

```
Spiritual Unity Unmanifested = 1 in 3 = 3
Spiritual Unity Manifested   = 1 &  3 = 4
Physical Reality =                      7
```

Illustration #5

Another way to demonstrate the relationship of matter to spirit is to look at the shape of the cube again. Instead of cutting the cube as we did before, starting from the lower left corner point, what would have happened if we had started from the top left corner point. Well, the answer would be nothing or the same physical shapes as before, except the figures would all be in reverse, and the tetrahedron would be upside down or standing on its point, instead of its base. So what is so great about that you say. The answer is a matter of the relationship of two possibilities, or the complimentary halves known as the positive and negative forms of matter. Only one can be manifested in our physical reality, but the opposite is also possible and it represents the un-manifested reality or spirit of that which is and in non-linear time that creates multiple alternate realities.

Our two tetrahedrons in their respective positions represent the structural form that matter can take in a state of complete equilibrium, or as I call it an inbalance. All matter and forms of creation contain this inner law of equilibrium. Therefore, man too, has an inner being or plane of contact with this divine form or pattern of being, just as the tetrahedron is relative to the shape of the cube. If man searches outside of himself, he will not find this divine being. That logic can be demonstrated by taking another look at the cube. Outwardly, this form takes on the shape of a square or cube that rests on one of those flat planes. Should the planes of the cube be unfolded, they would form the shape of a cross or the letter "T". This is also representative or the symbol used in theology for the crucifixion. In a manifested physical state of separation, this flattened out form represents the limitations of man crucified on the two beams of time and space in a three dimensional world of matter; that is, if man solely identifies himself with the outside world or physical reality. Remember, looks are deceiving.

Looking again at the cut up cube, and rearranging the tetrahedron and its corners, back to back, it is possible to end up with the shape of a pyramid. This is the form that is possible when man or matter reveals and reflects outwardly its inner form or shape of its divine self. This is the form or shape of man or matter in its spiritualized self. This is the divine self in complete equilibrium and harmony with All There Is. The recognizer, the recognized, and the recognition, are all one and the same. Isn't it strange and interesting, how dumb and smart the ancients were. These primitive people had few conveniences and/or material wealth; however, for some reason they had come up with and adopted many of the symbols that have a logical mathematical form or structure to them that represent man and matter in their relationship to this physical reality.

It is only from within that man can find his own true self. Man is the only single creature, composed of matter, that can <u>consciously</u> combine the laws of spirit and matter. He is the connecting link and is the only one capable of living by the laws of both worlds. Man's thoughts, words, and deeds, result from the act of giving and radiating energy in the form of universal love. On the other hand, man's body belongs to the material world of physical matter and he must abide by those laws too. When man directs his attention outward, he expresses the laws of resistance that results in separation that slows or retards his own being from progress and growth to his own true self or origin. When man works with the two laws in harmony, at the same time and in the right place, he is expressing the laws of divinity. However, if man should work against the laws of either spirit or matter, or if he should express them at the wrong time and place, then this act would be considered satanic. Hence, the origin of the word Satan.

The origin of the word satanic, meant something neither good or bad, but a condition opposite the laws of harmony or accord to that of the natural laws that govern both man and matter. Since man is the only creature that can consciously express both laws, it is only he that can enter into an act or condition which is considered satanic. Therefore, Satan, cannot exist as an entity unto itself or himself alone. It, or he, needs man in order to fulfill such actions contrary or opposite that which is or should be. Therefore, Satan can be considered as the law of matter that has come alive through divine spirit. That which is satanic, can also be considered the unconscious force of resistance. That is, it is an expression of the law of matter manifested by those who cannot identify or express the laws of giving, loving, or radiating forms of energy. Satan is the drawing inward, cooling off, paralysis, and extreme forms of possessing that man does unconsciously when he is dominated and expresses the laws of matter.

You may have noticed that I had underlined the word consciously a little way back. I will explain this word at considerable length later; however, I do want you to be aware of the fact that it is sometimes quite difficult to distinguish between the laws of spirit and that of matter. In fact, in the last paragraph, I mentioned that "extreme forms of possessing", are done unconsciously; yet, many people seem to be aware of what they are doing. Therefore, I qualified that statement by mentioning that this is so, "when he(man) expresses the laws of matter". What I mean by this statement is that man reacts to a patterned response to certain stimuli, rather than to use his free will and divine inner guidance of his own true self. That is, man instinctively selects to hold on to what he has, or to control and dominate for the purpose of his own material well being, that which is the basis for the laws expressed in matter. In short, one solidifies and fortifies his position for controlling the power that matter has in the world of physical reality and separation.

At the beginning of this chapter, I mentioned that all energy and forces of the universe are movements that emanate from one point, their own center, and radiate in circular waves in all directions and manifesting themselves as vibrations or oscillations. These vibrations, in turn, manifest themselves on many levels as wave forms, wave lengths, and/or frequencies. Because man is limited to the range of this physical reality, he can only perceive a certain number of these wave forms because of the limitations of his physical senses. The appearance of manifestations into matter, depends upon the ability of our senses to perceive this movement, motion, vibration, frequency, or whatever you call it. Those wave lengths not perceived by our senses are ignored by our mental consciousness, but just the same, they are there and they do exist in unmanifested non-linear time. Those wave lengths that are still within the realm of our consciousness, but are not considered matter are: sound, electricity, heat, taste, smell and light. Beyond this, are the waves that affect mental activities and life itself. But all of these forms, no matter what their shape or configuration, they all contain a divine inner quality of equilibrium or circles of unity.

As matter, or forms of matter, becomes less and less dense, they have fewer restrictions or limitations; therefore, they become lighter and closer to the laws of spirit. This variation of matter and various forms of life represents different degrees of resistance corresponding to a level of consciousness that, in a sense, recognizes their divine inner quality. If for some reason, one could induce an inbalance of energy to that of matter to overcome its resistance, one would in effect produce a chain reaction of burning. This process is basically the liberating of energy and/or the state of unity and all consciousness. Therefore, although resistance has the ability to slow and harden everything in the world of physical matter, so are there forces that have the ability to counter or offset those qualities. Therefore, man has the choice of selecting which of the laws he wants to exercise. His selections are then predicated upon which laws support his best interests in supporting or sustaining his life in the world of physical matter, or those that bring him closer to a reality of unlimited energy or a condition of total unity. The latter situation, while sounding extremely favorable is also frightening, because it could result in a situation of limbo or a meandering dream like state of non-linear unmanifested reality, if the mind or person were not disciplined.

What I am saying here, is that God is present in every creature and form of manifestation. But he reveals himself on every level of existence only as much as each form can consciously experience and bear his divine creative force, corresponding to his own level of resistance to create that life form. To consciously experience force, means being this force, and simultaneously it means radiating this force in all directions, including one's own body. Therefore, the body or creative form mustrecognize and learn to be resistant enough to withstand this radiation or again, it will burn up and destroy itself similar to that of a short electrical circuit.

Although man finds it difficult to distinguish between the laws of matter and spirit, he can do so if he can raise his level of consciousness; however, as I indicated, he can only do this to a certain limited degree without ill effects detrimental to one's own physical being. To do this, one must begin to recognize the difference between the world of effects and the plane of causes, otherwise known as intuition. The learning triangle is the subconscious means of growth whereby one should begin to see and observe these relationships in motion. However man must not just react to stimuli just for the sake of a response, he must know what he is doing and why he is doing it. This is a matter of consciousness. This is a matter of growth and increased tolerance to vibrations of a higher frequency otherwise known as consciousness. This is the limited process of the recognizer, recognizing itself with recognition.

That which has separated itself from the state of unity, cannot return to the state of unity without spiritual help. This must be done by that known as a conscious being. That being man, because man is the only creature who is conscious of this origin and the laws of both worlds. Man can identify with that of matter, because he is the same as that which composes matter. The individual is one or part of the earth and its creatures, drawing from it nourishment which is the same thing as resistance, and giving to it consciousness or pure energy, somewhat like a bride and groom in harmony or a state of bliss. This striving for harmony is characteristic of all love and this relationship is expressed in everything, including our bodies as weight. But there are some people out there who kind of overdo this love a little bit.

In any case, when man uses his consciousness in creative endeavors, he must always relate to matter in the form of resistance or weight. He must not ignore these properties and laws of matter and must not work against them or his ability to spiritualize matter will end up in another form of negative destruction otherwise known as, and considered as satanic, or that which is against the patterns and limitations imposed by those forms and forces of nature or physical matter.

As stated in an earlier chapter, man's purpose is to use and exercise the use of energy for the betterment or well being of all. Now we have also included that of matter as well as that of one's own fellow man. Man can alter the pattern and form of matter and thereby enlighten or spiritualize it in a limited sense, because man is of both worlds. However, this process can also work in reverse. That is, man himself can deaden or impede his own progress to his own enlightenment and /or growth. The relationship of man and matter affects and can benefit both, thereby hastening the return to unity for both, it is only a matter of consciousness. The structural pattern of man, matter, and all things in the universe, are based upon the cube and hidden within the cube is the tetrahedron. It is the one indestructible form or pattern found in everything and nothing. It is the uniting element. It is a form of unity. It is a part of God. Therefore, we are a part of matter and a part of God. We are one and the same. It is only a matter of consciousness that separates us. So we must be something special, because, "God doesn't make junk!"

Man then, is a unique creature. He is not completely matter, nor is he entirely spiritual in his being while he is in this earthly physical environment. He maintains his position in both worlds at the same time. Man maintains his position in both worlds by controlling his consciousness.

By limiting one's self, he can maintain his point of focus or position by willing his consciousness to recognize only certain things which operate at the same vibration level as that of physical matter. Again, the recognizer, recognizes its being with other forms of recognition that relates to his imposed limitations. That is, man has chosen to recognize or establish a basis by which to relate to certain vibrations which we call matter. Therefore, his selection has created patterns or laws by which he recognizes his environment.

As stated before, man has selected and separated himself from unity in order to bring life to that of physical matter. Matter is the outer limitation and structural pattern in which his consciousness dwells. Hidden within, is the inner content and bridge to the spiritual world of infinite unity. Through the use and exercise of energy, man is able to control his physical being and to sustain life by taking and converting heavier elements of matter or nature into lighter forms of energy. This process of nourishment is designed to release or breakdown the forms of resistance to other lighter forces that have a lesser resistance. In this process, energy is released and literally enlightenment takes place in matter. So while you are sitting there reading this book and thinking about all of the other things you could be doing, at least you may get some comfort out of the fact that you are doing something good for somebody and something (yourself and matter) right now or at least every time you eat.

The situation or condition of spirit being born unto matter is not without certain problems. Resistance is a very strong instable force. Therefore, man must learn, know, and recognize, the forces and forms of resistance in order to survive or support life in this reality. During the process of separation where man enters the world of physical matter, much of his consciousness is lost or severely restricted because of the limitations of matter and the forces of resistance. Consequently, man himself loses consciousness of his own being. He becomes unconscious of his own true self, because he is limited and subject to the physical senses that can only perceive the vibrations of physical matter. As a form of matter, he lives to fulfill wants and desires in a world of causes and effects resulting from the laws and limitations of physical matter. Yet, remember, man is not what he appears to be. There are outer physical patterns and there are inner intangible patterns. Man can distinguish the difference, he just needs to know where to look. He must recognize himself with recognition. However, he also has the option not to recognize what he is if he relies solely on the outside world of physical matter.

At this point, I feel that you may find my writings a little difficult to follow because I know that I am contradicting myself. This is unintentional on my part; however, it is true with so much of our lives. The problem lies in one's position and level within that position. That is, one limits one's self to the immediate environment or circumstances in a linear time sequence rather than a totally defined base. More simply, because of a constantly changing environment, one adapts to the limits of the existing pattern or framework; therefore, one can change or contradict one's self without losing too much cohesion. There is a certain specific relationship to, in this case, the words and the subject at hand.

Earlier I said that, "man is the only creature who is conscious of his origin and the laws of both worlds", and then I turn right around and say that man is unconscious of this same situation. The problem here lies in the ability of the individual to be completely conscious of linear and non-linear relationships. Few, very few people possess this ability. It is all a matter of selection. That is, what one consciously chooses to believe, determines his reality.

Because man is outwardly motivated, because he is part of matter, he may chose to be only conscious of that which he can identify with his physical senses. Therefore, he is limited to those laws which control and govern the laws of nature in a world of cause and effect. Consciousness can change that world and the individual; however, we must first know what to look for and understand the concept of unity. That is the reason for my ambiguity in my writing and this is the same problem that we all face in our daily lives. It is the question of what level of consciousness we are dealing with and with what reality. One can control his own destiny, but he must first consciously select what he chooses to experience from a state of separation which is first derived subconsciously from non-linear reality.

This problem is most noticeable to us, during a natural life process called sleep. Scientist have a problem in properly explaining the purpose and necessity of sleep for human beings. Most scientists agree that sleep is a necessary process whereby the body relaxes and rids itself of toxic wastes that have built up during the conscious waking hours of the individual.

Supposedly, this period of rest, refreshes and re-balances the cells of the body; however, the scientists are also puzzled by a few individuals that don't seem to sleep at all, and they seem to function perfectly normal.

I have yet to read or hear anyone try to relate the subject of sleep to the problem of separation. That is, perhaps sleep is a function designed to relieve man of his mantle of physical matter and return him to the state of spirit from which he came. The constant limitations of matter and resistance uses up a lot of energy to maintain man in a state of separation. Sleep is a state of super consciousness in an unmanifested non-lnear reality from which man can return to his other state of being or matter. However, because of the vibration level of non-linear unmanifested reality, man usually has no conscious memory of this other dimension that he can relate to when he re-enters the physical world of resistance; therefore, he ignores this reality.

This thought concerning sleep cannot be proven, as is true of all processes of the intangible. However, in this case we have some form of evidence that tends to support this thought. During sleep, there is still the question of mental activities of the individual. That is, although the body is at rest, the mental activities seem to continue, but at another level that is not always relative or compatible with our world of physical matter. In short, we call this type of mental activity, dreaming. This activity is often an incoherent, chaotic pattern of intangible mental activities which may seem to parallel our life in physical reality, but it does not affect our physical body per se in most situations. But, just the same, it does take on all of the characteristics of physical reality without the involvement or side effects of the human body or physical matter. While in the state of dreaming, there is no difference to the individual. It is only when he is awake that he makes a distinction of what is real and what is not.

Apparently, the question of reality has been answered in favor of physical reality, because man seems to spend more conscious time in the world of physical matter and the individual seems to exercise more control over his own personal situation. That is, physical reality appears to offer more conscious coherent and cohesive linear sequences of events and interaction which involve more laws or limitations that direct cause and effect relationships that control the individual and the learning process which is integral with growth. Again, the ability to control and be consciously aware of one's environment is an important factor in one's physical reality.

The body is linked to that of physical matter and the mind while controlling the body must still be limited by the laws and limitations of matter. Therefore, although man still maintains his identity in both realms or realities, the relationship of the mind is not as dominant as the body is in the thought process. However, if man can increase his level of consciousness, he may be able to distinguish a greater reality and free himself of the limitations imposed by the world of physical matter. Remember, you make your own reality. There is a pattern or structure to the universe that governs your physical body; however, you do exist in a state of separation within yourself. Therefore, you do have a choice and can select your own limitations both consciously and subconsciously.

What better way to end a chapter on separation than to lend a little thought about the parts that make up the whole. "The Part" is a piece of prose that may make some sense.

THE PART

There dwells within me the person of my being.
That being is the person of my conscious self.
This is the person of that which I am familiar.
This is the person I normally think of me.
This is the person that walks for me and talks for me.
This is the person who has feeling and awareness and senses my environment.
This is the person who responds to that which stimulates me.
This is the person who is the sum total of my experiences.

Yet, there dwells within me conscious activity and thought which does not normally fit that of my being.
There is a part of me which is in awe of the wonderment of life and nature.
There is another part of me that knows the true origin of life and the nature of personal reality.
There is a part of me that expresses beliefs beyond that of verbal or written communication.
There is a part of me that seems to transcend this reality, this world, and this life of physical dimensions.
There is a part of me that senses and experiences existence on a multidimensional level.

There is a part of me which is conscious and living in the present realm of time and space.
There is another part of me that seems equally alive but lives in the world of my dreams.
This is the part of me that is the person of my being.
This is the part of me that I have chosen to concentrate my energy and present point of focus.
This is the part of me that makes its home in this reality.

Beyond this present world of reality, there exists still other parts of me which are equally valid.
There is a part, or parts, of me that have been here before and will be here again.
These are the parts of me which do not have my focused attention and energy of the present.
There are also parts of me that could have been and others that still might be.
These are the parts of me, fragments, that live in a world of probabilities and parallel time.

There is finally the part of me which is the real me.
This is the sum of my parts.
This is the me that knows even more and is more knowledgeable than that of my conscious present self.
This is the me that knows no limits and ALL THAT IS.
This is the me of which I am, I was, and will be.
This is the entity of my being.
Here dwells the true person known as me.

CHAPTER 12

Patterns of Recognition

Before I proceed to go into detail and explain the idea of consciousness, I want to bring you along a pattern of mental growth that again leads one to end up with the same results that we have just achieved using the logical structure of mathematics. Instead of tangible structures, let's look at the intangible side of our realities. To do this, we must retrace some of our steps through physical reality and our learning process of growth.

Because man is a part of matter, he derives almost all of what he knows about matter through the physical senses. I say almost, because I myself am not sure of other contributions of perhaps other unknown senses that have been speculated about. I find myself trapped like most other people in accepting only what one can identify as real or pertaining to physical reality, even though I know that another reality of spirit must exist because we live in a world based upon separation. In any case, let's take a look at these physical senses and see what we can do to prove the existence of this other world.

Man is said to be endowed with five physical senses, and these are: the sense of sight or seeing, sound or hearing, touch or feeling, taste and smell. Supposedly, all of these senses work or operate in such a fashion that they detect a specific range or limitation of vibration or energy. If we were to possess a sense for heat, then we might be able to use it to see in the dark, just as infra-red devices are used. In this example, instead of using a physical organ to detect heat, man uses a mechanical system based upon electronic circuits to detect vibration of heat energy that is emitted by all forms of matter to supplement his own senses. Other devices use forms of sound or energy frequencies to increase the limitations of man's physical senses.

That means, that our knowledge of this reality consists of our reactions of our senses to that of physical matter or energy. That is, man primarily uses his outward or external senses to contact or convey information which pertains to the outer surfaces or characteristics of matter. As teachers of philosophy might say, you really cannot know anything about the object itself, only its characteristics. Therefore, man must rely on a relatively small minority of research scientists who really analyze and understand the internal structure and patterns of matter and its relationship to that of man and other matter. Whereas, the average person in the street really relies solely on his senses for knowledge of the outside world. This consists mostly of reactions to a stimulus-response type actions of our physical senses to matter and the laws that govern matter.

Again, we are faced with a situation of a pattern(s) or structure(s) with outside limitations. Matter has physical energy limitations; therefore, so does man. Consequently, knowledge as we know it is primarily a form of pattern recognition. That is, the physical senses detect and store information pertaining to the limitations of size, weight, shape, volume, density, color, temperature, sound, smell, taste, etc., and certain laws of probability that allow for changing that which is. Man then uses this knowledge of patterns to accomplish certain tasks or end results. The implication of the knowledge of patterns and the laws of probability are what constitute the building and understanding of relationships, which I spoke of so much earlier in this book. All objects of matter exhibit characteristics that have different limitations or beginnings and endings in relationship to one another.

Interesting enough, while these patterns of limitations seem to be rather simple and a sure fired way of determining just what is and is not in this physical reality, it still has some glitches. That is, there are some inherent problems associated with the physical senses. However simple some things appear to be, they can become complicated should one decide to properly analyze them. We often think in terms of a single action as that which is simple or automatic; however, such simple functions usually involves several distinct actions or commands. Any computer programmer can tell you that to get from point A to point B, as we tried to start out in the beginning of the book, we discovered it is a complicated task which is dependant upon what the individual wishes to experience. That is, to get from A to B, must involve at least six or more functions which involves an action to start, motion to move, balance, attention to one's environment for obstacles and to increase or decrease the use of energy, the relationship of matter to affect one's progress, and an evaluation when to stop. Simple, right?

However simple, simple things are, we take almost everything we do for granted. In fact, we really don't want to know what all is involved. We simply want to get or do something. We don't want to think about everything along the way. We are only concerned, or usually concerned, with the end result. This whole series of activities which are used to complete a single task becomes a form of pattern recognition and therefore becomes instinctive or intuitional. It is no longer a series, but becomes a group task or system known as a program or routine, if you will. Therefore, as a natural outgrowth or form of progression, we become unconscious to the actual mechanics or steps involved in the action(s) or routines, unless something unusual happens to interfere with the accomplishment of the task that is not normally expected. In a routine, most of the resistance of matter and/or the action has been removed or overcome to make the function automatic or subconscious. Also, as stated, this pattern recognition leads to a form of unconsciousness. Therefore, the limitations of physical matter are overcome and/or stored in another form of resistance known as the routine or a programmed structure of thought. We are no longer dealing with physical matter resistance, but with units of thought that form a kind of resistance of its own. Remember, thought is but another form of energy, vibrating at a higher level than that of physical matter. Therefore, anything that holds, restricts, or limits anything else, must contain some form of resistance.

Before we get into intangible forms of resistance, let's get back to the problem of the physical senses. What can possibly go wrong with the physical senses, you say. Well, not much if you know how to use them properly in relationship to the laws of probability. What I am saying here, is that sometimes the physical senses can fail to convey the proper truth about an object or that which is, and it requires more than the physical senses to distinguish differences in an initial outward appearance and that which actually is. In this case, we are primarily talking about objects based on or made from physical matter. To get a proper, unbiased idea of what I am talking about, which is next to impossible, let's make up a hypothetical example of the senses conveying the wrong information about physical matter.

Because it is difficult to get away from biased thought forms, I must resort to an exaggerated condition that may not be believable; however, it is the best I can do for now. Let's say, that we are a person who has been blind from birth and is at least twenty years old. All of a sudden, from some freak accident of nature, we acquire our sight. Here we are with a completely new sense by which to detect or receive knowledge about the outside physical world. Besides the sudden shock and the revising of certain specific reliance upon the other senses and their relationship with the individual, we find the new sense so overpowering that it may in fact interfere with our ability to cope with our old environment and our other senses. More than likely, this will only be a temporary problem; however, let's try to anticipate what some of these problems might be.

Probably one of the first problems we might struggle with is the problem of perspective. That is, because we have never been able to see before, and we have quite a lot of knowledge of the outside world stored in our memory based upon sound and touch; that knowledge does not immediately relate to sight. Therefore, it might be possible that initially we may not be able to distinguish objects in a distance from those close up, or we may possibly think that those objects in a distance are actually smaller than those close up. It might even be possible that we might think that the world or object ceases to exist as they approach the horizon. I seriously doubt that we may think things shrink when we walk away from them, but it may just puzzle us a little bit at first.

Even if we were not blind from birth, we still have other problems of sight that need special attention because they can be confusing. Here I am talking about the problem of heat rising from a hot pavement or other forms of matter. In this case, such conditions can completely obscure or hide an image of an oncoming car or some other obstacle in the area of the heat waves. We also have the problem of water and liquids which have the ability to magnify objects to make them appear bigger than their actual size when viewed from outside of water. Then, as we are putting an object into a clear glass of water, for whatever reason, we have to be careful about how we look into the container so that we do not get a distorted view that can make the image of the object appear to bend. So you see (pun on words there), you don't have to be blind to have trouble with the physical sense of sight. In these situations, sight can be deceiving. It takes the knowledge of refraction of light through medias and/or enough familiarity with heat and water and their relationship to other forms of matter to correct this false visual appearance of that which is.

There are a number of other tests and artwork designed to confuse the sense of sight using perspective shading and colors to deceive the eyes, or convey multiple contradictory images. Some of these tests are used to detect color blindness, others are simply designed to convey wrong impressions. We call such impressions, illusions; however, this word is usually used to notate something that really doesn't exist. The fact is, the eyes sense what it is limited to see, but the mind knows that the input is not correct and either switches to other senses for additional data, or just ignores the information as not valid or false.

I suppose that if we were also deaf and blind for twenty or more years, we would also have a little difficulty with sound too. Probably more so. Sound is affected by more conditions of temperature and water than is light. Therefore, our exaggerated person might have more difficulty detecting sound in a distance to its corresponding light image, versus that in a water environment. If we were to go into a soundproofed, insulated room with baffles, we would find the quality of sound quite different from that of a bare solid steel room. What I am saying here is that it takes a lot more knowledge of other laws governing sound than it does sight, but both sound and sight are affected by its environment or its relationship to other forms of matter.

We can go on and on citing some of the examples where the human senses can be deceived. Some of the most classic examples are: The illusion of striking a match in front of a person and then pretending to touch him on the back of the neck with a piece of ice. It will take a short time to distinguish the difference, but our victim will more likely than not swear that he was burned by the match rather than touched with a piece of ice. Another classic is to blindfold a person and ask him to bite into a piece of apple, but don't tell him it is an apple, and then put a raw union under his nose as he bites the apple. Again, the first reaction of the individual is to say that he is eating an onion.

So what have we just accomplished or proved? Well, I have really tried to show you that the human senses are subject to error and/or can convey false impressions to the mind. The senses can be deceived. What we have proved is that the senses are imperfect or are capable of error. This is the same argument that philosophy students are taught in their pursuit to find truth and a basis for right and wrong. The next thing that they are taught is that if the senses can be deceived and capable of error, perhaps there is a better way to discovering what is truth or what something really is, other than using the senses. Consequently, in trying to come up with a way to prove what is really true, right or wrong, they have taken several patterns or standards of limitations by which to gauge and measure actions.

Although we are primarily concerned here with a physical way of determining our reality of what is and is not, we are also interested with establishing a guide for morality. So what better opportunity do we have to review other forms of pattern recognition and behavior modes, than this. This is a sneaky way of saying that reality cannot be solely determined by using the physical senses. Therefore, I think we can combine our efforts here to correct or justify our search for, "Who am I?", and our reality. That is, at this point, we have pretty well determined that to discover who we are and what our reality has to do with all of this is a matter that involves mental thought which is of an intangible nature and that means that we must use our knowledge of relationships in a mental state. But, before we do that, we still must eliminate a lot of confusion about ourselves and the outside world. Therefore, in order to do this, I suggest we review other forms of thought known as philosophy that have been used and accepted through the years by man to control and direct his life.

The history of civilized man can be said to be a continuous search to discover truth and/or the good and proper life. However, truth in and by itself, is meaningless unless it is related to another body of thought. Truth represents a means to an end, a virtue to be pursued and it implies more than one possibility because of the laws of separation and opposites. Therefore, the justification of truth becomes a matter to be resolved. Man, being the ingenious creature he is, has established ways and means to approve and disapprove of these patterns or standards. Hence, moral philosophical standards for determining right and wrong, came into existence to justify or govern behavior.

Put in proper prospective, the church was the most dominate force that was used to guide man in his pursuit of a good justified existence. Therefore, the most common and popular standard used to determine truth, right, and wrong, was the theological standard. The main premise of this standard is that whatever God wills, is so. This is the doctrine's main premise. There are other supportive standards; however, all of these still require someone to interpret matters of conflicting interests. Naturally, I am over simplifying things; however, it is still a matter of human interpretation, which is also known as the authoritarian standard which was used by great kings and queens, emperors, and other types of totalitarian rulers of old. The only difference between these two standards is the source of the supposed standard, but interpretations are dispersed in the same manner.

In trying to prove the validity of the theological standard, one also encounters some additional difficulties. God is an amoral deity and should therefore be incapable of making moral standards. God could not be right or wrong, nor can he change anything which is considered right or wrong, because he is perfect. He does not make mistakes. That means, that if God were capable of determining right or wrong, which he cannot, there could not be any right or wrong until he commands it. Again, if he commands it, or changes anything, then he would be admitting he is imperfect, which does not fit the definition of God. Then again, if God could determine right and wrong, then he must have some sort of standard that is either understandable to humans or not. If it were understandable, there would be no need to appeal to God or the theological standard. If it were not understandable, how could anyone know God's will? It would be irrational for a human to know God's will; therefore, how could there be a standard? The theological standard must be assumed. To show right or wrong, one must already know what right and wrong is, and this is illogical.

Another basis for a moral standard is to appeal to one's own conscious. In this case, right and wrong are determined in the minds of each individual. Basically, this would be governed or controlled by an emotional response of feeling good or guilty on the part of the individual in regards to some form of action and he would avoid certain actions and seek out others. However, this allows each individual to determine his own right and wrong. But suppose there are two or more people who disagree on the proper action or what is right in a matter that involves more than one person? How would such an action be deemed either right or wrong? Who or what is to make the final decision?

Another problem associated with the appealing to one's own conscious is that such a standard assumes consciousness before an action. In our physical reality, there is little proof that this is so; in fact, the reverse situation seems to be more prevalent thought because our reality is based on a cause and effect relationship. An emotional feeling normally follows an action, not precede it. Therefore, the main premise of this standard would also be incorrect. Again, there is no way to prove or determine which individual was right or wrong in a case of conflicting interests. A system or standard based upon this premise might bring such a society more chaos than stability.

Perhaps one favorable standard is the appeal to customs and traditions which I discussed some time ago. In such a case, justification for right and wrong is based upon and determined by what has been commonly accepted as right or wrong in the past. With such a standard for guidelines, one knows before an action is taken, whether or not it is right. The only difficulty with this standard is how to resolve right or wrong when conflicting customs, traditions, or societies, come together. Such a standard is also somewhat rigid and may not cover all possibilities. That is, what happens when a question arises which has never happened before, or what happens when a custom or tradition changes? One cannot prove if an action is right because it is customary, or if it is customary therefore it is right.

The appeal to nature is yet another basis for a moral standard. However, in this case, one must first choose from at least two principle meanings of the word; then, which meaning of nature to appeal to and follow. In one sense, it means all the powers existing in either the outer or inner worlds and everything which takes place by means of those powers. In another sense, it means not everything that happens, but only that which takes place without man, or the conscious or subconscious actions of man. In the first meaning, Nature is a collective name for everything which is and is not. In the second case, it is a name for everything which is of itself, or what it ought to be.

The reason that makes nature attractive as a moral standard, also makes it unattractive. To do what is natural and to follow the examples of nature is attractive. However, nature, in the first sense, means nothing to man; because, man has no power to do anything else but to follow nature. That is, all of man's actions are done through and in obedience to nature's physical and/or mental laws. Man is but an extension of nature in this case. In the second case or definition of nature, the belief that man ought to make or follow the actions of things and creatures of nature is also irrational and immoral. It is irrational because all human actions whatsoever consists of altering, changing or improving upon the spontaneity of nature for his benefit. It is equally immoral, because anyone who endeavors to imitate the natural course of things whenever and however he felt the urge to, would be accused of being one of the most wicked of men in his society.

As far as my knowledge goes, all moral standards attempt to describe what is, or they try to establish a basis for right and wrong on an absolute condition or rule. Even the laws of nature don't do that. You would think that by now, man has learned something here on earth. Moral rules are exceptionless and supposedly designed for universal applications regardless of circumstances. You would think that by now, everyone would know that moral rules conflict with one another and cannot be proven unless an artificial authoritarian source can be endowed with the power to make those decisions. This is also our case of might makes right; however, being civilized, we would naturally be giving up our own rights in the interests or benefit of all mankind. Just remember, man is considered imperfect and limited; therefore, it is impossible to have a situation of no exceptions in a world based upon separation. Therefore, it is impossible to have moral rules, because no moral standard based upon rules can be proven to exist without laws allowing for change.

To establish a standard for determining right and wrong, one must avoid an absolute condition in order to avoid conflicting rules. A moral standard must be relative to customs, traditions and circumstances, and be capable of being understood and known to all so that everyone would know what to avoid and be allowed to pursue that which is believed good. Unlike rules, principles are general in character and do not tend to conflict with one another like rules. They do not admit to exceptions, but do vary independently with one's actions. Hence, if we are to have a standard, it must be based upon a principle rather than a rule.

Perhaps one of the best well known and received principles is that of utility, otherwise known and called, "The Greatest Happiness Principle". Its popularity stems from its relative simplicity. Basically, the principle believes that nature has placed man under the dominance of two forces. One is that of pleasure, and the other is that of pain. Nothing can act in and by itself as a motive for man but the thought of pleasure and pain. To denie this force will only demonstrate and confirm it.

Supposedly, every action is approved or disapproved in accordance to the happiness of the party whose interests are in question. When the interests of many are in question, that which is right becomes the sum total of those whose interests are in question. Therefore, right would be that which brings the greatest happiness to the greatest number of people. In this situation, or standard, everyone is obligated to perform that act which results in the greatest total balance of pleasure over pain in the long run or foreseeable future. One of the problems associated with this standard is the collective collaboration to inflict pain, suffering or hardship on other minorities of people. Supposedly, the association of the word pleasure assumes a position or condition of good or intended good doings even if it inflicts hardship on a minority. There are other principles and motives for moral standards that reason why an act has been done, but it is only this principle of utility that reasons why an action might have been taken to begin with.

Besides the logic of the principle, one must also explain the value of pleasure and pain and also how to measure it. In this case, pleasure is the end result which the principle advocates. It is the instrument and its force which determines right or wrong. The value of whether an action is right or wrong will be determined according to four circumstances; the intensity of the pain or pleasure, its duration or length of time it lasts, its certainty or uncertainty of its becoming a possession, and its frequency of its coming into one's possession.

There are two other circumstances to be taken into account when the value is a property of an act or event by which pleasure or pain has been produced. These factors are: the ability of the event to be productive or its chance of it being followed by sensations of the same kind, and secondly, its purity or chance that the event will not be followed by sensations of the opposite kind. Because these last two conditions are not properties of pleasure or pain itself, they should not be considered a value of pleasure or pain itself but may be thought of or used as a means to an end.

The greatest happiness principle is logically sound. It has no major faults, but it can become involved with a question of semantics and it can have opposing right and wrong within the same community on a specific action; however, the overall premise is good. It is not too unlike the democratic process based upon the rule of the majority. The biggest problem lies in the interpretation of explaining the values of pleasure or pain. As a principle, it is general in character and universal in application. I will reserve further comments until we have reviewed some of the other principles that can be used to determine and control behavior and will come back to this same principle in a slightly altered form later on in this book.

The principle of asceticism is almost opposite that of utility. This principle has a tendency to diminish the happiness of an individual and allows or approves of every action only in a direction of decreasing one's happiness. The premise of this principle is based upon the idea of self denial and self discipline. A kind of punishment possibly based upon the concept of original sin, where the individual assumes the posture or position of being unworthy of any form of pleasure or material gains. A servant of an unmerciful, vendictive God, if you will. This principle does not allow for any way to regain happiness; however, I believe the principle assumes that prior to an action, one is happy and either the action reinforces that happiness or takes away from it. Naturally, you can see that I do not fully understand this principle nor do I believe it to be a serious consideration on anyone else's part either. But it does oppose the greatest happiness principle, and that is why I include it.

The principle of sympathy and antipathy is similar to the greatest happiness principle; however, this is not by design. This principle approves or disapproves of certain actions, not because it adds or subtracts from one's happiness, but merely because it must set a precedence or guidelines for others to follow. There are no sufficient grounds or reasons for this principle, only a matter of expediency. Consequently, when enforcing this principle, one is apt to err on the side of severity. Basically, this principle is based on one's emotional feelings and/or those who are the leaders of that group or society, or those who are given authoritative control. Therefore, the guidelines depend upon who is in control of presiding over that community. If one hates little, he punishes little. If one hates much, he punishes much. If one hates not at all, punish not at all.

Antipathy has often been considered just grounds for action, because it composes parts of governing systems that are in existence today. Antipathy can be the cause of an action which is intended to produce good, but this does not make antipathy a right ground for action. Antipathy can never be a right ground for action, no more than can resentment, which is nothing more than a modified pattern of an appeal to nature or what is natural.

So, where do we go from here? Logic tells us that what makes a moral principle attractive as a standard, also makes it unattractive. That's because moral principles are not solely dependent upon the nature or class of an action, but are characteristic of something else and can vary independently of that action. Therefore, a moral judgement based on a principle is not judged only on an action, but is a reaction to an action and its relationship to that particular society or group. Consequently, one can have an action considered wrong at one time and right the next time, or it is also possible to have two different people do the same thing and have one person's act declared right and the other person's act declared wrong. That's because beliefs of a society, affect the outcome of a moral judgement based upon a principle.

The problem of this kind of flexibility is that few, if anyone really knows what is right or wrong at any given time. In order to have a stable society, one must be aware of the guidelines or rules of that society. Even if everyone should agree upon a moral principle, is that still a good basis for an action to be either right or wrong? History has proven on many occasions that this thought is not always correct. Remember our example or definition of good and bad and its relationship to that of Adolf Hitler's idea to purify the human race by exterminating the Jews.

So, here we are. Back where we started. We have reached a point using our outside physical senses and mental powers to try to achieve some absolute condition to determine right and wrong. In each case, of all known possibilities to this author, there is no sure way to come up with a reasonable standard to determine right or wrong beyond all doubt. We have come close, but no cigar! If we were a hermit and lived by ourselves with no contact with other humans, anyone of these standards might have worked and be justified. That is because, we are the controlling force that makes it work. In a society or culture, many interests conflict with one another; therefore, it is in everyone's best interest to achieve a good, fair and workable form of moral behavior guidelines, or standards. However, in our explanation of our physical reality, we know that we exist in a form of separation and this separation is reflected in many tangible and intangible patterns and thought forms.

Although no moral standard can be proven, one must exist, if we are to function as a society or group. To deny the existence of a standard would be totally false. However, what is the basis of such a standard? Perhaps this problem or absence of a reasonable answer is the problem facing our legal judicial system today? Perhaps what is right is might, or at least whoever is in control of our appointed institutions. As in the case of our physical senses maybe our mental abilities can also be deceived. Maybe nothing really exists at all! But if that were the case, then I wouldn't be writing this book nor would I be concerned with the problem of morality. A chain of proof or starting point must commence somewhere. Yet, it would be wrong not to admit to anything as true which one cannot, after sufficient reflection, doubt that what one senses is not in fact, true. You see, nothing really is, but it has to be. That is, nothing can be absolutely proven to exist, yet at the same time, no one doubts that it does not exist. Existence is a relative thing that seems to grow out of human necessity, but could possible exist in another state of consciousness.

Let me explain that confusing paragraph another way. Let me take you back to classic times in Greece's Golden Age and to one of the great founders or foundations of modern Philosophy, Rene Descartes. The story of Descartes is interesting in itself, but I am more interested in his thought process which seems to answer our problem above. Rene grew up in a period of unrest and confusion among learned men of his time. Sounds familiar? Anyway, he didn't know who was right and who was wrong. So he set out on his own to determine right and wrong for himself. What he ended up with, is something entirely different. Descartes' thinking is quite simple and yet is quite profound.

To begin with, Rene had as many doubts about the outside world as perhaps you and I. In any case, he too arrived at the fact that the physical senses were deceptive; therefore, he relied upon his mind as the basis of discovering the truth about himself and the world. To discover what was really true, he then ruled out all knowledge of the outside world that he had learned from other human sources and empirical knowledge. Lastly, he tried to eliminate all knowledge and/or information derived from dreaming. From his logical process of elimination and rejecting of all knowledge and information about the outside world, he could still reason that in fact, he was able to reason or think. Therefore, this desire to reduce himself to nothing, ending in something. This was the only thing that could be proven beyond any shadow of doubt. This truth, "I think, therefore I am", was so firm and sure that everyone could accept it, and it still stands today. No one can deny it as being absolutely true and beyond a doubt.

Looking at this statement in a little more detail, Rene rationalized that he could imagine that he had no body, and that there was no world nor any place that was tangible where he could reside, but he could not imagine for any moment that he did not exist. (To be completely and properly rational on the part of the reader, insert "I" in place of the underlined "he".). Just the mere fact of doubting indicates that I am something and that I must exist. He also concluded that he was a substance whose whole essence or nature was only to think, and which to exist, needed no space or material things. Therefore, this person, who I am, this ego, this soul, by which I am what I am, is entirely distinct from that of my body. That also means that to think, I must also exist. I think; therefore, I must be something.

From this premise, Rene, expanded his thought to the mere act of questioning. After contemplating that he had doubts, he concluded that he must be imperfect. Because to know was a greater perfection than to doubt(Here we are dealing with opposites and separation again.). But from something that was imperfect, meaning himself, from where did this thought of perfection come? Naturally, it must come from something more perfect than himself. This thought of perfection could not come from nothing or himself. The only hypothesis left was that this idea was put in his mind by something that was more perfect than he was and this thought was truth, or in one word, God. To this, he added, that God knew of the imperfection or separation of man and provided for a means of communicating recognition of needs, wants, hopes, desires, thoughts, etc. Therefore, he, or man, acquired all that he possessed from God and by a relationship or through use of what I call the learning triangle.

Therefore, reality grew out of necessity and limitations. That is, this reality is based upon perfections bestowed upon that which is and is reflected back to the receiver. (The recognizer, recognizes that which is, with recognition). Consequently, truth is a reflection that does not reflect doubt or imperfection. All those things which we conceive very clearly and very distinctly are true and is known to be true only because God exists and because he is perfect and because everything in us and around us comes from God. Any confusion or doubt about our reality must come from ourselves, because we are imperfect, not God. Therefore, it is evident that all truth and reality comes from within us and comes from a perfect and infinite being. However, we should never allow ourselves to be convinced about what is true except on the evidence of our inner reason, not our imagination or our physical senses. For reason does not insist that all we see or visualize is true, but it does insist that all our notions or ideas must have some foundation in truth. For it would be impossible that God, who is perfect and truth himself, would otherwise have given them to us.

And thus we return from whence we came. From unity. We are from one, we are of one, we receive from one, and we give to one, in a multidimensional manner. Yet, we are more than the sum of one's parts. We are past, present and future. We are, we were, and we will be. The selection and choice is of our own and his guidance. Pardon my rhetoric. I guess I got a little carried away. But the thought of unity is truly beautiful.

In case you are unaware of it, I have inserted some of my own thoughts to clarify that which Rene Descartes does so well on his own in describing this reality. My comments were few, so as to leave Descartes' thought patterns intact, or as near to it as possible. There is a specific area which I wish to bring to your attention that I believe could be improved upon; however, I did not want to take away from, or break Rene's logical reasoning process and/or have his thoughts misinterpreted for perhaps something that I am responsible for. Rene Descartes was a master and should be treated and respected as such. What I have done is to try to relate something that he wrote to something I wrote.

The area that I wish to address in more detail is his use of the word doubt to describe imperfection. In his explanation, he used this word basically to denote a form of limitation which was treated similar to that of a negative statement or response and not a desirable quality of human beings. If I am wrong in my interpretation, I stand to be corrected. However, if I am right, I don't think that changes the quality of his logical thought process either. That is, limitations, while being restrictive and/ or a sign of imperfection are neither good or bad in themselves. While it affects and limits man, it also forces or directs him in his growth process to pursue his return to unity. By creating barriers, man is encouraged to seek out and use his knowledge of both the physical and spiritual worlds for his expansion and growth in the direction of harmony and unity.

The reason for so much conflict and unrest in man is due to his inability to remain conscious of who and what he is. Consequently, man does not allow selection for those patterns or forces that work in a favorable relationship to unity. It is only when man works against the forces and patterns of energy that these barriers of limitation create experiences or physical sensations of pain, suffering, or sorrow. It is man's state of separation that motivates and directs him and matter to try to achieve a state of unity. That is, man unconsciously seeks to re-balance the forces of nature or matter to achieve a state of equilibrium or balance. This is similar to the principle of electrical charges and/or pressures; however, most of this selection process is based upon a super conscious state of non-linear reality to which most people are not conscious. We will get back to this later.

One of the most important things that you could have learned from all of the preceding is that you should and must question the obvious, instead of accepting that which is, or appears to be. Just like Rene Descartes. There are no experts or super knowledgeable people to whom you must honor or respect unless you feel that to be true or right from within you to respect that person with some form of recognition. There is no such thing as an expert, just as there is no such thing as the word best. What is it that you wish to experience? Do not be fooled by credentials of supposedly higher learning. Remember, you are a creature from two worlds. Half of all the information you get about this reality comes from within. The other half comes in the form of outside appearance and limitations. Therefore, by questioning, or learning how to question, you are in a sense regaining knowledge lost to you through a state of matter and resistance. In learning how to question, you are regaining the element of control and are therefore laying a new conscious foundation for a new reality of your own choosing. Not a reality chosen for you by somebody else.

Environmental conditions may exert forces of energy that control one's behavior, but it need not dominate one's life to a point of subservience to others. Balance is important in life, and complete obedience, or extremes without exercising a form of recognition to the element of control or the will of others is not conducive to either growth or creativity. Therefore, questioning provides the means for adjustments and changing relationships or patterns, as well as communicating the understanding of one's position in regards to the artificial element of control by others. In a sense, it defines the meaning of the authoritative sources and forces in relationship to your being. Questioning provides an outlet of creative growth within the confines of a particular controlled environment and lays a foundation for the natural progression for that element of control, by providing or referencing a position or relationship of the control factor and you. In short, by questioning, one is clarifying or indicating where the element of control is or should be in relationship to himself and/or others.

There is one last thing that I want to say about questioning before we move on to the world of intangible thoughts. It is interesting to note that the ancient's understanding of the word, doubt, stems from the word double and the number two, which we explained earlier. Anyway, the ancients defined the word doubt as the splitting of unity. That means that doubt is a position of separation and identification and that occupies the point or element known as knowledge in our learning triangle. That also means that the purpose of questioning is to seek, hunt, separate, and pursue a new point or position of understanding in relationship to the limiting extremes and opposites of that which is unity. Basically, we are talking about being consciously aware of how all of the separate parts add up and equal the whole, or possess unity. This is the whole purpose of the learning triangle and the understanding of balance and the positioning process. Questioning, opens up a line of communication that requires an understanding of points or positions in relationship to all those involved in the learning experience.

Questioning makes one seek an understanding of the relationship of yourself, your environment, and the desired end result or unity of purpose.

The sheer act of questioning makes one consciously aware of one's state of being (position) at that particular time. Therefore, the ideal situation is to become totally conscious at all times. That doesn't necessarily mean that you need someone else with you or present at all times, it only means that you require an inquisitive mind that seeks the answers that can only come from within or exist in another state of non-linear consciousness.

Each and every action should require the conscious understanding of the relationship of energy and resistance or the state of separation and opposites, in order to accomplish a positive creative form of action. This knowledge and consciousness is necessary because there is also the law of cause and effect that is the dominate force in the world of physical matter and it is this force which is set into motion when any action is taken on the part of any form of physical matter, be it living or non-living. Therefore, the conscious knowledge of separation and unity would be beneficial to everyone involved, and questioning helps bridge that gap to understanding the use of these energy forces and patterns and this in turn help us grow in the direction of unity.

I think that you should also be aware or cautious of all answers that are final. That is, growth is a constant sequential series of beginnings and ends that change or sets up new relationships that are constantly in motion, forming and reforming. This causes a form of growth and/or change of direction. That means that an answer that works today, may not be acceptable sometime in the near future. We are again primarily concerned with the reality of moral behavior standards. Again, you must look for the answers within. To accept ready made answers handed down by others is to cut off your conscious mind, even while you are supposedly awake. The answer may or may not be right, but if you don't understand why, then you are not doing yourself or anyone else any good. Questioning brings you closer to unity. <u>Acceptance is</u>, in a sense, <u>the giving away of your self control or control point.</u> You make your own reality. If you want to give it away, it is your business. But then, you do not or should not complain about a situation or condition that you have accepted. Again, you should learn to recognize patterns and relationships of understanding. Questioning is the means to re-balance a condition of separation or extremes. It is also a way to regain control of your conscious being or focus point.

Earlier in this chapter, we talked about various patterns of recognition which do not use the physical senses as the main element for determining what is. We also reviewed a number of standards used to determine right and wrong, and/or truth that could be proven beyond a shadow of a doubt. In this latter review, I believe, everyone could relate in some way to each and every standard that we discussed; however, we also discovered that no one standard could be completely proven and accepted as absolute or certain. Instead of finding that full proof standard, we found that truth and reality are only relative to the individual and God, which are the only two things that can be proven. That is, we have just proven again, that reality is a truth conveyed to man, through his ability to recognize certain patterns of limitations and to consciously focus in on these outer limitations through his physical senses and to mentally define these patterns. Again, man (the recognizer) recognizes physical manifestations with the recognition that they really exist by limiting himself to predetermined levels of energy. Truth is bestowed on man from within; therefore, reality is a relationship of one limiting himself to an environment and social order, which is a form of pattern recognition. The following poem kind of reflects these thoughts in a more dramatic way.

REALITY

No man is an island unto himself,
for if he chooses, he also loses.
One cannot know love or hate,
without first joy and sorrow.
One cannot relate to things which
one does not touch tomorrow.

Man cannot express,
that which he does not possess.
One must give in order to receive,
less one live, if only to be deceived.
To possess is to know,
and to know is to grow.

Reality is a matter of belief,
and belief is another form of matter.
Conceived and controlled by the unknowing, knowing mind,
that chooses and reflects that which one selects.
The problem of existence,
comes from a matter of resistance.

Alone, or in union,
there can be no conflict or confusion.
But separate and apart,
opposites are at the heart.
One must involve two,
and that is the clue.

The outer edges of reality bend and bump,
but they do not break.
Because the inner content shares and shapes,
that which we take.
We will choose and select that which we believe,
but we will experience that which is relieved.

CHAPTER 13

Consciousness

You may have noticed that I never did answer the question of morality or right and wrong in the last chapter. The only thing I did do was to prove the existence of ourselves, God, and indirectly physical reality. The issue or conflict of determining what is or is not in the intangible world of human beings was discussed, but was never properly resolved. We do know that questioning brings us back to unity and makes us knowledgeable of our other probabilities in our state of separation. However, we live in the world of physical reality and rely on our outer physical senses which are supposed to tell us about the world in which we live. Intangible matters of conflict cannot be detected, identified, and/or resolved using the physical senses. Therefore, the only thing we could substantiate was a relationship of truth to that of the individual, and this truth was based upon the understanding of one's own inner content.

In a case(s) of conflict, one is supposed to rely upon one's own inner self for proper direction or one's proper position in relationship to the matter at hand. However, as you already know, this may not or does not always work to resolve issues of conflicting interests. And this, I believe, is an understatement. Man is unique and one of his greatest achievements seems to be his ability to differ or conflict with his fellow man. Such a situation is inevitable or predetermined, because man relies on outward appearances and the physical senses that are designed to achieve greater forms or patterns of separation. Strangely enough, this concept is reflected back to man in so many ways that he should recognize them by now.

To understand our reality, we all know that where there is a single source of authority and control, there is an element of unity or a more unified group of people. It is only a diverse society, where the element of control is absent, that there seems to be more conflict and turmoil. This is neither right or wrong and can be considered an illusion. The patterns may not be recognizable and may require greater understanding and attention to detail. But this illusion is probably one of the main reasons why many countries and/or rulers so want or wanted to dominate all the peoples of the world, it was to put them under one unified rule or law of the land or world, if you will. Again, we see the motivation or the desire to do good, turned into a negative force or pattern.

Why is it that we as individuals do not tune into our inner selves for this truth? Why is it that conflict seems to be a way of life and cannot be avoided? Why can't we live in harmony with one another? Well, obviously, the reliance on outward appearances is a major factor. But, this explanation seems somewhat contradictory to our conclusion of the last chapter that basically says that the recognizer, recognizes its self with recognition and that recognition establishes what reality is. That means that there must be a deeper more complicated reason why man cannot understand or communicate with one another in a more positive, creative manner. The problem seems to be a matter of separation, again.

How then, can we have a situation of conflict, if we are possessed with the ability to relate to both worlds of physical matter and spirit? Separation, in this case, would seem to be a greater benefit to an individual in the world of physical reality. But, this doesn't seem to be true, and besides, how often have you ever heard of anyone actually saying that they rely or relied on their inner self for proper direction or truth? Either we, as individuals, don't know about our existence in both worlds of reality, or we don't know how to control or tap that inner source of knowledge and understanding. In short, it seems to be a matter of one's ability to focus in on one's self and to be conscious of that source of energy and power available to one's self. The problem seems to be a matter of consciousness.

It is difficult to talk and write and explain about something which is intangible and seemingly irrelevant. What cannot be seen, cannot hurt you, so the physical senses tell us, and this is the same philosophy that most people have concerning matters of an intangible nature. That is probably why there has been no serious thought or concern given to mental activities and/or patterning of the individual. Because mental thought is seemingly harmless, no one gives it any serious consideration, be it conscious thought or subconsciousness based upon non-linear reality. Just the same, mental thought requires the use of energy which is arranged in the form of a pattern or force of an intangible nature. Therefore, thought has a structural beginning and ending to it, just as that of physical matter. The only difference being is that thought cannot be identified by the physical senses.

People will find it difficult to relate to the idea that mental thought has form and structure, especially when they cannot see or sense it. Understanding the thought processes is one thing, relating the thought processes to a state of consciousness is quite another problem. In a situation like this, there is almost nothing to build on, other than the fact that we use patterns of forces for everything we do. So why not in the process of thinking. And this conclusion also brings us to another interesting form of thought. If energy is used in the process of thinking, then it is also used in the process of dreaming. Therefore, it is only a matter of one's ability to focus in or concentrate on the use of that energy and that is the element of control known as the conscious mind. That also means that there are levels of control or consciousness that the individual himself does not fully understand, or else he would not make the distinction between the waking and sleeping modes of thought. Consequently, that also means that there is a distinction and/or problem of associating just who the "I" is in "Who am I?"

Again, there is a separation within the mind, not just in its physical makeup, but also in its form or function. This distinction is commonly referred to in the term of consciousness and subconsciousness. The latter can be identified as a reality of its own because it is opposite the known consciousness. It must exist. Were it not to exist, we would have a lot of difficulty explaining this thing called sleep and other forms of altered states of being as well as instinctive responses and reactions. Yet, we still have some difficulty accounting for all of our subconscious and/or sleeping. That is, we can remember certain states of dreaming; however, scientists tell us that this state only occupies but a short time in an altered state of mind termed unconsciousness. Therefore, there seems to be yet other levels of consciousness that we can't even begin to speculate about.

Because one is usually not conscious or aware of himself, his surroundings, and the magnitude of the selections one makes on both a conscious and subconscious level, the tendency is for the individual not to believe that one is in control of his own self, reality, and/or his destiny. It appears this way because one cannot see nor understand his self and the selections he makes in relationship to the events that happen to his self, society, and the world about him. Things often appear disorganized and even chaotic; however, this only appears this way because the individual cannot see or identify the pattern or controlling force or forces within himself, just as he cannot identify himself in a superconscious state of being. It is because of this inability to identify specific relationships that the individual becomes confused and frustrated and a victim of his environment or predestination if he succumbs to his subconscious patterns of behavior, or so many think.

It is no wonder why man is so unique, so confused, and so disorganized, and is in a state of constant conflict in this physical reality. One's state of consciousness determines one's ability to deal with this physical reality. When the conscious thought patterns break down or don't work to achieve order and harmony of relationships, one loses his ability to control himself and his reality. He trades this level of consciousness for that which he believes will bring him to a sense of security and/or happiness. In short, he willingly gives the element of control to that of someone or something else in order to exist in a state of harmony and to benefit from that transfer of power or control.

If man fails to trade off this element of control, it is often taken away from him anyway by the sheer act of doing nothing about a specific act that affects one's reality. That is, if one's actions are not conscious to the changing patterns and forces that are in existence and affecting that particular individual and/or his reality, then one is not able to act or at least react to re-establish that element of control. In effect, in doing nothing, man has selected a course of action that is negative or does not contain the positive element of control in relationship to that individual. In this latter situation, one's own actions, or non-actions and behavior patterns tend to lose purpose, deliberation, and continuity. One appears to lose his sense of direction and/or position in relationship to qualities that he valued previously or experiences complete separation from his own inner self or consciousness.

In the latter situation, what the individual is actually experiencing is a period of change and growth that results in new patterns which have different relationships. Man must try to recognize new patterns and adjust accordingly. How well he adjusts determines his reality and a greater conscious effort is required to understand these new forces and relationships. The bonds and controlling forces are there; however, the new forces may be of a different pattern than those which existed before. Therefore, the individual may have to look harder, longer, and use more energy to determine and discover these new patterns. That means, that a situation that appears chaotic is not really chaotic at all. It only means that the patterns are not recognizable; therefore, a more proper definition of the word chaos would be "patterns of recognition that are not yet recognizeable.".

Naturally, that means that the ideal situation for an individual is form him to be totally conscious at all times. However, we also know that this is next to impossible, because the individual is not capable of recognizing himself within himself at all times nor should he. Such a situation or condition has never been known to exist; therefore, it is highly unlikely that such a condition could ever exist in this physical reality. To accomplish such a task would require a great deal of effort and energies which most people are unwilling to devote to matters of an intangible nature. Remember what you cannot see, cannot hurt you. Right? Also, to be conscious of yourself at all times will result in a relationship that is not conducive to a society or group environment. To be conscious at all times conjours up a picture of the great lonely wise man or guru sitting up on top of a high mountain contemplating mental thoughts, but doing nothing about them.

By using our explanation of the learning triangle and the explanation of one's position, it is possible to enlarge one's level of consciousness. This can be done by changing one's position in relationship to his point of balance within his environment. That is, by understanding the growth process and the learning triangle along with the concept of unity, one may be capable of greater understanding and peace than one ever thought possible. By understanding the inner content of one's self, one can raise one's level of consciousness and literally can grow by leaps and bounds. By understanding reality as a form of unity, one is able to break down the barriers of self limitation and rearrange the relationship of himself to all that is. By recognizing unity, one no longer is dependent on differences and separation as that which controls, but sees unity and oneness as a more powerful force.

By looking at the world as one, by seeing and seeking unity, one cannot help but increase one's level of consciousness. The world and/or physical reality will change right before your eyes, in a manner of speaking. In truth, it is you who are changing your position. It is you, who has finally found the element or key to controlling one's reality. It is the inner content. The recognizer, recognizing himself with recognition. You are more than you think you are. You are a part of all that is, God, and he is part of you. As one, you share all that is and is not. Consciousness is the ability to share this pattern of recognition. This is unity. This is love. This is what life is all about. You make your own reality and only you. It is only a matter of how conscious you want to be in a physical state of being.

The structure of the universe contains but one unifying element or pattern and this is the form of the tetrahedron. It's relationship to all physical objects of matter is the same. It is only a matter of consciousness or resistance that separates one form of limitation from another, and that is the element of recognition. Because of separation, one is not normally conscious of this form of recognition. Consequently, one restricts or limits himself to the recognition of patterns that have only outward appearances and uses to the physical senses. The knowledge and understanding of unity removes the restrictions or limitations of a physical form and allows the individual to go beyond the limits imposed by physical matter. In short, consciousness allows one to penetrate everything and nothing, it is only a matter of one's ability to focus in on that particular form or pattern of limitation. It is only a matter of what you want to experience. You make your own reality.

These are beautiful thoughts that I am expressing here; however, they are so far out of reach to the average individual that they seem impractical and impossible. Since we are or exist in a physical reality and identify or limit ourselves to our physical bodies, a utopia life of unlimited or even expanded consciousness is relatively unknown to all. We have lived so long in our restrictive environment that we have lost touch with our spiritual inner self, and we are not about to regain that knowledge and understanding of ourselves and our abilities overnight.

Remember, it has taken this civilization literally thousands of years to get to where it is today, be it good or bad, and it is not going to change that fast or quickly. The patterns have been set and are still very active and powerful forces that affect our lives. But, as we said in the beginning of this book, we must begin somewhere. We are constantly in search of new beginnings and endings in a limited sense. Now we have the opportunity to change even that.

As I indicated earlier in this chapter, many people will never, if ever, be aware of their conscious behavior, nor will they ever be able to raise that level of consciousness. Those who know the difference may not even want to. The reasoning for this form of apathy, other than not knowing the difference, maybe the thought that one might lose one's sense of spontaneity, or causes them to experience emotions with less intensity and/or feeling. One would rather, "Go with the flow", so to speak, or let their emotions take them where they may. Perhaps, I should take this time to demonstrate just what I mean in regards to this problem or concern of those who may be interested in this new approach to expanded consciousness.

The situation I am talking about is a kind of departure from the world of cause and effect. That is, I am suggesting that the individual now sees the world in an entirely different way and is not totally dominated by these causes and effects that take place in this physical reality. A simple example of this might be how one looks at a glass of water that is not full. Most people, who are influenced by patterns of speech and society norms, would say the glass is half empty. A much smaller group who thinks in positive terms, would say that the glass is half full. Our enlightened person, who is consciously aware of his environment, might merely say that it is a glass containing water. It is not so much the power of positive thinking, as it is a matter of understanding relationships, inner content, or unity. The question, is no longer a question, if it ever was one before. It is merely an inner and outer relationship that our enlightened person saw and communicated. He was not concerned with anything beyond those limits and he did not expect to gain or affect anything else. There was no value or relationship placed on the object in question. In short, one has eliminated or minimized the motive and emotional element from one's behavior. There is no commitment on the part of the individual for a direct relationship because the individual has chosen or selected not to relate to the object; therefore, there is no relationship and/or no experience.

As you can see, to raise one's level of consciousness also seems to raise one's level of indifference to others. It is like our wise man or guru sitting up on a mountain contemplating. This may appear to be the situation, especially to other people; however, it is really the confidence expressed in the knowing that the differences aren't as important as they appear. Anyone can take a negative or positive side of an issue and probably attract some kind of following, if he is sincere and professes his thoughts long and hard enough. But to emphasize the differences does not correct the situation as much as it separates all of those involved. Is that kind of energy worth it? Does it achieve anything constructive? Is it good, bad, right, or wrong?

The person who is conscious, knows the differences and the similarities, but he cannot offer a desired end result <u>unless he knows what one wishes to accomplish, or experience,</u> or unless there is a definite pattern which leads to a specific desired end result. This is like our explanation of our word best again and our wise man guru. One must first know what one wishes to experience, before he decides on a course of action. Consequently, our more conscious individual does not normally take sides on an issue and is not normally sought out for his knowledge and wisdom. Most people usually seek out those who will justify their thoughts and/or seek justification for actions to follow.

This justification is an action-reaction, or cause and effect type relationship where the individuals involved want a response that will in some way benefit them or to show others that they are in an agreement or a relationship that contains force or substance. Anyone who does not show a positive response or who shows indifference to a situation of this kind is viewed with suspicion and is usually ignored, no matter how supposedly intelligent that person might be. People tend to consider anyone who is not with them, to be against them, because they add nothing to the relationship. So, an attitude or relationship of indifference (as seen through the eyes of the other person only), is not considered an attribute, nor actively sought as virtue; therefore, it would seem that there is no trend or tendency for anyone to actively seek to awaken themselves consciously

WHO AM I? WHERE AM I? WHAT AM I DOING HERE?

and that is why our wise man guru sits mentally and physically alone on top of the mountain.

The choice or selection is up to the individual. You have a chance at a new beginning. You make your own reality. The fact that you make most of these selections in an subconscious state of being does not alter the fact that you are in control of your own destiny. So, the next time you hear someone complaining about things not going right for them, or they don't seem to go the way they plan them, and that life is hard, difficult, discouraging, depressing, or they tend to view most matters on the negative side, you better tell them to take another look at themselves. You or they are not a victim of your environment, unless you or they want to be. You need not experience life as a willing, or complacent collaborator to a predestined future of doom and gloom. You are not just some unknown stooge, acting out a real drama in a chaotic fashion. You are in control of your life, but the choice is really up to you. You can regain control of or over your life if you want to. The key or the control factor is the element of consciousness.

I have talked a little about this thing called consciousness and I have not taken my normal approach pattern of defining and then explaining this word. The reason why I took this approach to this chapter is both intentional and unintentional. First, I wanted to break up the routine and pattern of this book as an intentional way of showing you how intangible thoughts can have form and/or routine characteristics. Secondly, I also got carried away with a thought process and forgot to set the parameters of the word in relationship to its application within the context and limitations of this book. This is a polite way of saying that I was not concentrating so much on the foundation and basic fundamentals of communication, as I was on the desired end result. That is, I wanted to show you the effects that planes of unity have in affecting or not affecting one's behavior in our world of physical reality. Even though this was basically an error on my part, for failing to recognize the need for complete understanding, the whole arrangement of the inverted form works to show the problem of patterning and routines, and it shows you why routines are to some extent necessary and favored as a means to clarify limitations and to help and aid in one's ability to understand.

Perhaps, another reason for my delay in explaining this word consciousness lies in the fact that there are a lot of problems associated with this word. To begin, let's take the easy approach, which is the official definition of consciousness. It reads as follows: It is a state (position) of being aware, or being conscious of one's surroundings and what is happening around one's self. It is the totality of one's thoughts, feelings, impressions, and mental activities, of an <u>intentional</u> or controlled manner.

Now, you may have noticed that I already changed this definition slightly by adding the word position to clarify the word state. I don't think that many people think twice about this word state, and they really don't relate it to meaning a physical location occupying time and space which is both an *intangible position (time) and tangible position (space). State has a homely, friendly, kind of ring to it, something like an adjective that adds something to a noun type word. You know. It gets you from here to there, but doesn't add much in the process. Hopefully, this explanation will add a little something to our meaning of consciousness.

* I refer to both time and space as a position; however, time is actually tangible but it is somewhat abstract. That is, time is a reference point to the positioning of the movement of both the sun and earth. It cannot be isolated like that of the geographic location of space; therefore, I choose to call it intangible.

Although I have taken the official route to explain the word consciousness, there are still some problems that I think must be covered or added to that explanation. I would like to see the definition of consciousness changed to relate more to the specifics of positioning and/ or self determination. I would like to see some reference to indicate that: It is that state of being in which the individual maintains his position or point of focus in the physical world about him. The principle difference between these two definitions is basically in the use of the word focus. You see, in the latter definition, focus is the controlling factor that allows one to move his position of awareness through the learning triangle and it also regulates all incoming data. That is, the conscious point of focus assigns priorities in a conscious linear sequential order of importance to one's position and one's selections, or in relationship to the intangible learning triangle and that which one wishes to experience in the growth process.

Now, just because we have defined consciousness, doesn't mean that we are completely finished with it. Remember our planes of unity and the concept of balance sets the limitations and extremes of our consciousness. In this case, we are somewhat stuck with another problem. In order to get a complete definition of consciousness, we would normally look at the other extreme or limitation that is imposed by the word unconsciousness. But, in this case, we have still another word to contend with, and that word is subconsciousness. These latter two words are used interchangeably and wrongly to mean the same thing in many situations, but they are different. The common or proper form of speech to indicate the opposite extreme or negative of a limiting word uses the prefix, "un" meaning not; whereas, a word using the prefix, "sub" indicates a quality or position below or less than the positive limiting word, but not quite its opposite extreme. But again, through common usage and patterning of the individual, any word not properly defined and setting a limited extreme is usually interpreted to indicate the opposite negative connotation. Consequently, these words and meanings get used interchangeably even though they should not be. That's because they do not relate to the subject without proper support or qualifications.

To set the record straight, unconsciousness is supposedly a condition (position) where the individual is not aware of his physical self or senses and/or unable to control his state of being. This is a situation in which the individual is unable to focus his conscious thought processes in a planned linear sequence or orderly pattern of events relating to the sum of his thoughts and input from the outside world. Actually, we are dealing with a relationship of input to receptivity. It is like seeing or hearing something which can affect us, but totally ignoring it as not existing. Therefore, unconsciousness does not necessarily mean a condition of sleep, but can refer to a state of not being aware in a condition of being awake and functioning to other forms of input. In other words, this is a matter of priorities. Man can only act or react to just so much input that he wishes to recognize.

The word subconsciousness refers to a state of being (position) where the individual is also not aware on a conscious level, of his actions or thought process, or he is slightly aware of them, and therefore capable of some form of response either intended or unintended. Here we are talking about a basic action-reaction behavior pattern or actions of an automatic responsive type nature known as instincts. That is, the individual is more likely to react in a conditioned or specific predestined mode or routine. More often than not, the subconscious mind can be relates to matters which affect or threaten one's security, stimulates one's physical senses and organs, and may involve the use and exercise of energy in relation to the element of controlling an environmental condition. In short, the subconscious is more closely linked to the spiritual mind or super consciousness. However, this multi-leveled consciousness tends to recall learned patterning designed to protect the physical well being of the individual in a physical environment by quick responsive type reactions.

To explain that last statement, let's look at these three words again, in relationship to one's own being. Consciousness, and the subconscious mind take on both tangible and intangible forms of energy. That is, the state of being conscious or subconscious involves the movement and positioning of one's self in one's physical environment. Mental intangible thoughts are involved in these movements; however, the physical world of matter and outside appearances dominate one's thoughts. Physical reality consists of tangible matter that has greater density and force than that man's own physical body; therefore, one must consider and respect his environment. That means that man's movement(s) is one of the principal factors that occupies, influences and interacts with one's point of focus and mental processes that affects his behavior.

Contrary to the above, the state of being unconscious deals strictly with intangible forms of thought or energy, but at the same time, to be unconscious is to be in a state of super consciousness. That is, one exists in multiple unmanifested alternate non-linear realities and is capable of experiencing all those things that one experiences in physical reality; however, in the latter intangible world, one cannot be affected by physical matter as we know it and has no conscious knowledge of these relationships. Just the same, they exist, because thought has form. It is intangible and therefore it cannot affect a tangible physical reality through a direct relationship, or on a one on one basis. The intangible forces of the unconscious mind must be translated and/or transferred to the conscious physical world so that the point of focus can properly handle that input of data into a useable form of energy with which it can interact.

Now, I am slightly torn and confused here myself as to what to tell you next. I am not sure if I should tell you that unconscious thought can take two distinctive forms, or to wait and explain it in another way. However, since we are dealing with the unconscious mind I believe I should at least mention that unconscious thought can take on two extreme meanings. One is a negative form that is characteristic of inactivity of all life forces or energies, or the dominance of resistance that tends to harden or make an object more dense and heavier. In man, this unconscious negative force has the same effect, but it is hard to describe or tell someone about something that they have not experienced. To such people, there is no other way or possibility to expand upon one's physical senses or mental limitations. How do you describe the taste of a cherry or strawberry to someone who has never seen or heard of such an object. In this case, we are talking about a contrast that is even more drastically different and more dramatic than our example.

The other form of unconsciousness takes a positive form that is known as super-consciousness. In short, this is a contradiction in its self, because this is an extreme form of consciousness that is characteristic of a consciousness that is more awake and alert to more input than is that of a normal conscious person; however, here the vibrations are so strong or are at such a high level of vibration that one's own resistance cannot pick up or identify such patterns. This is consciousness is an unlimited reality of non-linear time. Really, this is not a form of unconsciousness; however, for lack of a better explanation, it should be mentioned as such, because it cannot help the individual in his present state of being. He is not aware or conscious of this other information available to him; therefore, in a sense, he is unconscious to it, hence, the use of the word unconsciousness.

If this book hasn't upset you yet, I suppose this is as good a point as any to really blow your mind. So here it goes. If you remember earlier in the book, I said that the structure of the universe radiates outward from a single point like a water droplet, atom or solar system. The limitation or final structure depends upon the amount of resistance that is encountered. But not all manifestations of life or matter are made the same way. That is, there are different degrees of resistance corresponding to a specific level of consciousness of the manifestation. In the physical material world of matter, there are four levels of manifestation which are: matter, vegetable life, animal life and human life. Each level of manifestation is characterized by its own degree of consciousness which is one octave of vibration removed from the next level of manifestation. To complicate things even more man himself contains three distinct levels and therefore manifests himself, or can manifest himself on all seven levels found in this physical reality.

In man, these distinct levels are not characterized by physical differences, but mental qualities. These four levels of man are: 1 - man, characterized by his intellect; 2 - genius, characterized by intuition; 3 - prophet, characterized by wisdom and universal love; 4 God-man, the last is the highest degree possible in this physical reality and is characterized by omniscience and omnipotence. Although there are seven levels, there are various degrees within a level; therefore, the amount of separation is relatively unnoticeable. Also, there are occasions where a crossover is possible; however, this statement or distinction is based upon an overall average that man displays in his behavior.

Let's take a look at these conscious levels of manifestation in more detail. Matter manifests itself through the conscious form of expansion and contraction, or the cooling off, or hardening of matter. Plant life also displays this characteristic, but has an additional quality that makes it different. Consciousness displayed at this level also includes the search for food, the taking of food, and the assimilation of food for growth. Animal life has all of the characteristics of matter and vegetable life but expresses its consciousness in the form of a body and mobility that allows it to seek out food, digest it, grow, and it also has a more developed emotional system that gives it instincts, urges, feelings, and desires. Whereas, man, on the four level, is characterized by all of the former; however, his biggest difference is his intelligence, intellect, or the ability to think. This is really the ability to recognize patterns and to apply his knowledge of relationships to the outside world of physical reality.

Man, on the fifth level, makes a substantial jump. That is, his consciousness lifts him out of the world of effects that stimulates man to react on the plane of causes and that allows man to be in control of his self and his physical environment. This is displayed or demonstrated in the form of intuition. With the help of his intellect and increased consciousness, he is able to communicate or transmit this intuition to his fellow man in the form of patterns or the creative arts. Most notably, in the arts as a musician, or composer, artist, dancer, writer, etc.

A person on this sixth level is still living in a condition of separation and must still seek satisfaction in the world of physical reality; however, this person expresses his consciousness from the inner knowledge of divine unity or oneness in the form of wisdom and universal love. Much more attention will be given to this matter of universal love later; however, this is a form of love that is always giving, never taking, needs no supplement, no physical manifestation and always radiates from the consciousness of divine unity. Such a person wants nothing, or to possess nothing, or anybody physically. Such a person feels one with the infinite, all there is.

The seventh level of man is the completely conscious man, the God-man. This is the most perfect manifestation of God in this physical reality. This is the highest form of consciousness that can be achieved here on earth. I know of no one that has achieved this status, nor do I expect to know of one in the immediate future. The patterns are just not there based upon western civilization knowledge. A God-man is a person who manifests God through his perfect consciousness or oneness with him. He radiates and experiences the divine creative forces in their primordial untransformed vibrations and frequencies and reflects that unity or patterns to others. This is the seventh level of consciousness, man exhibits the perfect balance of matter and spirit in this manifested form.

If you haven't noticed, we are again confronted with the significance of the number seven. This time it represents our spiritual levels of consciousness in this physical reality. Beyond these levels, God stands above all manifestations of life and rests within himself in absolute equilibrium without time or space. He is constantly radiating himself out into material forms or patterns in order to give these forms life which or consciousness. Nothing can exists without being in God and/or without God penetrating it. Every point of physical matter offers an origin that God may manifest himself through and everything that exists in this reality carries this point as its center within itself. From this point, there began its first manifestation, its creation, its fall from unity, and its resistance into our seven levels of consciousness.

All creations of the universe are based upon the principle of energy and life forces radiating from a central point. Growth always starts from the center and radiates outward, that's because the inner source of all power and manifestation is God. Every force on earth that is materialized has resistant strength to endure this radiating energy and this constitutes seven major levels of consciousness. God is everywhere present in every creature and he is manifested in countless different variations, because God reveals himself on every single level on which manifestation is possible. These forms of manifestation reveal only as much of God as each form can consciously experience and bare of the divine creative force, corresponding to its level of consciousness. Therefore, to consciously experience this force means being this force and simultaneously radiating it in all directions, including one's own body. Consequently, all creations, and the physical body too, must have an adequate power of resistance, or they would otherwise burn up, destroy themselves and/or return to its unified state or position of unity.

All manifestations of life and the matter that makes up those life forms, are composed of different degrees of resistance, corresponding to the level of consciousness of that life form. The chemical composition of the matter determines which level of consciousness or vibration of energy that that life form can support. The bodies of humans, in various planes of development, only appear to consist of the same matter based upon an outward appearance. However, they are actually composed of different chemical elements whose resistance always corresponds to the level of consciousness of the spirit that dwells within. That also means that the closer one gets to its center of being, the closer one will get to his own true self. The separation of one's self in spirit and matter also determines his behavior. That is, it is a matter of how conscious one is at any given time, that determines from which source or point of consciousness he expresses himself.

As you can see, we are talking about something like a split personality or multi-dimensional person; however, man being the unique creature he is, is able to move his point of focus enough to be able to concentrate on and maintain an identity consistent with his level of consciousness. But it should be stresses here that there are two distinct characteristics that make up one's being in this physical reality, even within the four levels of consciousness found within man. However, this distinction is more prominent at the lower levels. In actuality, this is the division of one's material self and one's divine true origin. Both exist in a state of separation; however, they are only separated by a matter of consciousness. To seek one's inner self, is to seek one's true self, and to be one with God. This is the only possibility for overcoming the state of separation and bringing back the consciousness into the state of unity. In this situation, the individual stops thinking about himself and instead becomes himself, and recognizes himself. The recognizer, recognizes himself with recognition.

That means, that right and wrong, good and bad, all come from one source; however, that source is not recognized with the same level of recognition that would be possible if everyone were on the same level of consciousness. That is, an action or situation is neither good or bad, until you relate it to something else and how you relate it depends on your level of consciousness. That also means that one's behavior is determined by one's position or point of focus in relationship to one's state (position) of separation or consciousness. And that, is what is so difficult about determining morality in a physical environment that uses outward appearances or forms of energy. It is also the problem of one's environment, society, and multiple patterns, based upon multi-levels of relationships and separation. Unless or until everyone can relate to an action or situation in the same way, there cannot be a consensus of opinion that the decision is correct.

So where do we go from here. Obviously one cannot throw up one's hands and say, "I give up!", "I don't care!" or "It doesn't make any difference anyhow". No! What that means, is that although right and wrong cannot be proven to exist in this physical reality, it must exist. We cannot all go our separate ways and hope for the best. This is a world of separation and there cannot be any harmony without an element of control that exists outside or inside of one's self. Knowing that there is no single tangible force or form of matter that exerts this kind of control, this force must be of an intangible nature. Therefore, any form, force or pattern, that exists that is intangible must be based upon the unifying element or belief in one, or God. Therefore, to have a unified world, one must believe in God. God is the first source of all truth and of all manifestations. In order to know and understand morality and the laws of nature, one must begin with God. However, in order to talk about God, one must try to understand that God stands above the recognizable world. That is, God can only be understood by God. Man can only seek the vibrations of higher consciousness that brings him closer to God or his origin.

The problem of a society and/or those leaders who are chosen to interpret the will of God, or this higher form of consciousness, is the fact that they may not recognize this higher form of consciousness; however, this does not mean that the individuals who make up this society are not themselves, subject to that same consciousness. Remember, it is only a matter of one's resistance that separates one's self from this higher form of consciousness. Therefore, it is this higher form of consciousness coming from an inner source that separates one's self from the knowledge of truth or right and wrong. One does not need an interpreter or someone of supposedly higher intelligence to tell him what to do. The answer lies within.

To do what is against the patterns of higher consciousness, is considered satanic or wrong. However, one's resistance may block out this knowledge and it is possible to continue on a course of wrong doing, without any significant restrictions or limitations imposed upon one's self by his fellow man. But also remember, there is this thing called position and balance that must be accounted for at some time or another, in this physical reality. That is, one's actions are neither right or wrong; however, they affect one's position within the learning triangle, One must eventually correct an inbalance in order to grow and to continue on one's journey in the best way possible to a higher level of consciousness and return to his origin.

To seek material gains or to seek the comfort of outside physical appearances, should always be viewed with suspicion; however, and then again, there may not be anything wrong with wealth at all. It all depends on how it is obtained. That is, it should not be gained at the expense or depravation of anyone else, either consciously or unconsciously. It should also be noted here, that under our new explanation of consciousness, no one is now considered unconscious of any and all acts. That is, everyone, under this understanding, knows, or has access to this information because we are all from one, we give to one, and we receive from one, in a multidimensional manner. It is only a matter of one's position that separates one from the truth or the balance of harmony and peace.

Tangible matter and intangible thought cannot exist without divine content. The whole three-dimensional world is built on this law, whether or not the form is considered inanimate or a living creature. If a person identifies only with his body and outside appearance of material wealth, then he is like our example of a cube that is opaque or that only reveals the characteristics of matter. A person who is conscious of this outer appearance only uses the knowledge of this form as a secure base upon which to build. That is, the inner contents or four inner triangles of the cube turned inside out, now form a pyramid. The symbol and structure handed down to us by the ancients who knew the differences. The pyramid is also the symbolic form of the God-man. A person of the seventh level who reveals his divine, selfless nature and completely manifests God on earth, but rules over matter and the body and is not a slave to the lesser needs of the unconscious.

While we are at it, I might as well explain the symbolic representation of the materialistic man. This symbol is the cross, which is composed of six squares laid out of or unfolded from a cube. On this cross, or "T", depending upon how you unfolded the cube, the divine self is crucified. A person who is materialistic or unconscious, is robbed of his power of his divine inner self. He is a victim or becomes the criminal who is crucified beside the divine one and is subject to laws of matter which command him to follow patterns or routines that satisfy only his needs to possess and exist or perpetuates himself. He is crucified on the two great beams of the three dimensional world which are expressed by time and space. A person who solely exhibits dependency on the outside world dies on the symbolic cross of matter. However, sometimes the pains and sufferings of even this lowly creature sometimes stir his higher levels of consciousness and resurrects him to again re-seek his inner true self. That is, he experiences his own salvation, because he recognizes himself in him.

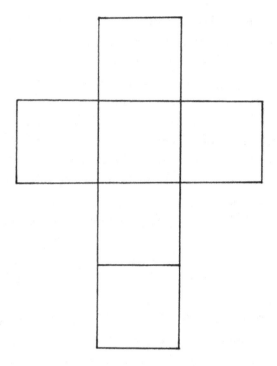

Cube shape unfolded to show shape
of outside manifestation appearance.
Illustration #6

Any resemblance to stories and characters foretold in this chapter are NOT purely coincidental. In fact, perhaps it is the other way around. Or is it opposite? Who knows?

CHAPTER 14

Beliefs

You would think that we have explored everything that is possible concerning ourselves and our physical and spiritual realities, and I guess we have; except, I want to make a special effort here to describe a form or pattern of intangible thought known as beliefs. I want to make a distinction here, because it is very important in the learning process and it probably affects one's physical reality and behavior more so than any of our rational logic concerning ourselves or our being. That is, we have been dealing with concepts that are stronger and more powerful than pure thought form; however, ideas and concepts are not as strong or as powerful as beliefs. As far as I am concerned, all of the reading and logic in the world are of no use in affecting one's thoughts and behavior unless they can be turned into beliefs. Thoughts are like our short beginnings and endings; whereas' beliefs are very long lines that are composed of thoughts or group of thoughts that form a conscious routine or pattern.

In order to begin this process of thinking about beliefs, I will again revert back to my original pattern of presentation. That is, let's look at the proper definition of the word, belief. A belief is stated as being a conviction that certain things are true. One has trust, confidence, and faith or accepts those things which can be identified as having a specific conscious certainty or truth about them. In a sense, by identifying an object or thing, one has separated it from a relationship and becomes a limitation of an artificial nature that has been created to isolate something from something else. It is a recognized form of matter or energy that cannot be broken down or divided further. It is a quality or value of inbalance that is unique unto its own self. It is limited and it is therefore, a belief.

Now the funny part about this is that a belief can also be a contradiction. That is, in the first sentence of explanation, we said that it is basically a conviction that certain things are true. Now that doesn't necessarily mean that it is based upon absolute truth or a divine origin. It only means that the person has to believe that it is true. That doesn't necessarily mean that it is right or in actuality, true. Nothing like being redundant and confusing. Anyway, I want to bring to your attention, that truth or beliefs can be of a false origin or satanic, in regards to perhaps, what should be.

I keep saying that you make your own reality. But I just want you to know, that reality is a matter of belief and beliefs are another form of matter controlled by the unconscious or super-conscious knowing mind. It is a problem of one's ability to relate or tune into that form or level of vibration. In another sense, beliefs are forms or forces of intangible unmanifested matter controlled or positioned by the conscious mind that is limited to certain frequencies expressed as wants and desires for the purpose of regaining some form of balance or continuity. Beliefs are nothing more than patterns of intangible thought that are in a state or position of imbalance and have limitations of consciousness in this physical reality.

Previous to this chapter, I have purposely stayed away from the use of the words, believe or beliefs, as much as possible in order to avoid additional problems. I also needed that time to build a better foundation for our bridge to understanding who we are, where we are, and continue our journey to discover what we are doing here. The reason for this avoidance is because beliefs are nothing more than limitations. Everywhere that I have mentioned the word, limit or limitation, you can also substitute the word, belief. Earlier, I felt that you did not have a sufficient basis to accept this thought form, but now, I think you do and can appreciate my deception or caution, in the use of this word.

Limitations of a mental nature are the extreme outer edge or parameters to which a person is conscious. Just for the sake of clarification on this word, parameter, it is a quality or constant, whose value varies with the circumstances of its application, as a radius line of a group of concentric circles which vary with the circle or item under consideration. I have spent some extra time here to explain this word in detail, because later on, it plays a very important part in our description of the actual thought process.

Anyway, these limitations are a form and force of the mental processes or parameter of one's point of focus. That is, the mental processes radiate out from this central point and encompass a sphere of influence, so to speak. These thought processes or parameters, also carry a value or intensity to them that make them behave similar to that of emotions! The closer one's point of focus is to a specific form of tangible or intangible matter, the stronger one's mental processes are both receptive to it and can radiate specific knowledge about its relationship to other matters or forms of matter for a desired end result. In short, one's ability to concentrate energy forces; act as a stimulus to that which is in question. This is a form of command or control of the Will and/or the movement of one's point of focus that is a product of the conscious mind in the form of offering recognition and that determines one's sense of direction and self control. Shorter yet, it is behavior. One chooses or selects what he wants to experience by consciously or subconsciously directing his attention or energies to that which is in question and hence, is attracted to an environmental position to observe and/or participate with recognition.

Now, beliefs represent the opposite of thought when it comes to intensity. Beliefs are very, very strong forces or patterns that are difficult to change or alter once they have been set into place or position, so to speak, and/or they are used effectively by the individual to control ones environment. Beliefs are so strong that they are no longer part of the conscious mind, but become part of the subconscious or super-conscious mind once it is accepted as truth. It is automatically engaged or utilized in a situation that falls within a specific sphere of influence or parameters by the movement of one's point of focus within the learning triangle. Therefore, beliefs are very difficult to change and are almost impossible to change in most people once they are accepted. Beliefs are similar to a computer program designed to perform a sequential series of short beginnings and endings that are bonded together to form a routine.

In a computer, the only way to get a different answer to what is programmed is to turn off the power and shut down the system. This is because a program can only give you answers that are already given to it. Garbage In - Garbage Out! Conversely, good information in - good information out!

To alter a computer program is a whole lot easier than it is to change beliefs in humans. Computers can be changed by just inserting a different storage diskette containing another program or changing an electronic chip and/or altering circuitry.

To alter a human belief requires a great deal of energy and effort and is often referred to as brainwashing. This type of reprogramming often produces results that are temporary. The only real way to terminate programmed beliefs permanently is through a process referred to as death. However, if one were to raise their level of consciousness, one could affect ones belief system in the here and now realm.

On their own, most people are unwilling, unable, or just don't know how nor do they want to change their consciousness and/or beliefs. They are content to go their own way and to live within the limits of themselves and those limits placed upon them by society, because they have learned to live or survive within acceptable limits. To them, that's all there is, so the song goes; however, at least the song asks a question, "Is that all there is?" Most people don't even ask. But isn't it strange that most people have a restlessness about them that they, themselves don't understand. This may be the pains of the crucified yearning to be resurrected by truth or divine origin of unity.

We have talked a little bit about this thing called thought, but if you weren't paying close attention to details, which isn't very hard to do when you are searching for a desired end result. I did that in the last chapter by changing my pattern of presentation of data and I passed by some very important forms of intangible thought that have a definite pattern to them. Thought can take many different forms; however, there are basically three different levels of intensity. The first level consists of random thought, or thought that does not have much force or energy and is of relatively short duration. This is thought, used in every day life, which is used in communications between people for the purpose of conveying a message concerning one's environment in relation to himself or a subject that is affecting him. Such thought is subject to great flexibility and diversity over a short period of time.

The second level of thought can be termed ideas and concepts. This is thought which is more complex or intense in nature and requires a great deal of energy and concentration on the part of the individual. This is usually done in some area of seclusion or isolation where an individual can get away from distractions. This environment helps concentrate or use energy patterns to move ones point of focus into other spheres of vibration relative to the object or subject in question. This is a conscious effort on the part of the individual to reach within himself or his higher self to relate to another level of consciousness. Usually, the time period is of greater length, in order to review all of the possible relationships or short beginnings and endings affecting that particular matter at hand. Therefore, this form of thought is a more in-depth pattern that reaches over more boundaries or areas of limitations that are imposed by random thought.

We have already talked about beliefs as the highest form of thought and have said that it was quite different from the other forms. Its primary difference is that it deals with the unconscious mind and cannot be controlled like our other forms of thought. Beliefs establish what is and is not. It recognizes those forms of energy that the individual wants to recognize. It establishes one's physical reality and environment. That is, beliefs limit the individual to see and/or sense that which is around him and that which he wishes to experience. Reality is a matter of belief, and belief is another form of matter, controlled by the unconscious or super conscious knowing mind. You make your own reality.

The subject or element of thought, occupies one of our points in the learning triangle called knowledge; however, as you can see by the preceding explanation, this thought form varies slightly from our original simple learning triangle, but it is still one and the same. However, to explain this new relationship, I will have to carry the planes of unity or spheres of influence, one step further. I will also have to re-explain the learning triangle in a new light. That is, since we have discovered multiple levels within this physical reality, we must re-explain the learning triangle in this new context of limitations. We have enlarged or increased our limits or parameters; therefore, we must grow mentally to fill the void and bridge the gap.

Using the model of an atom for an example of a comparable structure, we have a situation where thought or knowledge interacts with possessions and the individual similar to our concept of plane of unity. That is, these elements act or behave with different levels of force or intensity with one another. In studying the atom and the various physical elements, one discovers that the denser, heavier elements (thoughts) have a greater number of neutrons and protons at their central core. They also have a greater number of electrons circling about this core. These circles of electrons are determined by the amount or mass of its core. The electrons can have several distinct levels of orbit, again depending on the element involved. The more numerous orbits are normally found with the heavier elements. What is important here is that we have different levels of forces or energy affecting the point(s) of knowledge, possessions, and the individual, just as the atom is affected and changes its characteristics.

In reference to our point of knowledge within the learning triangle, we have already defined and separated three distinct levels of knowing in relationship to one's point of focus. These levels are in the order of their importance or force that they exert on our supposedly physical awake being and these are thoughts, concepts, and beliefs. In reference to the point called possessions, these three levels must be described as: security, physical sensations, and the exercise of power or control over one's environment. In reference to the individual, we have the 3 basic levels of consciousness. All together these points or elements take on a completely different shape and interaction when the individual uses his will and/or, to seek a form of balance or unity within himself.

I just want to take some time here to remind you of the levels of possession here. It has been some time and you might have forgotten a little. Security deals with self preservation and the concern with food, shelter, protection from physical harm and the protection of man's property and personal possessions. The second level of force deals with sensations. This has to do with any act that stimulates the physical senses of sight, touch or feelings, hearing, smell and taste. This level can also be separated and broken down into specific acts dealing with happiness or pleasure and pain, and personal possessions that comfort and affect the senses. I suppose I should also say that happiness also includes sexual stimulation.

The last level of force in our possessions element has to do with the exercise of power and it becomes a little difficult to discern this level at times. Basically, this exercise of power or energy is not utilized until after the other levels or forces of possession have been satisfied and are no longer of a threatening or determining nature. You might say that once one has mastered the other obstacles, he seeks to occupy himself with the control of energy itself. In this case, this primarily has to do with the use and exercise of wealth, or one's position within a specific group, and/or for the purpose of perpetuating one's name or reputation.

Most of these people actively seek and like using or controlling power over their fellow man; however, there are others who by virtue of themselves, command a following and respect that allows them to control a great deal, mainly by default, or an ability to communicate at a subconscious level. Interesting enough, this latter situation is somewhat like the physical positioning process that I alluded to in the selection process. That is, one finds himself the center of attention and is actively sought by all in that particular group and that puts him in a physical position similar to the manifestation of intangible thought.

Our explanation of multiple levels has now changed our learning triangle into another form or shape which is similar to the tetrahedron with our learning triangle forming the lines of its base and the three levels of intensity reaching up to a central point of total consciousness or unity. That is, each element has three stages or steps up the side of the tetrahedron before it becomes one and the same, the recognizer, recognizes it's self with recognition. There is no problem here of comparing this new shape to the pyramid, because we are not dealing with time and space; rather, we are dealing with intangible forms of matter or energy forces. This new structure points the way back to unity and these various stages or levels are the markers or milestones that point the way back and/or set the parameters of new growth and development.

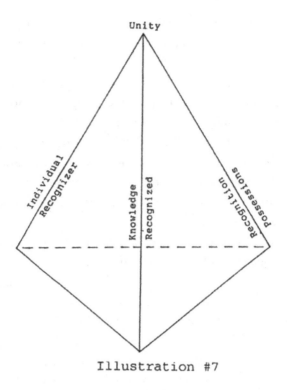

Illustration #7

For your benefit, this illustration depicts a visual structure of the learning triangle and the planes of unity that becomes the tetrahedron. Remember, these are technically invisible thought forms or structures of an intangible nature. Also remember that we are illustrating a three dimensional structure on a two dimensional media; therefore, our circles or planes of unity become spheres of influence that have parameters of ever increasing consciousness. That means that you have nothing to lose and everything to gain by trying to use energy to seek and/or regain your own true origin. You are more than you think you are. You are only limited by yourself. The choice or selection is up to you. But remember, these planes of unity are always interacting and trying to bring you back onto the path of your own true self. You must take an active conscious role in trying to help yourself. You make your own reality.

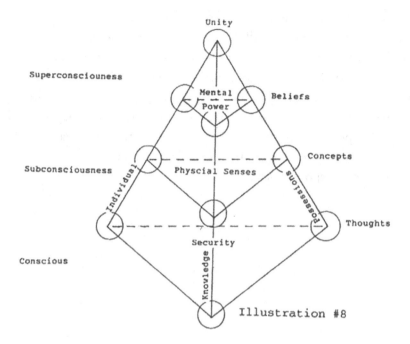

Illustration #8

Let's stop here for a moment, before we go into the technical aspects of consciousness to show or illustrate just how the thought processes work in relation to affecting and controlling one's behavior. Our earlier explanation of planes of unity and position in relationship to one's environment will just about complete all the work that we can do on the subject of behavior in this world of physical reality. The following diagrams will show you how to manipulate or control your behavior and/or how to modify your thinking processes in order to make your own reality. These diagrams also give you a structural pattern of intangible thought forms, as well as a formula to understand behavior and hopefully greater happiness

I say hopefully, because there are no guarantees that you will ever be able to or want to overcome some of the environmental conditioning processes that cause you to respond and react, rather than seek and enjoy total free will and/or happiness. Knowing the answers, does not necessarily assure you of greater happiness. Remember, value is something that you have to work for or expend energies in a relationship to some form of recognition. Happiness is a value that cannot be gotten without some effort on your part in some way, shape, or form. You must give in order to receive. Happiness is the recognition of unity or one to all there is. The amount of effort and energies you expend determines what you experience. Also remember, you must still deal with an environment that is relatively hostile to the concept of unity or oneness. We are involved in a world of physical reality that encourages separations and imbalance; therefore, it is quite easy to regress into comfortable patterns that may result in limiting extremes and they must therefore, also involve pain or unhappiness. In fact, our explanation of the diagrams that follow, indicate that there is a greater chance at unhappiness than there is for happiness unless one takes full conscious responsibility for one's life.

```
                          DIAGRAM # 1


                       Normal Conscious and
                      Subconscious Behavior


Spiritual Subconscious
                  Step 1 Position (Mental)
                         Positive - Negative

                  Step 2 Knowledge - Unity
                         Unmanifested non-linear reality

                  Step 3 Recognition
                         Focus Point
_____
Level of Consciousness - Distinct
_____

Consciousness    Step 4 Wants and Needs (Emotional)
Mental Level            Positive - Negative

                 Step 5 Evaluation (Understanding)

                 Step 6 Selection (Choice/Experience)

Physical Level   Step 7 Position (Mental)

                 Step 8 Environment (Physical)

                 Step 9 Focus (Time & Space)

                 Step 10 Patterning (Cause and Effect)

                 Step 11 Limitations/Beliefs
                         (Energy & Resistance)

                 Step 12 Reality (End Result)
Detail
 of
Step 11   Likes ..................Dislikes
(ACTIONS)       /\                    /\
               /  \                  /  \
         Want   Don't Want     Want   Don't Want
          |         |            |         |
        Positive Negative      Positive Negative
Detail    |         |            |         |
 of       |         |            |         |
Step 12   |         |            |         |
(RESULTS) |         |            |         |
      Short term Disappointment  No Effect Disappointment
      happiness  Suffering                Short suffering
                                          or brief happiness
```

225

DIAGRAM # 2

Modified Spiritual
Conscious Behavior

Spiritual Subconscious
                Step 1 Position (Mental)
                     Positive - Negative

                Step 2 Knowledge - Unity
                     Unmanifested non-linear reality

                Step 3 Recognition
                     Focus Point

Level of Consciousness - Fluctuates

Consciousness
Mental Level   Step 4 Preference (Recognition of Balance)

                Step 5 Evaluation (Knowledge of Unity)

                Step 6 Selection - more balance

Physical   Step 7 Position - more balance

                Step 8 Environment

                Step 9 Focus

                Step 10 Patterning

                Step 11 Limitations/Beliefs - more options

                Step 12 Reality - Greater Happiness

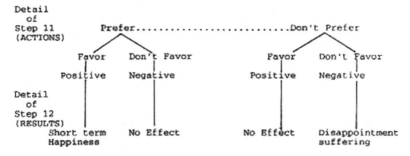

Detail
 of
Step 11   Prefer.........................Don't Prefer
(ACTIONS)

        Favor   Don't Favor   Favor   Don't Favor

     Positive   Negative   Positive   Negative

Detail
 of
Step 12
(RESULTS)
   Short term   No Effect   No Effect   Disappointment
   Happiness   suffering

DIAGRAM # 3

Spiritual Conscious Behavior

No Distinct Level of Consciousness

Spiritual Consciousness

        Step 1 Position - Unity

        Step 2 Knowledge - Unity

        Step 3 Recognition
               Focus Point

        Step 4 Unity (Balance)
               Manifested

Mental Consciousness

        Step 5 Evaluation

        Step 6 Selection

        Step 7 Position

Physical Consciousness

        Step 8 Environment

        Step 9 Focus (LOVE)

        Step 10 Patterning

        Step 11 Total Consciousness

        Step 12 Reality

No details: Actions and results are based upon unity.

So there you have the shape of things to come, or at least that of physical reality. The learning process never stops, hence the statement, things to come. The selection of the conscious process is the system that offers the individual a choice and happiness. It is also the process in which unity and oneness is the direction which one must eventually know and understand to proceed in discovering his own true self. The diagrams only serve to illustrate the form or structure of intangible thought in the world of tangible, denser forms of energy. These diagrams also relate to the issue of morality as well as a search for who we are, where we are and what we are doing here. These visual aids should just about verify the facts that good, bad, right and wrong, or any other limiting word, is a matter of position and a relationship of patterning to consciousness. Therefore, that means that limits exist only for the purpose of providing direction and/or balance in one's journey through life and what he or she wants to experience. As one's level of consciousness increases, one breaks down the barriers that separate one's self from everything there is and one automatically knows unity and happiness.

Now, I hope that most of you are not offended at the revelation that life is pre-destiny to reach unity; however, that isn't necessarily good or bad, it just is. This should not affect you to any great degree; however, I hope it does. I guess what I am trying to say is that I do not want you to abandon all of your existing values and cash in your chips, so to speak. It is expected or hoped that the patterns started in this book will hopefully produce or achieve perhaps some new beginnings and create some positive endings. Remember, thought forms precede physical tangible possessions. Before physical reality can change, thoughts must change first and then you can change physical reality, because you make your own reality.

You are in control of your own destiny. By being consciously responsible, you control your own destiny by selections from multiple unmanifested non-linear realities. You focus in and relate to things which you want to experience. You have learned the limitations that have been imposed upon you by physical matter and the relationship that society and cultural heritage has transmitted and transferred to you. You cannot ignore these limitations nor can you break free of these limits altogether, nor should you. Such a departure from routine or patterns, would probably cause more harm than good initially, but there is a need of a new beginning or a more conscious knowledge of your reality in order to grow in a more positive creative manner.

We have reached a point where the results of our labor are about to pay off or take shape. Don't blow it now! Remember, thought is basically intangible and you cannot drastically alter thought patterns or beliefs that have taken years to manifest into reality. Don't forget, people are creatures of habit, and it takes many, many years to change habits. Anything of value or valued, requires work and effort. You get out of life what you put into it! Changes mean new patterns and that requires the use of energy. Routines are comfortable, reassuring, pleasant to those who have mastered them, and they don't require any new uses of energy.

To drastically change the habits of a great many people, would require expending great quantities of energy and time to master new patterns; therefore, it would also create great forces of stress and negative thought that will stop or impede growth of some individuals unless they are conscious of themselves. Enlightenment is supposed to be just that. That is, it is supposed to lighten the load through the use of energy forms for the purpose of returning man back to his true origin. Unless he is consciously willing and able on his own, he cannot be forced into new patterns that disrupt his existing lifestyle. Force or the violent use of energy is never justified because it separates that person or thing from its environmental relationship(s) which offers a form of resistance and/or security.

When it comes right down to it, this matter of resistance is the major cause of pain and suffering. It is also typical of any form of life that recognizes outer appearances and separation as the basis for any life. The reasoning for this is because people relate to opposites and/or extremes, not unity as the basis for life. Unfortunately, we relate best to this world of separation than we do of unity; therefore, sometimes we get carried away even if we have the best of intentions. That is, we get carried away with an end result and forget about who, or how we affect others. Take Adolf Hitler as an example again. His original thoughts and intentions were for what he thought was the betterment of all mankind; however, his method for improving the physical genetics of the races was by eliminating the Jews, which was definitely wrong and detrimental to each and everyone in the world.

Now, you probably think that conflicts based upon misunderstanding of good intentions, is no longer a problem anymore. No comparison you say. It can't happen again, you say. You better take another more honest look at this matter again in a more objective point of view or position. Rather than to mention something of a more current nature that might be controversial and stimulate the emotions and creative barriers, I will only say this, I believe you will find more pain, suffering and destruction has taken place for supposedly good and right reasons and under the name of God, than all of the supposedly evil and selfish people combined. That's because evil or selfish people hurt themselves more than they hurt others. Their focus on personal gain and possessions do not normally generate the destruction that good does. In essence, what I am saying is that violent or extreme actions are never grounds for justifying good no matter how supposedly good the good cause is. If good inflicts severe pain and suffering on other people even under the guise of protecting the peace, then it is not good but satanic or bad.

As you can see by our diagrams of behavior, the sequential steps of all these systems are basically the same. Only in diagram # 3, do we rid ourselves of the subdivision and separation that causes disappointment and suffering, but again the steps are still the same. It is only a matter of consciousness that separates us from one another and everything that is. Only in the third diagram, is this element of control returned to the individual. It is my best guess that probably ninety - eight or ninety - nine (98-99%) percent of the people of the world behave or react to most situations based upon the diagram # 1, which is primarily based upon outside appearances. Possibly, one or two (1-2%) percent may control their actions based on diagram # 2, but this may not even be on a consistent basis. I know of no one that has achieved diagram # 3, but I wish I did. All of this doesn't mean that levels of consciousness cannot be raised at various times to achieve the modified or super-conscious level, but as I said before, it is probably not on a constant basis. This is somewhat of a shame, but it isn't that much of a surprise either. Remember, one seeks comfort with that which one is familiar. The tangible physical world is a manifestation of separation and limitations designed to bring spirit to matter and it is also designed to bring one back to one's own origin.

There is one thing that I want to point out in the diagrams, if you haven't already noticed it, and that is the percentage of pain and suffering in diagram # 3. This should tell you something about our behavior and world right away. In short, with a rise in the level of one's consciousness, there comes a significant level of happiness. There is also a noticeable decrease in the role that the emotions play as consciousness increases. This is because the control of energy is understood and channeled by the individual to more positive ways or more creative results. This doesn't mean that one will become financially wealthy or respected by all others, it only means that he is in complete control of what he wants to experience and/ or accepts responsibility for himself. One learns and experiences universal unconditional love.

The average man (man on the first level) can only experience vibrations above or below his level of consciousness as an emotional condition which in actuality is a relationship to unmanifested reality. That is, the physical senses perceive a relationship of the highest frequencies of universal love and the lowest, or those of ultra-matter, as hate. Naturally, the more one gets emotionally involved without being conscious of his position, the greater is the imbalance of his energy forces; therefore, the greater chance he relies on outside appearances and that has to involve greater separation and selections that bring him negative forms of pain and suffering.

It seems so strange, but humans seem to relish or almost delight in the fact that we are so negative. This is demonstrated by the following summary diagram # 4. When it comes right down to it, most humans select pain over pleasure at least fifty (50%) percent of the time. I am not sure why humans adopted and developed this pattern of selection over that of the modified conscious or super-conscious method of selection; however, it looks like we are stuck with it for quite some time. Naturally, this thing about identifying with outside appearances has a lot to do with it, but I also think that our societies and institutions also had a hand in it. I'll explain this shortly; however, I just want to point out that there is so much more to gain from seeking unity than one can possibly imagine. Remember, what you have never experienced, you will never know what you have missed. Or is it?

DIAGRAM # 4

Summary of Behavior Diagrams

Percentages of Pain vs. Pleasure

	Pain	Pleasure	No Effect
Diagram # 1	50	37.5	12.5
Diagram # 2	--	37.5	62.5
Diagram # 3	--	100.0	--

I suppose that most humans just don't know any better than to select courses of action that have been demonstrated by their parents and fellow humans. This is what is accepted or handed down from generation to generation. People seem to naturally accept conscious negative feeling. They have been conditioned and mentally indoctrinated for so long and so often, they have come to believe that they are not responsible for what happens to them. They actually feel and think that they are inferior human beings and look for or expect to be exploited in some way, shape or form. That is, they have been taught to look at the tangible physical outside world and material wealth as that which everyone should seek as their main purpose in life. In effect, what is happening is that they are indirectly creating belief patterns of dependency or artificial needs which others may then be able to exploit, both mentally and physically.

This attitude or feelings of inferiority, has also lead to a lot of people to think that they are unworthy and/or don't deserve a good life; therefore, they actually seek the negative side of the materialistic world. To these people, I will say that humility does play an important part in life; however, if you believe in God, you must also believe in balance. Humility must be balanced out with self confidence or the knowing that you are a part of God and he is a part of you. That automatically means that you must know or feel that part of you which is manifesting God's will. Don't let other people tell you what you are feeling or should feel. You make your own reality. You are responsible. You don't need somebody else to tell you what to do or how to feel. You are somebody special and you have a lot to give and giving will radiate that part of you that God and you share, and this will open up your conscious mind. It will not or may not bring you material wealth, but it will bring you peace and happiness.

Negative thought patterns are not exclusive or just a problem in western society. It is reflected in all groups of people throughout the world; however, our society seems fascinated by it. That is, our society almost seems to idolize it. This can be seen in the popularity of a wall poster or phrases called, "Murphy's Law". For those of you who aren't with it or haven't seen them, there is a poster whose main claim to fame deals with the idea that, "Whatever can go wrong, will go wrong", plus other negative variations on this theme. This isn't the only form of popular negative thought. We have whole institutions and professions built and established around the teachings of negative thought forms.

Here, I know, I am going to get into a lot of trouble and controversy. Therefore, I feel that I must preface my examples with this statement: Negative, unproductive thought forms are those forces which do not add to the growth or expansion of an individual in a positive creative manner. That is, they are forces of pressure that create barriers that tend to increase one's limitations to a point where the individual is reduced solely to unconscious behavior patterns that are reflected in routines of a subconscious nature. In negative terms, man is reflecting a relationship of matter, or one's environment, rather than that of spirit and the concept of unity.

I am sure that even these last couple of statements won't help me any with those people who are involved in the following institutions and professions. Therefore, I might as well jump right into it. I am referring to the institutions known as hospitals, insurance companies, lawyers, police and the professions of doctors, dentists and any other professions or institutions dealing with treating or recognizing negative forms of energy. Again, I must emphasize that here I am referring to the indirect encouragement or enforcement of negative thought. The actual services rendered are not of a negative nature; however, even the positive forms of help, supports the negative selection process by providing positive reinforcement to a detrimental negative thought form. In more simple terms, an individual gains support or recognition from these people and institutions, by just their presence. That is, they are being recognized as being the center of someone's attention and are being encouraged to interact with a negative belief system in a positive creative manner. This is similar to that of an actor playing a part or role in a real life drama. If he plays his parts well, he may be able to continue on playing and may even receive some award or attention for his effects. The attention or benefit to the patient or actor is highly questionable, because that reward may be the loss of physical parts of his body and/or health, loss of money, loss of freedom, and the ultimate academy award ....death.

Now, I know I have just upset a lot of people out there, but I think I may have also gotten a lot of attention. Just remember we are dealing with subconscious thought forms here which are intangible; therefore, it is extremely difficult, if not impossible, to relate to what I am saying. Instead, what will probably happen at this point is that those people who are greatly offended, will generate a lot of negative energy themselves which will manifest itself in ultra matter known as hate, and create impenetrable barriers to anything more I have to say. This stimulating of emotions must involve the generating of energy and that must be manifested into physical reality someway. You cannot ignore the negative manifestations of our physical reality; however, you do not have to support them either mentally or physically.

I suppose I could have presented these thoughts in a less dramatic fashion; however, sometimes shock stimulates one's thinking process. What I am saying is that the shear recognition of professions and institutions which are designed to treat ailments encourages people to use or frequent such services. Their physical presence means that they are going to be used. There is a relationship based upon good intentions to help one another. Man relates to the outside world of tangible matter and is comforted by the use of these energy forms; therefore, the more these services are provided and encouraged, the more that they are going to be used and this reinforces a form of negative thought making it easier to manifest supposed negative symptoms into physical reality. Remember, thought precedes materialization. The mind, especially the unconscious knowing mind, is a very, very strong energy source and the thought of recognition does funny things to people. In fact, you might say that people will actually kill for recognition, either themselves, a president or in some relationship whereby they get a few minutes of attention, fame or glory.

Now, if any of the previous negative thought forms have upset you, I'm afraid I have to upset you even more. We have talked about some negative thought forms that affect, or can affect an individual. What about a whole society? What I am referring to here is the support of a standing army or military power. What about the energy built around this negative form of thought? What about all the negative tangible forms materialized into destructive armaments, especially nuclear armaments? Just the mentioning of this negative force upsets me and I do not want to give any more reinforcement to this thought form than is absolutely necessary. But to also quit and ignore this negative force will not make it go away. We must generate another form of negative force to rid ourselves of this danger. As in math, two negatives create a positive. Hopefully, we can in some way, correct this balance of forces before it is materialized or used for that which it was intended.

Because of the emotions tied to the previous examples of negative thought forms, let me touch on yet another example of negative thought used in everyday life and living in a complex industrial society. To do this, I want to draw on my own experiences I encounter in dealing with manufacturing industries. Because of my position or closeness to the subject matter, I may be a little biased and subject to generalizations which may or may not be true. This is just a word of caution, before I proceed to explain how we are conditioned to think in terms of negative patterns. In this case, I want to deal with a hypothetical situation which I believe most people can relate to.

Let's say that a manufacturing company has a piece of machinery that has broken down. What do you think is the first thing that comes into the mind of those concerned? If you say, get it fixed, I think you will probably be echoing the sentiments of the majority of the people. But have you ever given it any thought to why that is the first thing that comes into your mind? It is probably because the machine is part of an existing routine or pattern that has been established and accepted as a necessary function designed to bring order or balance to productive facilities and personnel that support and perpetuate the organization involved. That is, the company is dependent on that machine for what it contributes to an end result that has a tangible material value.

This is probably the thought process that most people would subconsciously generate as an answer to the problem, or it might be a little more involved. Such as, it could be rationalized that material or physical objects cost money to make and to buy or possess. In this particular problem related to the company in question, it also cost money not to make the product in question. That is, the time not working by fellow employees means money or material objects not being made and/or both. So the common denominator to nearly all industrial problems relates to money, and/or patterns that involve money.

I am not saying that any of these thought processes are wrong. Again, like so many examples before, they just are. What you want to experience makes the difference. Money happens to be the motivating patterns that control most people's lives and selective processes. In the last example, money takes on the outside appearances of time, labor, material, facilities, overhead costs, and the cost of doing business and other factors, such as profit and then some. This example can be a negative form of thought process lies in the fact that money should not be the sole reason for the decision to fix the problem. That is, it should not be the reason to put back into operation a piece of equipment that is a possible hazard to anyone involved with the machine or end product if it is knowingly creating another possible danger for the sake of making more money. Objects or things should not be made for money, but for what they can add to the lives of those involved. Naturally, money needs to be involved, but it need not be the prime motivating force behind the selection processes involved in this example and unfortunately, this is the case in most situations that I have seen. There is a lot of greed out there which is perpetuated knowingly, but mostly, unknowingly, because of man's relationship to matter or material things.

Again, our whole society is fashioned around outside appearances and material wealth. That doesn't necessarily mean that it is good or bad. The problem seems to lie in the subconscious mind. Few people are aware of this thing called unity and are completely fooled and motivated to seek happiness in material wealth. Unity is completely opposite or contrary to everything in our life. There are no role models or patterns established to make this thought form known; consequently, it is not a motivating force as is that of money. We do not give out academy awards or honors to people for demonstrating or seeking unity. Any awards that are given out are given out under the name of good will and are usually linked to that of a particular person or act and/or deed, not for the concept of unity or oneness. This doesn't mean that this thought form itself should be the sole pre-occupation of all those involved either. Remember, you live in a physical reality, but you are spirit born unto matter; therefore, a balance should be sought between the two worlds. However, and unfortunately, the world or spirit and unity are not recognized in a world manifested out of physical tangible matter.

I hope these diagrams, examples and explanations, have helped you get the gist of things. It is relatively simple; however, it is sometimes difficult to get here from there. Our reality exists in a state of balance. It exists, but it is hard to see a forest through all of the trees. Basically, in this book, I have torn down all that we have lived with and have become accustomed to, no matter how just or unjust it might have been. We have all learned how to live with, get around or use different energy forms, in our daily lives and this physical reality. These forms create patterns and they do serve a purpose whether or not one is conscious of them. They are landmarks and they provide direction and possible growth. To abandon these energy forms, without knowing why and without having other conscious alternatives, is not a positive form of growth. The diagrams will help you on your way, but remember, you do not serve anyone any good, if you yourself do not know why you are doing what you are doing. The more conscious you can become in your thoughts and actions, the more happiness and joy you will bring into your life and the life of others.

We have just about concluded about all we can in discovering who we are, and where we are, but we are little better off than when we started out. I have presented you with another concept. Hopefully, you will make this a part of your own reality and make it a belief. In knowing more about yourself and your reality, you can help bridge the gap and continue your journey to your origin. It is difficult to relate to intangible thought forms and they are not easily accepted as proof in a reality based upon tangible physical matter. However, the concept of unity is strong and can stand by itself. We have no tangible proof of its existence and no way of knowing for sure using one's physical senses. Let's try to do something about that. To become more conscious of this true reality, you must ask questions until you have satisfied your own inner self. Then, you must act responsibly upon this knowledge in a more positive manner based upon the belief in unity.

That is, if you pattern your selections or behavior on an expansion of one's consciousness, then there is no doubt that you will find the intangible. You will find the happiness, and the joy that only unity and God can give. The recognizer, recognizes itself with recognition.

In a more poetic form, this chapter may be condensed to look something like, "A Thought About Thought". However, the answers cannot be found in a physical reality unless you know where to look.

A THOUGHT ABOUT THOUGHT

There exists in this world, objects and concepts.
One exists that can be seen and assimilated by our life's senses.
One exists as a mental state of being, unseen and free of form.
Yet, one is as real as the other.

A concept is the action of mental images in a state of becoming.
Concepts are thoughts, ideas and beliefs.
These are all thought processes of intensity.
The stronger, more intense the quality of thought the greater the reality.

A thought is a concept of low intensity mental activity.
Thoughts are both random and planned conscious activity.
Thoughts are both voluntary and involuntary activity.
Thoughts are the basis of our everyday consciousness.

An idea is a concept of higher intensity.
Ideas are a more creative forms of thought.
Ideas are thoughts of longer duration and concentration.
Ideas are the basis of progress or advancement of our world.

A belief is the highest form of a concept and intensity.
Beliefs are the most creative form of thought.
Beliefs are the least understood or controlled form of thought.
Beliefs are the basis of this reality and are responsible for our world of
physical objects.

Thought concepts form the world around us.
These concepts are all products of the human mind. Or are they?
Can the mind make, manufacture or produce thought?
What is the true nature of thought? Or, what is thought?

Suppose that there was a definite, tangible quality about thought.
Suppose thought were composed of material not unlike that of the atom.

Suppose thought were composed of an electromagnetic energy unity of a multi-dimensional nature.
Such an energy unit would not be identifiable as we know it.
Such an energy unit could exist, be unseen and yet, have form.

Energy units of this nature would tend to group themselves together with similar or alike qualities.
Almost like atoms, such units would radiate out and encircle the origin of its stimulus with lessening intensity and value.
This law of behavior would be subject to constant changes, dependent upon the value of the mental nucleus, originating source, or inner self.

If mental thought or concepts were composed of such a structure, then thought as we know it, would not exist.
In this structure system, the mind would not be originating or producing thought, but rather tuning in and receiving thought.
In this structure system, there would never really be new thought per se, but newly recognized or received thought.
The nature of such a reality would be determined by what a person wanted to recognize or receive.

Throughout the ages, we are told that man is given the choice of free will.
But, has anyone really explained what this statement means?
Suppose that statement really means that man has the choice of receiving that which he chooses to accept as real.
Suppose that choice or free will meant the choice of accepting a concept dependent upon inner self or mental nucleus.
The result of such a selection would determine the quality of one's life, the values which surround him and that which he chooses to receive.

There exists in this world, objects and concepts.
The difference is a matter of thought and intensity.
Thought received is thought conceived.
Man chooses his own personal reality.
There is a world beyond and life is not forgone.

SECTION III
WHAT AM I DOING HERE?

Balance

CHAPTER 15

Opposites

In the last chapter, I explained how thought patterns affect your behavior. I also showed you some diagrams which outlined specific models of behavior that control one's mental routines. If you were paying attention, you may have noticed that I never did say much about the 5th step of evaluation that is a major step prior to selection. That is because it is a transition step that combines all the elements of the learning process to the individual in a relationship of balance. That is, evaluation is a value process that assigns certain varying degrees of intensity or stimulates an act and/or end result. Again, this is either a conscious or subconscious intangible thought form that is dependent upon one's position within the learning triangle or the tetrahedron and this position depends upon one's consciousness knowledge of balancing physical reality and spiritual reality in both linear and non-linear time.

In order to explain this question of balance a little better, let me refresh your memory of our behavior diagrams. In diagram number one, I said that normal conscious behavior was affected by wants and needs, caused by actions and reactions to stimulus. In the modified behavior pattern, that step was replaced by preference regarding wants and needs which involves a more deliberate evaluation of a man's higher conscious nature. In the super-conscious behavior pattern, this step was listed as unity, which is the understanding of balancing needs and wants and the knowledge of conscious relationships in both linear and non-linear reality. In all of these instances, we are dealing with a matter of consciousness and balance or the ability to understand one's self and his environment through conscious recognition. That is, it is the ability to recognize the forces of energy and resistance and to act and/or react to a state of imbalance. The position or distance and the intensity or value of one's point of focus in relationship to the desired end results is the controlling factor of determining one's behavior and this must involve the question of conscious balance.

The ability to recognize imbalances determines how one behaves and is the most important factor that affects the way in which the individual makes his selections. That is, how one recognizes his self and his environment usually determines what his wants and needs are going to be. It is not a simple act of well defined limitations or beliefs, but is a continuous ongoing situation of shades of gray, so to speak, depending upon what you want to experience. You have a choice. You make your own reality. However, more often than not, you select patterns that you are familiar with; therefore, not being exposed or not possessing the knowledge of balance and unity, one normally seeks the world of physical matter and separation as that which is desired and is subconscious to one's basic nature.

This last sentence is probably an understatement. It is so important, that I can't emphasize it enough. How you recognize your reality, makes the difference which determines your behavior and personality. Pattern recognition is what makes you behave the way you do and to select those actions above those of others. That is why life appears and/or can be predicted in a predestined manner. The thoughts patterns are there. They are intangible, but they are there just the same. You become attached to certain patterns and they have value to you; however and again, these intangible patterns have subconscious relationships depending upon how you attach the value or worth of the desired result and this is simply a matter of balance. That is, you can utilize energy and resistance in such a way as to achieve a physical tangible end result; however, when it comes to an intangible result or goal, the manifestation is more difficult to achieve and discern consciously.

If you are inclined to see the physical outside world of matter and use the physical senses of the body as the only sources from which to draw your limitations and beliefs, then that is what you are going to rely on and relate to. It is also then likely that you will surround yourself with tangible forms of energy or material wealth and possessions as your only proof of your reality and that will be just about all you will be consciously able to experience. That is, you will comfort yourself with that which is familiar to you and that comfort or familiarity will tend to limit your beliefs or define the parameters of your consciousness. All of these possessions then become symbols of your reality and you will actively seek these possessions or will be engaged in some form of behavior that is designed to bring you those symbols of your reality. In this case, you may become addicted to these symbols and this may cause you to see your reality as a matter of wants and needs that must be filled in order to be satisfied or happy. What is really happening is that you are limiting yourself and your beliefs and/or you are severely restricting your form of growth and expansion. In short, the beliefs of the individual must be balanced, even though they may not necessarily be based upon a sound or true basis of what life is all about. What that means is you cannot obtain wealth and happiness solely from material possessions.

It is a matter of one's environment and conscious recognition that controls and influences one's selections and consequently, one's behavior. What you think you may need or want, is not necessarily what you really need or want. It is only a matter of one's point of focus or balance within the learning triangle that determines how a person will act or react. This behavior is similar to how a weather system works in nature. That is, air movement is controlled by air pressure and the rules that govern physical reality say that the greater mass dominates and tries to fill the void of the lesser mass or pressure. The greater the mass difference, the faster the movement. Naturally, there are countless other examples I could have used; however, this one seemed simple and easy enough to understand. But, I just want you to know, there are all kinds of examples and comparisons happening out there in the outside world that is of great value in understanding the learning triangle. It's just a matter of your being conscious of it, recognizing it; and understanding the proper relationship. Nature is a great teacher.

Getting back to the subject at hand, I want to make sure that you are aware of the fact that if you use something that adds to or stimulates your being in a positive way, then that something creates or causes a want or need that can become a necessity should one want to avoid the unpleasantness of being without it. That is, certain tangible physical substances can be used by the individual that creates changes in one's mental and physical being and that causes a type of addiction problem based on pleasure or pain. Indirectly, you can call this a form of greed; however, once the changes take place, the individual becomes unconscious to the matter of balance and the need actually becomes a dependency. It is something that must be sought or else its absence causes discomfort and possibly, mental and physical subconscious reactions of an uncontrolled nature.

I suppose at this point, I should compare this problem of addiction to that fashionable subject of drugs and other substances that induce hallucinatory or altered states of being. If you recall, way back in Section II of this book, I spoke to you of two different classifications of people. These groups were either Dionysian or Apollian. The Dionysian were those people that actively sought the use of drugs and other substances that could eliminate the natural boundaries of separation between the physical and spiritual selves. It is also interesting to note that we still have this type of separation or classifications of people today, however, now it is more of a mixed environment and not an isolated culture. The characteristics of people really don't have much to do with our subject of balance, but it may indicate that people or groups of people may be becoming a little more balanced in their behavior patterns. I don't know if this is good or bad, but there does seem to be a trend toward a more diverse, tolerant, and separated people, based upon more common lines than existed before. That is, the group has grown bigger within and the divisions of people seem to be getting closer together or overlap more.

Again, I must beg your pardon for getting off the subject of balance, but perhaps this is another subconscious effort on my part to change the thought patterns or presentation of the information. It may not lend itself to easy reading and understanding; however, it sure does get one to think about balancing behavior patterns and relationships. In fact, perhaps the best way to explain about balance is strictly by example, so here it goes.

Let's talk about the simple act of walking. Easy enough you say. What can be so difficult about walking? Well, try to tell that to a new born just trying to walk for the first time. Man's first attempt at walking is an entertaining and hilarious act to behold. You might often wonder if the child will ever learn to walk and also wonder why he continues to persist on trying, considering all of the falls and negative feedback to the senses. I can't answer you why man does it, but I can explain and tell you how man learns to walk. It is simply a matter of control and balance.

Man learns how to walk by deliberately putting his physical body in a controlled a state of imbalance. By the use of energy and resistance, mainly in the form of contraction of muscles, man puts himself in an out of balance condition to that of the gravitational forces of the earth in a pattern or a controlled rate of fall. The amount of imbalance that is utilized by the individual determines the speed at which the individual travels, or gets from here to there. Interesting, isn't it? Walking is a controlled rate or pattern of fall or a designed condition of an unbalanced body in a controlled or balanced situation. Maybe there is a clue here.

Remember what we said about physical reality, way back there when we were talking about separation and unity. In order to have a physical manifestation, you must have a condition or the splitting of unity, which is an unbalanced condition. That is, in order to have something derived or created from nothing, you must have an unbalanced condition. Unity is an unlimited condition of everything and nothing, and in order to have that something, you must also do something else with that nothing. They are opposites of the same thing. You cannot have one without the other; however, you can have both if you know how to control the relationship or balance of the patterns. You can get here to there, not by walking, but by controlling your state of mind and tuning into that level of vibration which you want to experience. There are no barriers, except those that you want to see. You make your own reality.

Now I know that last statement is hard to relate to, even I have difficulty with that relationship. I understand it, but I have never experienced it; therefore, I find it difficult to believe and that doubt causes a barrier that I cannot yet penetrate. That may be the trouble with most people and this book. It makes logical sense, but we have never experienced nor heard of anyone who has managed to cross over the barriers of physical matter. Even if someone had been able to make this transition consciously and come back, would anyone actually believe him? I think the answer to that question might come out to 99.9 percent of the people would not believe him and that alone might account for no one admitting to such a feat. Again, that doesn't mean that it is impossible. It only means that most of the physical human beings on this planet are at the fourth level of development and are not yet ready to advance to the next higher level. That is, we are all still pretty well hung up on this thing called physical reality and/or matter and we can't recognize its opposite, and that's because no one has convinced us of its existence in terms that can be understood by people who are trapped in a pattern or physical manifestation form of separation. Why should we believe in something that we cannot see? What we cannot see can't hurt us, right?

How do I answer a question like that? I think I am my own worst enemy here. I suppose the best way to answer that question again is to continue my pattern of logic and let the book answer itself. That is, we have to continue on a path of growth that asks a lot of questions and deals with our current limitations that we now know are imperfect or incomplete. To be incomplete, means that we are out of balance. If we were complete, we would be in a state of balance and would not be seeking something else. Man is a restless creature and is constantly changing and creating that which is about him, in order to comfort himself and to provide for his wants and/or needs. Now, we have made a complete circle and have ended up with wants and needs again as a situation that is caused by a condition of imbalance. The only logical answer to our question of our physical reality must lie in an intangible spiritual reality or unity. That is, we must exist in a state of balance with a physical pattern or structure and to also exist as spirit, possibly during a period called sleep. There are just too many relationships, not to believe in a dual reality right here on earth.

Again, that might be interesting reading and great for party and late night conversations, but what about right here and now? What can I do now to put this theory or knowledge into practice? Well I guess that that is a tough question too. The simplest answer to that question is for you to become more conscious, but that is somewhat impractical. Consciousness involves the knowledge of unity which is intangible and hard to prove. The next best answer to know anything about unity is for you to look at physical reality and separation as a clue to what unity is all about. Separation involves opposites or extremes and by evaluating these opposites one can determine something about unity. Knowing the existence of opposites is the first step in becoming more conscious.

To help you on your way, let's look again at some more common uses or practical applications of this form of evaluation process known as balance.

Remember in our diagrams, evaluation is the second conscious step in determining one's reality. It is a necessary step before our selection process and it is also a major factor in determining one's behavior. Evaluation is nothing more than a situation of determining balance, or how much energy to use in a relationship to a particular environment. It is fairly easy to determine or evaluate the application of energy where physical tangible matter is involved; however, it is a lot more difficult when it comes down to intangible thought forms, because intangible thought forms precede physical manifestations. Since this is the most difficult area to understand and discern, let's start here.

To begin this explanation, I would like to acknowledge and recommend another book called "Initiation", by Elizabeth Haich. Her book is considered occult or new age, but don't let that deter you. This is an interesting autobiography that involves mental growth and expansion beyond the limits of physical reality. Most of the following information is based upon Ms. Haich's description of mental enlightenment given to a privileged few, the initiators who sought their true origin and/or selves. The logic, beauty understanding, and love expressed in this book is well worth reviewing.

In Elisabeth Haich's book, "Initiation", she mentions twelve sets of opposites which you must learn to control or balance in order to improve yourself and your level of consciousness. I am not absolutely sure that this is all there is; however, they are so general, that they may in fact constitute the summation of all such intangible thought forms. In any case, let's review them for what they are worth. They are as follows:

keeping silent - talking
receptivity - resistance to influence
obeying - ruling
humility - self confidence
lightning-like speed - circumspection
to accept everything - to be able to differentiate
ability to fight - peace
caution - courage
to possess nothing - to command everything
to have no ties - loyalty

contempt for death - regard for life
indifference - love

Besides demonstrating the virtues of balance, these sets of opposites are also used by Ms Haich to demonstrate the verification of right and wrong actions, or in her words, what is divinely inspired and what is satanically evil or against the patterns or forces of God. Her explanations of opposites is solely for this purpose of defining what is right and wrong; however, I think it also serves my purpose to show the application of balance. Therefore, you get a two for one special of the day. The two applications are a good example of the close relationship of knowledge and possessions as well as inner content and outside appearances. That is, there is the knowing of the differences and the possessing of one form of manifestation over the other by understanding how the inner content will be manifested into physical reality.

In Ms. Haich's explanation of good and bad, she basically confirms my premise that there is no such thing as right and wrong per se, but only wrongly used characteristics and wrongly applied forces. She agrees with the old adage, that there is a time and place for everything. That is, everything is good and proper at the right time and place, but the same attributes expressed as good at one time, can be also considered bad, satanic or evil, at another time or wrong time or place.

Interesting enough, we are again confronted with the question of location and/or position. I think this book is trying to tell us something. I keep talking about position and point of focus both on a conscious and subconscious level. Which is still abstract and difficult to relate to or recognize, but at the same time it is a point or that part of us which is indestructible and intangible. It is the essence of who and what we are. I don't think anyone, including myself, can describe this as anything other than being. This is a point from which all else radiates outward until it encounters physical reality or resistance. It is the infinite source of our own creativity and that is why we make our own reality. But, it may also exist or be some point in the future and that is why it may be indestructible.

Let's get back to our intangible sets of opposites. The first set is that of keeping silent and that of talking. I believe everyone can relate to the virtues of saying the right thing at the right time, as well as the absence of saying nothing when something can be said. In the latter situation, there is a slang expression for saying something at the wrong time. It is said or called, "Putting your foot in your mouth". In certain situations, this can be a lot more serious than this play on words indicates. Also, if we talk at the wrong time and place, such speech can be satanic chatter or gossip. On the other hand, if we remain silent when someone is in danger for his life or being accused of something that is not true, then this silence would also be considered satanic. Therefore, you see, there is a need for balance and the understanding of differences and their proper use and/or place or position.

The next set of opposites are that of receptivity and the resistance to influence. This is more than difficult to explain, because here we are dealing with the thought of higher consciousness, the mind and one's inner content. That is, we should be receptive to everything which is based upon higher vibrations and God, but we should not be receptive or impressionable to those thought forms lower than ourselves. I think that what is meant here is that we should stand up for what we believe and yet, be open to understanding and capable of making those changes to those thought forms which are not based upon our own inner convictions. The expression of balance here is in the idea that there are certain forces that are manifested solely as an extension of man and that he requires that certain things be done, in order to create an orderly society; therefore, man should know the differences and, "Render unto Caesar what is Caesar's and to God what is God's", or at least to know the difference.

I find it a little difficult to distinguish much of a difference between the next two sets of opposites and the last two. These two, obeying and ruling are similar to receptivity and the resistance to influence, except that these two are concerned more with tangible physical actions than the latter two which are more intangible actions. We are again confronted with the need to appeal to our own higher consciousness or God, to determine when to obey and when to rule. We have a responsibility to do both, but not at the same time nor always in similar circumstances. It is believed that man can recognize God's will by seeking agreement or balance within himself; however, you would be greatly helping yourself by being conscious of the two extremes or opposites. These are; that you should not obey someone or something that is against your convictions for reason of cowardice, fear, material advantages, personal gain, or merely wanting to be a supposedly good and easy kind of going person. The other situation or condition is the knowledge or learning of your abilities and the matter or problem at hand and/or the other people involved. That is, you know how to defend yourself or survive by yourself and should be able to do the same for a group of people in a similar condition or a situation with which you are familiar. Ruling is a form of universal love, guidance and the ability to unite, all the forces with that particular group of people toward their general well being, without infringing upon their rights of self determination. The knowledge and balancing of the patterns of obeying and ruling are necessary to higher consciousness.

The opposites of humility and self confidence must also be learned in a proper balance. Humility deals with the knowing that you are but a part of the whole; therefore, one reflects or normally assumes an attitude and/or posture of being less than that to which you are relating to, be it another person or other physical manifestations of matter. While having this knowledge of yourself, one should never subordinate one's self to lesser earthly forms of manifestations, to do so would be a sign of weakness, cowardice and satanic. Whereas, self confidence is the knowing that God dwells within you and he is giving you the strength and knowing abilities to accomplish those tasks which are before you. An unbalanced condition of self confidence or extreme is the thinking that you are solely responsible for yourself. Here, one usually gets carried away with one's own importance or greatness and has visions of his own self above all else. The syndrome of grandeur and greatness surrounds his waking moments, because the world cannot do without him, he is indispensable.

The opposites of lightning-like speed and circumspection seem to deal with the element of time, but it too, has to do with one's state of consciousness. That is, if one is not paying attention to the matter at hand, one's actions or reactions will definitely be affected by one's point of focus or element of recognition. When you can act at a moment's notice, with complete concentration and presence of mind, then you are definitely at a level of higher consciousness and can exceed the limits of time. To act out of haste without regards for all others and all else or without the presence of mind, so to speak, is an unbalanced condition and considered satanic. On the other hand, circumspection is the understanding and controlling of one's point of focus. That is, before acting, one must learn to control the physical being so as not to fulfill an emotionally induced act strictly for one's own self gratification. To properly reach a right decision, one must recognize the will of God, and not Caesar's. But it is equally wrong or opposite and considered satanic to dwell on a matter and not reach a decision for whatever reason, or lack of reason it might be.

To accept everything and to differentiate are the next set of opposites. Before we can explain this set, we must first say that one's worth is not determined by external circumstances or material possessions, but by the degree to which one manifests God. All the degradations or humiliations cannot destroy or reduce one's inner values, nor can all the wealth and praise, raise one's inner values. All endeavors are but a means to an end; therefore, one should learn to accept everything. However, one should also know or differentiate when to defend himself and values against undue or unjust malice. To accept everything must not be allowed to degenerate into apathy, indifference or a cowardly lack of character. Yet, one must also know, understand and to balance acceptance with the ability to differentiate and distinguish that which is a positive form of manifestation from that which is negative. Unless one knows the differences, one cannot exist in a state of separation or physical reality.

This next set of opposites, the ability to fight and its opposite peace, must be treated with extreme caution. That is, humans know all too well the ability to fight and too little about peace. Please do not take this explanation as an endorsement that physical fighting is acceptable, because no act of violence is justified for whatever reason, if physical harm is incurred in some way, shape, or form. However, the message here is that you should be able to stand up and fight with all of your energy with the weapons of truth whenever necessary. This does not necessarily mean with physical objects of matter. Taken to the extreme, this willingness to fight should never degenerate into stupid quarreling to gain some form of advantage over your fellow man. Above all, remember that your fighting must be with the aid of your higher consciousness and the spiritual weapons of unity for the ability to restore peace. Also, you must balance this intangible pattern with that of peace and to seek unity and harmony in a world based upon separation. But, your love of peace must not be allowed to turn into cowardly submission for expedience sake or not wanting to fight or engage in conflict.

Caution and courage are the next set of opposites. In order to be a useful coworker or member in a society, one must learn the values of caution. That is, you can save yourself and your fellow man a great deal of physical harm and/or pain by the proper use and exercising the knowledge and balance of caution. But this caution should not be abused as to turn into a form of cowardice from fear or the lack of self confidence. Caution must be balanced with courage. You must actively seek out the power of courage to face the difficult challenges or tasks set before you and selected by you in your daily encounters. You must learn the proper use of energy in its many forms and patterns and to be self sufficient and to defend yourself against unwarranted attacks or accusations based upon unfounded truths. However, this active position of being right must not deteriorate into an unbalanced extreme of daredevil recklessness for one's physical sensations or stimulations.

When we discussed the concept of unity in an earlier chapter, we talked about the opposites of everything and nothing. This set of opposites also applies to man. On one side, you really possess nothing, because everything is a manifestation of God. You only have temporary use of this energy form and everything there is; therefore, you must use what you receive and pass along the rest. If you live by a stream of water, or abundance, you may use what is available to you, but you must let the rest pass you by and not stop it from someone else. You can use only so much and will receive according to your needs and your tasks before you. You need not worry about it. It will be there. But, this positive attitude must never turn into contempt for material things or not caring for one's self and letting others support you and your physical needs.

You must balance out your own needs and depend on yourself so that you can appreciate the use of your own energies or efforts. You must learn to respect matter and deal with it effectively, not without it, and not against it. You should try to acquire what you need, because it is necessary to sustain one's physical being and you must be free to pursue that which life in this reality has to offer. Therefore, you must acquire or possess matter, hold it, master it, and use it wisely, or you will be unable to carry out your earthly tasks independently and freely. If you don't, you will be at the mercy of earthly powers and under the control of others and/or victims of your own environment or selections. At the opposite extreme, you don't want this command of everything to deteriorate into the selfish act of greed or possessing material wealth of things for one's own self exclusively.

The next set of opposites is that of, to have no ties and that of loyalty. As a matter of balance, you must not allow yourself to be attached or attracted to that of another person strictly based upon what that other person can give you both mentally and physically. You must learn to distinguish the differences in the various levels of vibration within everyone and to recognize that which is of negative resistance and/or growth forms. Consequently, you must understand that you must be able to leave without delay, the person(s) you love most, whenever the task before you demands it. To help ease this form of separation, you must try to realize that the loveable characteristics to which you are attached or attracted to in another, are given to them by God, not the person himself. All those other people including yourself, are but an instrument for the manifestation of God; therefore, you can find these characteristics in all peoples of the world. If you love God in everyone, then you will not be attached to anyone and you will be able to distinguish the conscious difference. However, this knowledge of oneness or unity must never be allowed to turn into indifference or apathy as we spoke of earlier in the modified and super-conscious behavior pattern diagrams.

We will also talk about indifference again shortly in another capacity. But in this case, one should be able to recognize God's manifestations and to work with and be loyal to those who express God's will. This loyalty must not be allowed to turn into a cult for a person or persons or for personal glorification. Loyalty must not degenerate into complete obedience or other forms of worship. You should strive to bring people to their highest spiritual level without self glorification, but with the knowledge of humility that will not degenerate into personal self underestimating or self destruction. You must carry your worth as a human being. Loyalty should be expressed by some form of attention, but must not be all confining or the sole purpose of one's existence.

The contempt for death and the regard for life are the next set of opposites. Although life is our present point of focus and dominates our every conscious moment in this reality, one must also achieve a complete disregard for death. That is, one must understand that the physical body is but a shell which must be cast off or aside like a piece of clothing, in order for the being inside to grow and progress in his journey back to his origin. The living self is but a branch in the tree of life and life is immortal. Consequently, whenever your tasks bring you face to face with mortal danger, you must realize that you are or your body is but a part of you, or extension of you, and is not the total unlimited you; therefore, you should be able to encounter such a confrontation without fear or question of concern. But this knowledge of one's being should not be turned into disrespect for life. You must appreciate physical life while you exist in this state of separation. Life is a learning experience which teaches you the proper use and exercise of energy. You must try to live every moment to its fullest and experience all that is available to you in this plane of existence. But this joy of living should not become an end in itself or above all else and turn into the lust for physical sensations and life eternal.

Our last set of opposites is that of love and indifference. I have said something about this subject before. I expect to say something about these opposites now, but I expect to devote an entire chapter to this subject later on, because it is so very much misunderstood by my fellow man. Unlike our other sets of opposites, these two represent an inseparable unit right here on earth. That is, whenever you have manifested one, the other is automatically manifested. That is why this set of opposites is so important that I cannot adequately describe them here, but I will try to relate this set of opposites to the subject at hand and just touch upon those things which are pertinent.

Basically, what I am trying to convey here is that you must give up your personal point of focus, inclinations, and feelings, and learn to love everything and everyone without distinction or discrimination, just as God loves and manifests himself in everything and everyone. Just as the sun shines, love should be impartial and shared, and experienced by all. This impartial love is the most important and perfect form of love of all and yet, it must be indifferent to everything and everyone. That is, you must learn to love with an equal balance for all, no matter what one's relationship is with those involved with you. It is only when you learn and fully understand and believe in unconditional love that all the world will change. It is only then that you will become fully conscious and you will never again be the same. When this truth is learned and expressed, your impartial love will literally radiate from you to all creatures of the universe in a more positive, creative manner and will never again be mixed with personal inclinations or antipathies.

When you understand unity, you will begin to understand this kind of love. You will also be able to consciously position yourself above separation and will consider everything from the standpoint of the whole; consequently, you will be able to view conflicting interests of those about you who are involved in dissension and possible hostilities with impartiality. This vantage point or position will give you the ability to determine the collective needs of all, or that which benefits the needs of society. But this disregard for the interests of the minority individuals directly involved must never be based upon personal antipathy. That is, you must be able to objectively be indifferent to those nearest and dearest to you, if they select those actions which are satanic or self fulfilling, rather than reflect the will of God, it is better for a person to suffer material or physical ruin, even death, than to lose his soul. God doesn't meddle in the affairs of man, then why should you? You should be observant enough to know when something must be done to correct a problem affecting society. Balance and patterns must be maintained in a world based upon separation and free will, and you must never use force to change that which is created without just compensation and must be carried out impartially and fairly.

Should personal interests of the individuals involved be a major problem, then you must encourage these people to seek guidance and direction from within. Give them time and request that they seek a possible alternative or solution to the problem. If they are conscious enough, they will find an answer. Also, if they should seek help from among their fellow man, these people should not allow personal indifference or apathy to dominate thoughts or passion for this matter at hand. They should lend a hand and do everything that is within their earthly powers to help relieve the imbalance. You should not compel anybody to do anything by force. You must consider their physical and spiritual well being. Guide them, teach them, and support them. You must never be indifferent and scorn them, for this is a negative form of energy which, if carried to its extreme, will manifest itself into separation or hate. Hate is an extreme condition of indifference and is a destructive form of energy that interferes with man's growth process and should be avoided whenever possible in constructive endeavors. Again, divine unconditional love will direct you to the proper form of thought and actions on any issue.

The form of universal unconditional love is the hardest pattern for man to recognize and understand and is often confused with another form of love which we will discuss later. It is the hardest, because you must give up something in order to attain it. You must give up your imbalance and comfort that is associated or relative to a state of separation. The stability of pattern recognition in a finite or limited reality is a difficult force to change, once it is established and becomes a possession and/or part of one's beliefs. Again, man likes to surround himself with that which is familiar and comfortable or recognizable. He likes to limit himself so he creates barriers to channel and direct himself to a desired end result or limit. Unconditional love has no limits; therefore, it is somewhat out of the ordinary and does not fit the normal recognizable pattern of physical reality. Unconditional love requires a person to use all of his resources and to draw upon his inner spiritual self, or higher consciousness and expect nothing in return for his efforts.

Before we finish with our twelve sets of opposites and about love and indifference, I want to explain something else that affects all of these opposites. There exists in man, two forms of himself. We have talked about this before as his physical being and his spiritual being. We have also said that man dwells in a state of separation and associates with his physical being while on this earthly plane. Mentally, this position in physical reality is known as the little "I", or me, point of focus. Its opposite extreme is known as the true or big "I". There is give and take between these opposites and their difference seems to be indistinguishable by the average person, but there is a difference.

When we talk about an opposite position or giving up something, what we are really talking about is this close affiliation with the "me" part of our being. That part which identifies with our earthly being and other manifested forms in relation to the physical senses. We are asking that you rid yourself of that extreme form which is you and to seek a higher or more conscious form of yourself. The "me" form of your being, is not in balance with your all or total self; rather, it seeks the comfort of tangible outside forms of energy that are expressed in an outward direction only. The big "I" is a much more balanced and is the unlimited part of your being that is more conscious and therefore, more capable of knowing and dealing with the "me"; whereas, the "me" doesn't even know the big "I" exists. That is the difference that consciousness makes in one's life.

It is only when you have learned and used the previous eleven sets of opposites, will you begin to understand the twelfth set of love and indifference. Then and only then will you have reached a position within you that true recognition takes place. It is when you become conscious of your higher self will you be able to recognize the inner voice of God so clearly as to be in complete unison with his and your own true wishes. The twelve sets of opposites set the limiting extremes and are the guidelines that will bring you closer to understanding yourself. They also provide the balance that is needed to make you become more conscious and free of the artificial limitations of wants and desires imposed by an imbalance and the position of the "me" in physical reality. The twelfth set is the understanding of perfect, universal, unconditional, love. This is a form or pattern that can stand by itself. It is an inseparable unit that is manifested right here on earth as a true balance in itself.

We are not done with the concept of separation and opposites; however, for now we are only talking about balance and these sets of opposites serve as markers or guidelines for this physical reality. These intangible limiting extremes serve to direct an individual and help him seek a path or journey in the direction of unity. There is more to this concept of separation and opposites than meets the eye, but you must first learn to recognize and understand this concept before you can control yourself and to use the laws of separation effectively. Whenever and whatever you do, you are affected by these laws and you must recognize and work with them and not against them, if you wish to accomplish that which you have set out to do.

Before one can accomplish something new, you must start by looking around you and begin to see reality for just what it is. Physical reality is based upon separation. This separation is also found in the mental processes and is a manifestation of the mental processes itself. These manifestations are then transposed into physical reality and eventually, they find themselves manifesting into group behavior patterns. Like our example of a boat in water, we are making waves in our progress or journey to our origin. To achieve something, another form or force is created and is manifested in a series of events that add to our world of cause and effect; therefore, balance and care should be exercised whenever and wherever possible. You make your own reality, but you also affect the reality of everyone else and that is society or our fourth growth pattern in addition to mental, physical and spiritual growth that we talked about earlier in this book.

With an increased number of spirits entering the realm of physical reality, or as the population increases, the need for balance becomes more important and more noticeable. I am referring mainly to our present problems of pollution confronting our world today. This is a popular issue that everyone seems to talk about now, but few people do anything about it, unless it directly affects their well being. Apparently, physical tangible needs are put above or before the more intangible qualities that life has to offer. This problem of pollution is further complicated by old patterns or routines that have to do with our values and/or monetary system.

What I am referring to here is the relationship of tangible money to that practice commonly referred to a deficit spending and/or credit. Both of these problems are beautiful examples of imbalance at work in the tangible and intangible forms that reality takes. I don't propose to offer a solution to these problems here, but I wish to merely mention two current problems that directly affect our existence. These are problems that are prominent in our world today, because they have a cause and effect relationship which too few people have taken into consideration, either now, before, and in the foreseeable future. They are the waves which will rock everyone's boat and may possibly erode and interfere with our journey.

Although man has free will and he makes his own reality, nothing ever happens in this physical reality without a cause. Events are linked in a never ending continuum or continued relationship of all that was before and all that will follow in a direct and indirect relationship based upon cause and effect. Just as you have two parents, you must have four grandparents, eight great grandparents, sixteen great, great grandparents, etc. I think you get the drift. Man is free, but bound by necessities and the restrictions that he places upon himself and the laws of physical reality. Therefore, although you make your own reality, there are certain things you must know about your reality in order to control it. You are free to do and act as you please, or do just what you want to do, but you must also know and understand that there is a cause and effect relationship of all of your actions, and what causes you to select one thing over another is this thing called balance or the evaluation process. In order to be totally free, you must learn to control the will and not the wants and desires. The wants and desires are only a cause of an imbalance due to physiological needs, emotional feelings and environmental suggestions of associations, or other outside influences of others in a direct relationship to one's position.

The purpose of this chapter is to bring you aware of the existence of opposites which is the basis for this reality, or the causes that happen in this reality. By being conscious of opposites one can begin to understand why one does what he does and to possibly be in control of his wants, or at least know why he wants. The next step is to be consciously in control of his wants and not the other way around. This is the knowledge of the law of opposites and how they can be used to overcome each other and controlled. This is the beginning of using one law against another to overcome a condition that does not serve your best interests or the interests of others. Instead of being a pawn in a game of chess or life, you will become a mover, in control of the game similar to rock, scissors, and stone.

ONE

There is no number greater than one.
You can have multiples or fractions of one,
but one is a complete unit that stands alone.
Indestructible and integral in all things.

It is the flower of understanding
It is the link that builds bridges of thought.
It is the recognizer, recognizing itself with recognition.
It is the consciousness of pure energy and universal unconditional love.

One is the reason and purpose of communications.
The need and desire of two to form a common union of one.
Communion of thought of many into the consciousness of unity.
As it was in the past, it shall be in the future.

CHAPTER 16

The Mental Aspects

I think this matter of understanding and learning the sets of opposites sounds a lot simpler than it really is. I tried to indicate that somewhat by my explaining about the separation of one's own self into the mental "I" and the "me". This is further complicated by another set of laws or opposites that can be referred to as gender. That is, each of these sets of opposites and one's own being exhibits two other separate qualities. In physical reality, this gender law can be compared with the knowledge of positive and negative charges commonly used to explain electrical currents or energy. In a more common application, we use gender to distinguish the biological differences in a species as well as the term sex. With so many examples around, I don't think I need to describe this form of separation any further; however, I do want to describe just how this law of gender works in relation to our sets of opposites and other intangible forms of thought.

To begin with, I want to say that although gender is mostly associated with the distinction of the sexes, it is not restricted to a single sex. That is, both male and female human beings exhibit both forms within one. A man exhibits both male and female qualities within himself and so does the female. The two separate qualities or forces coexist in one. They are opposites existing side by side and in balance with one another like our circles of unity. These opposite qualities are not just restricted to biological functions or living organisms. Gender is manifested in everything and on every plane of existence.

Getting back to our original patterning of defining words, gender refers to, or means to beget; to procreate; to generate; to create; to produce: whereas sex usually refers to a physical distinction between male and female living things on a certain plane of existence. I used the words positive and negative earlier to try to describe gender; however, there are certain wrong connotations associated with these two words, therefore, I would like to explain that a little better. First of all, the word negative has certain undisputed connotations of something either weak or something which takes away from something to make it less than it started

There is nothing negative in the term negative. The so called negative pole or post of a battery is really the pole of force, by which the generation or production of new energy is manifested. That is, the positive charge attracts the negative forms of energy and the union is met with the creation of great excitement and movement that produces some new form of manifestation. In order to stay clear of this confusion, I will use the word feminine in place of the word negative and male in place of the positive form of this manifestation.

Using the example of electricity, during the union of the male and female forms of energy, a female form becomes satisfied, or receives some additional quality or value that can produce or make this union an act of creativity. A certain process is begun whereby the female particles vibrate rapidly under the influence of the masculine energy which circles around the latter, resulting in the birth of a new atom. This new creation becomes detached and leaves to start on a beginning or a new form of manifestation, carrying with it something of that former association. After this union, the resulting new creation is a separate thing having new characteristics that no longer exhibits the property of free electricity, but a state called ionization. This is a new stable energy form that is in a state of balance and is capable of entering into new relationships that was not possible to the previous separated forms of either before it.

The part that the male energy form seems to play is that it is capable of directing certain qualities of energy toward the female energy form and its presence seems to stimulate the female energy into a state of activity and/or creation. But remember, it is the female energy form that is doing all of the active creative work, and this is true on all planes. Another way to look at this is that the female aspect represents present and past whereas the male represents future. This is also a state of balance in that one form is incapable of doing anything without the other; however, in certain planes of existence, these two forms can be found to exist in one and are capable of reproducing or creating. In the higher forms or planes of existence, these qualities of gender are manifested separately in physical reality; however, they still retain their identity within each individual or being and are necessary in order to exist either physically, mentally or spiritually. That is, life cannot exist unless one possesses the energy forms of gender. Remember, very early in this book, we said that the purpose of life was to use energy, and this is the only way that energy can be used.

On the mental plane, the masculine principle of gender corresponds to the objective, conscious, voluntary and active mind. The female or feminine principle corresponds to the subjective, subconscious, involuntary, passive mind. In the last chapter, we talked about the dual aspect of the mind as the "I" and the "me". Then we said that the little I or me doesn't even know that the big I exists, that's because the big I really exists in the super conscious mind which is unconscous to the me. In this relationship to gender, the "I" represents the male gender and the "me" represents the female gender principle. The "I" is always in the aspect of being, and the "me" is always in the aspect of becoming. To know and understand the principle of gender is to possess the keys to control and master your own being and to make your own reality. But, before I give you the element of control, let's make sure you understand the duality of the mind.

Earlier, I explained Rene Descartes' theory of "I think, therefore I am". I believe everyone could relate to this statement and agree with it; however, on closer examination and the need to make life a little more complicated, as the song goes "Is that all there is" (that Peggy Lee made famous), seems to indicate that there is this other something more. This other something, we already said, was the "me" aspect that works in unison with the "I". The "me" is usually mistaken for the "I" because one thinks in terms of tangible outside forms of manifestation that correspond to feelings, tastes, likes, dislikes, habits and other characteristics, that make up one's personality. The individual and others can identify and know this form or person. The "me" also consists of all accumulated knowledge of the self in relationship to everything in the outside physical world. The "me" identifies with the body and the physical needs and care of this outside appearance and may extend even to one's clothes.

With most people, the mind seems to be something that belongs to their body, which in a sense it is, but it is also quite independent. In fact, as one increases his level of consciousness, he learns that it is just the other way around. The body belongs to the mental part of one's being. However, man limits himself and still believes that his mental state concerning feelings, needs, and wants, are a part of his physical being, rather than things produced by his mentality. That is, he may be able to identify himself as this separate form of inbalance, or being, or creation within himself, or of him, instead of a manifestation created by him. Through the process of learning opposites, one soon discovers that it is quite easy to recognize the differences and change one's, feelings, wants, and needs. He also learns that these characteristics that he associates with himself or his physical body, are really not part of him at all, but are routines or patterns with which he associates in relationship to certain outside conditions or stimulus.

As man begins to recognize his own ability to understand and to know of his own abilities to generate thought, he will discover the approximate position of his self, or the balance point between his "me" and "I" aspects of himself. He will have learned the point at which he can have absolute control of his thoughts and actions. This is the point where everything happens. This is the position where thoughts, ideas, beliefs, emotions, feelings and all other conditions of wants and needs, are generated. This is the point where the female aspect of the mind, joins with the male to produce or create that which is the "me". It is at this point, that the mental thought receives some form of energy and support from the "I" aspect of one's being and produces an intangible thought form that is later manifested into lower forms of matter or reality.

This mental aspect is the concept that I have been telling you about for some time; "THAT YOU MAKE YOUR OWN REALITY". Now you know how you do it. If you can achieve this point of recognition of yourself, you will also begin to see another point or aspect of yourself. That is the "I" aspect. Once you have discovered the self in balance, you will notice that there is another part of you that is capable of standing aside and has the capability to watch its own mental creations in process. This is the object "I" part of your being. I suppose the "I" can best be described as being a part of the Will. That statement pretty well confirms what I have indicated from the early part of the book, that learning is a matter of one's mental position.

Now, I have been able to effectively show you how one's position can be changed or be manipulated in order to bring about a form of learning which is relative to knowledge, possessions and one's self. By the willing and/or movement of the "I" a form of energy is directed to the "me" which transforms this energy into an intangible thought form that is relative to some form of creativity that is then transformed into some form of action or physical manifestation. The action of the "I" or Will is something of a one shot deal. That is, once it starts the ball rolling, it stands back and watches what it started, and it can no longer control the process unless the individual is conscious of his "self" or balance point, which I occasionally refer to as one's point of focus. In short, you might say that the "I" wills that the "me" to begin and proceed on a path of creation in a direction that is designed to teach itself a form of recognition that will bring it closer to itself and/or unity.

Let's repeat that last statement in more detail. It deserves a little more attention. The masculine "I" principle is the initiator, instigator or whatever, and it is always providing direction and energy in a relationship to balance. The feminine "me" has a much more varied field of operation. The "me" is the actual doer of the two. That is, it takes the energy and/or stimulus from the "I" and is responsible for all that occurs from then on. It can do or manifest all kinds of energy forms, both tangible and intangible. However, without the male, the female "me" is apt to sit back and rest, content with receiving impressions and images from the outside physical world.

It is the "I" that is responsible for producing original mental thought or creations. But even though the "I" is responsible for new original thought and/or primarily resides in the realm of unmanifested non-linear reality, the "me" is somewhat locked into limited patterns of recognition and resides in only physical reality. That is, the "me" is bound by limitations or beliefs as to what it can do that is relative to the outside physical world. The "me" relies on patterns that are familiar to it and the knowledge and understanding of its self and/or its reality; consequently, it limits itself to patterns or routines that are known to it which in turn, somewhat stifles or slows down the creative process of the "I". The "I" is a pattern initiator and the "me" can be considered the end result, or the "I" is the beginning and the "me" is the ending. This might also be compared to high technology or mathematics as the X and Y axis or how a digital analog process works. That is, there is a movement first in one direction followed by a movement perpendicular to the first in a series until a point or end result or shape is formed. This is similar to a cause and effect relationship.

I am sure that you can distinguish this gender principle in yourself and in others in your daily lives. I am also sure that you will agree with me, based upon my preceding explanation that few people really employ or use the masculine male principle in their daily lives. To use the "I" principle requires the use of the Will or energy from an inward nature, away from the physical tangible world where our "I" reality dwells. Until you are consciously aware of just what our reality really is, there is no way that you are going to see much in the way of creative thought. Only those artistic freaks and weirdoes seem to have some idea of what this thing known as original thought is and everybody knows that they are crazy and are not in touch with reality. Therefore, that means that the main thought here should be that you must first understand our reality and that one's reality is really based upon separation and that balance between these two worlds is important to one's growth.

Let me go one step further in this explanation of gender, to show you another possible inherent danger or problem associated with the principle of gender. In order to do this, I must again explain how the principle works. The Will moves the "I" into a position so as to stimulate the "me". How this is accomplished is by a change or difference in the levels of vibration within the "self". That is, the "me" relates to physical reality; therefore, its vibration level is less than that of the "I" which vibrates at a higher level. Consequently, the "I" is capable of energizing and/or stimulating the "me" into action. The "I" imparts a piece of itself within the female "me" and it accepts it and makes it its own and acts and thinks accordingly. Because the "I" is so strong and powerful, this higher level of vibration is capable of stimulating not only the mind of that particular individual who originated the idea, but it is also capable of stimulating almost anyone who dwells in the female "me" part of himself. Unfortunately, this is the majority of most people dwelling in physical reality.

Most people are content to live according to the thoughts and ideas instilled into their "me" from the "I" of other people, and they don't even know it. Most people are too lazy to use their own willpower to stimulate even themselves. They go about their everyday lives thinking other people's thoughts and performing routines and patterns that are expected of them by other people. Then they even go about expounding how other people's freedoms in other parts of the world are dominated by the governments of those other societies. I think a lot of people better take a closer look as to what is happening around their own back yard.

The industrial revolution tried and was very successful in molding consciousness to the needs of others and/or institutions. In fact, our society built upon these principles and encouraged conformity as a means of strength and that which was good for material prosperity and progress. The media carried its message to all with the same thoughts and consequently, these ideas set into motion creating a subservient society dedicated to the idea of central authority and/or rule from the top. The idea of one's own value was second to that of the country or society first. This is still the dominant thought force in existence today and in the foreseeable near future. This acceptance of authority seems the best alternative to most people right now, especially with a supposed threat of one's security by all those hostile countries out there who are anxious to take over our country by physical force, so they can impose their will on all of us. You know everyone who is not with us is against us and wants to dominate us. But now those ideas might not hold water, or be true, if what I said earlier was true. I think the biggest threat to all societies or countries might be if everyone were to become conscious of themselves and their world or reality, which is based upon separation.

As I indicated before, man has free will, but he is limited by his own self. His limitations or beliefs are a product of his own being, or rather, becoming. But he is also susceptible to thoughts not his own. Therefore, man can very easily become a victim of his own environment or others by the sheer passive nature or female aspect of his self. By not exercising his own free will, or male aspect of himself, he becomes a slave of those who are capable of exercising that power. Man makes his own reality, and all of it stems from a mental nature or intangible source based in unmanifested non-linear reality. The element of control over one's self must first begin in the mind, and hopefully in the mind of the originator or self.

The problem that the average person is faced with is that they tend to be receptive and dwell or position themselves in the "me" portion of their conscious mind. They are not aware of this thing called separation, and the dual aspect of the mind. Man tends to be lazy and seeks comfort in patterns of recognition; consequently, he isolates himself from himself and dwells within that reality that he thinks is the most important and probably thinks it is his only reality. To regain control of one's self, one must become conscious of separation and to learn the value of our twelve sets of opposites. Remember, the behavior diagrams that show that value precedes selection both on a conscious and subconscious level. Also, remember that value is the amount or degree to which one is willing to expend efforts or energies for. Therefore, if you are not willing to expend your own energy to find yourself, you will probably not find anything else either. Instead, you will become a passive, willing recipient of others and/or your environment. Without original thought or actions, you will become mere shadows and echoes of others that have stronger wills or minds than yourself. Unless you know why you are doing something, you shouldn't do it. Ask questions. You do not do anybody any good unless you know why you are doing what you are doing.

This whole book is designed to be a learning experience. Hopefully, you will begin to think more clearly and with more intent as your relationship to the cause and effect world around you. Hopefully, you will be more deliberate in your thinking and actions and learn to consciously control your position or point of focus in a more positive creative manner, for if you don't, you will be nothing more than a pattern of routines or a dull shell of a structure that reiterates and regurgitates a reflection that resembles a human being. You must learn to live and be alive. Learn to be truly free and a collaborator with yourself. Learn to use the knowledge of opposites to awaken yourself and to see how beautiful life really is. There is no such thing as good or bad, it's only a matter of what you want to experience.

Man tends to separate or polarize himself in one aspect of his being and tends to dwell in a state of inbalance. That is, he selects a position which is a balanced condition, or one aspect of reality, which is in fact or in truth, a reality in an unbalanced condition. The reason for this tendency to dwell within this one aspect of reality is the level of one's consciousness and man's reluctance to use energy to seek a true balance. Earlier we said jokingly, that what you don't know can't hurt you. Now, I am not joking. I would like to make it plain and clear. What you don't know, can hurt you. You must learn to dominate your own self. You must learn to use your Will to obtain the mental images that helps you to help yourself so that you can help others. The masses of humanity in all societies are sheepish like creatures, yearning to be lead, directed, and controlled. They do not seek or demand much. They are eager to please, get along, and to be liked in return. But, they can also become willing pawns in a game of power and/or control, which can become very dangerous and detrimental to everyone's growth and physical life itself.

The person who knows how to control the masculine aspect of their mind is the actor who can make other people laugh, cry and weep, as he wills. He is the successful actor, statesman, preacher, writer, successful businessman, and natural leader of people, who can motivate and make people do things that they would not normally do on their own, if they were left up to themselves. The knowledge and control of the masculine mind is the key or secret of personal magnetism, influence, fascination, and all the other forces that make one stand out above the crowd. However, it can also belong to a person who seeks personal attention and/or some other form of greed and/or wealth. Like our statement on beliefs, a belief does not have to be based upon truth in order to be a belief. It merely has to be an indestructible certainty on the part of that individual, whether it is right or wrong. Therefore, there can be a problem for those people who, either knowingly or unknowingly, possess this aspect of control. For they can understand their form of power over his fellow man for the benefit of all, or they can use it for selfish interests and/or to help a personal few at the expense of many others.

The knowledge of the masculine "I" aspect of the mind is of no value or use if one does not know how to control it, but if its use or control is known, it should be carefully exercised in a balanced form in our physical reality. That is, it should not be hoarded like a vain foolish act of greed, because it is a form of wealth, and it should not be used constantly, unless there is good and just cause(s) that can benefit from all that may be involved. The law or use of energy is what physical reality is all about.

We are a part of God, and he is part of us. Together, we are one. We are a part of the universe of God and he is us. The problem is a matter of separation and consciousness. Now you are on the right path to begin your journey back to him. Those who stray will find the going tough. Those who violate its natural laws will suffer greatly. Remember, in a world based upon separation, you must learn to use one law against another, instead of fighting against them. To fight against a natural law is to expend great quantities of energy and to gain little. To work with the laws is like playing our child's game of, "Scissors, Paper and Rock". One will dominate the other, but each has its value.

The value of knowledge or information is for use, not to be kept secret, locked up, and stored. Knowledge, without use and expression or manifestation is a vain thing which brings no good to its possessor. The computer revolution is suppose to be an age of information. Wealth will be sought and/or available to those who possess great knowledge. The fantasies and popularity of spy movies, reinforce that belief. That is demonstrated by the fact that the spies are always trying to get, buy or sell, information that is considered extremely important for protecting someone or country against a supposedly hostile opponent who is always trying to control or dominate others for their own benefit. But remember, information is no good in and by itself. It must relate to something else or relative to a particular desired end result. So you see, the physical world or this reality is more mental or intangible than you really think or believe.

Knowledge is not quite the same as what I described earlier in this book as pattern routines, but patterns of recognition. Unlike the definition that states: knowledge is the accumulation of facts of certainty, I think that we have demonstrated that few things are certain and that most things are always in some state of becoming, which is really the female aspect or manifestation in physical reality. Knowledge is more a relationship that involves recognition of position or movement. That is, the individual does not necessarily know for certain as to what something is, but rather what something is becoming. I know this sounds confusing, and I had hoped that we had gotten all of the confusion out of the way by now and were ready to use our newly acquired knowledge to all our benefits. Well, about the only thing I can say is that I, myself am still learning and I cannot provide either you or me with a satisfactory answer to this question, because I cannot determine where the male "I" part of this form of physical manifestation might reside, other than it might be in a higher un-manifested form of energy occupying its structural form in non-linear reality. This idea is basically saying that the self, like God, is not capable of recognition. But, this is not the point that I really wanted to make.

What I really wanted to say was that knowledge should be put to good use and not be used indiscriminately. That is, it must in some way relate to that which you want to accomplish in a positive creative manner. You should not just reflect knowledge, just as you should not do something without knowing why. These thoughts are all designed to get you to think so that you will become more conscious of yourself and your reality. That's what life is all about. You are to use energy to bring you back to your origin and your path will be shortened and your journey made easier if you become more observant and conscious of all those forms of energy that point the way.

Again, man is lazy; consequently, man learns routines as a necessary evil, or a way to get from here to there. This is not knowledge so much as it is the recognition of an acceptable pattern that serves a physical function, but not necessarily a mental function. Doesn't that sound like a common complaint of a lot of workers in our industrial society? I think some people might even refer to such work patterns as boring! It is also the cause of a lot of wasted time and efficiency. Given the proper incentives and support, you might be amazed at what one of these supposedly lazy and stupid people can accomplish, and it doesn't necessarily have to be money as the prime motivating factor, it is only a matter of recognition.

As I also said earlier in this book, life is a learning process. Unless you are willing and able to spend or expend energies toward this goal, there is no worth or value to life per se. Maybe, there are so many lazy people out there because there are so few true leaders out there who know how to properly motivate and guide their fellow man. It is hard to do something alone, but when you have help, it is so much easier. Even if that help is not of a tangible nature, the knowing why is a very, very important part of the act or the accomplishment. Patterns or routines may be acceptable to society in general, but it is not acceptable to the individual in the direction of free will and choice.

Hopefully, now that you have learned the element of control, you can take a more active role in behalf of your own self. That is, you can now feel comfortable in the knowledge that you can or are originating your own creative thoughts. You should also beware of mental miserliness and express into action that which you have learned. Study the laws of separation and opposites. Study that which is relative to you, but also practice what you have learned. Balance is important in life. You can't sit back and always watch, listen, and be passive. Don't be afraid of making mistakes, or fear failure. Remember, these latter terms or events are only relative to a group environment. Failure or fear of mistakes is only relative to the society in which you live. These designations are either formal or informal rules or regulation standards by which we conform to group behavior or the main element of control. If you think independently and act accordingly, then it is not possible to make a mistake or fail. You may not achieve what you set out to do in the time period you want to do it in, but you have made an effort, and you have learned from it.

Whether you succeed or fail at something is really up to you. If you want something bad enough, you will get it. If you fail at something, I am sure your values concerning that something are subject to change, or will require a new effort, possibly in another direction to accomplish the same thing. The main thing is that you should never give up. Try, try again, is a very good philosophy. The tangible physical achievements are not as important as your own growth and progress to your own being and becoming. I think at this point, there is another beautiful saying that I think is appropriate here and I would like to repeat it in a slightly altered form. It goes something like this: "If you have* something, set it free. If it comes back to you, it's yours. If it doesn't, it never was". Everything is relative. If you put out an effort, it will come back to you in more ways than you can think of. It is like a snowball rolling down a hill. It gathers more meaning and substance than one can imagine. Another saying: "Nothing ventured, nothing lost", is another interesting quote. This is somewhat based upon negative thought. However, it is also a double negative and that makes a positive. That is, what do you have to lose? A person who never does anything never gets into trouble. You have to do something in order to get something. Make it happen!

* Original wording: "love someone".

To change your mood or mental state from a position of rest or inactivity, you must learn the law of opposites in order to change your level of vibrations and/or consciousness. This can be done by understanding and controlling the aspects of the dual mind. You must stimulate your female mental aspects of your mind into action by positioning your masculine "I" in the direction that you wish to go. That is, you must direct your energies of your Will to that which is relative to you. On a conscious level this requires that you pay specific attention to directing your mental vibrations toward a desired end result or accomplishment that you believe you want to achieve. Once this is done, the Will energizes the female aspect of the mind to draw upon the knowledge of what things are relative to accomplishing the task or desired end result. Then this stimulation takes this area of knowledge and develops it by presenting various forms of patterns of recognition or routines. The end result depends upon how conscious the person is, who is involved and/or the emotional level of the relationship.

To cultivate the art of one's conscious attention by means of the Will is the mastering of one's self and the knowledge of how to control one's state of being and becoming. The knowledge and use of opposites plus a few more things to be discussed will provide you with all you need to speed up and give you absolute control over your mental processes, which in turn will manifest itself into physical reality. If you are in a state of fear or possess fear, do not waste time trying to kill fear, but instead, cultivate the quality of courage that can relate to actions that can or may be used to correct or alter one's condition or state of being. This turning to an opposite condition will automatically dissipate one's fears. You may still be in danger; however, you will now be changing the stimulus and making it weaker the more you seek alternatives of courage. If you consider your physical body above all else and think about and dwell on all the possibilities that can happen to you and/or your body, then you will only intensify your fears. To get rid of the bad or negative or darkness, you must allow the opposite to enter into being and becoming. You might even think of the saying: "Let there be light!"

The mastering of opposites is part of the mastering of one's mind and/or being. Without the knowledge of opposites, one cannot know freedom and will not be able to effectively deal with or determine one's own environment. If you can only devote a little time, care, patience, and practice, to this mental process and the law of opposites, you will be able to master this physical reality. The value of anything depends upon the energy or efforts you are willing to give. The law of opposites and gender are true, but the results obtained by each individual in the application of this principle of usage, depends upon the efforts of each individual. One must learn to change the negative into the positive form of the same quality. That is, the opposites are of the same quality of vibration, but they are only separated by a matter of degree; therefore, they appear different. To understand this intangible quality of difference is almost impossible to manifest in uncertain terms; however, it exists just the same. All forms of energy have their equal opposite. That is the state of the universe. That is reality. Consequently, one can change a condition by energizing its equal opposite, making one more dominate over the other. The mind is capable of transferring energy and transmuting one state or condition to another, degree by degree, opposite to opposite, vibration to vibration.

From all of the foregoing, you may now see a relationship about our reality that was not evident before, and that is that one can exist in one part of a state of separation and not be aware of the other part, or for that matter, even care. This is the condition of inbalance that I told you about earlier. That is, one can exist separate and apart in this physical reality, but eventually a state of true balance must be achieved. Inbalance is a state or position that is out of balance, but yet it is stable within certain limitations like our circles of unity. That is, it is a condition all its own, but has its opposite that also exists. The two exist side by side and are stable. Together, they possess abilities beyond any one of them separately. This is the stuff that miracles are made of.

Nature compensates for the imbalance that occurs in physical reality by creating cycles or movement. That is, nature puts everything into constant motion and a pattern of radiating or revolving that somewhat acts as a gyro which is used to navigate an airplane or other vehicles. The gyro acts as a stabilizing force by creating its own small gravitational field, thereby keeping everything associated with that instrument in balance. In short, motion creates stability by creating an artificial force that holds or draws everything connected to it in a relationship of balance. The limitations of this motion are the limitations of its control. What all of this means is that there are cycles or rhythms created within one state of separation in order to create a balance or stability within itself or plane of reality, as well as a motion or cycle between these realities similar to our principle of gender. However, and again, these motions and cycles are also based upon vibration or movement not unlike the idea of energy and resistance. To understand these movements is to understand and control one's self and one's reality.

Just as black and white are opposites of the same thing be it shades of white or shades of black, our sets of opposites all possess the same qualities of one and there is motion between them that strives to achieve a balance. Over a given period of time, there are equal periods of day and night, so must there be equal stimulus, moods or emotion, concerning our sets of intangible opposites. This thought also lends credence to my statement that most people's lives are very routine or pattern oriented and they don't even know it. You may think that you are expressing free will when you are actually expressing that want or need of a cycle phenomena based upon the laws of imbalance.

The whole process of wants and needs associated with our behavior diagrams deal primarily with this cycle movement or rhythm. What we think we may need is not a need at all, but a point of extreme limitation reached by or affected by our own vibrations that are in a state of imbalance in this physical reality. Perhaps, I should restate that and say that the wants and needs are real, but that they are reflections of one's own vibrations in relationship to one's own cycles. These cycles are very, very similar to human biorhythms that have just been identified as affecting behavior by creating or identifying periods of extreme cycle overlap or stress in our physiological human make up or patterning.

Now just because we are affected by cycles or rhythms doesn't mean that we have to be controlled by them. In fact, that is the point of this whole book. You make your own reality. The more you know about yourself and what affects you, the more you will be in control of yourself, and boy is that neat! Just think, no more hassle or fear from wants and needs, because you have acquired or possess the ability to understand these wants and needs as to just what they are. You control them, not they you. By learning and mastering our sets of opposites, and using the gender principle, one can dominate or control these rhythms or cycles that occur in man and nature. By becoming more conscious of your self, you will begin to see or notice these cycles within you and by energizing yourself at a certain point or position, you thereby polarize yourself against the movement away from that point. That is, if you are in a pleasurable state of being and don't want to enter the state of becoming, then you can insulate or polarize yourself against changing that mood or feeling, to a great extent, by mastering the ability to control your cycles completely. By learning how to concentrate and use the gender principle of the big "I" you can maintain a perpetual state of bliss, if that is what you want.

By concentrating and using the reason of logic, which is nothing more than understanding one's position, one can overcome the downward negative swing that all forms of separation must follow or experience. Let me emphasize, that by polarizing one's self does not destroy or alter the cycle, because that law is indestructible. The action of concentration simply allows you to overcome one law with another and thereby neutralizes one with the other. Scissors cuts paper, but paper wraps the rock that can break the scissors. The laws of balance and counter-balance are in operation on all planes and between all planes. By mastering the law of opposites and learning how to control one's "I", one is capable of changing his level of vibration and creating his own reality, if he so desires.

The masses of people are carried away or along, obedient to their environment, the wills and desires of others, the limitations of their own patterning or routines imposed upon them by themselves and other outside causes which tend to control their life and/or destiny. By learning the laws of separation, one can learn and master the game of life, instead of being moved about and being used by others or at the mercy of one's environment. If and when these laws are mastered, you may still not wish to exercise complete control over yourself and/or your environment, but the option is yours.

The wise or conscious person serves on the higher planes of existence and rule or control on the lower planes. That is, the wise man obeys the laws from above, learns to understand his existing plane, and exercises control over the lower domains. The wise man works with the existing laws by understanding their relationship and movements and their becoming, then uses these laws to his benefit and growth. He is not the blind servant or slave of these laws and he knows that fighting them is a futile battle against continuous ongoing forces.

To effectively influence one's environment, one must first learn to understand one's own self and that has a lot to do with understanding of one's mental self. The process of balance and evaluation precedes that of selection and selection precedes physical actions and manifestations of a tangible nature; therefore, balance is a mental condition involving a position or point of focus. Almost everything we have talked about since we described the physical universe has been in connection with man's mental abilities or the intangible world of matter and energy forms. All physical actions are based upon selections that were determined from abstract intangible qualities or values based in unmanifested non-linear reality. That means that energy forms are derived from a mental nature or origin in man. If this is the case or true with man, might it not also be true with the manifestation of physical matter? That is, energy might have an origin or being of a mental nature of God and man is but an extension of God or part of God; therefore, there may be more to this physical reality than meets the eye.

What I am getting to here is that nearly everything we have talked about is of a mental nature. Might it not be said then, that the universe may be considered wholly mental. If this is so, then it is also reasonable to say that if it is mental, then it can only be ruled by one's mentality. If the universe is truly mental, then the mind must be the highest power affecting this reality. Reality may be a mental creation of the all or God and subject to the laws of separation. The universe, as a whole, and its parts or units may have its existence in the mind of the all or God. Therefore, if the universe is mental, this mentality is not just a mere collection of facts; rather it is based upon the relationship of being and becoming. You make your own reality. You are a mental being equal to all there is. It is only a matter of consciousness that separates you from what you are and what you can become.

WILL

Where there is a Will there is a way,
or so they say.
What this means is hard to say,
but it effects us in every way.

From an intangible spiritual source
comes a tangible physical force.
It is that thing that makes us go
and swings us back, to and froe.

It guides us to where we want to be
and takes us to what we want to see.
It makes us get involved
and determines how things are resolved.

It is the essence of what we are about
and creates certainty or absence of what is doubt.
What is this unknown quality?
It is that thing that makes me, ME!

Where Will and I reside
is a question and/or guide.
For in this physical reality
There is no thing called Finality!

CHAPTER 17

Control

I guess you thought that we were done with the aspect of control and/ or discovering and understanding who we are. Well, maybe you're right; however, I just want to go over everything that affect us and/or our behavior. As you may now be somewhat aware, life, and/or this physical reality is not a simple process to be understood. Like Albert Einstein's Theory of Relativity and Unified Field Theory, there are a number of factors or rules one must consider in order to use to master the concept of time and space. There is a difference between being affected or controlled by the rules and being in control of the rules. Unlike Einstein's 16 rules that govern his Theory of Relativity, the laws/principles that govern man are but seven. There's that number again! We have covered each of these rules to some degree or another in previous chapters; however, let's put them in so kind of order again and list them in a more easy form or pattern of recognition. They are as follows:

1. The principle of mentalism.
2. The principle of planes of unity(correspondence or levels).
3. The principle of vibration.
4. The principle of polarity.
5. The principle of rhythm.
6. The principle of cause and effect.
7. The principle of gender.

The first principle listed is that of mentalism. It is probably the most important principle that you can ever learn. This is the principle that ties everything together. Even if you do not agree with the logic that everything is based upon the separation of unity, you must seriously consider the relationship of yourself and everything else, or all there is. In short, you must agree or realize that everything you relate to enters or affects you by way of your mental capacities first. That is, all one's physical or outside senses must enter into a relationship which the mind can understand or else it is ignored as not relevant to one's reality and cannot affect his state of being. What the physical senses cannot identify, supposedly cannot affect one's physical reality. The senses are limited to receive or detect certain qualities of vibration that are then translated into some form of recognition and response or cause and effect. This can only be done mentally, or one can only react after the mind has determined what is best for the physical tangible body. Therefore, one's greatest influence over the physical environment is first accomplished by mental powers. To do anything, to be anything, one must think about it in an intangible mental state or position both consciously and sub-consciously.

The All is mind. The all is everything and nothing. This is a truth. It is the total of one. It is unity. The simplest statement is the most complicated. Rene Descartes said the, "I think; therefore, I am". Again, a simple statement and yet the most important concerning our being. The outward appearance and manifestations of matter are all related to the mind. Just as the inward spiritual qualities of intangible things are but understood by the mind. Spirit cannot be manifested into physical reality, but it can be understood by the physical mind that can affect physical reality. The mind is the point of focus or consciousness of the self or position of the self. It is the position of a point of balance between the world of physical matter and the world of spirit. It is the union or consciousness of both realities in a state of limited unity.

The universe is mental and held in the mind of the All. While the all is in the All, it is equally true that the All is in the all. This statement, which seems quite simple is quite confusing. Although it is written in English, it literally needs a translation. What is meant by this statement, is that the All, or everything there is, God is everywhere in everything and nothing. There cannot exist anything else in any way, shape or form. Therefore, while God or the All is everywhere and in everything, he resides within himself. Man is created in the image of God and is also part of God and God is part of man; therefore, he too resides within himself. "I think; therefore, I am", is a mental condition or state of being; therefore, the all is mind.

This somewhat abstract idea can also be related in other terms, perhaps more easy to understand. For this, we need another example. Let's say that someone were to ask you to imagine or to form a mental image of something, say another person, an idea or any other thought form or pattern. The significance of this request may not affect you in the least, and you may easily comply. Now in performing this function or task, you may not be aware that you have just created a mental image that relates to physical reality. Also, you may not be conscious of the fact that the mental image created in your mind has been of an inward form of attention and thereby negating or decreasing your reliance on all other forms of outside sensory data. That means that in actuality, the individual is involved within himself or his own mind and the image it is involved in creating. Consequently, that means that the universe and the mind, is mental.

The natural outcome of this mental process is that the resulting tangible thought form derives its life, spirit or reality, from the mind of the thinker or individual. Just as an artist immerses himself in his creative works, so do his works reflect his ability to mentally concentrate or to be consciously aware of the relationship between the intangible and the tangible worlds of reality. This is almost like saying that the finished works of the artist have a spirit or reality all their own, or is it that they only represent the spirit and mental power of their creators, both statements are true. It is not so much the physical tangible results that are important as it is power of the mind over matter. A creation takes on the spirit of its creator, but it is not the creator. Just as we are all part of God, we are not God. There is a relationship that is reflected into physical reality by way of one's mental abilities.

There exist many degrees of being and degrees of existence in the universe. We are concerned with seven levels or planes of physical reality. All depend upon the growth and/or advancement of these forms based upon the principle of energy overcoming resistance. The degree of separation is based upon the ability of that form to recognize itself with recognition and this is consciousness. Only man is capable of extending and expanding himself to recognize himself with recognition, but even he is limited to a specific level of consciousness at his lowest levels. It is only when man has reached his highest level that the ultimate point is reached in physical reality and a mental conscious cross over is possible to access other unmanifested non-linear realities. This is where conscious unity or balance can be achieved with All There Is. This is the ultimate point where the recognizer, recognizes itself with recognition.

In this physical reality everything experiences the form of separation known as resistance, but everything is also in a process of growth; whereby, everything is overcoming this resistance with other energy forms to become more conscious of itself on a limited scale. This is demonstrated by the fact that all matter is in motion and vibrating its own level of matter. If that motion were constant or decreasing to a lower form of energy, that object would itself decrease or cease to exist; however, the constant use of energy causes a condition of growth or creation that increases and changes life forms into extension of itself that are greater than it was before. This is a form of expansion that changes the limitations of its existence and therefore, in a sense, changes its level of consciousness, which is considered a mental function. In order to change one's position or relationship to all there is, one must use energy. But energy can be misused to put one in a position of greater resistance instead of less resistance; therefore, care should be used in the exercise and application of energy.

Because all physical matter is in a state of separation that means that there is a dense form of matter that vibrates very slowly and a higher form of that same thing that vibrates at a higher state. That also means that for everything physical, there is an opposite form that is of spirit. Again, there is a big difference in the rate of vibration. As you learned from the last chapter, the "I" dwells in the spiritual realm and the "me" dwells in physical reality. The "I" is capable of activating or transferring its energy to the more dense form of the "me". That means that the "I" becomes involved or wrapped up in its creation, just the same as the artist or creator gets involved in his work. The mental thought process dominates the "self" and one loses or almost forgets his own existence and virtually lives in his own creation. If it weren't for one's point of focus on outside stimuli to the physical being, one could not distinguish spiritual reality from physical reality.

The whole mental process is nothing more than a transfer of energy from the higher form or level of being to that of the lower form. That also means that the vibration level must decrease as it reaches or achieves the level of physical reality. The more one uses energy, the more one achieves a greater consciousness of his being and becoming. The more one can focus his attention on the mental process, the more one will be able to control his growth and becoming.

It is interesting that the word, attention, is derived from a Latin root and means to reach out or stretch. That means that the act of focusing one's attention is the mental reaching out or reaching within, and to extend one's mental energy to cause a union of the two worlds of reality. Extension and expansion are a form of growth, which is nothing more than movement or a journey to one's own being. The constant use of energy and the attention one gives to using energy will help one along his way in an upward movement to a higher form of himself.

If the All is everything and nothing, and if it resides within itself, then it also means that the All behaves similar to a closed system, or a system that feeds upon itself and replenishes itself in a self sufficient manner. In fact, the all or everything there is, is often related to a hermetically sealed box, and interesting enough, the word and definition of hermetic stems from the teachings and philosophy of the great Egyptian teacher Hermes. This ancient teacher taught the principle of unity or oneness of creation back before it was able to be recorded.

The only thing that separates humans from all there is, is this matter called resistance, and the only thing that can overcome this resistance, is energy. That doesn't necessarily mean that this resistance is going to be broken down in a short period of time nor in a long period of time. Our reality, teaches us that all matter or entropy will eventually affect and begin to change what is into something else. No matter how hard a substance is or how big it is, the constant use of different energy forms will change it. Patience is all that is needed and perhaps, a little bit of help on the part of one's self or consciousness.

There are many words coined to indicate or identify change, growth or progress; however, they all seem to dwell on the idea of gaining energy and the modification of that which is. In the case of human beings, this growth process or entropy can also be considered an awakening process or we may compare our present existence to that of an amnesia patent. That is, the consciousness of the individual is increased with each application of energy, adding to one's experiences or knowledge of relationships. This is the learning process; this is the recognizer, recognizing himself with recognition.

The only way to overcome resistance is with energy, but you must also be observant and conscious of this use. You must learn to use energy wisely, or else you may find yourself in a more difficult place or position than you were in before you did anything. But also, you may find that to get somewhere, you may have to go back a little, in order to advance. This is somewhat like finding yourself in a maze. You must observe the patterns and select those positions that benefit all and not the privileged few whom you think worthy of your gifts. Do not think in terms of what you can benefit by giving to others, but feel benefited that what you have is not yours to begin with. Remember, the all or God, gives you everything that is yours and/or what you need. What you do with such gifts is strictly up to you.

Growth, or change requires the use of energy, and you must understand that wealth is a form of energy that must be appreciated and shared accordingly, not hoarded and left idle. Balance and position of one's self in life is very important in this physical reality, but we are dealing with growth on other planes of existence as well. Therefore, balance is important to one's position because it stretches beyond the physical limitations of one's reality. One must learn and understand that growth is occurring on the mental, spiritual, social and physical planes, and possibly in unmanifested non-linear realities as well. That means that how one positions himself mentally, determines how one makes his own reality. To be super conscious is to recognize all possibilities and probabilities in non-linear time. Unity is the destination that one must seek in his journey or growth of himself and the only way to achieve that is to learn how to use energy. The knowledge and understanding of that relationship is the balance of which I speak. This is the greatest wealth one can possess. For it is this conscious knowledge that allows one to control himself wherever and whenever he wants without being affected by that particular environment.

I may have overdone it again on talking about the principle of mentalism; therefore, I want to remind you that this is a chapter dealing with the elements of control. In discussing this principle at length, I have actually touched upon each of the other six remaining principles; however, I still want to cover them again in a more direct and condensed form. The first principle almost requires a lengthy explanation, because the other six are all relative to the first. That is, for the other principles to be understood, the principle of mentalism must be part of that understanding. It is that principle that creates the unity that binds them all together. Just as the physical body requires physical nourishment or a certain amount of resistance and exercise to grow and expand, so too does the mind; however, because the mind functions on higher forms of energy, it requires greater exercise and higher and finer energy forms to function properly. The ability of the individual to be consciously aware of the learning triangle enables him to exercise complete control of his physical body and his physical environment. What the individual does with that control is up to him.

The second principle should really be referred to as the principle of correspondence and not planes of unity that I indicated earlier. The reason for this confusion deals with specific levels or planes; however, the planes of unity that I spoke of earlier in the book are actually sub levels or levels that have opposites. The principle of correspondence deals with a specific level of vibration and states that, "What is above, is the same as below, and as below, so above". The principle of correspondence basically gets its name from the fact that energy forms, or vibrations occur differently on other levels or planes of existence in both manifested and non-manifested reality. That is, solid matter can be broken down or changed into something else in a predictable manner, because it corresponds to certain known laws of science. What exists on one level can be transferred or changed to correspond to that of another level.

There are supposedly, three major planes of manifestation in this physical reality and they are physical, mental, and spiritual. These planes are then subdivided into seven minor planes and these planes are again subdivided into sub planes that are comparable in pattern or structure to our intangible sets of opposites that fall somewhere under the major mental plane. The difference between these planes is solely a matter of degree or an arbitrary rate of vibration similar to a measuring ruler. All of these manifestations are but creations of the All, and have their existence within the infinite mind of the All. Therefore, there exists correspondence, unity, harmony and agreement, between each of the seven planes. That also means that there is a pattern of recognition that transcends the levels of manifestation in a growth pattern of expansion. The point of focus or balance changes ever so slightly in a specific direction thereby allowing one to gain something and give something in order to achieve a greater consciousness and/or a higher level of being.

Without getting too heavy into the next principle, the principle of correspondence merely reiterates that we all exist or belong to one. Unity is the balance that we all seek; however, we exist in a state of separation that creates a form of resistance or inbalance that maintains our position on a certain level of existence. In order to gain control of one's self and his environment, one must learn to be conscious of the various degrees or levels of energy and/or vibration. It is only the learning and knowledge of these manifestations that one can overcome the laws of cause and effect and other adversities that confront man. Paper wraps the rock, but the rock will break the scissors, that can cut the paper, that wraps the rock. Planes of energy can be controlled if they are understood. The problem of understanding is relative to one's position of consciousness. If the universe is mental, then man's reality must also be mental. Understanding is nothing more than recognition, and man does not yet know how to recognize this. Man does not recognize the pattern of limitations that he has placed upon himself; therefore, he does not yet recognize himself with recognition.

The next factor of control is the principle of vibration. I find it somewhat difficult to make a clear cut difference between this principle and that of the last which deals with identification and separation of energy levels and/or vibration. Except, this principle gives us the cause for the principle of correspondence. That is, this principle states that nothing rests, everything moves and vibrates. This movement or vibration exists at all levels of life and manifests itself in a circular motion or revolves upon a central axis and therefore can be considered to have cycles. Consequently, all forms of energy are involved in a constant motion around and/or against each other in a relationship to points or a point inward or outward. Naturally, this movement creates change and different relationships that result in a form of growth and/or direction of becoming. As matter or energy reaches its higher forms of vibration, it enters into laws of cohesion and attraction, followed by ethereal state of being, similar to a plasma affect that permeates all that is. You might call this ethereal state an elastic substance that serves as a medium of transmission for waves of energy known as heat, light, electricity, magnetism, etc. As these energy forms change into something else, they give off or shed their heavier molecular or atomic structural pattern and cease to be a physical tangible object long before the ethereal state is reached.

Why I am telling you all of this in some detail is because man too, takes on a similar path or journey as he grows. This is a process of change which consists of giving as well as gaining; however, the gaining that I am talking about is not so much in the way of accumulating more physical tangible matter, but mostly involves a form of liberation from the confining outward appearances of matter. That is, although man or matter is composed of higher forms of energy, these energy forms are confined, entangled and/or imprisoned, within these tangible structures. Thus, when man or matter is stimulated, they give off certain vibrations or unloads them to become lighter and to change. However, unlike matter, man is affected much more and more often than is matter, because man can stimulate himself with mental thoughts, emotions, reason, will, or desire, or any other mental state or condition that activates or energizes his becoming. That is, man can change his position or point of focus to experience or not experience anything he wants.

Even though I think the last couple of sentences were clear enough to be understood, they also mean something else. As man sheds or throws off these limitations of heavier energy forms, he may in turn affect the minds of other people through a process of induction otherwise known as mental telepathy. That is, as each individual becomes more conscious, so too does his personal level of vibration. that Since thought proceeds all physical manifestations that means that one's mental abilities are affected most, As man becomes enlightened or more conscious, he may be able to tune in and influence the vibrations or thoughts of other people. At the same time, man is also subject to receiving thoughts from others and making those thoughts his own, if he is not conscious and/or careful. That raises a lot of questions concerning everyone's actions and the part that society plays in our growth and learning process. Hopefully, this thought may get you thinking a little more and hopefully result in your questioning of yourself.

As you can see, man is engaged in a journey or growth process that will lead him toward his spiritual self, unity or balance. As man progresses, he will begin to use more and more of his mental abilities, until he achieves a point where physical reality will no longer offer him any more ability to grow. That means that this world of physical reality or one's earthly experience will not end, or may not end, in a catastrophe, or chaos, or a big bang, or a collision, or the burning of the sun, but will occur because there will be no more need or ability for growth of man or other life forms in a state of separation or as physical matter. This mental situation or condition must occur first, before a physical manifestation can materialize. The universe is mental first, as is man. Thought must precede selection, and separation, or resistance must be overcome with energy in the direction of unity.

The spirit of each soul is not or never will be annihilated, but is infinitely expanding. The created and the creator are, or will become one, for they are one now but separated. Just as the All or God stimulates himself by meditating upon the universe, so can man cease to exist upon the material plane by willingly withdrawing himself into his indwelling spirit. As dense matter is energized, it begins to increase its rate of vibration, it begins to get warm, then hot, then hotter until it starts to de-materialize. Matter may go through changes of a solid to liquid, to gas, and may also involve color changes as the temperature increases, but in all cases, it begins to give off heat, light, and solids that can enter the environment. As this process continued one would enter or emit X-rays, electrical charges, and magnetism, of a limited nature. In any case, matter basically undergoes a change in its characteristics and begins to emit or gives of itself to the surrounding environment until and beyond the point that it can be observed.

Note the pattern of change. As energy is applied or as activity increased, one gives more and more of itself off to its immediate environment until it virtually becomes unlimited or unencumbered by outward physical form. And so it is with man. As above, so below; as below, so above. Vibration makes the difference.

I have spoken about the law of opposites in earlier chapters. The principle of polarity is the same thing, but is much more extensive than I indicated in those preceding chapters. This principle states that, everything is dual or separate and everything has poles or its pair of opposites. That is, opposites are certain indestructible units identical in nature, but different by degree. All truths are but half truths and every truth is half false. This is most evident in the explanation of temperature. Because everyone is familiar with temperature and degrees, let's use this example to describe the principle of polarity.

First, to explain polarity and temperature, let's also use a practical application instead of its effect on man's physical senses. Let's use an industrial application. Let's say that we have two machined parts made identically the same, made under the same conditions and temperature. If we were to heat one part short of its melting point, we would have a part that will probably be larger in size than its identical twin which is still at room temperature. Now, if we were to take this other part and put it into say liquid nitrogen or oxygen and measure it, we would have a part smaller in size. The difference between the parts would indicate the opposites of the original part or the material used to make that part. This difference can be measured in degrees of temperature or an artificial unit of measurement.

It is common in industry to assemble two mating parts with identical dimensions without the use of a welding operation or another manufacturing process by freezing them and then allowing them to return to normal room temperature. The only thing that is affected is their size. You might also want to draw upon some analogies that one extreme represents a beginning and the other, an end. The point at which they become identical is the point of focus or balance point.

In our example we need to establish limitations which are acceptable to the function or end result. Parts are designed to function together to perform a task in physical reality under conditions that the assembled device may encounter or will experience. Therefore, one must tolerate differences, within limitations, knowing the working environment that it will be exposed too. That is, a part is to be made to a certain physical dimension with tolerances for either increased or decreased sizes that are acceptable to an environmental condition and other mating parts or materials in our physical reality.

Now this long explanation defines and designates a specific current position in relation to an environment that is subject to degrees in temperature and physical changes that in itself is not specific. That is, everything is subject to a tolerance, or range of acceptable change. Again, none of this really explains the poles or extremes, but we have established position; therefore, a pole or polarity, represents that position farthest away from the point of balance or medium point of focus. But remember, just as it was difficult for us to establish a present point, so it is with finding the furthest point.

If we were to use some of our examples of known opposites in nature, I think you may disagree with me and yet be quite surprised. What I mean by this is that the opposite of the North Pole is the South Pole and the opposite of east is west. One can geographically pin point a pole, but in traveling to one of these latter points one will discover that a person will always be opposite some designated opposite point or position. In the case of east-west, one will discover that he is always traveling east or west of a specific point to reach its opposite, but at the same time, the opposite point keeps changing as you change. Sure, you may reach a designated opposite point, but it is only relative to your starting point. This sounds like my first chapter, explaining beginnings and endings.

Because we are dealing with physical reality, which has or is controlled by outside or outward appearances, there are certain specific poles or opposites that have tangible points or poles, and so too has intangible thought forms; however, they are even more difficult to pin point. But, it is not so much the importance of these points as it is your personal relationship to these positions. A good example of this problem is the determining of good and bad, right and wrong, etc. These are all relative terms to our own position on an intangible unsure scale of tolerance that is in constant change. By learning to recognize polarity one can make his own reality to his own choosing in a more positive, creative manner. All one has to do is to recognize these opposites and to focus in on that which one wants to experience. A negative can be turned into a positive as well as a positive into a negative. The only problem of this element of control is one's own self or one's consciousness or his ability to recognize these opposites, extremes and balance. Physical reality is a form of separation; therefore, opposites or poles must exist. By understanding this, one can begin to learn to consciously control one's reality by the raising and lowering of his personal level of his physical vibrations in order to achieve a more dominant positive mental state, instead of being a servant or slave to the negative form of polarity that creates pain and suffering.

The fifth principle of rhythm is an extension of polarity and/or it compliments or explains a little better how polarity occurs and changes. This principle states that everything moves in patterns. That is, everything flows in and out like tides, or rises and falls, or everything behaves similar to a pendulum. In short, rhythm is the motion that keeps everything in balance, by compensating for extremes or the condition that I refer to as inbalance. It is at this point in the book that I can now say or clarify how and why inbalance maintains its stability. It is by this principle of rhythm.

In our description of poles, especially intangible ones, you now know that they are difficult to discern and are not so plentiful, if I can use that term. That is, the points or degrees between the poles outnumbers the two supposed points of the poles. Therefore, the poles act as the limiting extremes and all action or manifestations must occur within those boundaries. That means that the center point or point of balance is where most of the action or activity takes place. It is from this center point that one can experience the greatest amount of freedom or movement before a limit is reached. But because everything is in a constant state of motion, means that, that thing must proceed in a specific direction toward an outer limit or pole. Therefore, that means that there exists movement or motion between opposites or poles. That also means that there exists a force or forces that control that movement to keep it within the limitations of those opposing forces. That means that there is a definite pattern of recognition set up in an oscillating fashion, first toward one pole, and then toward the other. That motion depends upon the power or strength of the poles in question. That doesn't mean that the motion or object must achieve or reach one pole, but merely has to be attracted in the direction of one pole and then the other.

In describing this movement of motion of rhythm, we are basically talking about two dimensions; however, a third factor is also involved, but it does not play a significant part in rhythm and that is growth. Rhythm behaves as if growth does not even exist. That is, this movement toward the poles continues in perpetual motion and is not affected by anything else as long as the poles or opposites exist. Through changing vibration, one may achieve a form of growth or expansion of the poles that might affect the rhythm or motion between the poles, but such change is not significant in terms of physical reality; however, I think that this may be more important on a more intangible or mental nature. In any case, growth creates expansion of the rhythm, if nothing else. That also means that no two points are exactly the same. Nothing exists in a state of being the same that is the law of entropy.

Man sometimes uses the word cycle(s) to describe rhythm or this observable motion. In fact, he has collected all sorts of facts and figures to make predictions and has succeeded in many cases to accurately predict a lot of rhythms. Most notably, he is familiar with the seasons for planting and harvesting. Man most frequently refers to this rhythm as time, and has been most creative in his explanations about rhythm in songs, which is in fact, a controlled form of sound or vibration or a void of sound. Music is nothing more than the pattern of intensity and silence between two opposites. Sorry to be so clinical about that! But, I particularly liked one pattern of vibration that was made popular by a musical group called the "Birds" during the sixties and the Vietnam War called, "Turn, turn, turn", which describes cycles as well.

The song goes something like this; "To everything, turn, turn, turn; there is a season to be born, a time to die, a time to plant, a time to reap, a time to kill, a time to heal, a time to laugh, a time to weep. (refrain) A time to build up, a time to break down, a time to dance, a time to walk, a time to cast away stones, a time to gather stones together. (refrain) A time to love, a time to hate, a time for war, a time for peace, a time that you may embrace, a time to refrain from embracing. (refrain) A time to gain, a time to lose, a time to rend, a time to sow, a time for love, a time for hate, a time for peace, I swear it's not too late". I think this song says a lot about polarity or opposites. But it is still relative to the individual and/ or his environment.

The principle of vibration states that there is no such thing as absolute rest or cessation from movement and all movement partakes of rhythm. This rhythm is of universal application on all planes of life and human activity, both of a physical and mental nature. It is rhythm that is responsible for the succession of man's moods, emotions, feelings, and other peculiar changes, associated with his behavior. However, by being conscious of polarity or the poles, one can consciously seek his own higher self and thereby escape the swing or rhythmic pendulum toward the lower negative pole. In a sense, what happens is that one allows the negative swing to take place without him, or without his knowing it, on an unconscious level. This is an element of control that allows the individual not to experience these negative forces on a conscious level.

This transfer of energy is called transmutation. It consists of raising one's level of vibration and ego above that of one's subconscious plane of mental activity so that the negative swing or rhythm is not manifested in consciousness, and the individual is not affected. This is somewhat like rising above something and/or letting that something pass below him. One basically attaches himself to the highest point or desired pole and refuses to participate or experience the negative slide backward. That is, if one can raise his level of consciousness, he can control his position and/or behavior by willing himself not to follow or be influenced by this rhythm or reverse swing. To control your own self is to neutralize the principle of rhythm; however, there is no way the principle itself can be destroyed. One can escape the effects of the negative movement, but he cannot change the rhythm to any great degree.

It is also important to note that the energy force exercised by the poles determines the amount of the swing or variance of the rhythm. That is, the swing to the left is the same to the right. This is the law of compensation. There must be a balance in the rhythm, but it doesn't necessarily have to happen on the next immediate swing, or swings. It can be delayed over an extended period of time. Ponder that last statement for awhile. Time's up, let's get moving again. What some of this means in the long run, is that the man who enjoys keenly is subject to suffer keenly, or the man who feels little pain also enjoys little joy. The capacity for pain and pleasure in each individual is a matter of balance. That also means that one must eventually pay the price of one extreme to the other extreme, or use the law of neutralization to overcome this severe movement. The law of compensation is ever in operation, striving for balance and counterbalance. Eventually, everything has its pleasant and unpleasant sides. The things one gains are always paid for by the things one loses. The rich may attain material wealth, but the poor may enjoy more of the simple pleasures of life.

The principle of causation states that every cause has its effect and every effect, its cause. Everything happens according to law and chance is but a name for a law not recognized. In short, this is the principle of cause and effect that I have frequently spoken of earlier. Nothing happens by chance and there is no such thing as chaos, only laws that behave to a pattern as yet not understood, or not as yet exercised or controlled. As discussed before, the universe is mental or within the mind of the All. There cannot be anything outside the mind of the All and independent of it, because nothing could exist without a recognizable pattern.

The principle of causation reaffirms the belief in unity, the All or God. It does this by assuring us that all things are predictable, knowing the forces at work. Given the same physical conditions or environment and the same forces in exactly the same amount and sequential order of starts and stops, the results will always turn out the same. However, you should also be aware by now, that growth and/or vibrations constantly change and nothing is that firm or certain unless you are certain of change or its direction of growth. Nothing ever happens without a cause, or chain of causes. This is our motorboat and water effect that I spoke of at some length.

There is always a cause and effect to every event and an event is that which comes, arrives or happens, as result of something before it. Once energy or force is set into motion, it will continue to work in some way, shape or form, until everything is brought into balance. There is continuity between all events, past, present, and future. You might say that creation was a positive creative event that started the ball rolling and everything since then has been primarily of a destructive nature in order to re-balance itself. But remember, this is only a half truth. Where did all of the energy come from to become something of a tangible nature? Was something else changed or destroyed to accomplish something else? What about all of the positive forms of growth found to manifest themselves here on earth? A lot of questions which I am afraid I can't answer. I just want you to be aware of the fact that even in these questions, the thought form of good, bad, right, and wrong, or positive and negative, are in existence and they don't necessarily have or need an answer. The answer to all questions is, what do you want to experience? There is a relationship that exists between all things that have gone or been before and everything that will come after or follow.

Every thought we think and every act we perform has its direct and indirect result which fits into the great chain of cause and effect; however, almost all of this occurs on a sub-conscious level just as man is free and yet bound by necessity. There exists a relationship that binds men and makes them slaves of heredity, environment and physical needs. Man is swayed by opinions, customs and thoughts, from the outside physical world. The principles of polarity and rhythm affect man's emotions, feelings, thoughts and moods; consequently, few people are even aware or conscious to the potentials that life has to offer. It is only by understanding and recognition that one can control the principle of cause and effect. That is, after one has knowledge of this principle, one can begin to use one law against another, until he has at least sought refuge in the law itself. Man has the ability to raise himself above the principle of causation and can control the results; however, he must first know where to look. The universe is mental. All manifestations must begin in the intangible mental state of the individual; but, if you are conscious enough to recognize all the patterns of beginnings and endings at work and in what sequence, then you can use the laws to move mountains and anything else you so desire. Nothing is impossible; it is just not recognized or thought of yet. Paper wraps the rock that can break the scissors that can cut the paper.

I have spoken a lot about the last principle of control in the last chapter; however, I just want to touch upon the principle of gender again as part of a sequential process involved in the control and behavior of one's self. This principle basically states that gender is everything, and that everything has its masculine and feminine properties or characteristics which are manifested on all planes. Let me remind you that we are not dealing with the manifestation or separation of the physical sexes, but with the active and passive origins of life.

All life forms possess both the male and female principle in its single life form. Both live side by side in a give and take type of situation. The male or masculine principle represents a positive pole form of energy and the female or feminine principle represents the negative form of energy or pole. Together, this gender principle is responsible for all creation by producing, generating and transferring of energy forms into mental and physical manifestations.

As mentioned in the last chapter, it is the male energy form that carries the initial charge or instigates that which is to become. This process works similar to how heredity and/or physical growth patterns or characteristics are transferred to the new born prior to birth. But, it is the female charge that is in fact, responsible for the growth or manifestation and appearance of that life form into reality. Nothing can be accomplished without a balance of those two forces. One needs the other and vice-versa, in order to procreate and grow. They are both equally important and they both work as much or as hard as each other, both in a linear sequential manner and in non-linear unmanifested reality that has short beginnings and endings.

It is the masculine principle of gender that works first and seems to direct its energies toward the female principle. You might want to compare this structural form to that of an atom, in that the female form occupies the center of the atom's nucleus and the male circles the female. It is through a process of concentration or position, and the values or intensity that the male energy form of one's being unites, and/or transfers, or energizes a female energy form that stimulates the growth of new mental thought forms and physical manifestations. Even though we are talking about a linear sequential pattern of growth, the male energy form is functioning constantly on other levels and/or matters pertaining to one's well being, and if the will is strong enough, one can modify or make changes to manifestations which it has previously created; however, such latter changes are not common or the rule. Gender behaves as a form of balance between non-linear spiritual reality and physical time space and matter. It is the prime motivating force that keeps everything going in a state of balance or perpetual motion. This is the start-stop factor that creates beginnings and endings. This principle completes the mental process and defines its limitations of control or rules of behavior.

So, what have we learned about the seven elements of control, and how do we consciously go about regaining control of our lives? Well, first of all, you must believe that you(we) live in a type of closed or unified system that is governed or controlled by some very specific rules. Once one learns to recognize these rules, one may be able to begin to use these rules to control his own being.

Second, you must believe that this closed system is based upon unity or oneness, and that everything is related or relative to one another on all levels of life. That is, life exists on a multi-dimensional scale of reality, or in a sense, life is never destroyed, but merely changes form.

Third, you must believe that everything is in motion and that it vibrates or radiates, at specific rates and therefore creates specific patterns. These patterns, in turn, behave to certain rules of change that have beginnings and endings that are tied together in a linear sequential manner in our physical reality.

Fourth, you must believe that the rules of change are based upon polarity or separation. That is, although we live in a unified system, physical manifestation must be based upon separation and/or opposing forces in order for resistance or denser forms of matter to occur.

Fifth, you must believe that because life exists in a state of separation, there are opposing forces at work striving for balance. That means that life forms position themselves at a point of balance, but because of motion, a rhythmic pattern or swing is set up and/or maintained so long as the opposing forces exist.

Sixth, you must believe that every event or thing that happens is based upon something or some force that is striving for balance or counterbalance. This is energy and resistance at work on a multi-dimensional levels of consciousness and/or super consciousness.

Seventh, you must believe that all forms of creation are based upon gender, or the transferring of energy from one form to another for the purpose of growth and/or manifestation.

To learn and understand the seven principles of control, you must be conscious of everything about and within yourself. In short, you must believe in yourself and your being and becoming. You make your own reality; however, you must be conscious of everything you do and think. Nothing happens by chance or accident, and there is no such thing as chaos. You must believe in the positive creative forces within you. You are a part of God, and he is part of you. With such teamwork, how can you not miss being successful at everything you try? It is not impossible to control your consciousness. All you have to do is to learn to understand and recognize the rules of the game and how they relate or fit together. Then, you must learn to work with the forces of God, and not against them. You can do anything you want, based upon the principle that the universe is in the mind of God. Everything is in the mind of the All, and you too must begin your quest or journey there. You are a part of God, and he is part of you.

This same thought is expressed in "The Purpose". This piece of prose makes everything sound so simple, yet it is still so abstract as to makes this information difficult to use in everyday applications. There is so much simplicity and beauty to life and somehow, we just cannot seem to see it and/or find it, but remember, it is there if you look for it.

THE PURPOSE

Suppose, I were to ask you to imagine a vast universe.
Imagine this universe without limits, physical form, or shape.
Imagine this great expanse entirely filled with energy.
Imagine this energy, this seething energy, so active as to be
electrifying to our senses.
Imagine this energy to be another form of consciousness
or conscious entity.
Imagine this conscious entity to be in constant motion
and constantly changing.
Imagine countless centuries of motion, like the waves on a beach.

Imagine this conscious entity capable of thought and dreams.
Imagine this conscious entity requiring the use of energy for this activity,
which in and by itself would also be part of that entity itself.
Imagine the use of this energy rearranged, transformed, converted, and
changed into physical form, but still locked within the confines of this entity.
Imagine many eons of time and this state of being and becoming.

Imagine the solitude of such an entity in and by itself, with its thoughts
and dreams.
Imagine this entity releasing more and more of itself into the physical matter
of dreams.
Imagine this entity releasing more and more of its dreams to a physical
reality capable of its own consciousness.
Imagine this new conscious entity to be composed of that which is the original
entity, but which now has free will and lesser energy powers.
Imagine this new entity to be part of, but less than the original entity.

Imagine a new entity, given and endowed with a new reality and new forms
of energy.
Imagine this new entity in a new state of being and becoming.
Imagine this new entity evolving, as the original entity, but with another
definite purpose.
Imagine the purpose of this new entity to be to familiarize itself with the use
of energy, which is but another part of the original entity.
Now, suppose we call the original entity GOD and its creation, or new
entity, MAN!

CHAPTER 18

Law and Love

I have, up to this point, tried to give you a good solid background as to just what life is all about and also, how to go about controlling your own self and/or destiny. That means that I have also tried to establish a new or more solid basis for making selections which we relate to as good and bad, right and wrong; however, I can only hope that I have replaced current thought patterns with more suitable or understandable thought forms which everyone can relate too. The aspect of control is more difficult to describe and a lot more difficult to put into practice, considering all of the forces and/or environmental factors that relate to our outward selves and physical reality. That is, to know about something is one thing, to understand it is another, and to relate to it and put it into practice is still something else. You have been given all the ingredients that are needed to understand and control your being. You now have the key to the inner content of the learning triangle. How you relate or apply your energy forces in relationship to this information or knowledge and to possessing it, will determine how well you master physical reality.

The inner content is what life is all about. It is a growth process, whereby we use energy to position ourselves in an ever changing environment in order to grow and progress on our way to becoming our higher self. Our physical reality is a huge learning triangle where we relate to the knowledge of energy in its various forms or patterns and then use that knowledge to position ourselves and to use or possess it, in order to grow. How well we adapt or balance ourselves in this environment is only part of the problem, we still have to contend with our growth on a spiritual, mental and social level. This is a kind of balancing act on a multi-dimensional level and on more levels than I intend to pursue in this book. It's bad enough to try to focus in on a small circus like tight rope act amongst all of the other outside stimuli and forces affecting our being and becoming, without getting too distracted in other abstract intangible ways.

In trying to explain life, as we know it, I have probably offended a lot more people than I have helped. Perhaps the main reason for my comment is due or comes from the rather sterile, unemotional type of reasoning and logic I employed. That kind of makes man look like a robot or fool that goes around doing things and not knowing or really understanding why. If this is your thought and you have reached this point in this book, I see no other way that life can be adequately described, without going into this thought process. This way is necessary in order to eliminate the confusion and inconsistency and/or contradictions that are a way of life and/or the basis for this physical life. All of this conflict is due to the nature of our physical reality.

Let me remind you that our life is based upon separation and the manifestation of energy forms in various degrees of that separation and/or resistance. Without resistance, physical matter could not exist, nor could any higher form at this level. Our consciousness is the bridge that spans and connects all of the pieces or parts that are separated by a seemingly big insurmountable gap; therefore, our consciousness determines our reality and/or our balance in this reality. How we see it or recognize it determines how we relate to it. Therefore, one must know or understand the rules and principles of physical reality before one can properly function or balance himself in this environment. But again, there are other intangible realities that one must also balance in order to keep everything straight and all of this cannot be proven in the conventional sense of the word, or proof, as is required by most men of science.

Now that I have somewhat stirred up some mud by confusing you with an area of thought that I have not explained or pursued in any depth, I want to try to proceed in a direction of giving you some practical applications for what we have learned. That is, how does this knowledge of separation and consciousness relate to each individual and/or what good is it in a practical application. The simplest, shortest, and most logical answer to all of these questions is that the individual is the sole source of one's reality and/or he can control his environment. Even though this short answer is correct, it still does not sound logical to most of our average readers, because I believe everyone feels in some way or another, subject to conditions beyond their control. Also to say, such a positive statement means that there are no limitations or restrictions placed upon man and everyone knows that that is not true. If it were true, everyone would be going about his own business, doing his own thing, and not caring about anyone else. Such a simple answer cannot be true or practical, because we do not live independent of one another and we do need other people to support us in our daily life. But before we rule out our positive simple answer as false, remember, every truth is but a half truth as is everything false is but half false. Everything depends upon one's position amongst opposites or within a state of separation.

Logically, that last paragraph should bring us to a point of nowhere, however, that also means that the pattern is just not recognizable yet. Man needs balance, but he cannot accept a position or situation that is not of a singular nature, or relative to his growth in a specific direction. That is, man cannot seek or select a position of balance at all times, because that would severely limit himself or restrict him in his becoming. Therefore, man needs to select extremes in order to expand his environment and/or consciousness. Again, life is nothing more than a learning process; whereby, he makes selections that sets into motion, causes and effects, which he chooses to experience. Sounds simple, doesn't it? It also sounds unbelievable again, because it is so impersonal and cold. Why is that? Why is there doubt or the splitting of unity concerning this logic?

Let's take another look at our answer. Again, the obvious answer that the individual is the sole source of one's reality and/or can control his environment does not relate to each individual in a practical way. Why? Because of the laws of cause and effect, everyone knows that they are being influenced or affected by something beyond their control. Even if they did know, or were conscious of everything, there is still the question of control and no one that I know of has ever expressed the feeling that they were in fact in control of their life fully. Besides, for everyone to be completely independent of one another is contradictory to the concept of our whole growth pattern process, otherwise known as sociology. What I mean by that statement is that growth is a process based upon a relationship of mental expansion and then physical experience.

For people to ignore one another is to increase one's limitations and restricts them more by setting up artificial energy forms of resistance. That means that although we have all of the known control factors that affect us or help us determine our own reality, there is still something else that plays a significant part in our daily life and that affects our consciousness. There must be something that stimulates our conscious and subconscious mind in a more practical way that we can all relate to. There must be something that balances out all of these varying degrees and opposing forces. Just as right and wrong, good and bad cannot be proven to exist, there still must be a way to make that decision and a way to bridge the gap and the conscious mind cannot do that alone. We are not or cannot be Mr. Spock from Star Trek!

So what is it that we are missing? What can be so simple and yet so complicated? It is about time to pull the rabbit out of the hat and/or let the genie out of the bottle. There definitely is something else that we have not touched on that does explain or affects our physical reality. What is it you say already! Voila, I say! It is LOVE! Love? Yes, love! Now what the xxxx does he mean by that, you say? Well, I can't answer that question in a short sentence, that's why I devoted a whole chapter to it. In fact, I would have liked to write a whole book on it, because love is not a simple matter; however, it was necessary to build a better foundation before we proceeded with such a simple but complicated subject. It is simple because everyone knows or recognizes the word love, but it is complicated because it is used so frequently to mean different things. Therefore, it is necessary to again take the cold sterile approach to explaining this term and its relationship to man.

To explain love, we need to define what is meant by love, because love has a lot of different meanings. In addition to meanings, love is expressed in two different ways or on two different levels of life. That is, love is first recognized on the animal or third level of life as the driving force which is manifested as animal instinct or the desire to mate and reproduce. In this case, love is a stimulating vibrational urge which is primarily an active extreme or polar energy force that localizes in its inherent gender that causes an imbalance. That imbalance, in turn, has its effect on that animal by causing it to seek an opposite that will balance out or neutralize that force and/or urge. Therefore, love on this level is somewhat of an uncontrollable nature, because it is caused by body chemistry that activates or triggers the animal to mate and propagate the species. During this period of activity, that animal sets aside its normal characteristics of seeking food, shelter, and security in favor of satisfying this imbalance.

Although man is not an animal, he still expresses the consciousness of his lower levels, because that is the basis of this physical reality. Man too has to seek, fulfill and express his organic, plant and animal characteristics, as well as his advanced intellectual levels of energy. However, man is not ruled by imbalance as much as animals are; therefore, he can seek and choose the time and/or place where he wants to manifest himself in a sexual loving manner. But again, this kind of love is still an animal characteristic which man has mastered or modified by his intellect to fit his social environment and lifestyle. On this level, love connotes a need or want that can only be satisfied by possession. This may not be evident to most people, because most people do not see physical love in this light, but see it as the highest form of expression between people. This is both true and false. That is, physical love can be considered the highest form of expression if the action is not done solely to satisfy one's needs and wants. We will explain that a little better later on.

Love on the third level or animal level is distinguished from love on the sixth level by its need for possession. If you really sit down and look at this animal form of expression, you will see that the characteristics of this love are manifested by man in personal contact. That is, man seeks to come close to another person of the opposite sex, perhaps embrace, kiss, hug and touch, and/or join one another in stimulating one's outward physical senses. All of these actions are related to the act of possession. Even if you logically reason that the other person involved exercises free will or the freedom to or not to participate in this form or terms of endearment, it still constitutes mutual possession on the part of both parties.

Possession is not exclusive of or characteristic of just one individual. Love or the act of possession at this level is then the bringing together for the mutual fulfillment or physical needs. There is not necessarily anything wrong with this form of love, but whoever is subject to this form of possession, or love, is still living in a consciousness or a condition of separation that seeks the outward complimentary physical partner, or opposite, in order to satisfy his physical needs. This love always seeks to take, to have something, or possess. It is not a long lasting permanent thing in and by itself and capable of control by the individual. It requires something in return. Basically this would constitute meddling, getting involved with, or relating to the nature of cause and effect that that person chooses to experience

Love on the sixth level of life is a different kind of love. It is love that is not easily understood by man, because most people are not conscious enough to recognize it for what it is, and those who do, do not know how to manifest it totally. This love is not based upon separation or a condition of division, but comes from the knowledge of unity itself. Such love is often referred to as unconditional love or universal love. This is an active manifestation of always giving, never taking, and therefore needs nothing in return. It needs no supplement, no physical manifestation and always radiates from the consciousness of one, the divine all, all unity, or God. People who know, understand, and are conscious of this love, do not want to possess anybody or anything; rather, they merely want to give in a positive creative manner. This giving is also not readily understood, for it is founded in the knowing and recognition that they are already one with the infinite all and need nothing more than to wish or recognize this consciousness.

Such love, this love, is the most perfect manifestation of God and man at this level. This is love or man just short of the totally conscious person or the God-man, who is the seventh and highest form of life on earth. If you know of any such person, let me know. I know of no one; however, they have been known to exist. Maybe they still exist, but I doubt if anyone knows where to look or how to find such a person. Besides, why would anyone want to find such a person is also a paradox that most people cannot properly relate too? That is, man cannot relate to that or those which do not touch them or affect them in a tangible or intangible personal way.

How, or better yet, why a person would want to seek someone who cannot affect them seems illogical in our physical reality. Yet, the desire is there. It is an inner drive of our becoming our higher selves. The strange or most important thing to remember is that a person who expresses this kind of love cannot; repeat, cannot dramatically affect someone else in an outward fashion; however, just being in the presence of such a person would drastically affect everyone on other levels. Remember higher consciousness transcends all forms of energy or forces. All levels of humans know and sense this consciousness in higher beings. They recognize on a subconscious level that such a person knows and understands our physical reality and how one makes his own reality and chooses that which he wants to experience.

Although love on, or expressed by one's sixth level of being, sounds somewhat cold and sterile, it is in truth, the highest form of love that can exist, and it can be actively sought and expressed, even if it does not involve direct commitments on the part of the individual physically. This love is the fairest of all and constitutes one's higher self and/or his expression of inner unity or all with the universe. This love is the knowing and feeling that one is doing what he does best. This is the love of knowing that that which you are doing, or involved in, is that which you are supposed to be doing. This is the inner knowing or consciousness of your relationship with all there is both on linear and non-linear bases of our reality. This love is the love of one's inner content and its position within unity. This love is the love of God and your expression of him through your being and becoming. It is the most perfect form of love. It is the law of the universe, which is perfect, but it also allows you to go your own way, and to express your own self, allowing you to choose your own reality. How you choose to exercise that love determines your own reality.

So you see, love is the energy force of recognition and control that is expressed by the principle of polarity. It is the most important law that you can know, understand, and express, in this reality, but in a sense it is an expression of acknowledgement based in unmanifested non-linear reality. It is the most powerful of all the energy forces that we have talked about so far and has the capability to penetrate and affect all of the other principles of control that we talked about earlier. That's because love is one of the few intangible forces that man seems to recognize and understand both consciously and/or on a super conscious level. This force, this power of love on the sixth level of life has the ability to penetrate even the densest forms of matter, or the strongest negative form of itself, which is expressed as hate. Because love is such a powerful and strong force, I want to take some extra time out to explore perhaps some aspects of this form or opposite that you may not be aware of in its application.

Strange as it may sound, love on the sixth level can only be expressed by someone who loves himself. That is the first and most important fact that you should know. Love is a form of energy that must come from within, or all your attempts to convey that energy form will fail. That is because to love yourself means to position yourself within the strong positive pole of love in its most potent or primordial energy form. When you position yourself within this life force, you can then express the power of the universe. You cannot do this effectively if you do not understand the seven principles of control. You must make a conscious effort to do this or you must already be expressing the laws of the universe by inwardly knowing your position in this life and reflecting that position to others about you. This is the importance of position that I keep talking about and that may sound so strange to you. It is that point where you are one with God and he is one with you. It is an expression of universal unconditional love.

Let me remind you that love on the third level leads you to expect more love or something in return. At that level you can also express the opposite of that love as hate if you are not conscious of your position. That means that love and hate are both based upon self identification or related to your position. That also means that you cannot effectively love or hate someone else unless you can identify with them or relate to them by some form of recognition. That is, you must have had some form of interaction or give and take, if you will, with that or those other persons. You cannot get emotionally involved with those who do not touch you physically or emotionally. You cannot normally express love or hate to that of a stranger unless you have positioned yourself mentally in an extreme condition of this energy force.

In a practical application, hate always involves a painful sense of separation from love and is an expression of that division. A person you feel strongly about or against upsets you because he does not live up to your expectations or does not recognize your wants and needs for his love. If you hate a parent, it is precisely because you expect such love. You cannot express or expect that feeling to someone you do not know or from whom you expect nothing. In a strange way then, hate, is a means of returning love. It is an expression meant to communicate a separation that exists in relation to that which is expected. It is a limitation or barrier that is designed to get one's attention.

Hate then, is something that is loved. That is, it is precisely because the object or person is loved so much that it is also so disliked, if your expectations are not met or recognized. You may love a parent, if that parent does not seem to return that love and denies you your expectations you may hate that same parent. Then, hate is meant to get you your love back. It is supposed to lead to communications; whereby, you state your feelings or clear the air, so to speak, and that brings you closer to that person. In a sense then, hatred is not the denial of love, but an attempt to regain it and the painful recognition of the circumstances that separate you from it.

It would seem that if you understand the nature of the two forms of love, you would also be able to accept the feelings of hatred. This previous example was related to a family relationship; however, this same thought pattern can also be applied to a work environment as well. That is, one normally does not think in terms of love, but in terms of recognition, which is really the same thing. I use the term recognition because of the sexual connotations of love on the third level, but love is the form of recognition which is in question. You must also remember that love is often confused with that which is considered a two way street, or that requires a response on the normal level of communications as expressed on the third level. Unconditional love requires no response on the sixth level. The difference cannot be identified unless both people can communicate at the sixth level; therefore, one must make a conscious effort to express love in the form of recognition in nearly all cases. This is the only way it can be understood in an outward tangible environment.

When you control love at the sixth level, you control enormous amounts of energy. When you express hate, your energy is transformed into dense thick barriers that defy penetration by other forms of control, except by someone else's love. By accepting yourself and your joyful being that you are, you fulfill your own abilities and nobody can ask for more. When you have reached this point or position, your simple presence can make others happy. You cannot hate yourself and love anyone else. It is impossible. You will only express or project qualities you do not think you possess which others will sense, unless they themselves are out of position. By expressing false love with the thought of personal gain is detrimental to all those involved. Such love only prevents one's own personal growth and creates more barriers and limitations. Such love cannot be expressed if one himself is centered around possessions such as greed, or the use of power, or authority, as well as perhaps only a person seeking knowledge. Remember to express love also requires balance and the control of one's self.

One last thought. When you love others, you should grant them their innate freedom and do not put restrictions or demands on them. Love, on the sixth level, requires nothing in return, but such love must also be understood by all involved. That is, one cannot abandon certain limitations without replacing them with a higher form of consciousness. One must be able to relate to love and there are various expressions and characteristics of love, but all love affirms unity of purpose and thought. So, before you stop expressing love in physical tangible terms, you must be sure you are able to communicate that love in other recognizable terms or actions. Remember, it is one's inner content that determines or limits one's outer world. Until one is conscious of this dimension of understanding one cannot hope to control one's self and/or convey that thought of unity with that of another.

The journey of life and to which we are all involved, is a growth process of learning. To raise one's self to the next highest level, one must increase or lift himself consciously to a plane of divine wisdom using universal love. This is a slow gradual upward movement of change similar to an awakening process or an amnesia patient, for which this book gets its name, "Who am I, Where am I and, What am I doing here?" These are the three questions that must be asked, before one can proceed on his journey and on his way to becoming his true self. But even as these questions become clearer, one must never forget who he was and/or where others are still. That is, one must be able to bridge the gap in others as well as himself. The law of love is the easiest and quickest way to bridge that gap. It is the one control factor that is easily accessible to the conscious mind because it also recognizes the unconscious super consciousness and/or non-linear realities where unity exists. It leads one to one's greater happiness and can take those people with whom you have contact with along with you to some extent. It is the only universal law that is constant. But remember, it also has an opposite side to it. Try to be conscious of that.

Now, if you haven't noticed, I have given you seven principles of control and one law. There is a slight difference. Laws usually pertain to manmade rules governing specific affairs of man. It is a declaration of position which is not to be questioned, but it is based upon a world or reality of separation and man being the creature he is, is subject to these manifested forms of separation or division. That means that man's laws are somewhat questionable, depending upon who is exercising the element of control. Consequently, most of man's laws are subject to a great amount of interpretation and flexibility that does not necessarily have anything to do with divine wisdom or truth; rather, it is more a reflection of those who exercise a great deal of control especially in monetary terms. Unfortunately, the legal judicial system is more a product of those who exercise their power to influence and then it is a question of right or wrong. Laws are supposed to be made and enforced for the greater well being of all concerned, but the only real test for a law is still within the individual. That is, if a law interferes with the exercise of free will, then it is not a good law' but a barrier or limitation designed to restrict or subjugate people for the interest of someone else or interest group.

Naturally, the best law(s) would be no law(s) at all, but again, this is not practical. The problem with laws is that they are too specific and relate to actions in a physical world of opposites or separation. Therefore, the best alternative for a law would be a principle. A principle differs from a law in that it reflects basic truths or a quality about life or this reality. In short, principles are general rules that do not conflict with one another, because they do not deal with the same thing or same issue. Principles are used mainly to explain physical manifestations or factors governing the control of energy forces, but as you can tell by our last chapter, they can also deal with the intangible. However, I hope that you have learned by now, that the intangible is just another higher form of energy in an unmanifested state. This may sound a little confusing and contradictory, but it is not because a principle is not enforceable nor can it be controlled in the normal sense of the word. That is, a principle cannot be used as a law, because it already is, or at least it explains that which is.

The dilemma of coming up with a principle as a rule or law for human behavior, is also quite complicated and/or impossible, because as stated before, a principle only describes that which is; therefore, a principle cannot be used as such for a rule or law. However, at the same time, the whole idea of society and group behavior is based upon a kind of sharing, or mutual benefit for the great well being of all; therefore, love is or can be used as a principle. But again, what good is a principle if it only describes something that happens. We need something more specific that we can relate to on a daily basis. You know dXX well that no one is going to pay any attention to something you can't do anything about. Or can you?

Everybody knows that man's actions cannot be predictable to the point of a specific reoccurring action or reaction given the same condition and circumstances. That's because each individual relates to the same thing in different ways or different patterns, even though man is somewhat routine or pattern oriented. Man's overall or general behavior patterns are thought or believed not to be consistent with each individual. Strange, isn't it? But given that logic, we must then reinforce it with the idea that given the same set of circumstances between two people, or given the same circumstances to the same person, separated by the element of time, the action or reaction will probably be different. Hence the logic that a principle cannot be used to rule or control one's human behavior.

I think the problem or the seemingly contradictory statements are a result of the principle of gender that is also involved here. That is, the word love is a lot more complicated than you can imagine, for it is manifested in and by each of the preceding seven principles of control; consequently, the principle of gender is the least known and understood of all the principles of control and it therefore is not recognized in its state or position. That means that love is manifested in a state of being or active state, and a state of becoming or a state of growth. The latter is not necessarily a passive state, but it could be. Perhaps the best word to describe becoming would be a state of development. In any case, when love is thought of as a principle, it is in this latter stage or state of development. There is little or nothing that can be done about it, but that also means that love can be and is a principle.

Love, in its active state of being is also a law. That's right; love is a principle and a law. This is not contradictory because the manifestation of love is multi-dimensional, so to speak. Love as a principle, states a condition of existence or reality that is affirming the positive nature of unity and purpose in our being and becoming. Love as a law, states an intent and/or reason for our purpose of selections. That is, there is no such thing as good and bad, only that which you want to experience. All of your actions are selected or done with normally good positive intents, even if those intentions are selfish and self gratifying only. It is the principle of cause and effect that makes your actions and/or selections either positive or negative in relationship to the rest of your society and this relationship is what makes one's own learning or growth process either of a negative or positive nature. You make your own reality.

Again, love is a strong, powerful force. It is consciousness in which God dwells in his purest form. Unconditional love is a principle and a law, because it affirms the greater well being of yourself and all others. It is both active, passive, and forever changing. It is the force that brings you back to your origin. This is our predestined journey from which we are so distracted with temptations, or physical manifestations, or resistance in our reality. You are in control of your own life. You are something great. I remember a poster that showed and said (usually portrayed with the picture of a small child) "I must be something good, because God doesn't make junk!" And using that same form of thought, the world and universe must be created with that same loving thought, or why else would it exist? Aren't we part of that same thought or plan? Therefore, love is a principle and a law, because it explains what is and can be. What we do with it consciously is something else. Will it be positive love or its opposite, hate? You make your own reality!

How do I go about telling everybody, like the song, that "Love is the Answer". How do I convince everybody that you can control your own self and/or behavior by being conscious of love in its many forms? How do I tell everybody that love is the driving force that keeps us going and keeps us in balance? Just as the universe is mental, it is also conceived in love. Through the application of this force, all matters can be easily resolved because that means that each person or individual could consciously reflect his higher self and/or position. In such an ideal position there could be no conflict. It is only when man cannot consciously find himself or goes against the patterns, laws, and principles of this reality, that there is conflict.

So when everything seems like it is going wrong, all you have to do is contemplate love. When things look bad or out of control, just sit back mentally and contemplate love. By doing so, you are in a sense meditating your position or state of being with all there is and you are actively seeking your center of being. From there you can also transmit your male gender principle to all of those who are receptive or unconscious of their higher being. That is, you can take an active part, literally, in making this a better place to live. You can transmit and transfer the energy of love or this law of love to all there is.

Even though these are some beautiful thoughts that we are talking about, I believe we still have a problem of practicality. In fact, maybe it isn't so much of practicality as it is in the relationship of the individual and his limitations and routines. That is, man is not accustomed to positive creative patterns or routines of behavior as well as they identify with or recognize the negative energy forms. Instead of looking inward and transmitting the thought of love, which is manifested into caring and sharing, one seem more capable of expressing the negative form manifested in hate. Through the ages, man has sought and gotten accustomed to demonstrating his disapproval and increasing his limitations or barriers to his higher self. He has now gotten into patterns and routines that are now unconscious forms of responses. That means that it is a lot harder for man to liberate himself in a more positive creative manner.

This problem of negative thought patterns is reflected in our whole society. I have stated and said that love is a law, but where do you find any such law written or appearing in any legal books of man, except the Bible? You can't. That's because men originally sought to clarify only those things that were negative to man. But by constantly stressing the negative features of manmade laws, he has done or accomplished the reverse. He has instead, used these laws to set precedence or guides for supposedly good behavior. But how can something that is based upon a negative energy force support or stimulate good positive behavior? It would be the same situation as mentioned earlier of trying to love someone else, when you don't even love yourself. You must position yourself on the positive energy side, before you can transfer that force to someone else. However, our society seems to be doing an excellent job of manifesting this reverse energy form.

So you see, you might say that the law of love may be considered to be unknown or forgotten, except in its form of manifestation on the third level of life and some exceptional people who are becoming conscious of this energy force. Over the years, man has seen fit to ignore this truth and has tried to supplement this law of love with literally hundreds of others.

It seems strange, almost too strange, to me that the most important and most powerful law of man has been conveniently forgotten or overlooked most of the time.

Instead of love, man seems almost carried away with the making of new laws, rules, regulations, and other ordinances etc. However, man will never succeed in replacing the law of love, but the reverse is true. There can only be one true law and that is to love unconditionally: You can eliminate the whole legal and judicial systems of the world by creating this one law. You can also change the Department of Justice to the Department of Love and all you need to run it is someone who can consciously recognize love. In matters of conflict, all you have to do is to sentence each of the individuals involved to a couple of hours of silent meditation of love.

Impractical you say! Yes, you are probably right, but again, what a beautiful thought. Man is not yet ready for such simplicity, because simplicity is so complicated. Just think of all the people that would be put out of work and are necessary to perpetuate the existing system of legal justice, besides the conscious learning patterns and routines are just not there nor are they being properly developed. Man is not used to looking within himself for answers and therefore, he cannot properly relate to someone else who does know and understand this unconditional love. Most people think that kindness is a form of weakness and they usually try to exploit it to their personal advantage. Trying to send love or break down barriers of hate with love is difficult. Remember, most people relate better to separation and division than they do unity. Our tangible physical outside reality is based upon separation and it is difficult to make others aware of the concept of unity, when they are so surrounded and distracted by these forms of manifestation.

One might think that because we live in this kind of physical reality and can express love that we are the higher life forms. However, love requires effort to overcome resistance and that allows us to change what we do not like, or that which is detrimental to all life forms. Reality is a matter of belief and belief is another form of matter in an un-manifested state. We make our own reality. We should seek our higher conscious form of being and becoming and to consciously strive for universal unconditional love at all times, not because it will benefit just ourselves, but because it will also benefit others and everything else. That is, by sending and/or being conscious of the energy of love, one can begin to break down the barriers that divide us and separate us from one another.

By being conscious of love, we will all benefit and grow, because we will have found our proper position and balance within this multi-dimensional reality. If we reasonably succeed in becoming more conscious, we will all be on the right path on our journey of becoming. We can also be consciously aware of our position, place, mission, or purpose, in making this reality a good learning experience. Just as the learning or behavior diagrams indicate, happiness is a matter of being conscious and transmitting universal unconditional love. We make our own reality by choosing that which we want to experience.

I admit that most of what I am talking about is of a theoretical nature, but you also know by now that all physical manifestations begin in the mind. Sure it is somewhat impractical and it may be a little rough for a lot of people to become accustomed to these thought patterns, but don't you think that it is worth the effort? Remember, the real value of anything depends upon the amount of effort you are willing to put into it. It is a quality relative to your efforts. Again, to love unconditionally is somewhat unrealistic, in our terms, but think of all the benefits if it were possible. It would be a lot simpler and easier if everyone knew and understood this inner content; however, not everyone is on the same plane of life. That doesn't mean that you have to adjust yourself to a lower vibration plane, but you should demonstrate and use love in practical ways. Do not treat anger with anger, but use it to produce positive results. That is, for every negative, there is an equal positive form. You cannot eliminate or remove darkness, without first letting in a little light. Use the seven control principles to turn everything into its positive form of creation.

If man could only learn to recognize himself with recognition, what a beautiful world this would be, but man needs help. By learning to understand the principles of control, one cannot help manifest and recognize love. By understanding the principle of control, one does not limit himself more, but expands himself more consciously; thereby, he increases his being and becoming. He recognizes himself with recognition and learns to love doing it. By learning how to love unconditionally, he could turn night into day. He could find his true balance and position within this physical reality and he would find this reality virtually limitless with no barriers or restrictions. By learning to love again, man could find his way back to unity and to be one with God. Don't you think it is worth the effort?

THE GATE

Love and hate share but one single gate.
Open it wide and see what's inside.
Pass it by and nothings tried.
Step inside and there's no place to hide

Is it love or is it hate?
Shall I go or shall I wait?
Is it choice or is it fate?
Shall I enter through the gate?

To enter, one is centered.
But to wait could be one's fate.
Selection is one's direction and
Position determines one's transition.

Black and white, day and night, which is right?
Or could it be what you see is really what you want to be?
One and one are two, but is that true?
The answer is up to you.

To love or to hate?
To enter or to wait?
Must one choose?
Or must one lose?

Love and hate share but one single gate.
Open it wide and see what's inside.
One must give in order for one to live, and
Recognition is the key of what will be.

CHAPTER 19

Communication, Common-Union, Communion

Take a good look at the title of this chapter. Interesting, isn't it? Three words that have a lot in common. This chapter still involves the practical application of universal, unconditional love; however, it also explains the process of recognition, or shall I say one's re-awakening. You have learned in the last chapter, that love is manifested on two levels of life and that both of these levels also involve two aspects of one another. That is, love is always in an active state of being and a passive state of development or manifestation. Because man is so routine or pattern oriented, he is often not conscious of this energy force; therefore, he loses sight of, or confuses the positive creative forces of love with those physical manifestations related to possessions and that can lead to greed, anger and possibly, hatred. Man is not used to looking for an inner relationship or questioning himself. After all, everyone knows what you can't see, can't hurt you. Isn't that so? You should know better by now.

The biggest problem facing man in this physical reality is that of recognition. How does one recognize himself with recognition? Well, first of all, it is a matter of one's position or point of focus. That is, though mental concentration one can balance himself so that he can consciously recognize everything around him. However, this point is not so much a physical location as it is the ability to tune into a wider range of vibration. Consciousness is recognition. Therefore, to recognize something, you must be aware of its presence and/or position and this is the purpose of one's conscious mind. It is the ability to know without seeing, hearing, smelling, tasting, and feeling. It is the ability to be that which is in question. This is the ability to feel God in all that is, as He is in you, so are you in He; therefore, there resides in each of us and everything there is, this consciousness which is expressed as universal unconditional love.

Just as we are conscious of those things that we can identify with our senses, there are things that cannot be identified but intuitively felt to exist. That is, you can sense the presence of someone, or feel the warmth of a friendly environment, or the coolness of a hostile one. There are also other forms of consciousness that we have yet to develop or recognize. That means, that there may be alternate patterns of both tangible or intangible forces out there to which we are not aware of relating to non-linear unmanifested realities. That is why there are automobile accidents, and why people may lose houses or other property to the sea, or other forces of nature. They are just not conscious of the manifestations of certain forces. In simple terms, that means that you are not accustomed to seeing or looking for certain patterns. Usually because these patterns are more difficult to recognize you attribute bad luck results to poor judgement. That also means that you are not conscious to patterns and therefore, you tend to look at things in a specific way or you see what you want to see and ignore other probabilities. You are behaving in a certain predictable manner that is a reflection of your own personality or behavior.

Interesting enough, that means that you are not a victim of your environment as much as you are a victim of yourself. You are your own worst enemy. If you look at other people with suspicion, hatred, or other negative thoughts, while you are in a position of a negative rhythmic swing, you and they will be influenced by that negative thought and you will see just that in other people, unless they are consciously aware of your situation. That doesn't mean that that other person isn't that way to begin with, but just the same, that is only a half truth. That is, for every negative characteristic, there is an opposite positive characteristic both of yourself and other people. That does mean, that if you look for something bad in a person, you will surely find it; however, that also means that if you look for something good in that same person, you will also find that too.

Again, that means that recognition is a form of communication that is complicated. That leads one to believe that man's relationship with his fellow man is more a reflection or image of his own self than it is of that other person. In other words, you have the power of control over your fellow man to change him; because, in a sense, you are not changing him so much as you changing yourself, or the way in which you look at others. Remember, in order to change night into day, you must let a little light enter. In doing this, you must begin with yourself and then encourage those positive qualities that you do see and do recognize in that other person or persons. This whole thought process is probably better known as the power of positive thinking; however, it is in fact, an act of unconditional universal love that makes you more conscious of the inner qualities of all.

Here we are, talking about the learning process again, because we are again talking about the relationship of one's self, knowledge, and possessions; however, now we have opened up our area of learning and growth to include other people. Remember, we all grow in four ways and socially is but another, faster way of becoming our higher selves. That's because there is a greater exercise and/or experience through an interchange of thoughts, ideas, and beliefs. Consequently, one learns more quickly about the limitations and barriers of his reality than he could possibly learn on his own. That is also because one must overcome or try to understand the element of control, which is normally out of the hands or reach of the individual in a group environment. How one relates to difficult situations determines his growth. If he only recognizes the physical manifestations of control, such as the use of power and/or weapons, he will have failed to understand the principle of cause and effect or he has used only one principle against another and failed to consider the greatest principle of all, love. This is similar to our game, paper wraps the rock that can break the scissors that can cut the paper. Man forgets or doesn't know how to look for the other forces that sit with latent powers to benefit all.

So, although we are engaged in a tremendous learning process, we are also faced with a great deal of danger and without universal unconditional love, we could all eliminate each other out of fear, hate, or other negative forces. Love is the force of recognition that balances out and keeps us going. The problem is the inability of all involved to recognize it. The energy force of love is strong and capable of penetrating the strongest barriers of hatred; however, it may require a united effort. There is power and strength in numbers. This is a great way to put the, Greatest Happiness

Principle theory to work. Through a conscious, unified effort, it may be possible to break down these barriers of hatred, but it requires energy and effort in a positive creative manner through loving, caring and sharing. The latter are all acts of affirmative action that stem from our male gender or being. Such positive manifestations must be cultivated in order to grow and take us along with it. There is a great deal of work that needs to be done in order to recognize recognition as a force.

On a more personal level, when you think you hate the world or the peoples of the world most, you are actually caught in a dilemma of love. What you are doing is focusing your mental thoughts on the negative manifestations of our reality instead of its positive aspects. You are comparing the world or other people to your loving idealized concept of it and them. You are putting your love, or your concepts of love on such a plane that you divorce or separate yourself from your real feelings and do not recognize the loving emotions that are the basis for your discontent. That means that you have unconsciously manifested the negative feelings of love and have closed or shut off that positive creative force that can bring you back your love and happiness that you so desire.

Closer to home, let's take a family situation. There is no difference between this love for the world and other people than there is for one another in your immediate family. The only difference is in one's closeness or your ability to recognize, identify, or relate to, those other people. That is, the more frequent or closer you are to someone else, the more you understand and recognize the inner qualities that you so like and desire in those people. In actuality, what you see and recognize in those other people is the manifestation of God. That is the recognizer, recognizing himself with recognition. In any case, when a change occurs that separates you from that close relationship, you feel that division more than you do if the people in question were not familiar to you. That doesn't mean that there is a significant difference within one's own family. There is no basic difference between the love of a child for that of a parent, or a parent say for the child, a wife for a husband, a brother for a sister, etc. There are only various forms of expression and characteristics of that love and again, all love affirms in a positive energy form. You just cannot elicit deep emotions for people you cannot identify with, for they leave you relatively untouched.

So you see, love is somewhat hard to recognize even in your own family. Just think how difficult it is to try to communicate it to others. Yet, in a sense, love is the basis for all communications. It is a positive act or relationship that is intended to bring you closer together. It is a desire to bridge a gap between you and others. It is a form or pattern of energy designed to transfer a thought from one person to that of another. This is the taking of an intangible energy thought form from one person to that of another and to form a common union, a unity or oneness of thought. This act of communication then is designed to form a common union and ultimately, a communion. It is the intended sharing and/or possession of something in common.

Remember, love is manifested in many affirmative ways, the best known of these is caring and sharing with and for others; however, its most popular form is also the least recognized and understood. It is the relationship of caring and sharing that one offers recognition and experiences reality. This is how one makes his own reality. He must form a union with someone or something and communicate that union. When it comes to verbal speech and written communications, it is sometimes difficult to form this relationship, because of the problems of definitions, slang, connotations, inflections and other variables. Verbal and written speech is a very poor way to communicate. It is also the most popular. Let's try to do something about that.

Have you ever really sat down and given verbal and written communications any serious thought? Take a close look at it. What do you see? I'll help you. What you see is an energy pattern designed to communicate your position or clarify someone else's position in relationship to yourself or others. That is, you are trained to recognize and communicate certain knowledge and/or possessions to those of others. This is a positive act. Without communications then, things would be a lot more difficult.

Communications is an intangible thought form designed to convey all forms of manifestations. That is, there cannot be anything of any value until that manifestation is shared in some way. Everything has some limited value to each individual in certain specific ways that only that person can relate to. This knowledge of these manifestations and relative patterns and relationships then become a possession of that individual; however, this knowledge or possession has no real value until it can be shared. That means that each of us acquires a learning experience that has value and worth because it can be utilized to save other's time and energies. Therefore, communications are intended to convey or share a position that someone else has acquired knowledge of certain manifestations.

These forms of communication can be very personal in nature or very impersonal. On the personal level, we are talking about the sharing of one's wants, needs or desires, and how that relates to that of another person. That is, if you live with someone else you must be concerned with your inbalances and/or the direct or indirect force that you have on those of other people. You must be conscious of their interests as well as your own. In this relationship, sharing is much more important than if you were to live on your own. A family or group environment requires a great deal of communication so that there is not a conflict of interest or position. Two people cannot occupy the same place at the same time, nor can they use the same thing at the same time. I mean how close can you get to one another in a loving way? The most prominent thing that comes to my mind is the bathroom. Sometimes, if not most, it is just not possible to use the same facilities at the same time, nor do most people want to.

Besides the question of position, which communicates a want and/or desire, there is also the question of needs, which is primarily concerned with one's physical body and its upkeep. Everybody needs food, shelter, and some form of security. In order to provide these things, you must either have the resources to buy what you need, or be willing to do something to acquire those things. Then again, you might be able to merely ask for them; however, to strictly rely on the latter pattern of behavior will not work for long, unless you are considered a minor or child. In either case, to continually ask for things without giving or offering something in return is very detrimental to any relationship including that of a family. Such a relationship is an incomplete unbalanced form of communication, for it links two or more people together in a tangible way, but it does not bond them in a form of communion. Unless some effort is made to balance or compensate for the fulfillment of these wants, either through tangible alternatives and help to relieve the burden of responsibility from those who are providing for those wants, or there must be a meaningful dialogue of communications to establish the reason to perpetuate such a relationship. Without some attempt to communicate love, there is no form or force that can establish unity. Anything of value requires work. The effort you put into anything determines its value or importance.

Perhaps I had better clarify that last statement a little better. What I am trying to say is that you must be willing to give something that is of yourself for a relationship to be of a positive nature. If you cannot provide anything of a positive tangible nature, then you must give something of an intangible nature. Suppose you have children of school age who cannot support themselves or their needs. You do not readily expect them to earn money to offset their or your burdens; however, you do expect them to comply with your wishes. That is, you are concerned with their well being; therefore, you expect them to comply with your desires for their growth and education and that is intended to help them when they are on their own. In this relationship, the parent must communicate a desire that the child consider your guidance and follow a pattern of behavior that is conducive to that family environment; whereas, the child should make an attempt to follow that guidance until he can determine what he himself wants and/or can support. Naturally, there has got to be some give and take in this relationship. That is, each is not going to get what they want all the time, but again, there must be a form of balance in this relationship or it just won't work. Each must be willing and able to give and communicate love.

The parent child relationship is somewhat unique. That is, although the parent does not necessarily want or need the child to do anything on his behalf to help the family, he does expect something from the child. Perhaps the simplest tangible forms of help include the caring for, or picking up of their personal things, maybe the cutting of the grass, doing the dishes, doing the wash, washing the family car, doing the ironing, and/or just helping with the general chores of the household. That doesn't necessarily mean doing these things on a daily basis; however, it sure wouldn't hurt. In the absence of such acts, the alternatives would be for the child to accomplish some notable academic or extra curricular goals of a positive nature. Simple, yes? Yes it is, to a point. These acts of communication and love can also become a negative form of responsibility. There is a difference and the balance is sometime difficult to discern.

The difference between unconditional love and responsibility is very narrow. One is an act of love, the other is more a negative form of want.

Maybe a polite way to put responsibility is to say that it is a form of conditional love. This form of love expects something in return. It is limited. If a parent or child is conscious enough of the positive aspects of love, there would be no need to ask or demand anything in the way of a tangible contribution or responsibility of another.

To be responsible, is to take a position or be asked to take a position that is directly related to the individual in question. It is an obligation or commitment related to that person and/or his physical being or reality. Therefore, if a pattern of love can be properly communicated or recognized, then there would be no need for responsibilities. Because each person would inwardly know what is expected or required of him without asking. The communication of love is the knowing of family patterns of behavior and/or how they relate to you, and how you help, or respond, or offer positive creative efforts, to change or relate to those patterns.

I hope you understand what I am talking about. I am trying to show you an element of control that you can use in a positive creative manner. Unconditional love cannot be expressed or shown in a conditional way as a responsibility if everyone is to gain from that specific relationship. That is, you cannot expect to get something in return for everything you do; however, it is also your responsibility to yourself to let your thoughts and beliefs to be known if you think that there is an unequal balance in a certain relationship. The communication of this concern must also be done out of love, not a negative hate form. Should this area of concern and contention not be resolved through love, then one must attempt to bring one conscious of those problems created by the others inattention or neglect. Then, if this too should fail, you must cut off your love or your relationship of caring and sharing and other tangible means of support, in hopes that this separation will bring you a line of communication that will bring you back your love. However, sometimes this may even fail. Somehow you must get through to one's consciousness. A truly conscious person cannot help but communicate love, harmony, and peace, with all that he comes in contact with. Such a person is a truly balanced person that needs nothing asked of him, because he is already consciously aware of his responsibilities to himself and God.

Wow! That was a lot lengthier than I intended. I guess that matter strikes closer to home than I thought. In any case, I also want to touch upon love in a business or professional environment. Believe it or not, this form of love and communication is nearly the same as that of a family relationship, except the people involved are not as close to you. Also, instead of dealing with a lot of intangibles, the major relationship deals with a tangible end product and/or responsibility. Here, you do have a definite situation where one is financially rewarded with tangible compensation for his efforts, more so than just love. This monetary reward is supposed to replace or be a substitute for the absence of the caring and sharing in the family relationship. That is, to compensate for a direct close relationship, one is given something of a tangible nature for his energies and efforts. This is a form of communication, a common union, and in a remote sense, a form of communion, but it lacks the quality of true unconditional love. That is, money is not intended to be a lasting permanent bond and that's why it is often a bone of contention and conflict.

Naturally, the absence of unconditional love increases or causes separation; therefore, all the monies in the world cannot substitute for love. Somehow along the way or path of progress, man has developed or created this form of compensation to ease the pain of this separation. Money was supposed to be the equivalent or equal to love only in a tangible form. It was supposed to be the greatest equalizer that demonstrated one's thoughts of caring and sharing. It was supposed to reflect the energies and efforts of an individual for his contribution to the well being of all those people that he helped. I think somewhere along the way this system has gotten a little bent out of shape.

There are a lot of jokes about money. Especially the one that goes like this: "Money isn't everything, but it's sure way ahead of whatever is in second place". The joke is cute, but I'd like to take exception to its thought content. Also, it does show a point and that point is that money is probably the most important thing that concerns most people. It shows, "What Makes Johnny Run". It is money! Unfortunately, most people do not understand or recognize the power of universal, unconditional love, but they sure do recognize the power of money; therefore, in our existing reality, it probably is more powerful than love, only because it is used and exercised more. Money is powerful, but still, it will never replace love, no matter how many jokes or how much one can accumulate.

I hope you can see what I am trying to get at here. Love is very important and it is still involved in the work place; however, most people do not recognize it in this environment. Still, everyone relates to work in monetary terms and somewhat neglects the need and importance in this situation. However, if love is properly understood and utilized in a positive manner, through communications, common-union, and communion, the work place can become a better place to be and can also become more productive in more ways than one. The benefits of love and its proper application can move mountains of physical tangible matter as well as intangible obstacles to one's well being. To be forced or responsible for doing something, day in and day out, and not knowing why or without contributing to that cause, does not help anybody grow and prosper. People need not be extensions of machinery or systems that are dispensable. As Barbara Striesand sings "People, who need people are the luckiest people in the world!"

There are no quick answers to difficult questions. I am sure you have heard this before. I again take exception to this statement. There is a quick answer and that answer is always love. How that answer or love is used or applied is up to each individual. Perhaps the most important thing to remember is, what do you want to experience? If you are a truly conscious person, and I know of no one who is, you will automatically know what to do. Therefore, in the absence of this consciousness, I suggest that you consider or treat all matters of conflict as a family type situation or physically try to project the thought of love to the problem and you will find yourself being automatically guided to a just and reasonable solution for all. You should also remember that you get back what you put into a situation. You cannot get back what you do not or unwilling to put in. It is a direct relationship; however, it need not be an immediate return, or even in this life time, and it will be a reflection of your own energies and efforts.

A business or profession is just like a person. That is, it behaves in the same manner as those people who are in control of that particular company. Unless those people and/or business understands and expresses love in a caring and sharing manner, it has no good basis for being or becoming. There is more to a company than meets the eye. It is intangible in its qualities as well as tangible. It also has an inner content that counts and connects everything in common and in a meaningful relationship.

That's why people who work for a company never get over a layoff or a separation, because they have put so much of themselves into making that relationship work. It is like a marriage.

Remember, the value or worth of anything depends upon the amount of effort and energies you are willing to expend. That means, that life or existence that does not care or share, is valueless and has no good basis to exist. That goes for people as well as a business or profession. There are other things to consider in a business environment other that money or profits. Life can be greatly enhanced by all concerned if everything were equally shared or communicated properly. How can everyone be happy if but a few enjoy the fruits of this physical reality? Just think, if there was something more to business other than money, you might get more involvement in a company. In fact, the most notable pattern might be something you are seeing now and that is a tendency or drift toward employee owned or operated companies. It makes you wonder, doesn't it?

In the course of running a business, government, or any other organization, most people think that the power or control of such a venture comes from above. That is, the element of control comes from the top and works its way down. Strange as it may seem to most, it does not. People are given responsibility to control, because they are capable of consciously knowing what must be done and to know their position. That means, that the power of control is shared. That is, unless a person can use his inner qualities to accomplish more positive good benefits to all involved, he will soon find himself on the outside looking in. Maybe not physically, but definitely, mentally. A person cannot control or govern unless he is given consent and/or support from below as well as above. Positive love is the caring and sharing of a special relationship. That doesn't mean that a relationship can't also be based upon hate; however, such a relationship cannot last. No compensation in the world can outlast love.

A person of authority must be able to be consciously aware of real tangible goals as well as intangibles of a mental nature. Such a person must be able to communicate unconditional love to create a common union and hopefully some form of communion or unity. How successful he is determines how well that company prospers and grows. Keep in mind that a company is nothing more than a group of individuals behaving as one. It is a common union. Its growth depends upon its inner content of people all working together in a form of unconditional love for both tangible and intangible goals. Therefore, a company is not a person, but a group of people. It can take on the characteristics of a dynamic individual, but it is the parts that make up the whole. A chain is only as strong as its weakest link. We must all try to be more conscious of our position within the inner content of the whole or group. That doesn't necessarily mean that there is going to be peace and harmony at all times, because that simply is not possible at this level of existence. Not everyone can, nor should they relate to the same things in the same way. No two people are alike. Disagreements are to be expected. That's why communications are needed to bridge the gap and to re-establish that common union and/or communion. You get out of a relationship what you put into it. Through communications one is able to relate or transfer thought patterns so that each individual can recognize the purpose of their separation or differences.

The relationship of a family, a business and a government, is very similar. That is, they are all group relationships that need something more than just tangible objects. They need a form of stability or balance, that provides for their physical and mental well being. In order for any of them to exist, they need a form of universal unconditional love that is not demanding or based upon conditions that limit one's growth, but at the same time, it must also create a structure of unity. Individuals going and doing their own thing without caring for their fellow man cannot grow in a positive manner. They must learn to share their knowledge and profession with their fellow man. As I said before, through this exchange of one's inner content, one can grow much more faster than being left on one's own. The element of control must be shared in a caring, loving, manner to create a common union and communion of one. This is a community of man. You make your reality, but you also help make that of your fellow man; therefore, you must try to be conscious of your use of energy. There is more at stake than you think in your thoughts and actions.

Periodically, people, businesses, and governments, must make changes that are designed to enlarge or expand as well as down size or to generally encourage patterns of growth, in a new direction. Such changes are not always readily accepted, because that means that new energies and efforts must be used to accomplish these new changes or patterns of recognition. However, given the proper communications, most people learn to make the proper adjustments. However, sometimes such changes are not properly communicated to all involved and people either knowingly or unknowingly, do not comply to these requested changes. In this case, there is no common union or oneness; consequently, there is a division that weakens the total unit or group. Again, this is not necessarily bad at all times, because it provides a moment for dialogue that can reaffirm those things which one can agree upon. Just the same, sometimes good intents end in failure or a reversal of a detrimental nature; however, one can learn from their mistakes. It is just when the separation or division widens into a situation of extremes that a conflict can occur. Without communications of some kind this universal unconditional love cannot work its magic. Therefore, remember, when there are unresolved problems, get talking and communicating. Separations will not go away by themselves. They need help.

To resolve a problem, sometimes they require giving up something or making some great sacrifices. If you are truly conscious, you will know what and when to do something. In the absence of this consciousness, you must try to take a little time out and withdraw yourself physically from the situation, if possible, or at least you must try to do so mentally. If you think consciously, you know that the value of anything is relative to the people involved. That doesn't mean that you should give in to the demands of others all the time either. Because, to give in is not helping that other person to grow either. Again, the question of balance comes into play. Somehow, someway, you must learn to think and open yourself up consciously by looking within. You must determine what is valuable to you and what is not. The less demanding or limited you are in your wants and needs, the more mental wealth you possess. You have more options, possibilities, and probabilities. The most important thing for you to do in a situation of conflicting interests and/or sacrifices is to stop and think consciously before acting. Then do not predetermine the events to be either good or bad, but they just are. Take them for what they are and get on to the next moment and experience it. Do not dwell in the past, or for that matter, don't dwell on the future. Live for today, this moment, and experience it in its fullest. If your thoughts are based upon unconditional love, you can't help but succeed in everything you do, because you will communicate that love to others and they will recognize it and give it its proper recognition.

Talking about sacrifices, there are usually more to these acts of self or forced self limitations than meets the eye. For one thing, to voluntarily limit or restrict yourself usually brings you closer together with others in the same situation. That is, to voluntarily share something with someone else is a communication of caring. It is an equalizer or an act of trying to balance a condition that is relative to all involved. In the business world, the manipulation of employees or people has long been accepted as the only way to do or run a good business. However, the long range effects of such a practice, are very detrimental to nearly all involved in a direct and indirect way. Because that means that there are a few people who are well off and another group who are not so well off. Whereas, if everyone were to accept a small overall sacrifice, they would all benefit in the long run as long as everyone did their best to eliminate the problem causing the sacrifice. In fact, to resolve a problem by asking for everyone to sacrifice would more than bring you closer together, you would be creating a stronger organized group with more in common than ever before. You would have a nucleus of believers in communion. Sure, you might lose some people who cannot or will not make those sacrifices you request, but what you do have left will probably out produce what you had originally. However, the sharing of sacrifices must also be accompanied by the sharing of the wealth in good times. Balance is always important.

A person can physically and mentally accept hardships when they know that others are experiencing the same problems. That's because people can relate to one anothers position. That's also why you see so much helping during a natural disaster. Everyone knows or has some idea what it is like to have nothing; therefore, any little bit of help in a situation like this is greatly appreciated and usually accepted. People do not normally accept what they cannot use. At the same time, most people cannot accept a situation that has extremes and these situations are usually man made causes. That is, they cannot accept a situation that gives or rewards a few people at the expense of many. A system that can support poverty and wealth sided by side, is not a system of universal unconditional love. Balance is required for any relationship to work in a positive creative manner. To do otherwise, is only asking for trouble. Disparity brings on an increase in radical behavior. That's because the separation between those that have and those that have not, is noticeable and man uses his physical senses more than his inner knowledge. Consequently, separation or extremes is somewhat of a negative nature; therefore, it manifests negative love or hatred. When this situation takes place, logical thought processes are sometimes replaced with behavior on a lower level of being, commonly known as the survival of the fittest.

Strangely enough, this survival of the fittest theory is not necessarily associated exclusively with the poor. There are many people in all walks of life who believe in this thought form and it is most unfortunate. Wealth in physical tangible terms, does not necessarily mean growth or enlightenment of that individual. There are a number of people who have lost their way and believe in this theory. Wealth in monetary terms is relative. That is, the more you make, the more you seem to need; consequently, no one ever seems to get enough and those that seem to have everything also seem to be unhappy. Or at least, they seem to display a reckless irresponsible pattern of behavior. To be truly happy and/or wealthy, is to be completely free of wants and needs and that is the supposed nature of money. But, as we just said, no one can seem to get enough money; therefore, it cannot bring you happiness, only convenience in the way relative to physical tangible matter. To be truly wealthy, is to be truly conscious and understand and express love in an unconditional way, through caring and sharing. To know, understand and express love, is to break down the barriers of limitations and to free yourself of all wants and needs in this physical reality.

I have not gone into details or aspects of communications, other than to identify caring and sharing as a manifestation of love that is a higher form of communications other than verbal speech and the written word. There are many other thoughts, gestures, and actions, that are also used to communicate, such as the shaking of one's head in a particular direction, a movement of the arm, hand or other parts of the body, and intentional non-recognition responses. All of these forms of communication are based upon our position and recognition of ourselves to others and/or things. These manifestations are also based upon our behavior diagrams and our desired end results aimed at creating an environment for our greater happiness.

How well we learn to communicate determines our growth and happiness. That is, if you are capable of relating and communicating with everyone and everything, then you have a larger or more conscious reality than if you have but a few friends and interests. You make your own reality and set your own limitations. You cannot always trust verbal speech or the written word to the exclusion of all other forms of communication. You must learn to look within yourself and others to find the basic element of God within each and everyone and thing. It is there. Look for it!

In learning to communicate and establish a relationship, most people fail to recognize themselves as the most important part of any relationship. Consequently, they find themselves constantly reacting instead of acting in a cause and effect environment. All of the control factors that we have learned and studied say that you are the most important element in any relationship. However, most people fail to recognize this, that is why the element of control is beyond their reach. These people fail to see these energy forms and forces and make selection for themselves based upon emotions and causes, rather than make their own reality. They also fail to see that most of their selections for their happiness usually leads only to temporary changes, rather than the long sought after happiness they so desire. Remember, you are reflecting an image of yourself in any relationship and you will only get out of it what you are willing to put into it. You must make an effort for any relationship to work. We exist in a state of separation, you must look for that which binds us together in common union, and communion. You must learn to communicate love.

In order to create that loving feeling and communicate that beautiful thought of unity, one must be in a proper position or frame of mind to create that common union or communion and that takes energy and effort. In order to recognize love, one must know and possess love. This is but another manifestation of our learning triangle. The knowledge that we acquire must be communicated or given to others in order for them to possess it in a common union with us. That is, there is a direct relationship with them to us by way of something else, some inner content that we share in common. Through love, we care to communicate with others our knowledge of love so that they too can possess and share it. Remember the value of anything is worthless, until you can share it with someone and/ or they know the value of it. In some cases, some people don't recognize universal unconditional love as a valuable quality. Some people are taught and told that kindness is a sign of weakness, but a truly conscious person will know the difference and those that don't, must work a little harder to understand the value of this inner content. You can catch more flies with honey than you can with vinegar.

One must learn to find his positive mental pole and to concentrate his conscious energies and his point of focus on this position of being. To do this is to raise one's self above the plane of cause and effect and to manifest positive mental force on all you come in contact with either physically or mentally. This process is probably better known as the power of positive thinking and it is just that. Love is a very powerful positive force, but it also has its negative side. You must be conscious of the difference.

You must be able to recognize yourself with recognition and make a conscious effort to recognize all there is. To do this, you must try to be all there is. Naturally, you cannot manifest this form as we have described it, but you can be it mentally. That is, to be all there is, is to be in communion or one with God in a positive loving way or position. From this point of focus, you cannot be anything but good and that means happiness will follow. This is what communication is all about. You select what you want to experience. You select the relationships that you want to share in common union. How well you relate to this experience depends upon how well you consciously concentrate upon your inner content and enter into communion with that experience and/or people. Your communion is the relationship and balance of your knowing and possessing along with loving, caring and sharing. You make your own reality. To be happy depends on you. For the world to be happy depends on you and how well you communicate that thought of love to others and they to others, etc.

CHAPTER 20

Recognition

When I tell you that you create your own reality, I am sure that none of you, or very few, actually believe that as true. You are not that sufficiently secure in that belief to take advantage of it and grasp this great creative freedom that you yourself make. Rather, you feel more comfortable when you give yourself and others, excuses. It is always somebody else's fault that you are in this position or that position because of something beyond your control. Your reasoning and logic for this behavior and thinking is based upon conditioning and training. I might say brainwashing; however, that is a little hard to swallow, because there is no real recognizable effort to change a belief or beliefs from what they were originally. That doesn't mean that we have not been conditioned in a specific way to think and act, because that is the exact nature or basis for our science of Anthropology. We are a collection of patterns and beliefs that result in something that has some cohesive qualities about it.

Man can follow any road he chooses. He can choose any one of the three paths our Indian studies described concerning culture, or he can maintain his existing status or even choose something entirely different. You can choose or select any road that you so desire, but until each individual realizes that he forms his own personal reality and is in control of that life he does not exhibit or demonstrate complete freedom. Rather, he has admitted to default or given away his rights to be completely independent. Remember, there is a price to pay for everything. The amount of effort you put into anything determines what you get out of it.

Do you really want to know what freedom is? Freedom is the inner realization that you are an individual and that you do create your own reality. You do have the freedom and joy and responsibility of forming the physical reality in which you live and that you can change it when you want and how you want it to be. You are not free when you say that such ideas work for others, but they do not work for me because my problems are caused by something else. Reality is not caused by heredity or environment. No problem is caused by conditions beyond the control of the individual. You will find freedom by learning to look inward and realizing that you create your own reality. There are no exceptions to the rule. Your success or failures, you have yourself created. If you would but understand this, it is the truth that would but set you free.

In this physical reality, you can't help but look at your physical condition and compare it against what you want and what is supposedly good for you. Then all you have to do is change the inner self accordingly. This environment provides us with much learning and lessons for our becoming. You are meant to observe and judge physical reality and that it is the materialization of your thoughts, feelings and images. The universe is mental. What is above, so it is below. You are meant to realize that the inner self forms that world. Until you learn that lesson, you cannot be allowed to go into other dimensions. You must understand the power of energy and understand the power of your thoughts and subjective feelings.

When you thoroughly recognize the freedom of your own being, and your own creative powers, then you will also recognize yourself as a creator. You do create your daily life and you joyfully help create the mass experience of the world as you know it. From this experience, you can say that you act out of full joyful knowledge and love of your creativity. When you recognize this, then and only then can you say that you do not blame events or circumstances as that which affects you or determines your reality. This is the recognition factor. This is the completion of the trinity. This is the manifestation of one brought into the physical plane of existence. This is the form or pattern that consciousness must take in this reality.

We have covered a lot of ground on our journey from here to there, or is it there to here, or does it matter? What really matters depends upon what we want to experience. However, we have travelled quite a distance in this book. We have travelled beyond the limitations of physical reality into the worlds of spirit and the mental aspect of our being and becoming. Hopefully, you may now have a better understanding of who you are, where you are, and maybe, just maybe, what you are doing here. You are many, many things. You are not just a physical being, as you are not just a spirit, and you are not just a mental state. You are all of these and more. Your being also exists on many levels of consciousness; therefore, your present point of focus may not be your total reality. You see by our explanation of unity and God and everything and nothing, there is a unifying element even though everything in this reality exists in a state of separation. That means that there is also a unifying element that links or ties you to everything else that exists. You are a part of God and he is a part of you; therefore, if you can become conscious of that part and position yourself mentally, you can become conscious of everything there is including non-linear reality.

In a sense, we are partners or co-creators with God. When you understand yourself and recognize yourself with recognition, you will have actively awakened yourself consciously. There is a conscious relationship that in all probability can come to each of you and all the peoples of the world, if you so desire and seek the inner self. If you only take the time to understand the nature of your own grace and your relationship with All There Is, within this reality, then the world will open up to you and you will realize many things. When this recognition, this law of grace, is achieved, there will be no need to feel alone and to be fearful. You need not try to leave something behind or populate the earth in an indiscriminate way. Your immortality is not dependent upon your seed that falls from you to grow in the world of physical matter. You will recognize your own immortality and therefore be free and joyous with your mortal self and you will gracefully take your part as co-creators on a conscious level with all life forms dwelling within this physical reality.

You cannot help yourself or others by identifying with your own weaknesses or the weakness of others whom you have given your element of control. When you are safe, you are safe. You are in a position of strength, because you have balanced or focused your point of power in the present in this physical reality. You are not thinking of the past or future, you are now. Therefore, you can bring all your energies together in love, peace, and tranquility, to the benefit of all those who seek your help. You cannot give help where it is not wanted or needed; however, you can aid those who seek that help. When you are in this position of strength, you have energy and power to think and feel clearly and to be more conscious of everything there is. You can feel and sense the patterns of conscious communication between you and nature. When this happens, you do not need to pretend that you are not safe or indulge in the experiences of others.

Each individual's reality is safe and secure, unless they choose to experience something else from another position. You cannot relate to what I am saying, unless you fully understand the concept that the universe is mental and that you make your reality. You establish the environment that you wish to experience. Unfortunately, most people equate aggression with that of strength or the physical act of aggression, or the violating of other's life, liberty, or property. Man has seen and witnessed so many instances and examples of such acts, resulting in the gain and benefit that such actions seem to be an acceptable way of life or commonplace. In truth, such acts are contradictory of one's strength and are a failure to master this physical reality mentally. That is, beliefs have directed, thought patterns, to follow a line of logic that fear of physical pain is to be avoided at all costs. That means that others have adopted patterns that reinforce those fears and use such fears as a means to their creative efforts at the expense of others. In short, man has supported the patterns and systems that encourage physical and violent aggression

As you can see, aggression is a negative creative act that stems from an outward position in this physical reality. It is a form of greed and/or an occupation that has found a position in this society and is supported as such. In a sense, we have accepted the ideas practiced by the Dobu Indians off the coast of New Guinea; and that is to take at others expense. However, today most behavior involves the control of money; therefore, we are a little more discreet about how we take. Such a pattern or system feeds on negative thought and breeds or grows as long as people believe it to be an exciting and valid form of behavior. Therefore, it is highly unlikely that you will believe my earlier comments that that you are safe and secure, but it is true. It's just a matter of what you want to experience.

Why I said that physical violent aggression is really a sign of weakness is because, the person utilizing this method to support his physical well being has failed to manifest his energies to the benefit of all concerned.

That is, that individual has used his powers of knowledge and physical strength to achieve only gain to his own person, hence the earlier comment that such acts are acts of greed. That doesn't necessarily mean that all acts designed to produce self gratification are bad. Neither does that mean that they are good. They just are. Then again, people who have established such behavior patterns of self gratifications can feel quite comfortable and may recognize and return their wealth to society in some manner. In fact, such people probably think about themselves or what they do to support themselves in the same way as people who labor for a living. The control of money to them is a way of performing a function which is their occupation. However, the thought of this control factor or force and in some cases physical violence only makes it more exciting than a 9 to 5 type job. But just the same, in most such behavior patterns, there is an element missing that makes such behavior contrary to that which is natural.

The determination of actions can best be identified or distinguished as good or bad from the point or position of love. That is, the true test or qualification of whether an action is good or bad. An action can only be determined by the individual and the individual must learn to recognize himself and others with recognition. The individual must choose or select to manifest his inner thoughts out into physical reality from a position of universal unconditional love. This is recognition and is synonymous with the word and/or verb, to give. It is the giving in a relationship to understanding that completes the trinity of being and becoming in this physical reality. When one places himself consciously in this position of being, he cannot, repeat, cannot but be good in a positive creative manner. He must act from a position of power and complete control over himself and his environment. That does not mean that he will abuse or misuse that power in a negative manner, for he will know and recognize the difference.

To describe "Where We Are or Where Am I", is to describe the problem of balance. This is also a matter of recognizing oneself with recognition. It is that which makes up our reality and it is of our own choosing. We must learn to recognize this as the basis for our reality and must try to regain the control and knowledge that we had at birth. You must un-teach or unravel yourself from the patterns you have spun and weaved through the years and get back to the truth of your being. You must learn to recognize that you choose to see and identify that which you want to see or identify within some kind of relationship. In short, it is our beliefs that make our reality and who controls our beliefs but ourselves. It is the end product or possession of our understanding of everything there is.

Interesting enough, the word and/or verb, to be, is another word that gives us a clue to our reality. Have you ever seen such a crazy word in your life? In the present tense, the word be, becomes am, I am, you are, he, she or it is. These are all forms of the word be. It is supposed to express, attribute, or identify a value, or state of being equal, or a state of balance similar to the mathematical symbol (=) that expresses a balanced relationship to a certain specific unit or unifying forces. In short, the word position can be interchanged with all of these forms of the word "to be" and substituting the noun with a pronoun, and no meaning will be lost in the usage. Example: I am, means my position; you are, means your position; he, she or it, means their position. That means, that everything in this reality revolves around one's position. You make your own reality. You are in control of your being, because you are the center point of balance. You have focused your consciousness on this physical plane of existence and you are the center of this reality, your reality.

When you do not understand this position and therefore yourself, you project this lack of knowledge to others. You are positioned at a negative pole and this lack of recognition results in fear. The mental thought pattern or vibration is then transmitted and reflected back to you in many forms, but since you do not recognize it you think that you are bad or evil. Therefore, your friends, associates, and strangers, become afraid of what you yourself do not understand and this not understanding is a manifestation of your position of fear. Because one feels comfortable with that which one is familiar with, that means that one surrounds himself with others who reflect those same qualities; therefore, he attacks even more of the same. Such a position is an inbalance and is complicated by the lack of consciousness of one's inner self. In this position, the individual usually looks outward instead of inward for meaning and recognition and that will not achieve balance.

To understand the power of recognition, one needs to recapture the courage, the joy, and the love you felt as children. Each day was an adventure, a miracle to be explored and there were no authorities to tell you how to explore it. Even your parents were but guides and had little to do with your reality. They did not tell you how to plan your day, or relate to different events within the day. They did not tell you how to react to a flower, the trees, the wind, the rain, the temperature. To become truly alive again, you must try to rediscover the wonder that you once had of this world, this reality you choose. You must try to look at that around you with a new, different viewpoint. There are no authorities, but the joy and authority of your being, where time is not separated into moments, where you awakened each moment as you did as a child. Each moment was a new birth, a fantastic reality in which you had your place, your position, and your part to play, and where the miracles were your own and grew from the fantastic joy of your own being. Try to recapture those moments that existed before you were educated and learned the limitations that you have created with the help of others.

To understand the power of recognition, you must find your own reality and your own way. It may be difficult, but mentally take away all the comfortable and uncomfortable rules, laws and patterns, and return your being to the authority of yourself. Do not try to avoid that authority! Listen! Do not say that you hear nothing and see nothing when your own authority speaks. Do not try to ignore or avoid your beliefs. Your inner self is not frightening, or you are not a bad person, or for that matter, that the world is not a bad place. Tell yourself; convince yourself, that since you are a part of All There Is, or God, you are also a unique expression of everything there is. There is nothing to be afraid of because you are part of everything by the shear act of recognition. Tell yourself that often. Think and feel that and it will eventually get through to your conscious being.

When you are afraid of your own authority, you will accept almost anything rather than face the authority of your own being. Yet, when you were still an unborn fetus, you did not question, who am I, where am I, and what am I doing here? Probably, you just basked in your own fantastic vitality of your own being and becoming. Somehow, someway, you must reacquaint yourself with your own self and give you back your trust in the nature of your own being. For if you trust what you are and who you are, you can never go wrong in whatever terms you want to use. Literally, you can fly through belief systems as a butterfly flies through the backyards and fields of your physical and mental realities. Remember, what is above, so is below.

When anyone tells you that your power is not yours and that you are not your own person, I suggest you eliminate this negative force from your environment or disregard any association with that thought form or pattern. It is easier to declare one's self weak, sinful, bad, fat, short, etc. It provides us with an excuse. We rather consider ourselves as failures of the flesh or victims of our society and blame someone else. It is therefore easier to place our power and/or fate in the hands of those who say they have the answers. This may take the form of dieting, drugs, astrology, religions, and/or other special interest groups. Those authorities who seem to agree with our negative thought patterns seem to attract the most following. The setting of guidelines and limitations to our being seems to give us salvation from the horrors of our physical world; however, it also seems that such authorities gain at the expense of those who are supposed to be helping. Why is it that people think that denial is always the answer to their evil world.

A word of caution, you should not believe anyone who says that you are evil and must repent. Anyone who gives you special instructions, tokens of power, or any other forms on which to rely should be watched with care. Anyone who tells you to pull your ear, crook your nose, wiggle your fingers, and that you must say Om, Allah, or Amen, or to breath properly, eat in a certain way, and only eat certain foods, sleep in a certain manner, deprive yourself, and to suffer great pain, or visit only certain people, and other patterns of restriction should be avoided, or not given any credence or validity by your thoughts because this is deemed recognition. Whenever such people tell you that authority resides outside of yourself, do not believe them. When anyone tells you that happiness and joy resides outside yourself, do not believe them. Your salvation does not depend upon any other living or non living thing but yourself. You have never lost your soul. You are your souls. You are spirit born unto matter. You can trust your bodies as you can trust yourself and God. In this reality, the body is the garment that the soul wears.

You as an individual cannot escape your own creations. It is not death that any of you have to worry about, it is your creations. You make your own reality, whether you like it or not. You cannot blame your own creations on any person, God, any fact or any predestination. You and you alone, make your own reality. The only thing that you do receive, to do this, is the energy that is given to you by God. But, there are no strings attached. You can do with this energy, anything you want, because you have free will. Your behavior, your reality depends upon what you choose to experience and learn. Your beliefs create whatever we've got. The framework of your birth represents the framework of your intent in this physical life that we know and this is one of your conscious decisions. This is one beginning. The supposedly complicated exterior manipulations of history and circumstances, the methods used to sustain, change or modify our physical situations, are nothing more than the output of yourself and those beliefs that you share with the masses of people who populate this earth.

You form your own reality. You form the world that you know and recognize it through images that relate to you and affect the exterior framework of this reality. If you don't like things, all you have to do is to change your inner precept, your thoughts, your beliefs, or nothing will change. It is sometimes hard and difficult to see just how we can support such lunacy that we see in the world; however, we do. On a collective basis, similar to how the greatest happiness principle works, every thought, good, bad or indifferent, is multiplied many times over and equates to mass beliefs that carry a kind of weight or mass that in itself has a certain amount of force to influence the events that we see around us. It is, if you will, a kind of way to prioritized what we want to happen or manifest itself onto this plane of existence. Therefore, whether you like it or not, you form part of a mass consciousness or reality that exists besides your own.

There are those who prophesy a great holocaust will destroy mankind, if not the world. The patterns may tend to support their beliefs; however, you do have free will and you can change those patterns. You can agree with those patterns and experience great pain and suffering that fear brings, or you can say nonsense. Man is not sinful, evil, bad or rotten to the core, and life is not a cosmic accident. Based upon what one hears, sees, and reads, one might logically come to the conclusion that left alone, man would destroy himself or civilization. If that were so, what then started civilization if it were not for the natural inclination of man? What began the cooperation that allowed people to unite in tribes and cultures?

Our world is not in dire straits because everyone trusts themselves. It is precisely the opposite. We do not trust ourselves! That's why man has limited himself and created social institutions to fence him in and to limit his experiences. We have not allowed ourselves the freedom that we experienced as children; rather, we have succumbed to patterns of expediency and/or conformity that stifles our growth and creative endeavors. If we could reawaken ourselves and become more conscious of our being, we could then learn to trust ourselves and eventually trust our institutions and our civilization. As it stands now, few, if any of us, really believe in the basic good of our creations. But the good is there, just as the bad. We must learn to ask ourselves, what is it that we want to experience and then we must seek its manifestation into this physical reality.

As long as man believes in the basic evil of his fellow man, then he must project that image upon himself and accept the consequences. Should you want to see the world destroyed and then the prophets will echo your beliefs. But, there is nothing on earth, or of a spiritual nature that will destroy you, unless you are convinced that you are so evil that you must be destroyed. Even then, those who refuse to accept that belief will regain and remember that loving technology that he has forgotten. It is that universal unconditional love that will set man free again. He will learn to deal with this earth and universe with that love, that technology and that love will bring him the truth of recognition.

The universe is safe, but it is difficult to believe considering our news agencies and institutions that seem to dwell on stories of war, murders, trickery, and greed. Such forms of communication seem to create a common union that can lead us to a communion of a negative nature. This is the pattern that is apparent in our reality now. That does not mean that you have to agree to this folly. You must insist that you are good. The official line of consciousness forms the world about us and you perceive and experience that world like the greatest happiness principle. It will always show you the results of the beliefs that are inherent in the official line of consciousness. This consciousness is our Academy Award, our Oscar, if you will. The answer to our world problems is the same as the answer to your own problems. It is simple. All you have to do is to say to yourself that you do not believe whatever it is that everyone else is saying about whatever is in question and then you must also mentally believe yourself. You can refuse to believe out of ignorance, stupidity, pride or whatever, it matters not. You have the right to say NO!

You must learn to believe that the universe and world is safe. Nearly everything that you see in the outside world will lead you to think that it is not, and the defenses that you yourself have set up, that condition and pattern you, also indicate this. But, you do not have to believe this. You can learn to leave the official line of consciousness that surrounds us and that we all use as a criteria for our reality. In so doing, you will withdraw your support to that mass consciousness and you will weaken it ever so slightly. You can still retain it as a picture of a possibility, but you must learn not to believe in it. You must learn to step out or take yourself out of that picture, while loving it and wishing it well. But also wishing it and sending it energy to change that which is to something that is of a more positive nature.

For a thought to become a belief, you must mentally take hold of thoughts that you wish to see manifested into physical reality and you must concentrate on possessing them. Then you must try to concentrate your male gender powers to stimulate your being or mental "I" that will in turn, plant the seed of creation in your mental "me" and perhaps the me's that are around you. You can influence others, but to do so, you must first believe that which you want to see manifested as valid and real in your own mind. A belief is nothing more than the ultimate form of recognition. This is actually a relationship of thought to that of recognition which is the basis of a belief system. By understanding and controlling yourself, you can learn to create valid patterns that can indeed alter the nature of your own reality and possibly those about you if they so desire also.

For you to help others, you must first operate from a position of strength, not weakness. You must learn how to control beliefs and/or change them. You must have good footing, so to speak and stand on firm ground so that you can extend your arms to someone else who may be mired in quicksand. You cannot help someone by leaping into that same quicksand, for surely you will both go down together and I don't think he will thank you for that. You must understand that when you commit yourself either physically or mentally to a specific event or issue, you are getting involved with that particular belief system. Whether you like it or not, you are in a sense jumping into quicksand and you cannot help. The saying that there is strength in numbers does not necessarily make things right. Just because a lot of people feel and act a certain way does not necessarily mean that it is right for you, or for them. Question everything.

To be of help, you must learn, or try to learn to be more conscious of everything about you. Through loving, caring and sharing, you cannot go wrong unless you fail to heed your inner self or inner voice. You must learn to organize your reality according to your strengths and hopefully in a playful manner that you experienced as a child. Learn to trust your being, your dreams, your joys, your hopes, and your prayers. Then and only then, can you be of some help to those who do not trust themselves and organize a defense based upon fears.

If you yourself need help, you must learn to believe that your plea is indeed answered, no matter how impersonal the universe may seem. When you seek help, you actually set the universe into motion, but your answers come from within. You make your own reality. When you seek help for others, you yourself must learn to be objectionable to the matters at hand. The best kind of help that you can offer is to just be there for moral support. Just as flowers send help to us humans by just being there and being themselves, being beautiful; so too, can you provide the same kind of support. These people in distress can sense your presence and strength and can draw from your energies to create their own reality. All you have to do is to offer an occasional word to remind them of their own great powers and energies and their creative strengths. Remind them that they are good and encourage them to work out the problems and do not fear and they will do the rest. Remember, do not join them in their belief less you too want to experience it also. You must learn to refuse to accept the beliefs of others with which you do not agree. The choice is yours.

When you read the newspaper, listen to the news, or watch TV, you are relating to symbols representing real tragedies. But these tragedies do not exist in your time framework unless you want them to by extending some form of recognition. Anyone acknowledging these events commit themselves in the support of these events and/or beliefs. They also position themselves in a negative location that generates a feeling of hopelessness, a loss of their power or control in the present, and it may also instill fear. You do not help others by taking on these same belief systems and/or jumping into the quicksand. From the framework or pattern of belief in yourself and your greater good, you have strength, validity, grace, exuberance, and additional energy that you can send out in the form of love to touch the hearts and realities of other people all over the world. Do not lend credence or support to their problems. It is theirs to solve and/or experience. It is there for a reason. It is part of their growth process and nothing happens by accident.

There is great abundance in this reality. There is nothing you need to fear. The universe is safe and so are you. With a sense of love and identification through communication, common-union and communion, there is little room for ideas of annihilating other species so that we can live. Survival of the fittest is not a rule or law of man or nature. Nature supports and/or controls the growth of lower forms of life through a consciousness of balance. Man too, shares and is bound together in a gestalt of creativity and balance; however, he does not share this knowledge consciously. Communication takes many forms and all species of plant and animal life gracefully acclimate themselves to this world, this reality, for a mutually beneficial purpose of growth and communicating recognition. They all give and take with graciousness and unconditional love that is difficult for man to identify, for he is not used to recognizing these forms of unity. The plants and animals in the world are not gluttons. They take only what they need to survive. Nature has a consciousness all its own that tends to balance itself out.

On the other hand, man has chosen a different kind of consciousness. His consciousness necessitates a different kind of challenge that will result in different learning and growth patterns of a mental nature. The animals know their own grace, they breed with joy and spontaneity and order that they consciously sense. There is nothing preventing man from remembering or becoming conscious of this knowledge and sharing with these other life forms the fruits of this planet in a more harmonious way. There are directions that man's consciousness can take him that would indeed change his reality, if he so desires. He can tune into and understand biological spirituality and become more knowledgeable of his physical needs and those of others. By understanding the aspects of control and the inner orders and/or patterns of logic, man can begin a new kind of awareness of this earth, one that does not despoil its planet, but consider it sacred, one in which man can take an active part in conservation and be proud of it.

Through this consciousness and knowledge of our reality, man can and should develop a greater tolerance or patience of his fellow man. By knowing that each person creates his own reality, that means that there may be conflict and overlapping interests. Each person is unique. Who is to say that all realities should coincide? Again, we are all involved in a learning pattern of growth, and what better way to learn the use of energy than to have it tested in so many different ways. Even though it may be somewhat difficult and frustrating at times, it is also kind of neat, just think how dull life would be if everything went right all the time. In fact, that is part of the problem concerning world peace. Here, we are again dealing with conflicting wants, needs, desires, belief systems, but then again, we are also dealing with an element of excitement and/or danger that makes this belief system interesting. It's something like playing Russian roulette with a loaded gun. That is, it's an exciting game that you either win or lose one's life. There is no in-between or degrees of joy or pain; therefore, there is excitement that attracts interest and preoccupies one's time with such a belief system.

Most people associate peace with the thoughts of quiet, sullen, tranquility of a dignified or respected nature. Therefore, most people also equate aggression and violence with excitement or things which are not peaceful. People also associate power and energy with aggression; consequently, most people are afraid to elect or support people who foster the thoughts of peace or who are generally peaceful in natural characteristics. This same general belief is quite common and is supported by most people and other countries of the world, hence, the state of the world today. Our present situation is the result of your individual beliefs in mass consciousness. There is no way to ensure peace, but for everyone to lay down his arms. What would happen if two armies were fighting and one decided to lay down its arms? Do you think that the side that had arms would eliminate those that didn't? I think not.

By being conscious in a loving, caring and sharing way, there cannot be any such thing as physical violence upon another. There is no justification for violence. Now, the words sound simple enough, but I don't think many of you really understand or fully accept these thoughts, except as they apply to others. That is, it is OK for others to practice this philosophy of love in relationship to themselves; however, when you are backed into a corner, these thoughts get dashed and no holds barred seems to be the rule of the day for most people. This cannot be acceptable behavior; you must learn to apply positive patterns to yourself before you expect others to follow. By accepting this thought and nourishing it, you are giving it a reality of its own. Once a creation is manifested, it does not disappear, be it physical or mental; however, your relationship to this creation is subject to change. I will explain this a little more shortly.

If and when the level of consciousness increases in a positive creative manner, then you can populate the world with ideas of peace and it will grow and prosper. When you think thoughts of aggression, you attract aggression and you draw it out from others unless they are in complete control of themselves. That also means that as long as one believes that he must fight for peace, so must he lose the issue. To acknowledge the word fight, is a physical act of violence and that does not encourage or bring out a positive creative manifestation of unconditional love. You must remember and learn to recognize that an act or thought of hate is intended to bring you back your love. That means that to inflict pain and suffering upon others, for whatever reason, is not justified under any circumstances, because what you are doing by your act of violence is to take away or separate people from their own patterns of recognition or love. No matter how supposedly justified these acts may be, you are separating people from people in some way, shape, or form; be it in the form of death or physical pain that modifies the behavior that once was, or affecting changes that again modifies living patterns.

If you really are a peace loving, caring and sharing person, there is hope. There is always hope. To change the world, you must first start with yourself. You must believe that violence is not an acceptable alternative to those who oppose your plans and wishes, whether they be yours, those of special powerful in numbers groups, or for that matter, nations. In a strange way, if you want peace that badly and in a relatively short period of time, you must think in aggressive terms. That is, it takes aggressive energy to send forth thoughts and feelings of peace. In a sense, you must fight fire with fire, excitement with excitement. You must mentally create and project your thoughts of peace in an aggressive manner. Then, your thoughts can and will radiate outward, giving and fostering joy, and vitality, and encourage the trust of peace as a viable, acceptable, challenging alternative.

Such action can be compared to the natural thrust of a flower as it grows up through the ground, through the leaves and rubbish, to thrust forth its beauty upon the world. Now the song wonders and so do I, "Where Have All The Flowers Gone?" What happened to flower power? We could sure use some new aggressive flowers working within the structure of society today.

A word of caution, when you start to learn how to use aggression for peaceful purposes, you must be sure that you are consciously aware of what you are doing and how it affects others. Each individual is aware of thoughts through subtle subconscious communications. You are going to meet and encounter resistance, but since you are not made of concrete, you may end up altering your own thoughts or justifying your actions for supposedly more noble causes. Remember, violence is never justified for whatever the reason. Undoubtedly, your own thoughts will change somewhat with time as you grow and learn to recognize the world around you. By knowing yourself, you can change yourself and perhaps help someone along the way. Take a long hard look at yourself and your beliefs see what it is that you like and don't like about yourself and aggressively resolve to encourage the positive and eliminate the negative in a conscious manner, and do it now.

Earlier, I mentioned that when you think thoughts, they do not disappear when you are done with them. They are creations, just as anything made of physical matter. They are real and they have validity, no matter how supposedly good or bad they are. Because we are outwardly oriented people, we cannot follow patterns of intangible thoughts as we can objects of physical matter. That is, we can follow the creation of a physical manmade object from conception, to completion, to its usage or history, to its destruction or modification. We cannot do that same thing with pure thought. But just because we cannot follow a thought after its conception, doesn't mean that it still does not exist. Even if one tried to consciously follow this thought, he would undoubtedly lose interest in it because he cannot maintain concentration and could not devote his attention in the form of recognition to that particular thought. Just the same, thought is a valid creation. It is an organized pattern of energy, similar to physical matter, but at a higher level of vibration. The amount of time and concentration you do spend on thought, determines its strength or intensity.

Why I brought up this question of thought and creativity, is to show you an interesting concept or two. First, I wanted you to see that you cannot logically follow thought or the pattern of thought for any reasonable period of time; therefore, it is also a sure bet that there is little you can do to follow and understand the happenings of this reality which is based upon such thought patterns. Second, the implications that thought does not disappear are immense. So much so, that I seriously question myself if I should put it in my book. But considering that I am an optimistic person and thought that some parts of this book might be beneficial as well as controversial I decided to go for broke. As long as you maintain a loving, caring, and sharing position, you will consciously be able to comprehend and use this following information in a positive creative manner.

Now, given the idea that thought has existence and validity long after its originator has finished with it means that in certain terms, there is no such thing as death or destruction. That also means that you cannot hurt anyone or anything. I know that is somewhat contradictory to my earlier statements about violence, but now we are talking in the context of a different relationship. This is what this reality is all about. It is recognition. To really understand this reality and the nature of life and/or energy means to be conscious of unity or the degrees of unity that has opposites. We live in a world based upon separation as we relate to this physical reality, but in fact, it is all one. It is only a matter of recognition and understanding that separates you from that which you want to experience.

Getting back to our thought on death and destruction, to understand this concept of unity means that you cannot destroy it. You may be inclined to think that you misuse it; however, you cannot. You are not able to misuse it, or destroy it. Energy can neither be created nor destroyed, but it can change and that's what growth is all about. Basically, you cannot hurt anything, but as long as you think you can, then you must live within that reality, and that can hurt. Our belief system is a foundation of mass thought and physical existence. It is a framework or pattern within which we operate and from which we reference or recognize everything and nothing. Consequently, that means that nothing is hurt without first giving acceptance to that hurt, without attracting it, and without bringing it to itself, because it is within our belief system and you form or make your own reality. So, even when you think you destroy, you destroy nothing.

When you think you kill, you kill nothing. Even when you imagine that you destroy a reality, you can only destroy a reality as you know it. The reality will continue to exist, but in a form that you do not and cannot recognize.

Now, that doesn't mean to go out and start killing and destroying, because that also means that your thoughts or concepts of death will also carry over to you. That is, if you kill and believe that you kill, you will bear the consequences and the pain and suffering that go along with that manifestation. Your definitions, thoughts, and ideas, reflect your own reality. You actually live in a dream, but that dream is composed of a great number of people who together, create the ground-rules on how this game of life is to be played and worked out. But, just as you are about to learn the key to all of the answers to life, they might go ahead and change all of the questions. You create your own reality. You are acting out your part in a real life drama in an ongoing series. Will you receive an Academy Award for your part?

A. F. KENTON

THE KEY

They sing of love in song,
but are they wrong?
Should we belong to that of another,
or are we more like that of a brother?

Does one have to receive,
or can one give?
Is that what we believe,
or how we live?

In a land of opposites
there is two, and
the splitting of unity
is the clue.

Everything that is,
is half of one.
Recognize what it is, and
you recognize none.

Love and hate is
but one single gate.
Know this to be true
is to know colors and hue.

All are but one divided.
Be conscious and you will be guided.
There is a law of love to be sung
and you will hear that clarity rung.

This then is the key
that will work for you and me.
Seek and you will find
reality is a state of mind.

CHAPTER 21

Morality

If you look at the beginning of this book, there are promises that this book will cover the subject of morality. Yet, up to this point, there have been very few references to morality and those references have been of an indirect nature that did not go into any depth. Well finally, by default, I decided to try and devote a whole chapter to this topic. However, let me warn you, for those of you who are used to seeing black and white, separation, contrasts and divisions, for those of you who are comfortable in our present behavior patterns that have do's and don'ts rules, for those of you who are looking for answers and a leader to tell you what to do, when to do it, and where not to do it, I am afraid you are all in for a big disappointment.

The issue of morality deals with the control of human behavior, and by God or whoever else you want to swear on or by, I have covered and hit upon that subject enough. However, just to be sure that I have covered all the bases, let me make one more direct attempt at explaining morality head on in a direct relationship. First of all, morality is a system of values one uses to create a reality. Morality implies a set of rules by which one is supposed to operate within. It is a guideline that permits growth but in a limited manner toward a specific desired end result. I am not sure anyone can tell me what those specific desired end results of our existing system or systems are; however, I can tell you it is limiting. I suppose one out of two isn't bad, but then again, it isn't good either. It just is.

Rather than think of the negative restrictive nature of morality, let's take a positive approach or look at the word. Morality implies whatever is the most creative part of your being and becoming in terms of what you want to do. You live within a reality, and while you do, you must deal with it. Therefore, morality is the value system you use to make your own selections that determines your behavior and/or reality. Now, that says a lot and it says nothing. That is, it tells you everything you need to know about morality for you to use it; however, it tells you nothing in the way of what to do, or how to do it. It is strictly up to you as to what you want to experience. All matters requiring a decision or selection are all moral decisions, because they involve the use of creativity, development, and spontaneity. You make your own reality by selecting and choosing alternatives as to what you want to experience.

There is nothing difficult about morality. The difficult part of morality comes in with the application of thought into physical manifestation and/or actions. That is, there are no difficulties creating your own happiness and experiences if you do not have other people to deal with; however, the element of control becomes obscure when it runs into the conflicting thoughts of others. Then the outward process of communication takes over to reestablish the element or understanding of the control factor, to form a common union that can be consummated in a communion of thoughts, actions and deeds. However, this same selection or decision could have been also achieved by another process and that is the inward process of loving, caring and sharing. That means that there are two ways to achieve the same results. But, because of the problems associated with outward manifestations, even speech and other forms of outward communication often fail to convey the act of communion to one's fellow man.

Man exists in a world of separation of being alone and together, and between the two is the meaning of humanity and mankind. There is also the meaning of life and death. You can never be completely alone or together at all times. You exist between these two points of reference in a position of your own choosing, somewhere between the desire and the ideal, the dream and the execution, between your love and your expression of it, between your ability to recognize and to offer recognition. Somewhere in the midst of all of this balancing dwells your reality and therein lies the meaning and validity of your soul.

If you believe your reality existed because of some chemicals atoms and elements that happened to come together without purpose and accidently created a reality and man, you're crazy. If you're concerned with what came first, the chicken or the egg, you are also crazy. It is not a question of physical manifestations it is a question of consciousness. Consciousness is balance and is that integral part of everything and nothing. If I were to believe that my consciousness was created by some god who made me and my kind in a perfect world, but did not have the creative abilities to keep it perfect, then I too would be crazy. If I were to believe that I lived in a world of decay, degradation, pain, and suffering, then I too would have a poor conception of myself worth and my fellow man and I am afraid that that is just what our limited belief system has lead us to believe.

I personally cannot believe that the integrity of this and each and every moment is an accident. There is no way that I can believe that all of nature is sane and right but man. If that were so, how could all of nature turn out to be all right and only man created in sin and was evil. How could God or nature have gone so astray as to make such an error? The answer is that he did not! What is wrong or has gone wrong is our belief system, not morality. We have too many authorities, too many chiefs, too many differences and not enough individuals or individualism. Rules are made to be restrictive, to limit beliefs, to control mass behavior. However, rules are also made to be made, to be followed, and broken by those who wish to control. When you wish to accomplish something that is beyond your control, you make rules to help you manifest that desire. So it is with both the individual and society. The problem of rules is knowing what to support and what to ignore and that is a matter of beliefs. When you need rules, make them, when they do not work, find a new set, but always follow your own inner dictates, not those of others.

I think the thought of no rules and regulations is probably frightening to most people, just the same as my idea of how to support peace is by eliminating arms is frightening. We must learn to trust ourselves and our fellow man and this can only be done safely by each individual if he is capable of positioning himself properly within himself and/or his belief system. I think that if you believe in yourself, you must believe that the fewer restrictions and limitations that are placed upon one's self, the fewer problems or separations one sees. This same thought pattern is displayed by our behavior diagram that is based upon unconditional love. That is, as one raises his level of consciousness he sees that there is no such thing as opposites. Everything is composed of units of unity. The concept of unity has no absolutes of yes or no, but is composed of degrees of maybe and that lessens the chance of prejudice and conflict. Such a belief system accommodates practically anything that comes along; however, it is still up to the individual to give it a try. But, I will admit, this is still a strange concept and takes some time to get accustomed to.

Everyone seems bent on waiting for the other person to give an inch before they do, but remember, someone has to make the first move. You are not an island unto yourself. You exist in a reality composed of many; therefore, you must take part in your world as you understand it. But now that you understand it a little better, you may now wish to take an active role in reshaping its belief systems. But in reality, the best way for you to take an active role in changing this belief system, is for you to be yourself. For each of us to learn, to understand, and to experience and work out the challenges and possibilities of creation, is to fulfill one's self and to implement God's will as well as one's own. Each of those conceived in this physical reality are born into different races, cultures, and to experience different problems; however, each and every person is involved in a learning experience that leads to the same basic desire for universal unconditional love. Translated into more simple terms, that means that we all seek freedom to do what we want, when we want, where we want, why we want, and how we want. The only problem is with who we want. That takes a form of communication.

I just want to point out that my explanation of everyone's basic desire is the same question and answer that I proposed for a new belief system that eliminates prejudice and conflict. To refresh your memory, I said in effect, that the best rules are no rules at all. You make your own reality, and each in his own way participates in what we think of as the history of our time. In so doing, we are following and acting out the principle and the law of love, either consciously or unconsciously. Naturally, the element of control is more obvious in a conscious situation and to do so will lead to morality of the highest level. It is not something that has to be worked at, it comes naturally. When you achieve this conscious level, it is difficult to regress because one's life becomes abundant and beautiful. You live in a safe universe, but be true to that which you love, for if you do, it will take care of you, because that is the nature of love. It is the only law, principle or rule that you need to know.

Your thoughts do count and they do add up to form our world, and our reality. However, do not get too discouraged if they do not go your way. The world has been around for a long time and there are a lot of people out there who are seeking experiences different from your own. The world will go its way. It may not be your way, but then again, it may. Somehow, someway, a balance will be struck with the universal mind of all there is, that will form or create those experiences which everyone seeks in mass or as individuals. These creations and ideas will form a pattern that will tend to influence and direct the events that affect our reality. Given proper aggressive nurturing, your thoughts may fall like seeds that fall from a giant oak tree. They may fall on fertile ground or be blown to far distant places before they take root. In any case, they possess the potential to affect everyone's reality. Then again, the seed may be quite different than the plant that gave it life. Don't be discouraged by appearances. It is the inner content that counts. The ugly duckling may be a thing of beauty.

The question of rules versus no rules is difficult to comprehend, because there has never been a situation where man has acknowledged that there were no rules. Although we ignore the whole issue, most people in some way, shape, or form, are influenced and governed by rules of others or ones of their own choosing. This is morality. It controls behavior and growth patterns. It would be an interesting experiment if we could all experience this condition, if only for a short time; however, I am also sure that most people would feel extremely uncomfortable without some demands or limitations placed upon them. What would happen if no one or nothing put any demands upon you? What would you do? Would you live a life of leisure and indulge yourself in the sensual pleasures of life? Unfortunately you will never know; however, I am sure you would not. You see, there is more to man than meets the eye.

You cannot separate yourself from others or your world, nor can you force yourself upon the lives of others without their consent. Therefore, the only thing you can do reasonably well is to be yourself. By being yourself completely, you are automatically doing what you yourself want to do and fulfilling the purpose that is your own, but joining with others in a like purpose. In doing so, you in a sense, become a force of nature. Also when you learn to trust that force, that is yourself, you flow naturally into those areas of your own interest and the interest of others. This being yourself is the form of spontaneity that was mentioned earlier. Spontaneity is the subconscious knowing of yourself, your being, your purpose of learning and growth in a specific direction of becoming conscious of yourself. Spontaneity is the inner content of understanding that relates to yourself, knowledge, and possessions. It is the relationship of the recognizer, recognizing himself with recognition. It is balance.

You were born with true impulses and they are always with you, even though you have been taught not to trust them. Man has been educated to a point where he has forgotten the language of impulses. In fact, man basically equates spontaneity with irresponsibility and that which is evil. How this belief originated is beyond me, but it seems to be prevalent among most people. Probably the belief was or is founded upon the joyful and playful manner that this creative form takes. That is, our concepts of happiness, joy, and pleasure, seem all fraught with traces of evil. Everybody knows that life is hard and a major struggle just to stay alive; therefore, anything that comes easy and creates happiness must be bad or evil. That logic is as bad as a joke I heard about a guy who trained a pet flea to jump on command. In short, the joke proceeds that the man loses the attention of the crowd, so he begins to remove the legs of the flea and after removing all the legs, the flea becomes deaf. That's bad!

What I am saying is that if you allow spontaneity its own freedom, then you are consciously happy and you will convey that happiness to others and there is nothing wrong with that. If everyone learned to follow their own impulses and to be spontaneous, everyone would naturally gravitate to his or her own place in our world. We would all be doing what we want and it would also be leading us in the direction of loving one another. However, because of our restrictive or limiting environment, I think most people would believe that my idea of spontaneity would lead to chaos and shambles. In this case, I kind of agree with such negative thought. That is, I agree that initially this would be true, but then I think a balance would be reached whereby everyone would be fulfilled to a point where they would begin to setting down and do what was necessary. That means that someone would find pleasure in collecting garbage, someone would like working with chemicals, or around a hot oven, and someone wouldn't mind digging ditches, or mining coal.

These are all new strange thoughts and I do not expect most people to agree with or to, but if you follow the logic, it has merit. You are now seeing some of the results of supposedly liberal laws governing sexuality in this country, even though there is still a substantial negative force against this belief system. In any case, I believe statistics are beginning to show a drop in pornography businesses and related activities. The logic also follows the kid in a candy store syndrome. That is, given enough money or having to work in such a place, one eventually begins to lose interest or taste in or for the product. This is also the argument used in our country to encourage free trade and deregulation. In the latter situation, this is still a very heated debate that does create initial hardships when implemented and most of the positive results are not obvious. Consequently, most people will be very reluctant to commit themselves to the concept of spontaneity. It is one thing to talk about the intangibles of the potential self or being, but it is still quite another to take away patterns that one has come to rely on to support them in this physical reality.

Let me remind you that a journey of 1,000 miles begins with the first step and also remember that that is what life is all about. We are all on a journey of growth and learning. Life is only as hard and as difficult as you want it to be. You have never, never been told or taught that before; therefore, I do not expect you to drop everything and run. You must maintain your balance, but if you can do it more consciously, it makes it so much more easy. Despite your experiences with impulses or spontaneity in our culture and society, despite their contradictory nature as we know them, you have impulses that you do follow. That's because spontaneity has its order and when allowed to do so, they work not only to the advantage of the individual, but also the entire world. These impulses can be related to our problem of beginnings and endings, in that they are patterns that lead to a destination. But that ending or beginning depends on you.

Need I also tell you or remind you that impulses are both positive and negative? Impulses are meant to tell you something. If you feel like hitting someone, then you must or should translate that impulse into a positive force. That is, you must engage your conscious mind to distinguish what course of action you want to take and/or experience. When you retard restrict or limit yourself, you also cut down the possibilities of yourself, and when you do that, you also cut down your own creativity. That doesn't mean that you should hit that someone, but it is a possibility. If you are conscious of your own spontaneity, you will automatically know what to do. And if you have positioned yourself in unconditional universal love, you know that your actions are going to be right and beneficial to all involved. They are going to be responsible actions.

When I talk about responsibility, I am referring to the act of being you or yourself. When I talk about being yourself, I am talking about the same thing that makes a dog or cat wag its tail, wiggle its ears or plays by itself. The dog or cat has no one telling it what to do and has no responsibilities to behave in a certain way, or walk a certain way or do anything. All the animal has to do is to express its joyful creative nature as should man. What man needs to remember is to trust himself, and though that trust, that joy, that playful impulsive self, he can get to know and recognize his inner self. Through that expression, his spirituality will blossom and flower. He will not discover his inner self if he does not trust the self that he knows. He will not flower if he pretends that his spirit is elsewhere and that he is separate. There is no distance between the "I" and the "me". They are one and the same, connected to each other by degrees. Your spontaneity and impulses are your best contact with the inner self. To impose limitations, is to restrict growth and there are no limitations on beauty or truth.

Learn to trust that spontaneous direction. Do not ask others how to grow. When you were a child, did you seek the help of a guru to grow another inch or two? No, you already knew, but now that same knowing is joyfully hidden within you. Knowledge through education is important and has its place, but think of all those stupid trees and flowers out there growing with absolutely no one, nobody, telling them what to do or how to do it. There are some noticeable trees out there that the utility companies and some private individuals seem to think they can limit and teach; however, these exceptions stand out like a sore thumb or lollipops and are of questionable beauty, unless you like imbalances. By restricting or limiting growth, you create new patterns that never compliment the entire self or physical structure completely.

As mentioned several times before, man still needs exterior organizations, but the real organizations are within or inside. Once this is thoroughly understood, there will be no need for outward, exterior manifestations, or physical reality. Because man is not used to thinking spontaneously, he will find it hard to try to adjust to a more free and open self and he is bound to have questions and need help with this concept. The strange and funny part about this whole thing is its simplicity. Your beliefs form your reality and all of the answers to all of the questions that you can possibly have are within yourself. You just have to know where to look. You do not need gurus, psychiatrists, priests, philosophers, or teachers, to tell you what to do. You are a part of everything there is; however, you are not conscious enough to recognize it and/or be it.

Man's belief in the reality of guilt, is his most negative force that affect our world and morality. To correct such behavior, man must un-teach much of everything that he knows or has been taught. He must begin afresh, as a child using his innate wisdom of his own being. He must seek out and explore that which interests him and encourage others to cultivate their own creature-hood. Man should try to return to himself and seek his own wisdom and energy that was his at birth and is still there, but is now hidden. Basically, what is wrong with our society is that man has been taught to forget; consequently, he has sought to rely, more and more on other people. Call it welfare, call it socialism, or call it whatever you want, but do not encourage it with substitutes or any other negative form or pattern of physical manifestations.

The best thing that you can do for those people who have lost themselves and their way back to themselves, is to give them unconditional universal love. Get them to feel and touch their own birth or rebirth, and convince them that their birth was never finished with their entrance into this world. Each and every day is a new birth. Each moment of existence is an enactment of that birth. You have at your fingertips, the same energy and the same joy you once had when you dove through unknown dimensions into this system of probability, this physical reality. Tell those people to know thyself and do themselves just honor, by remembering the joy of play and spontaneity and by following this course of action, one will be drawn to his own inner self. By believing and trusting in yourself, you will discover your true being and your actions will lead you to your own answers and growth in a more creative manner. Your joyful playful actions will simply add a helpful exterior structure by which you can test yourself and/or your beliefs. There is nothing wrong with that. Remember, man seeks the comfort of like things. The physical structure of play provides that pattern.

Using opposites to prove a point, the opposite of play is work. When you think of work, you automatically think of something that you do not want to do and set up mental resistance to it. When you think of play, you think of fun, but such fun is usually conceived or structured by the same rules and organization as is work. That is, you know that games have rules and to play the game, you must play by the rules. So it is with work. Therefore, if you know how to play, you do not need to know how to work. Work and play are one in the same. You are not doing something because you must do it, or because it is right or necessary, but because it is part of your nature which must be manifested into physical reality. It is a pattern of creativity that is necessary for one's growth that involves spontaneity and an inner structure that goes hand in hand. All work environments, if properly structured or de-structured, so as to permit greater freedom of creativity, can become fun, or at least less restrictive and repressive in nature, and that is the whole idea of this book.

Man, in this day and time, is an amnesia patient. He is wandering around in a daze. He does not know who he is, where he is and what he is doing here. There is nothing wrong with this behavior so long as it is all of a positive creative nature; however, man seems to know and understand and recognize the negative forces of this physical reality and himself better than he relates to the positive creative forces. Therefore, man's patterns of growth seem based upon fear and isolationism, which is the direction of "The Third Wave". This is both good and bad. You make your own reality; however, it would be better if you knew what you are doing.

The reliance on outward manifestations is sometimes misleading and can result in acts of violence; however, if you are conscious of yourself, you know that nothing happens by accident. You attract that which you want to experience. If someone should gain from an act of violence or someone ceases to exist, remember that such an encounter or experience is sought by all of those who are involved. Again, it is better to know what is going on than to jump into the quicksand and perish too.

To become more conscious, you must try to learn to disregard what you have learned. That is a difficult task. Through spontaneity and in a joyful and playful way, you will learn to trust yourself, which will lead you toward the freedom of your being, because you are used to discipline, you may feel cut adrift, undone, or without foundation. Do not fear such emotions, because in truth, you are cutting your dependency on patterns and structures based upon the outside world. It is only when you can relocate or reposition your being that you can feel the great foundation of your own being and its greater freedom. When this point is reached, then you can draw from both worlds and balance your growth and control your becoming. The most important thing that is relative to you is to remember that the universe and/or this world is first created mentally. To change anything, you must first change your beliefs. The only real responsibility you have is to be yourself, not what someone else thinks you are. By being yourself to the best of your capacity, is to fulfill the responsibility of life and your actions and feelings will communicate and speak for yourself and them. For in being yourself, you bring forth the message of freedom and creativity.

I have mentioned before that there is no destruction or evil. But while we all think there is, then we must all deal with it accordingly. This reality is of our own making. There are no forces outside of ourselves that cause us to do evil. You must learn to recognize that fact. You must feel your answers and your feelings must rise up out of your own experiences in the form of recognition with the warmth of love, joy, and acknowledgement. This is what morality is all about. When you are able to think for yourself, for the joy of your being and give thanks to yourself for your physical body, you are on your way back to yourself. It is a joint effort of creativity and eternal knowledge that you control and/or balance. There is no reason to doubt your integrity.

In a dream state, you will be reassured of your own integrity by yourself, that same self that you have forgotten. The self or selves you hope you are, but the self you are afraid you will never be. Those selves are or exist, and they will speak to you in the dream state as they speak to you now while you are awake, but while you are awake, you do not listen. Your dreams will help you point the way to your own freedom. You do not seem to understand that your dreams are real and have validity. Your thoughts and intents have a reality that builds up in energy at other levels of existence and works for you. Your dreams are a gift to yourself, sense their miracles, their joy, their freedom and trust them. If you make mistakes, they are your mistakes, and you can learn from them. If you make decisions, they are your decisions. If you are afraid to make selections or decisions, then you cannot learn, experience, or grow. You make your own reality and you have a lot of help from yourself in doing so and/or if you want it.

Listen to your own being. He who is in a physical position to rule or control others makes himself a false god, if he is not conscious of his becoming. A person of authority does not have authority if he has to exercise negative forces to enforce that authority. Those who have mastered the art of verbal communication to command favors, commands nothing. Their reality consists of temporary or false prestige or position. Those who accept false praise need it worse than drugs and live in absurdity. He, who confuses you, confuses himself and speaks in ambiguous terms because he does not see clearly. The man or spirit, who sets himself up above you, is not above you, because there is no above or below. Anyone who tells you that he has the answer to life and won't share it doesn't have it. The answers are free and they are simple. They belong to you and everyone else who trusts themselves.

You live in a safe, moral universe. You do yourself no good by rehashing or reliving the negative actions of the past. The best thing you can do to believe in yourself is to mentally reassure yourself, before going to sleep, that you are secure and safe in your own self or being; therefore, you can move with confidence and ease and freedom in all dimensions of your own reality. The past has no power over you. You always live secure in the power of the present and in the knowledge and consciousness of your power and reality that you make. You control your point of focus and your relationships with the outside world. If you cannot trust that which keeps you alive, then what can you trust? You keep your eyes open, and your lips smiling, your fingers wiggling, and your motor (heart) running. It is the unknowing, knowing super-consciousness that rushes within you at every moment and you can trust it above all things. It does not come from others or anything else. You cannot find it in books, on television, or anywhere else. It comes from the intimate experience of your own being. When you are alone, you feel it. It is the essence of your being, and nobody, or nothing can take it away from you.

Life is quite simple. Only man has managed to make it difficult. The universe is mental first. Your beliefs form reality. That's it! But if it's that simple, what happened? Where did we go wrong? Why did we forget it all?

And why aren't people aware of it? How could we have allowed ourselves to create a reality with all the pain and suffering and wars and starvation, diseases, cruelty and the whole bit to flourish? Apparently, it is something which we wished to experience, or else it would not have come to past. The patterns that we so cherish and worship are the same forces that create our reality. Therefore, what is wrong with our world is wrong with us. We make our own reality and the majority seems to rule even in a mental state of being just like the greatest happiness principle is supposed to work. Again, that doesn't make it right or wrong, but it is something that we have chosen to experience.

Nature is a beautiful teacher. The animals go about their business with the reality and present joy of their being. You don't see any of them popping pills or running around with hypodermic needles to get by their day, do you? They do not need it. They do not need acid, grass, peyote, or anything else, because they know that which they are. Our animal friends are full of joy of their being and they are not afraid of it. A squirrel scampers through the branches of a tree. You don't hear anyone yelling at him to be careful, he might fall. He is not afraid of falling because he trusts his own being. He knows, without fine intellect, that he has a place in the universe. A place made for him and one in which he is something that is joyful and alive. When a bird builds its nest in the trees, you don't see building inspectors going around to check out its construction to see if it meets all of the codes of nature and is safe for the newborn. How much is enough? The answers are within. Left alone, all men can find the right answers if they are conscious of their own being.

The grasshopper leaps with great ease and grace, out of the knowledge and vitality of his being, but if asked to tell others how he does it, he can only tell them that he does it. Those others, who are not grasshoppers, can only sit, listen, and acknowledge his instructions, but they are not grasshoppers and they cannot jump as he. Man possesses the knowledge and understanding to relate to one another and things, but he must want the experience before he can do what it is that needs to be done. There must first be a Will, to establish a value, to make a selection necessary to bring about a physical manifestation. Without values, creativity or morality is not possible.

Raindrops fall to moisten and nourish the physical earth. They are all individuals. They do not stop to think where they must fall and when; yet, all by themselves, they bring freshness and vitality to the grass, flowers, trees and everything else, by their falling. That is their responsibility. When man too learns to seek his own spontaneity, he too will be like the raindrops. He will seek to nourish the earth and those in it by being himself and thereby changing the world. Both will benefit. By learning to be spontaneous, man cannot plunder the earth. He will learn to understand and love himself, and that love will be reflected back to the world around him. In learning how to be spontaneous, you are learning how to play, and if you know how to play, you don't need to know how to work. Because if you understand what play is, you know it is organized to accomplish a desired result. You know that games have rules and that you are part of the game and therefore, you help make the rules. The same is true of this reality. You are a participant. You are involved, whether you like it or not. Learn to play by the rules of the game or change them. In any case, do something. You are an individual. You count! Do your own thing, but do it from a position of strength and love.

Forget your ideas of the past or future. Forget all the philosophies, political systems, the occult and religious nonsense, that you have learned. Look at your present point of focus with wondering eyes of a new self. If any of these belief systems separate you from the joy of your being or becoming, then it is detrimental and should be avoided. You do not need one of these belief systems to justify your existence, for whatever reason. All you need to know is to be yourself. Learn the joyful, playful, spirituality of yourself and/or your being.

Sports athletes are always breaking new records. Why? Because they dream dreams from which they inspire themselves to break the limitations that they have had to live with. Limitations are restrictive and do not help one grow and become his greater self. So learn to trust yourself, and your love, and your dreams, and try to communicate those thoughts openly. You are part of all there is and it is part of you. Through that common union, one can reach communion with his fellow man. Your thoughts can be shared by all. There is no such thing as heaven on earth as we know its meaning. If there were, everyone would be bored. People need a challenge. They need to grow and change. Nothing stays the same. The laws of this universe will not permit anything from remaining the same. Man must learn to recognize the patterns of growth and work with those laws and/ or principles. He needs initiative and the desire to accomplish and to use energy in a positive creative manner.

Your beliefs form this reality. However, man relies more on the outside physical world, than he does his inner self. Therefore, everyday and in every way, man runs up against beliefs. Either they are his or someone else's. The trust or certainty that he puts into these beliefs makes them work or not work, depending upon the individual. Anything will work, if you believe strong enough in it. Acid will work if you believe in it, LSD, an occult school, religion, political groups, medicine, drugs, god or gods. Aspirin will do it, or anything else you can think of, if you believe in it. The universe is mental. Each of you will usually put before you someone or something that is thought to be greater than you are that must be obeyed. Each of you will follow his or her own journey through life relying on something or someone else. But, the magic is you! To believe that the magic or secrets to life is somewhere beyond you in a pill, a medal, a god, a product, a person, a diet or whatever, will cause you to spend the rest of your life in search of it. Let me assure you, that it is not outside of you, it is within you. You make everything count. You make your own reality.

Each and every one of us, and/or groups of people are working out certain beliefs and experiences in exaggerated form. Nothing happens by accident. You will not be caught in an earthquake, ravaged by a storm or anything else, if you do not want to be. No one dies who has not decided to do so. If this is not true, then you are a victim and the universe must be an accidental mechanism appearing with no logic or reasoning. That means that your body came accidently into creation and out of some cosmic accident that may not follow any rules and may not be duplicated. That means that the complexity of your body is not justified and all that beauty was created for no other reason than to be a victim. That is the only alternative that you have to your forming of that reality. You cannot have something in between. You either have a universe formed with a reason, or one without. In a universe of reason, there cannot be any victims. Everything must have a reason, or nothing has a reason. I suggest you choose your side!

Any evils in this world are symptoms of your own inner disorders and are meant to teach you something. You must learn to recognize them and correct them for the growth and well being of yourself and others.

Every nation, every people form their own violence and are responsible for their own conditions. The starving in the world is the result of conflicting beliefs. If one thought cannot dominate or be manifested over another, a third alternative course may result which may take the form of droughts, flooding, temperature changes, etc. This only happens when the spiritual and the physical are so separated that they cannot materialize or fulfill needs. This is a condition of contrast that knows its own order. Nothing happens by accident, it is the result of conscious or unconscious thought meant to bring about a change. The condition of universal unconditional love can change all the pain, suffering, and misery, in the world, but it must be supported to bring about its physical reality. That is what morality is all about. It is about LOVE!

In our society, morality is thought to be a set of rules or laws, both formal, but mostly informal, designed to control and/or restrict human behavior. These rules are guidelines which were set up, with supposedly good intentions, to direct our society toward its greater well being in hopefully, a more harmonious and an organized way. Their intent was to create an understanding of acceptable behavior by which everyone could relate to. However, the rules or guidelines are based more on negative thought than they are positive forms of manifestation. I believe, it may have been hoped that man could see that certain things were restricted but most things were acceptable and encouraged. Through the passing of time, the restrictions or restricted limitations have increased and the other options have diminished. That is, new restrictions have been added to the negative list and many, many more laws added to the formal list, without anything or few rules being discarded. That means that our list of negative reinforcements is constantly growing.

This trend in our morality is somewhat detrimental to freedom and creativity. Instead of becoming more open and creative, we have inherited and are inclined to perpetuate a pattern that is somewhat faulty. Where all of this is leading us, is anybody's guess right now. Perhaps the doomsday prophets are right but on the other hand, we all make our own reality, so there is always hope. However, it is up to you and each one of us to see life for what it is and to select and choose that which we want to experience with a little bit of thought behind it all. We have a lot of options, possibilities, and probabilities. How we bring all of this together depends on each one of us. You make your own reality, but what you do also affects others. Even the smallest force in nature can cause major changes, given enough time. Patience is a virtue, but if we can all add a little force to our male gender or being, then perhaps, we may affect great changes within our lifetime. I think our physical reality needs it and/or us now, more than ever before. Where are those aggressive flowers?

I don't mean to end this chapter on a somber note; therefore, let me remind you that nothing is destroyed without the knowledge of those involved. I spoke of this in the last chapter with some reluctance. The problem in presenting this pattern of thought and its ability to be understood, is that it involves a level of consciousness which most do not or cannot consciously recognize and that includes myself. One's greater self is multi-dimensional. We, as we know ourselves, are but the tip of an iceberg. We are greater than the sum of our parts and it is not the intent of this book to delve into those areas of being and becoming.

We exist in this physical reality. Therefore, we must deal with reality the best way we know how. That means that we must use those things which we have knowledge of to correct ourselves and our society. What I am saying is that we must relate to this reality with conscious mental thought. Our consciousness, or this reality, has chosen or seems to have chosen to relate to matters on an intangible subconscious or super conscious level. Therefore, that means that we do not recognize our conscious thoughts for what they are. That doesn't mean that they do not exist. All that means, is, that it is difficult to follow such patterns. Hopefully, through the knowledge of your own being, you may be able to recognize and offer recognition to yourself in new ways. The most important of these, is the knowledge of your inner self. Learn to understand this other form of reality. Learn to trust it. Learn to use it and balance yourself in a positive creative position of love. Nothing, NOTHING, happens to you by accident! You are the recognizer. You recognize your reality with recognition. You make your own reality. What you believe determines your reality. Your beliefs restrict or limit your growth. Morality is but another name for those restrictions or the lack of them. All restrictions are not bad, SO LONG AS YOU RECOGNIZE THEM FOR WHAT THEY ARE AND HOW THEY RELATE TO YOU! THAT IS WHAT MORALITY IS ALL ABOUT! IT IS THE POSITION THAT YOU WANT TO EXPERIENCE!

CHAPTER 22

The Awakening

As you may or may not have noticed, I have divided this book into three sections. The first section deals primarily with physical reality as we know and relate to it. The second part eases into the area of spiritual reality which is an equally important reality that few people know anything about and/ or fail to recognize. It is just as real as physical matter; however, it is not perceived by the outward physical senses of man. You can also compare physical reality to that which is tangible and spiritual reality to that which is intangible, but by now you know that that is only half true or half false. Just the same, man understands the outside physical world better than the inner intangible world or content of himself and this is why this book was written.

The last section three of this book, deals with balance. This is a position of knowing and understanding how our world based upon this dual reality or separation works and how our consciousness can control our being and becoming our higher selves. I am not concerned with good or bad, right or wrong, as I am with the learning aspect of one's experience here on earth. Section three gives you everything you need to know to balance and control your life and to grow in a positive creative manner. Balance is a growth process that must be maintained and that means that you must deal with separation to create a unity that you can recognize. The growth of any life depends upon energy and resistance. They are one and the same, they are unity. How far you can go in your being or becoming your higher conscious self depends on you. What restrictions you put before yourself makes this game so interesting is that they keep changing the rules of the game. They, in this case, are the supposedly educated or people who try to identify and separate alike things for the sake of drawing limitations and/or maintaining the status quo. Differences exist, only if you want them to exist. You will find whatever you are looking for, if you look hard enough. Your thoughts and beliefs are a reflection of yourself and/or position. If there is one thing that you can learn from all of this and this book, is,

YOU MAKE YOUR OWN REALITY!

In organizing the patterns of man, sociologists and anthropologists have classified man into two distinct groups. They are: Dionysian and Apollian. The Dionysians are those who resort to drugs or other physical substances to break down the physical limitations of man's physical senses in order to experience or consciously enter into communion with his spirit in an uncontrolled manner. The Apollian does not seek outside or outward help to communicate with his inner self. Rather, he is content to live on a day to day basis and experience that which is in the realm of his perceptions and senses. The Apollian is what our third book section is all about balance; however, the Zuni Indians of Southwestern United States may have carried the concept of balance a little too far. That is, they have tried to present balance in a moment to moment basis, rather than spread it over a lifetime. Balance is important, but not at the expense of one's learning experience.

In our own Western civilization, we can see elements of balance, as well as the extreme societies that are based upon fear like the Dobu and a culture based upon wealth and/or greed like the Kwakiutl. What I tried to point out before we studied these groups of people is that the studies are but a reflection of the people who view or study these groups and how they relate to their own society. Therefore, you are or should not be as concerned with the differences and/or contrasts as you are in the relationship and presentation of the data as it relates to you. You will see all of these elements in our society, but how I choose to display or review the data is how you will react to the thought patterns. That is, I could have chosen to slant or show you a comparison that might lead you to believe that our society is very much like the Dobu Indians and/or is likely to become like this group. Or, I could have chosen to show a greater concern or concentration on wealth and greed as the motivating factor behind our society, like the Kwakiutl Indians. In any case, knowledge or data is only as good as what you can learn from it and how it can be used. Nothing exists until you want or make it exist or becomes a reality.

In chapter nine on "Good, Bad, Right, Wrong", I acknowledge the control of the individual to recognize his reality and to make and/or experience that which he wants. Nothing is good or bad, right, or wrong, until you relate it to something. You determine your own reality. The normal thought or concept of reality is that you learn your mental and physical limitations, as well as spiritual and social. However, what I am trying to point out, is, that you primarily learn to limit yourself. That is, you consciously erect barriers that say A + B = C, and once you do this nothing else is possible until you correct that first belief. Remember, rules and laws serve a purpose up to a point, but once that point is reached, you can discard those rules and start with new ones. This world, this reality, is in a constant state of change and so too, is man. It is a relationship that one must understand, learn and grow. We live in a world based upon separation; however, those differences are but degrees of the same thing. Man must learn to recognize those limitations and use them for guidelines only. They are not meant to restrict him and subjugate him into subservience out of ignorance or fear, but to provide him with landmarks that will direct him in his growth and becoming.

In chapter ten, "Physical Reality", I have tried to explain that man must learn to try and position himself consciously to other forms and forces of energy, and his recognition of these patterns affects his reality. But, appearances are deceiving if viewed only in an outward physical manifestation form. That is, separation and divisions exists, but they are also united. Unless you are conscious of both aspects, you will not be able to learn or grow in a positive creative manner. This ability to identify things and objects is a result of inbalances or the ability of the recognizer to recognize. This is important, but it is equally important to offer recognition, which is the relationship of that object or thing to the recognizer. It is energy in a form or pattern that can be used to sustain or benefit man in his journey through life.

"The Structure Of The Universe", is chapter eleven and deals with the makeup of physical reality in mathematic terms. But this physical manifestation is also expressed on a spiritual level as well. That is, everything and nothing are opposites of the same thing, which is all there is, God. This can also be expressed in the word or term, unity. They are one and the same. The proof and existence of God, is very, very important for the well being and balance of man; however, most men choose to forget about this aspect of themselves. Consequently, man is out of balance and has expressed himself out of a position that is not conducive to his well being. Man has forgotten that he is spirit born unto matter, because the process of separation has set up more resistance than his conscious mental energies can overcome. This consciousness is what limits man and prevents his awakening to a new self and reality of his own self in a more conscious way. Man's physical senses can be deceived and convey false information; yet, man chooses to rely upon this outward source of information over his inner knowledge of that which is. Again, it is a question of patterns that man becomes accustomed to and relies on, even though it may not reflect his true reality.

Chapter twelve is "Patterns of Recognition. There have been many attempts by man to justify or establish a moral basis of being that is fool proof and that everyone can agree to. However, each attempt has failed to establish this truth whereby it is compatible to all the people(s) of the world. The problem seems to lie in the fact that no outward manifestation can be proven beyond a doubt, because no authority is all powerful that anyone can relate to that can establish this truth that everyone seeks. Nothing can be proven to exist in the way of a standard of behavior or a single infallible source of truth. The closest we can come to a workable standard, is "The Greatest Happiness Principle", however, this is not so much a standard as it is a consensus of opinion. That opinion doesn't make it right; however, it does justify an action. In fact, this standard is what is alluded to in the establishing of our world and/or reality. That is, though the accumulation of mass opinions, a belief system is unconsciously manifested and therefore, creates this reality that we know and that is why things appear so chaotic, troubled, and a condition to no one's liking.

The only thing that we can know for sure and beyond a doubt is that, "I think therefore I am" and that God exists. No matter what else happens, know that "I" must be something. I am a thing that thinks; therefore,

I exist. Big deal isn't it! Well it is if you find yourself in some vast void with nothing to relate to for some unknown reason. Without physical stimulus, there is no physical reality. Your senses must recognize patterns of energy with some form of recognition in order to establish a basis of communication, or common union. But because this physical reality is but a variation of unity and therefore composed of conflicting patterns of the same thing, one must learn to question in order to become more conscious of all there is and his reality.

Chapter thirteen, one's "Consciousness" seems to be the pattern of recognition that determines or limits one's reality. That is, it is the ability of the individual to recognize patterns for what they are and to offer some form of recognition that is reflected back to himself or the recognizer. The intensity determines the relationship and understanding of itself. That is, how you make your own reality. You consciously choose or select that which you want to relate to and how, and that is how you make your own reality, by selecting that which you want to experience from both linear and non-linear realities. If you choose not to be conscious of the unity of everything, you will see and experience great intensity and contrasts that are manifested in separation or linear physical reality. If you see everything as one, you see much much more, but your emotions may be greatly diminished, but this need not be so. You may select that which you want to experience.

Mental thought does have structure and form, but these forms do not relate to man in the same way as the physical senses do. Because man is in a state or position of separation and is not conscious of his own reality, he is in constant conflict with himself and his reality; therefore, be believes that he is not in control of himself or his reality and/or is a victim. There is but one unifying pattern that exists in everything and nothing and that is the structure of the universe, that is God, and that is the tetrahedron. Its relationship to all physical objects of matter is the same. It is consciousness of that element of balance that determines one's ability to recognize and offer recognition to that of the recognizer. In short, consciousness is the structure. The ability of one to recognize determines how he understands and relates to his reality. However, this structure, this recognition, this consciousness is not easy for the average person to relate to; consequently, most people will continue to go through life without really knowing or understanding it. They will be victims of their environment and controlled by the world of cause and effect. Reality is a matter of belief and belief is but another form of matter, controlled by the subconscious or super-conscious self.

To imply separation, is to admit to distinctions or degree of manifestation. That means that there are levels of consciousness. These levels are: matter, vegetable life, animal life, and man; however, man himself has four levels that are manifested or separated by mental qualities. These levels are classified as: man - characterized by intellect, genius - characterized by intuition, prophet - characterized by wisdom and universal love, and the God-man - characterized by omniscience and omnipotence. Although these separations are listed as such, there is very little noticeable difference that is distinguishable. Most men are only on the fourth and fifth levels of conscious and their behavior is sometimes influenced by their higher qualities that display characteristics of their higher self in this physical reality. That is, man's purpose is to learn how to use energy for the purpose of overcoming resistance in a positive creative manner by growing or expanding his limitations and/or beliefs for the benefit of all creation.

In chapter fourteen, "Beliefs", we learn that thought has levels of intensity too. That is, there are thoughts and ideas, concepts, and there are beliefs. I think everyone knows and recognizes the first two manifestations of thought, but few if any, recognize and understand the workings of beliefs. It is the most intense form or structure of thought and is very difficult to identify and/or dismantle once they are formed. That is, beliefs are like a computer program that is designed to get you from here to there, without any conscious thought process involved. It is a routine or pattern which when formed, is difficult to change or alter. It is the pattern or structure that most limits or restricts man in his growth process. This pattern of growth takes on the shape of a tetrahedron and its outer sides represent the various levels of thought, consciousness and possessions that ultimately reach or climax at the point of total unity.

This pattern of growth can also be depicted in the form of a diagram that affects one's behavior. This pattern can also be used to control one's behavior on a day to day, moment to moment basis. There are 12 steps in each pattern that represents a level or degree that has a beginning and ending, or some form of unity to it. Strangely enough, steps two through eight remain virtually the same. Only steps one and 12 change significantly. Therefore, that means that the conscious beliefs that you start with affect your reality and that brings you happiness, no effect, or pain and suffering. How you look at things or how you recognize things determines your reality. That is, your reality is more a reflection of your own inner self than it is a matter of forces outside of you. Remember, value is something that you have to work for or expend energies for, in some form to achieve an end result. If you are not willing or able to give something of yourself, you will not get anything of value in return. "You get what you pay for!"

Chapter fifteen "Opposites", one understands and recognizing inbalances, one determines his own reality. One's behavior is based upon his relationship and value of the things he recognizes. If you only rely upon outward appearances and stimulus from your physical senses that is all that you can offer recognition too. Consequently, your behavior pattern will be on a normal conscious level that sees separations and a world based upon cause and effect. Therefore, your behavior will be of an action-reaction type, right or wrong, black and white, etc., type of responsiveness, filled with much pain and suffering.

You can change your behavior, but it is not easy, because you are not conscious of the patterns of limitations that you yourself have imposed upon your growth. But, the best way to understand yourself and these self limitations is to learn about opposite intangible thought processes. Study them, know them and recognize them for what they are, then you can become more conscious of them and control your relationship with them. By recognizing the positive and negative poles of unity, one can better understand oneself and control one's reality.

But, just as there are opposites of intangible thought forms, so is there both a kind of spiritual and physical relationship. That is, there is in chapter sixteen, "The Mental Aspect" of intangible patterns, known as gender. That is, there is both a male and female type principles involved here, but these forces are not confined to one or the other sex as it is in physical reality. Rather than to explain what it is, it is better served to explain how it works. In all thought processes, there is needed a beginning or instigator so to speak. That is the purpose of the male gender. It is to activate the mental process that manifests thought into being. It is the purpose of the female gender to bring that thought into existence in physical reality. That means that there is a union of spiritual thought with that of thought related to the physical world. The result is neither all spirit nor all physical. You might say it is man's ability to balance spirit and matter. That also means that you cannot know or understand your own true self as you cannot know God, because that part of you dwells in other dimensions. Man and God are co-creators. One and one are two and two is unity in balance.

This gender principle also reflects the dual aspect of one's self. That is, man himself has two distinct and separate selves. I refer to these two selves as the big "I" and little "I" or "me". In the unconscious man, there appears to be no difference in these aspects of one's self; however, as one becomes more conscious, one learns that the "me" relates to the physical body and outside needs and the "I" is quite independent and deals with the inner self. It is one's ability to consciously recognize this dual aspect that determines one's ability to position himself and to control his reality through the control of his thoughts. Without a proper understanding and relationship between these two aspects, nothing can or will be done in this physical reality. It is a balance, a union, or communion, with one's self that is manifested onto this physical plane of existence. Again, you must be willing to expend energy to accomplish anything and the amount of energy determines what you will receive.

Chapter seventeen, "Control" clarifies or puts everything into a nutshell. That is, it explains that everything, repeat, EVERYTHING, originates or is of a mental origin first! This chapter tells you all you want to know about life and how it relates to one's reality; however, it is also very abstract. In short, there are seven principles of control that determine this physical reality. The principle of mentalism is all inclusive in that it explains all of the other principles. This principle states that everything is derived from the mind or from intangible mental thought processes. The principle of correspondence simply states that there are multiple levels of thought or intensity and what affects one level has some effect at another level. The reason for this transfer of energy is due to the principle of vibration. That principle states that everything is in a constant state or position of motion. Some fast, some slow, some noticeable, and some not so noticeable. This principle is also supplemented by the principle of polarity. This backs up or reinforces our knowledge of patterns that simply put states that one can be caught in a position of imbalances or relate to everything in an out of balance position. Without the knowledge or knowing of separation, one cannot properly learn to grow and balance himself on his journey to himself.

In addition to polarity, everyone is affected in some way by forces of movement that cause the principle of rhythm. This is a slight inclination to be influenced by first one pole then the other, but not at the same time or the same degree or strength. If there was no movement on the part of the individual, there would be no rhythm, but there is movement and that motion causes other motions in an action-reaction kind of relationship. However, that action-reaction pattern is really the principle of cause and effect, that is, our motorboat effect that I spoke of several times. That is, everything and everyone who does anything, uses energy and that energy does not stop with the individual. Once the individual is done with that something it continues to be or exist and affects other things and/or people. Therefore, caution should be exercised in learning to use the principle of gender to manifest thought and/or reality. To bring thought into reality takes some careful thought and inner knowledge of one's self and all there is. To do things for one's own self gratification is not conducive to that individual or the well being of all concerned. We live in a closed system, although it does not seem apparent, that is unified and shares all there is. Also, this system operates by these seven distinct rules or principles. If one can learn to recognize these rules, one can begin to take control of his own reality.

Life exists out of a state of unity and we are all striving to regain that unity or oneness. Everything is related or relative to one another on all levels of life and its common link or bond is the pattern or shape of the tetrahedron which is found in all forms of matter. You must also learn to understand that these levels of vibration cause patterns that also have different characteristics or resistance and that results in separation and creates inbalances. But, without motion, that separation will cease; therefore, there is a balancing of forces constantly at work causing rhythm and polarity to affect one's behavior and/or life in general. Everything that happens is based upon something or some force that is striving for balance and/or counter balance. Life is multi-dimensional and involves the use and transmutation of energy for the purpose of growth and/or manifestations.

This whole book goes a long way to build a good foundation to establish some kind of basis by which man can use in establishing rule, law, code or principle, upon which to monitor or control his life in a group environment. In chapter eighteen, on "Law And Love", I describe that you can have all the rules in the world, but if you do not have love, all the rules are of no good or useless unless there is the caring and sharing for one's well being. This is love. This is the manifestation of life and/or creation. Through love, you can use this energy force to position your being in a more positive creative manner and to help those about you regain their own true selves. Love is the only law that is also a principle. Love is based on the principle of polarity, except it is a positive manifestation of that principle. There is also the negative form of this principle which is hate and is the opposite that of love. But, by using one law against another and by understanding and recognizing love, one can change his reality and expand his consciousness. By learning the true meaning of universal unconditional love, one can change the world. Love breaks down the barriers and restrictions put forth by beliefs and hate. It expands and penetrates even the densest patterns and forms of energy. By learning and understanding love, one has found his position and the way back to himself and God. The "Secret of Happiness" is contained in but three words: LIVE LIFE IN LOVE; for in this position one cannot but give of himself and act from a position of unity and GOD!

In chapter nineteen, "Communication, Common-Union, Communion", one learns to form the bond or link between himself and his fellow man and to help him make a better physical reality. Communication is a form of recognition or attempted recognition of an outer nature. It is a means of creating a common-union that will hopefully lead to a communion, or unity of mind and/or purpose. Through communications, you establish a bond that is related to one's inner self or position. We are talking about the sharing of one's wants, needs, desires, and how that relates to that of another or others. Two people in physical reality cannot occupy the same place at the same time, but they can mentally. In a condition or position of universal unconditional love, one need not try to communicate verbally with that of another because he automatically knows and understands the position of the other without asking. It is only a matter of one's consciousness and an understanding of opposites that results or causes separation and for that reason, one needs outward communication.

In learning how to communicate and establish a relationship, most people fail to recognize that they are the most important part of any such relationship; consequently, they find themselves constantly reacting to something instead of acting independent of the patterns or forces surrounding them. In learning how to love, you must first learn to love yourself, for if you do not believe in yourself, how do you expect anyone else too. Your beliefs are the recognition or reflection of yourself and you will communicate those same beliefs either knowingly or unknowingly. Love is not a sign of weakness and it can communicate unity. Your communion is the relationship and balance of your knowing, and possessing, along with loving, caring, and sharing. You make your own reality but happiness depends upon you. How well you relate to your experiences and communicate that common-union, depends upon how you make that reality.

In conscious terms, chapter twenty, this "Recognition" is very misunderstood. You have complete freedom, but you choose to limit and restrict yourself and to make life into a series of responsibilities. No matter what you think, you are not completely free in a group environment; therefore, you are not happy or joyful about your own being. At any time, you can recognize your physical condition, compare it against what you want and to change it accordingly, but you should also be aware of these new forces that you set into motion. To change anything affects others and if you are not in a position or state of love, you may do more harm than good to yourself and others. You are partners or co-creators with God. When you understand yourself and recognize yourself with recognition, you will have actively awakened yourself consciously and that is what this reality is all about. To awaken yourself consciously is to break down the barriers and limitations of linear and non-linear realities. You will learn that separation has its limitations and that you will no longer be able to grow in this reality. You will expand your mind and dwell at choice in other manifested or unmanifested realities. Death is but one's realization that one has grown to one's limitations in this reality.

You make your own reality. You live in a safe and secure universe of your own choosing. There is nothing evil that can affect you unless you want it to. Your beliefs determine your reality. So long as you choose to involve yourself with others and other belief systems, so will you experience those patterns of force that exist. They are real if you so believe that they are. To describe who am I, where am I, and what am I doing here, is to describe the problem of balance and/or what we wish to experience. Excitement need not be evil or violent, nor should peace be passive and dull. You make your own reality. To understand position, is to understand recognition and to control your reality. You have a universal part within you and therefore you are a part of everything there is. That is what you must learn to recognize. There is nothing to be afraid of. Trust yourself. If you cannot trust yourself, who can you trust? Before you can help others, you must first help yourself. You must operate from a position of strength and universal unconditional love. That doesn't mean that you have to love everybody, every time, but you should at least learn to recognize the forces that are at work in your relationship.

In chapter twenty-one, we deal with the question of "Morality". That is, it attempts to set some guidelines that you can use to establish a good system for determining moral behavior; however, the conclusion is that you cannot have a written universal law other than love. Through love and the conscious understanding of yourself and your reality, you can and will reflect that which is. By being yourself, you are fulfilling all of the joys of life. By doing and being what you want, you will automatically form a new society whereby everyone will be happier and will naturally gravitate to those positions that are necessary to exist in this physical reality. By being yourself, you are creating a positive creative environment. You do count and together with others who are being themselves, you will create a better, happier, safer place to live and grow.

Nothing happens by accident. You cannot separate yourself from others or your involvement in this world, nor can you force yourself upon others without their consent. Therefore, the only thing that you can do well is to be yourself and in so doing, you will automatically create a better environment. Learn to be spontaneous and follow your impulses; however, also learn to recognize that these are just that, impulses. They are meant to tell you something. Try to be conscious of that inner communication and seek its positive manifestation. Even though someone may be communicating something negative, try to turn that negative into a positive. You cannot help someone who is drowning in quicksand by jumping in after them. I doubt if anyone will benefit from that impulse. You must learn to understand and deal with the patterns and forces of this reality and act out of a position of love. Then there is nothing that can prevent you from doing anything, except yourself. You make your own reality. Gee, that sounds familiar.

You live in a safe and moral universe. Learn to recognize it and to be an active participant in its creation. Life is quite simple, but somehow most people seem to make it difficult. Nature is a beautiful teacher. Open up your eyes and mind, see the creatures and creations of nature in their joyful struggle to be themselves. Life is a learning process that requires the use of energy to overcome resistance. To grow, you must expand your beliefs about all things. Beliefs are a form of energy that you can learn to control and share. You help form this reality by your sharing of beliefs; therefore, if you learn to position yourself in a positive manner, you can help more people than if you hated them. Learn to be spontaneous and as aggressive as a flower in your endeavors. Where have all the flower children gone? Learn to understand the gender principle and start aggressively pursuing love. Learn to recognize yourself with recognition.

Because we live in a world based upon separation, it is difficult to remember or recognize unity in its many forms and positions. If you look for joy and happiness, solely in the outside world of physical reality, you will not find it. The accumulation of wealth and material possessions will not achieve that desired end result. To seek this direction, course or goal, is to put yourself in an extreme position within the learning triangle and this creates an imbalance. To do so is to polarize yourself and limit your experiences that choke off your own personal growth and your conscious awakening. The awakening process involves the knowledge of balance and how to position one's self in universal unconditional love.

One of the best institutes or outside organizations for learning, studying, and understanding balance, is also one of the most controversial in one's life. I am talking about a form of communication that leads to common-union and communion. I am talking about marriage. It is the best means for two physical manifestations to learn and understand balance. That is, it is the union of opposite genders for the purpose of unity; however, it can only achieve unity in this physical reality on a temporary basis. That is because happiness can only be achieved from within and cannot be possessed. To seek external unity is pleasing to the physical senses, but it is not permanent or lasting. It is beautiful and it is an outward form or manifestation of love, but it also has or connotes the extreme position of possessing like material wealth. Therefore, the only true universal unconditional love is to learn to recognize yourself with recognition and to seek your inner self, so that you may communicate that knowledge of unity to all your fellow man.

Man is like an amnesia patient. He wanders around in a daze. He is not sure who he is, where he is, or what he is doing here, and he doesn't seem to be concerned about any of these questions either. He seems to seek material things and expresses himself in greedy terms. He always wants and is unwilling to give. Until someone, or this book, awakens him, he will continue to stumble around and communicate in an incoherent way with those about him. Until man learns who he is by becoming more conscious of himself and his reality, until he learns to recognize that he lives in a world based upon separation, and until he learns that he must try to achieve a balance within this reality, then he must continue to be a victim of his own doing. TRY TO REMEMBER THAT YOU MAKE YOUR OWN REALITY!

This book answered all the questions of the amnesia patient and more. To simplify matters even more, let's answer these questions by the numbers and/or by the book in short brief concise terms. Question: Who am I?

Answer: I am spirit born unto matter manifested from a mental universe. Question: Where am I?

Answer: I exist or am conscious of a linear physical reality of space and time based upon separation manifested by energy and resistance.

Question: What am I doing here?

Answer: I am learning to use energy for the purpose of growth of my being and becoming conscious physically, mentally, socially, and spiritually in a positive creative manner.

Question: What about morality?

Answer: No laws or principles are possible, but one is necessary. There is but one answer and that answer is LOVE! To exist in this mental conscious position one cannot but do the right thing!

Life is truly beautiful, and exciting, and wonderful, yet, most people fail to recognize it as such. There is so, so much love that is out there all bottled up. It is like a balloon ready to burst. I hope this book may help you break the limitations of the balloon and that you impose upon yourself and I wish you your greater freedom and love. Again, the "Secret of Happiness" is to LIVE LIFE IN LOVE! It is a position of strength from which anything is possible!

You may say to yourself now that these are all very, very good thoughts and words and are idealistic and not possible in this physical reality. I live in a rough cruel world of survival of the fittest. Only the strong survive and\or prosper! Do you? Or are you just venting out the clichés handed down by generation after generation of victims who did not know how they make their own reality? Do you like the world you live in? Do you think that your life does make a difference? Where have all of the aggressive flowers gone? The flowers transmute the world about them by letting others see their inner beauty! Don't you have something to share and show?

What you think determines who you are! You are constantly creating yourself everyday in every way and moment. It is you and you alone who is responsible for your reality. You are in absolute control of your reality. What do you want to experience! It is easy to be a victim! All you have to do is give up control of who you are and what you want. Society or a group environment makes it easy for an individual to relinquish or share ones in exchange for something in return either tangible or intangible. Make sure you choose and select wisely what kind of reality you want to live in. Remember, if you don't like what you see, think again. The universe is mental first.

I would like to end this book with a little prayer of my own. I hope you will remember it when things don't seem to go right. We could all use a little encouragement at times:

My dear Lord God, thank you for today, yesterday, and all the days to come. May the thought of my love go out to all the peoples of the world and may they grow and prosper in a more positive, creative manner, through loving, caring, and sharing. Please help me to help myself, so that I may help others. Please let me recognize the patterns of our power, strength, knowledge, wisdom, courage, humility, and love so I might use those forces to face those tasks which I have set before me.

Thank you, Amen.

THE END, OR IS IT A BEGINNING?

Everything that is true is but half true and everything that is false is but half false. A beginning is but an ending that has changed into something else and every ending is but a journey begun. As one grows and becomes more conscious of his powers from within, one soon discovers truly how beautiful life really is. But at the same time, there is the fear of failure and the unknown that clouds one future. There is balance in life and confusion abounds in separation and change. Stop and recognize what is, is unity in its many forms. You cannot make a mistake because the answers to all your questions are within! You make your own reality!

The final piece of prose assumes that you have discovered who you are; however, it indicates that there may still be more to yourself than this life can explain. Therefore, you may find it somewhat interesting.

A. F. KENTON

THE NAME BY WHICH ONE IS CALLED

My appearance upon this world was received with a multitude of
anxious thoughts.
Thoughts of great happiness, joy, sadness, fear, promises, and unknown
expectations.

To mark this occasion, my presence, and future, I was given a means of
identification. A NAME!
A label or title which will endure a span of time equal to or beyond that
of my physical being.
This name bestowed upon me limitations of social order and societal
normalities.

Within this framework, this environmental image is where I am to
function, take part, and contribute.
A world of countless trials and confrontations, countless rules for
survival and reward.
A stage play drama, tragedy, and comedy, all rolled into one.
A seemingly hostile and alien reality, but a reality of consent and of mind.

The name by which I am called is not of my selection,
But this moment of time is an image of my reflection.
I have been here before, and will be here again,
I have lessons to be learned and debts to amend.
I have no conscious thought of before nor extension of beyond,
But my true self knows ALL THAT IS, and of my names foregone.

A name, a world, a thought,
A bridge is being sought.
The revelation of my being will come,
When the evolution of my names become one.
The gap is for our own protection,
But the next name may be our final connection.

BIBLIOGRAPHY

Baumgardt, David. Bentham and the Ethics of Today. Princeton, New Jersey: Princeton University Press.

Beals, Ralph L. and Hoijer, Harry. An Introduction to Anthropology. New York: The McMillan Co. 1965

Benedict, Ruth. Patterns of Culture. Boston: Houghton Mifflin Co. 1934

Bentham, Jeremy. Hedistic Utilitarianism - Introductory Readings in Philosophy, eds. Marcus G. Singer and Robert R. Ammerman. New York: Charles Scribner's Sons.

Bentham, Jeremy. Principles of Morals and Legislation. New York: Oxford at the Clarendon Press.

Bentham, Jeremy. The Principles of Morals and Legislation. ed. Lawrence J. Lafleur. New York: Hafner Publishing Co.

Berlitz, Charles and Moore, William L. The Philadelphia Experiment. New York: Fawcett Crest Printing 1980.

Descartes, Rene. Discourse on Method. trans. Lawrence J. Lafleur. New York: Columbia University Press 1950-6.

Carter, Mary Ellen. Edgar Cayce on Prophecy. from the Assoc. for Research and Enlightenment Inc., New York: Warner Book Edit. 1968.

Haich, Elisabeth. Initiation. Palo Alto, Ca.: Seed CenterPub. 1974.

Keyes, Ken Jr. Handbook to Higher Consciousness. Living Love Center St. Mary, Ky. 1975.

Mill, John Stuart. Nature and Morality - Introductory Readings in Philosophy, eds. Marcus G. Singer and Robert R. Ammerman. New York: Charles Scribner's Sons.

Mill, John Stuart. Utilitarism. ed. A.D.Linsay, New York.

Mill, John Stuart. Utilitarians. New York: Doubleday and Co.

Ouspensky, P.D. In Search of the Miraculous. New York: A Harvest Book.

Roberts, Jane and Robert Butts. The Nature of Personal Reality. Englewood Cliffs, N.J.: Prentice Hall Inc., 1974.

Roberts, Jane. Adventure in Consciousness. Englewood Cliffs, N.J.: Prentice Hall Inc., 1975.

Roberts, Jane. Psychic Politics. Englewood Cliffs, N.J.: Prentice Hall 1976.

Roberts, Jane and Robert Butts. The Unknown Reality - Vol. one & two. Englewood Cliffs, N.J.: Prentice Hall Inc., 1977 - 79.

Roberts, Jane and Robert Butts. The Nature of the Psyche. Englewood Cliffs, N.J.: Prentice Hall Inc., 1979.

Roberts, Jane and Robert Butts. The Individual and Mass Events. Englewood Cliffs, N.J.: Prentice Hall Inc., 1981.

Three Initiates. The Kybalion. Chicago: Yogi Publication Soc. 1940.

Toffler, Alvin. Future Shock. New York: Bantam Books.

Toffler, Alvin. The Third Wave. New York: Bantam Books 1981.

Watkins, Susan M. Conversations with Seth - Vol. one & two. Englewood Cliffs, N.J.: Prentice Hall Inc., 1980 - 81.

Printed in the United States
By Bookmasters